EXILES

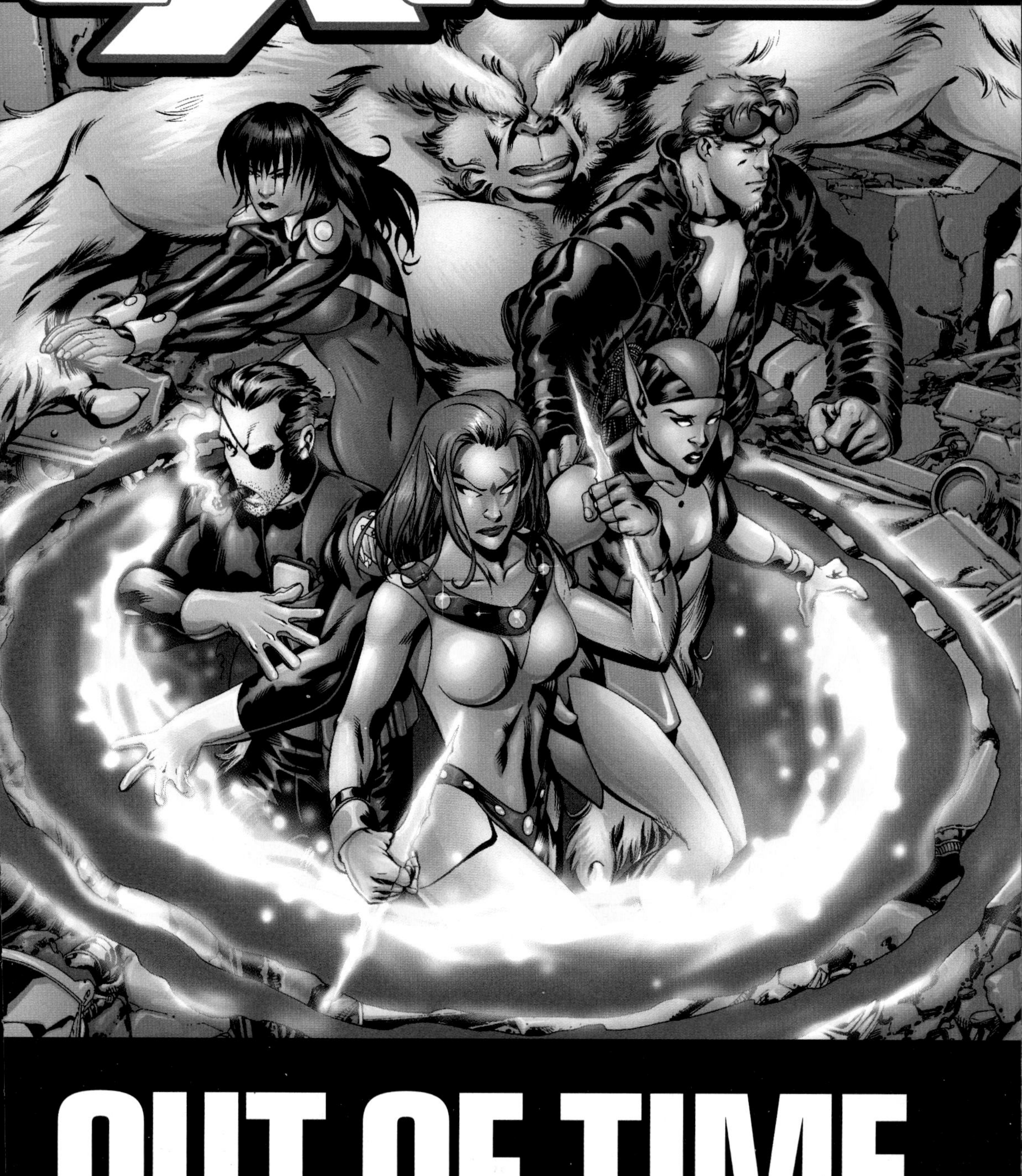

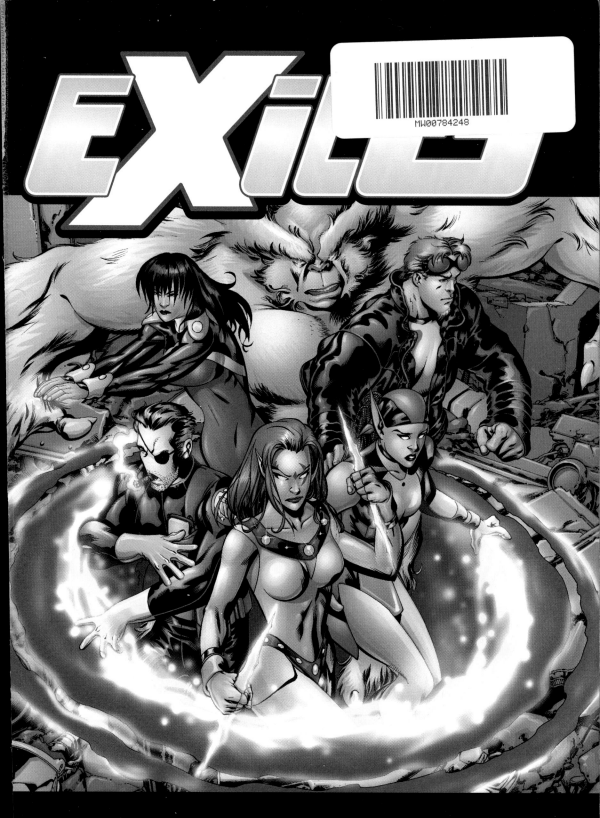

OUT OF TIME

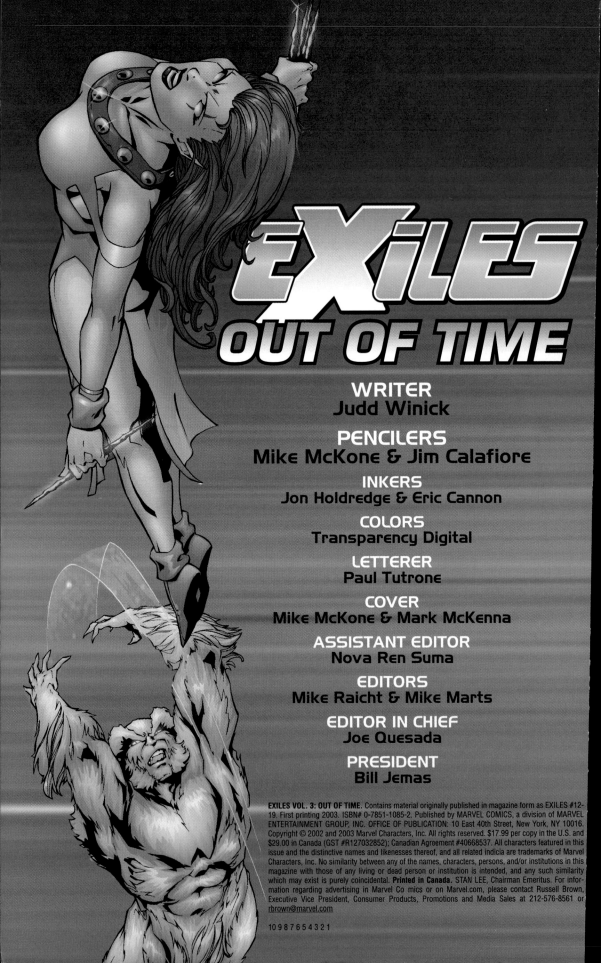

EXILES
OUT OF TIME

WRITER
Judd Winick

PENCILERS
Mike McKone & Jim Calafiore

INKERS
Jon Holdredge & Eric Cannon

COLORS
Transparency Digital

LETTERER
Paul Tutrone

COVER
Mike McKone & Mark McKenna

ASSISTANT EDITOR
Nova Ren Suma

EDITORS
Mike Raicht & Mike Marts

EDITOR IN CHIEF
Joe Quesada

PRESIDENT
Bill Jemas

EXILES VOL. 3: OUT OF TIME. Contains material originally published in magazine form as EXILES #12-19. First printing 2003. ISBN# 0-7851-1085-2. Published by MARVEL COMICS, a division of MARVEL ENTERTAINMENT GROUP, INC. OFFICE OF PUBLICATION: 10 East 40th Street, New York, NY 10016. Copyright © 2002 and 2003 Marvel Characters, Inc. All rights reserved. $17.99 per copy in the U.S. and $29.00 in Canada (GST #R127032852); Canadian Agreement #40668537. All characters featured in this issue and the distinctive names and likenesses thereof, and all related indicia are trademarks of Marvel Characters, Inc. No similarity between any of the names, characters, persons, and/or institutions in this magazine with those of any living or dead person or institution is intended, and any such similarity which may exist is purely coincidental. **Printed in Canada.** STAN LEE, Chairman Emeritus. For information regarding advertising in Marvel Co mics or on Marvel.com, please contact Russell Brown, Executive Vice President, Consumer Products, Promotions and Media Sales at 212-576-8561 or rbrown@marvel.com

10 9 8 7 6 5 4 3 2 1

They are heroes from different realities whose own timelines have become compromised. The lives that they once knew have been altered.

CLARICE FERGUSON, AKA BLINK.
The team leader, a survivor of a twisted reality dubbed the Age of Apocalypse. She is the acrobatic teleporter.

TJ WAGNER, AKA NOCTURNE.
The daughter of Nightcrawler and Scarlet Witch, she is able to fire Hex Bolts and also "possess" people for short periods of time.

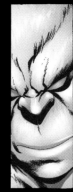

DR. HEATHER HUDSON, AKA SASQUATCH.
Field leader, chief medical officer and monstrous brute of the Canadian super team, Alpha Flight.

CALVIN RANKIN, AKA MIMIC.
He is nearly his own reality's Captain America, possessing the powers of five different mutants.

MARIKO YASHIDA, AKA SUNFIRE.
Japanese born émigré and mutant wielder of Flame.

And of course, there's the shape-shifting **MORPH**.

To return to their worlds and to be restored to their former selves they must repair the broken links in the chain of time.

They will travel together from one alternate universe to another, each time completing a mission to set right what has gone wrong.

The have battled Dark Phoenix, captured the Hulk, and defeated Galactus.

They have lost team members-- Magnus, son of Magneto, sacrificed himself in an atomic blast to save a reality-- and Thunderbird, who was instrumental in the downfall of Galactus, but was left comatose and near death in that reality.

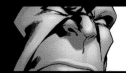

They have found love, experienced danger and formed friendships.

Their lives are unpredictable.

No one can say where their next mission will take them.

They are the **EXILES** and this is their fate.

12

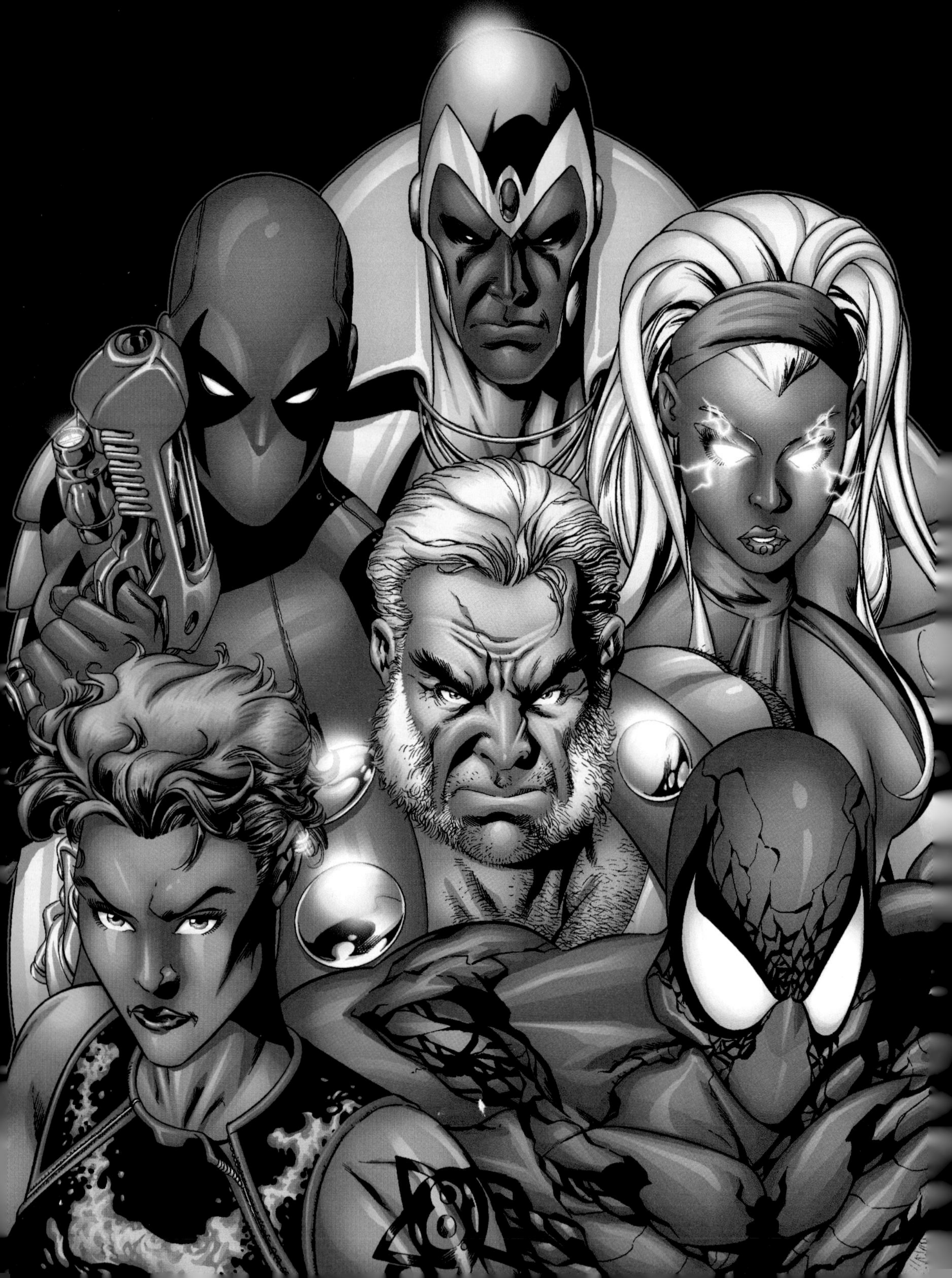

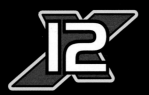

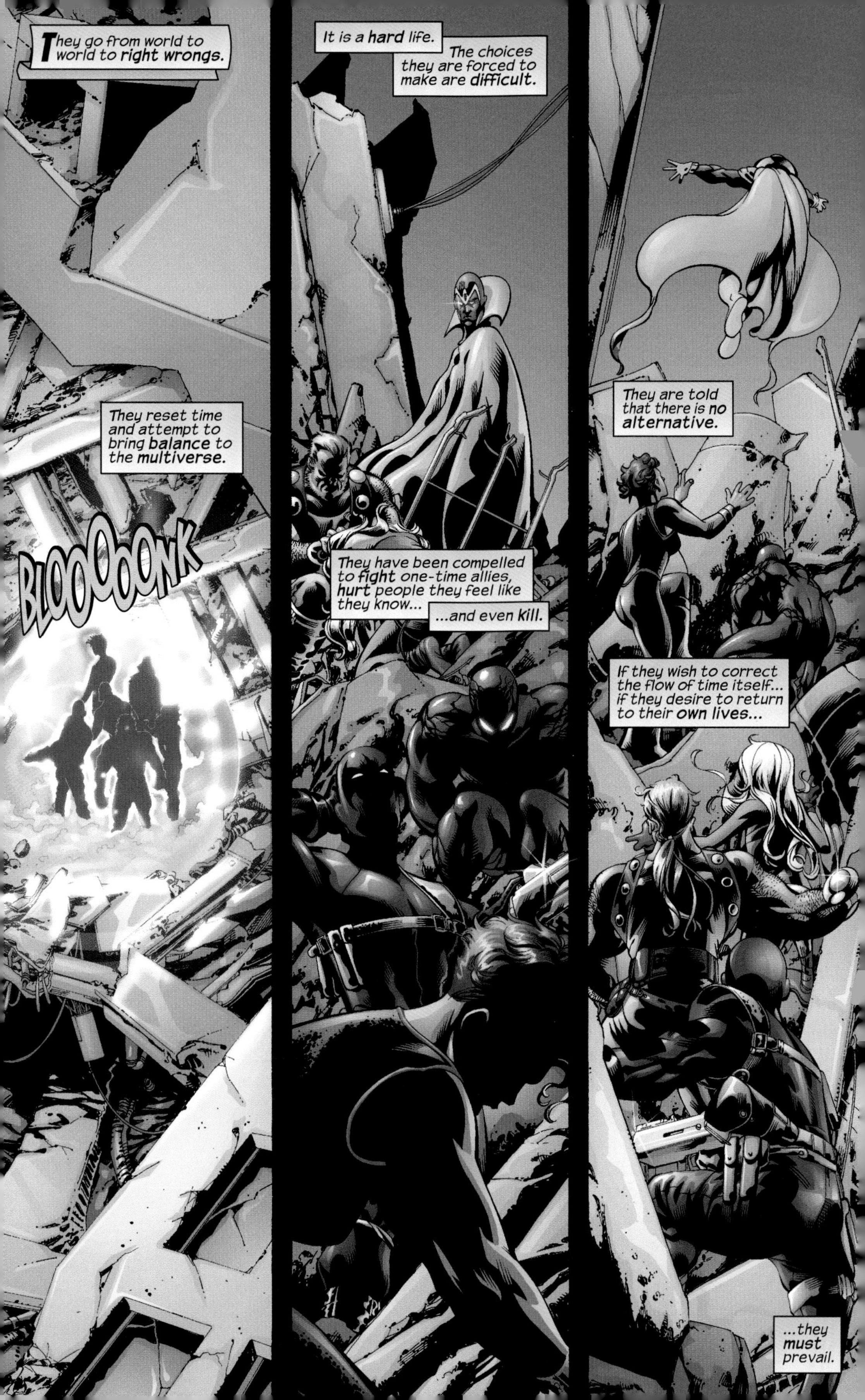
They go from world to world to right wrongs.
They reset time and attempt to bring balance to the multiverse.
BLOOOOOONK
It is a hard life.
The choices they are forced to make are difficult.
They have been compelled to fight one-time allies, hurt people they feel like they know...
...and even kill.
They are told that there is no alternative.
If they wish to correct the flow of time itself... if they desire to return to their own lives...
...they must prevail.

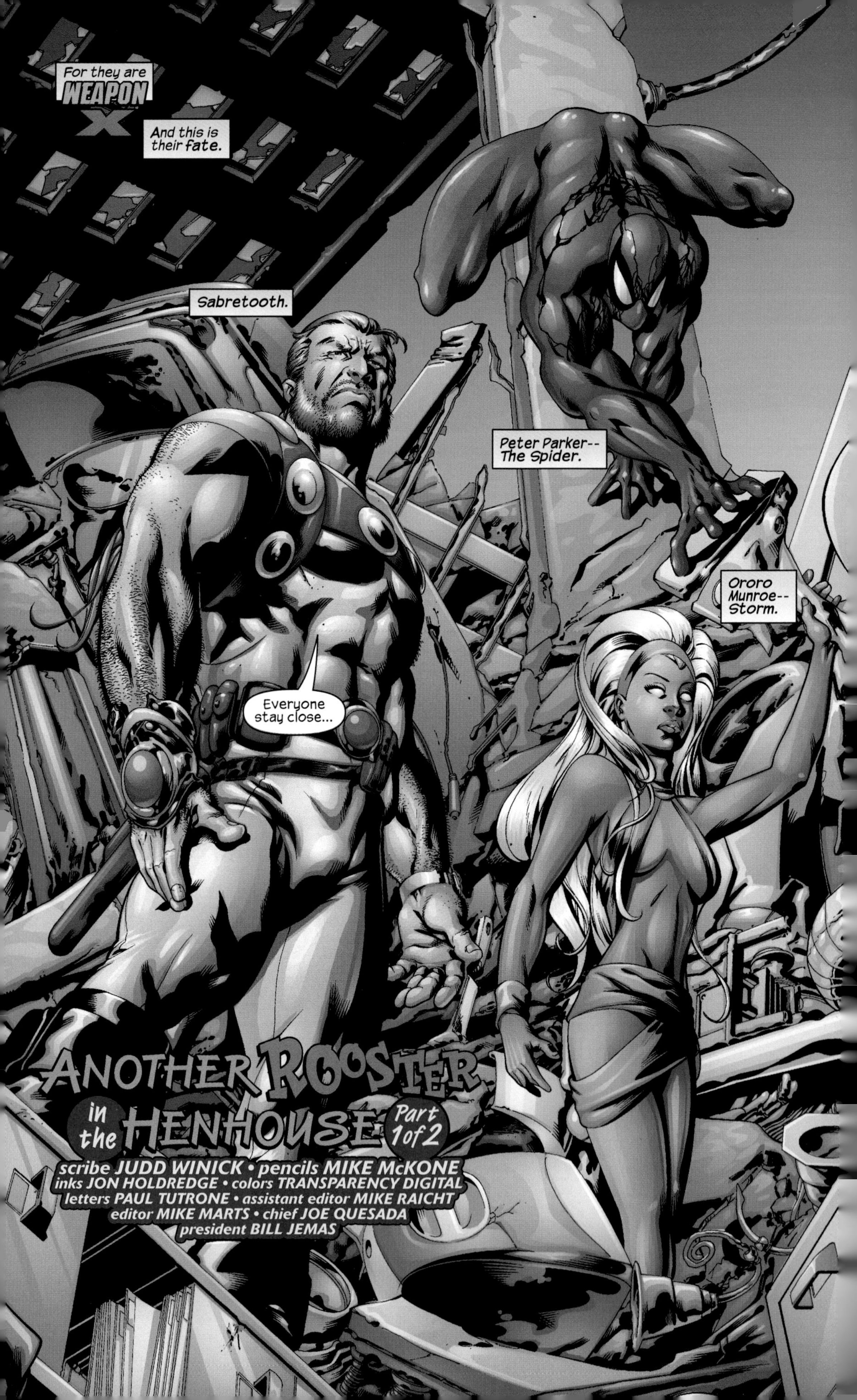

For they are WEAPON X
And this is their fate.
Sabretooth.
Peter Parker-- The Spider.
Ororo Munroe-- Storm.
Everyone stay close...
ANOTHER ROOSTER in the HENHOUSE Part 1 of 2
scribe JUDD WINICK • pencils MIKE McKONE
inks JON HOLDREDGE • colors TRANSPARENCY DIGITAL
letters PAUL TUTRONE • assistant editor MIKE RAICHT
editor MIKE MARTS • chief JOE QUESADA
president BILL JEMAS

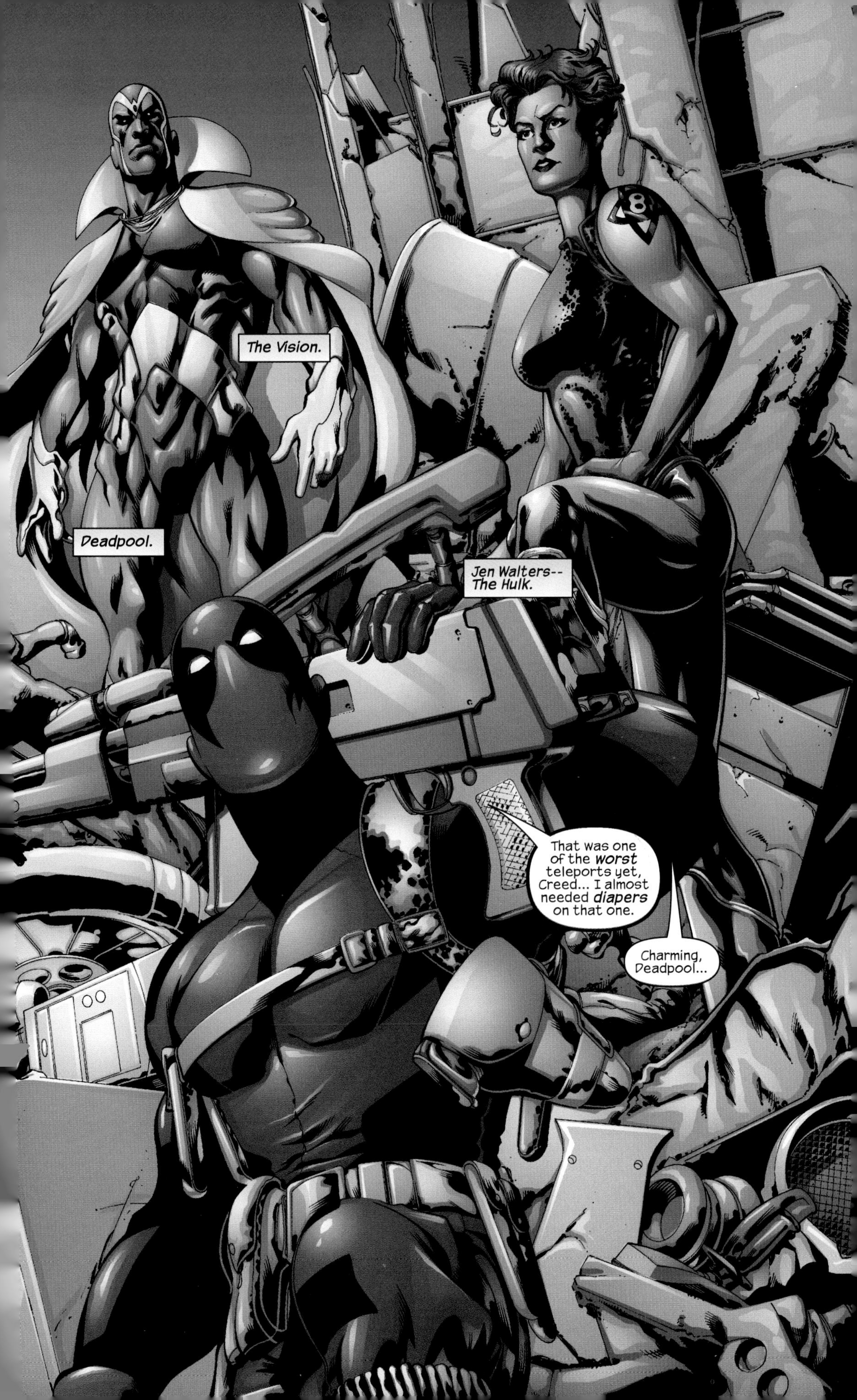
The Vision.
Deadpool.
Jen Walters-- The Hulk.
That was one of the *worst* teleports yet, Creed... I almost needed *diapers* on that one.
Charming, Deadpool...

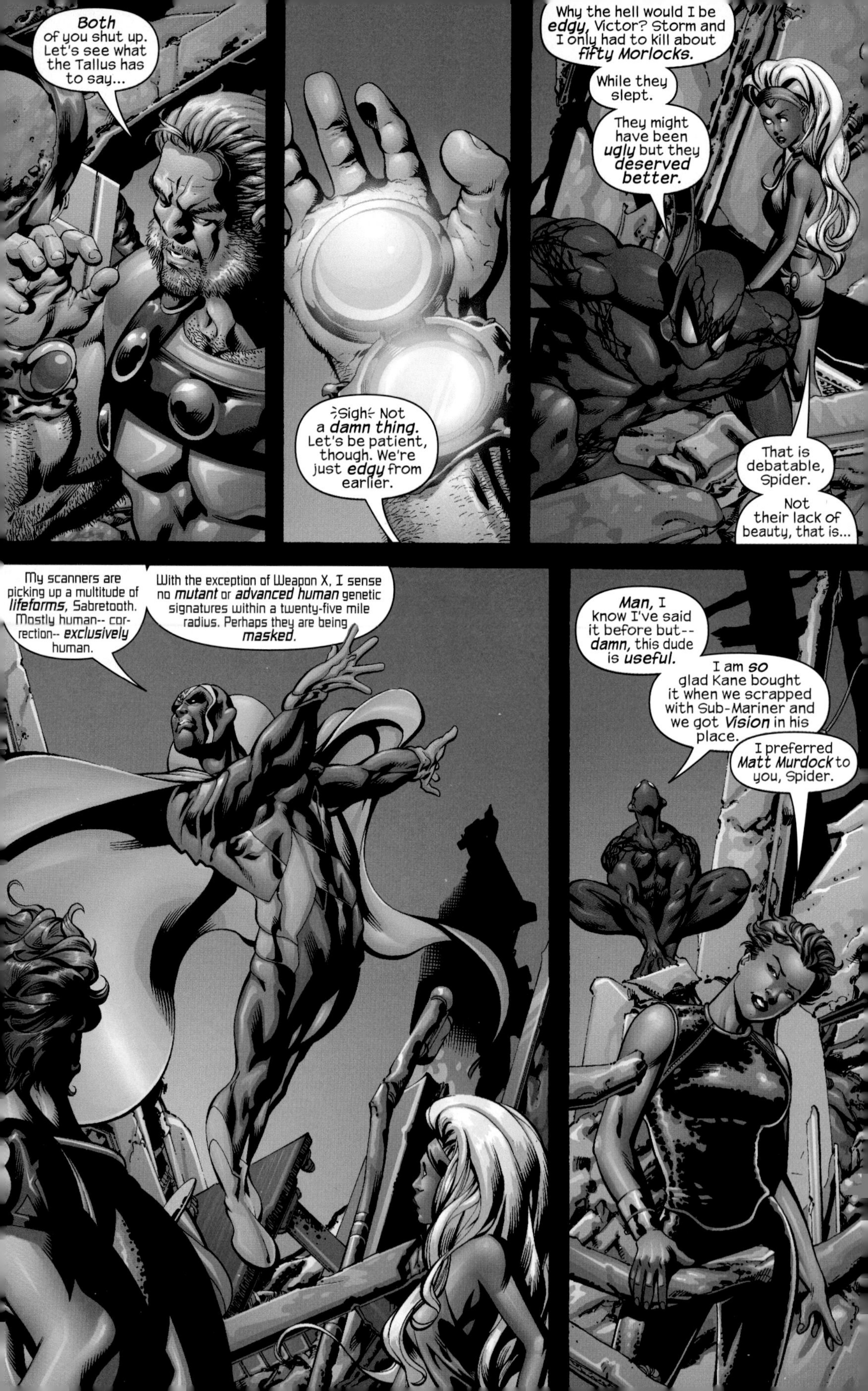
Both of you shut up. Let's see what the Tallus has to say...
-Sigh- Not a damn thing. Let's be patient, though. We're just edgy from earlier.
Why the hell would I be edgy, Victor? Storm and I only had to kill about fifty Morlocks.
While they slept.
They might have been ugly but they deserved better.
That is debatable, Spider.
Not their lack of beauty, that is...
My scanners are picking up a multitude of lifeforms, Sabretooth. Mostly human-- correction-- exclusively human.
With the exception of Weapon X, I sense no mutant or advanced human genetic signatures within a twenty-five mile radius. Perhaps they are being masked.
Man, I know I've said it before but-- damn, this dude is useful.
I am so glad Kane bought it when we scrapped with Sub-Mariner and we got Vision in his place.
I preferred Matt Murdock to you, Spider.

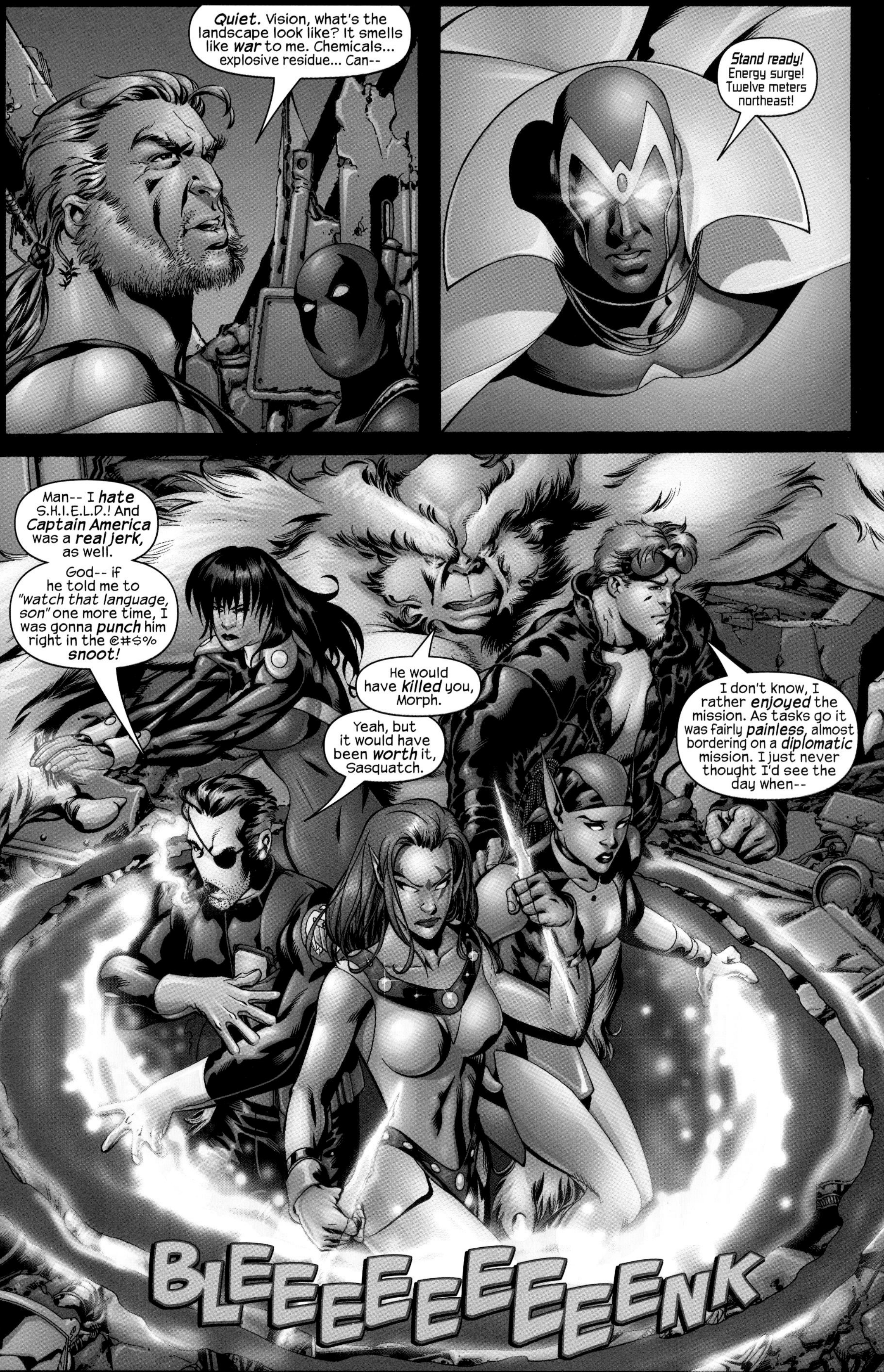

Quiet. Vision, what's the landscape look like? It smells like war to me. Chemicals... explosive residue... Can--
Stand ready! Energy surge! Twelve meters northeast!
Man-- I hate S.H.I.E.L.D.! And Captain America was a real jerk, as well.
God-- if he told me to "watch that language, son" one more time, I was gonna punch him right in the @#$% snoot!
He would have killed you, Morph.
Yeah, but it would have been worth it, Sasquatch.
I don't know, I rather enjoyed the mission. As tasks go it was fairly painless, almost bordering on a diplomatic mission. I just never thought I'd see the day when--
BLEEEEEEEEEEENK

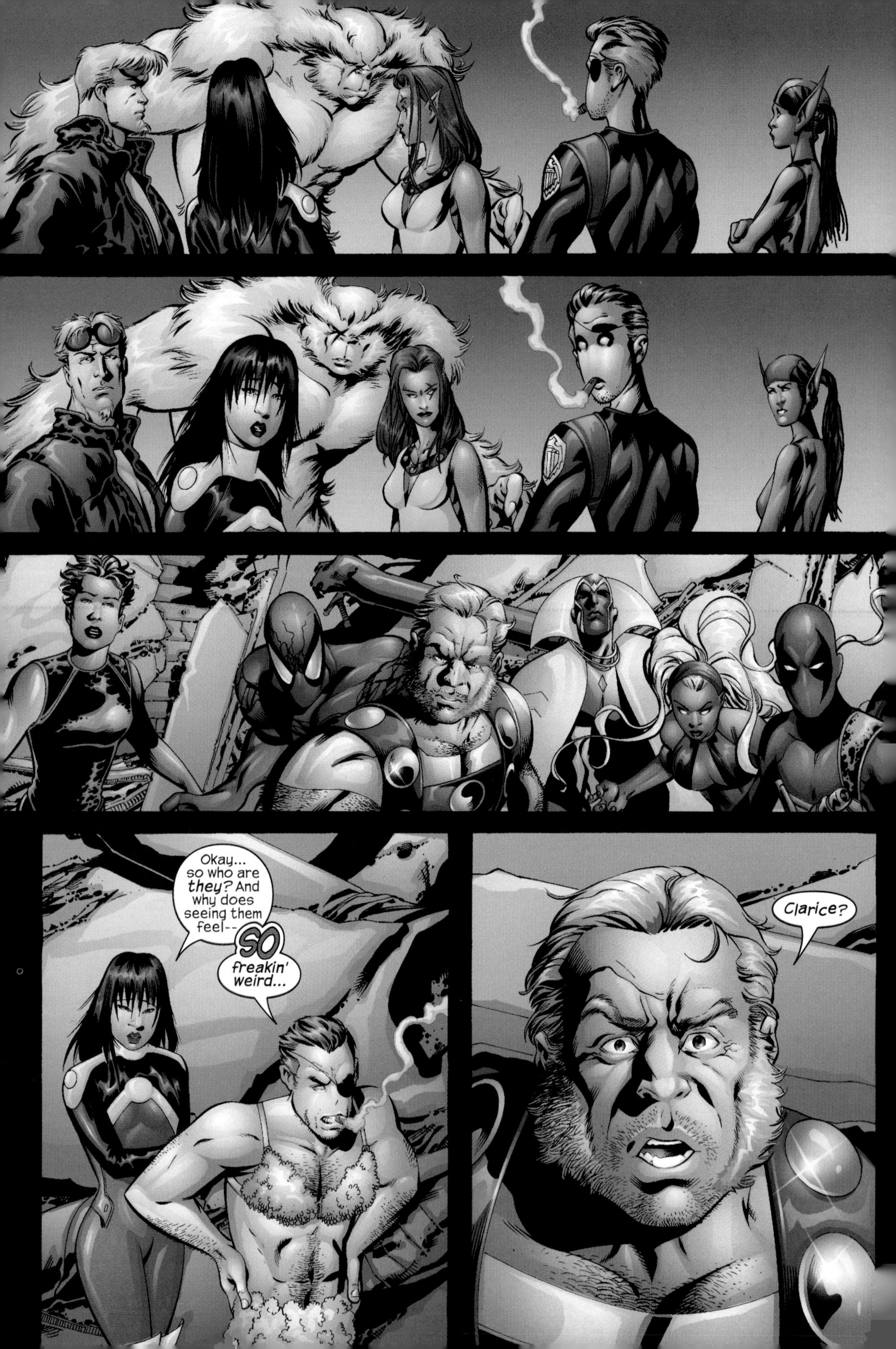
Okay... so who are they? And why does seeing them feel--
SO freakin' weird...
Clarice?

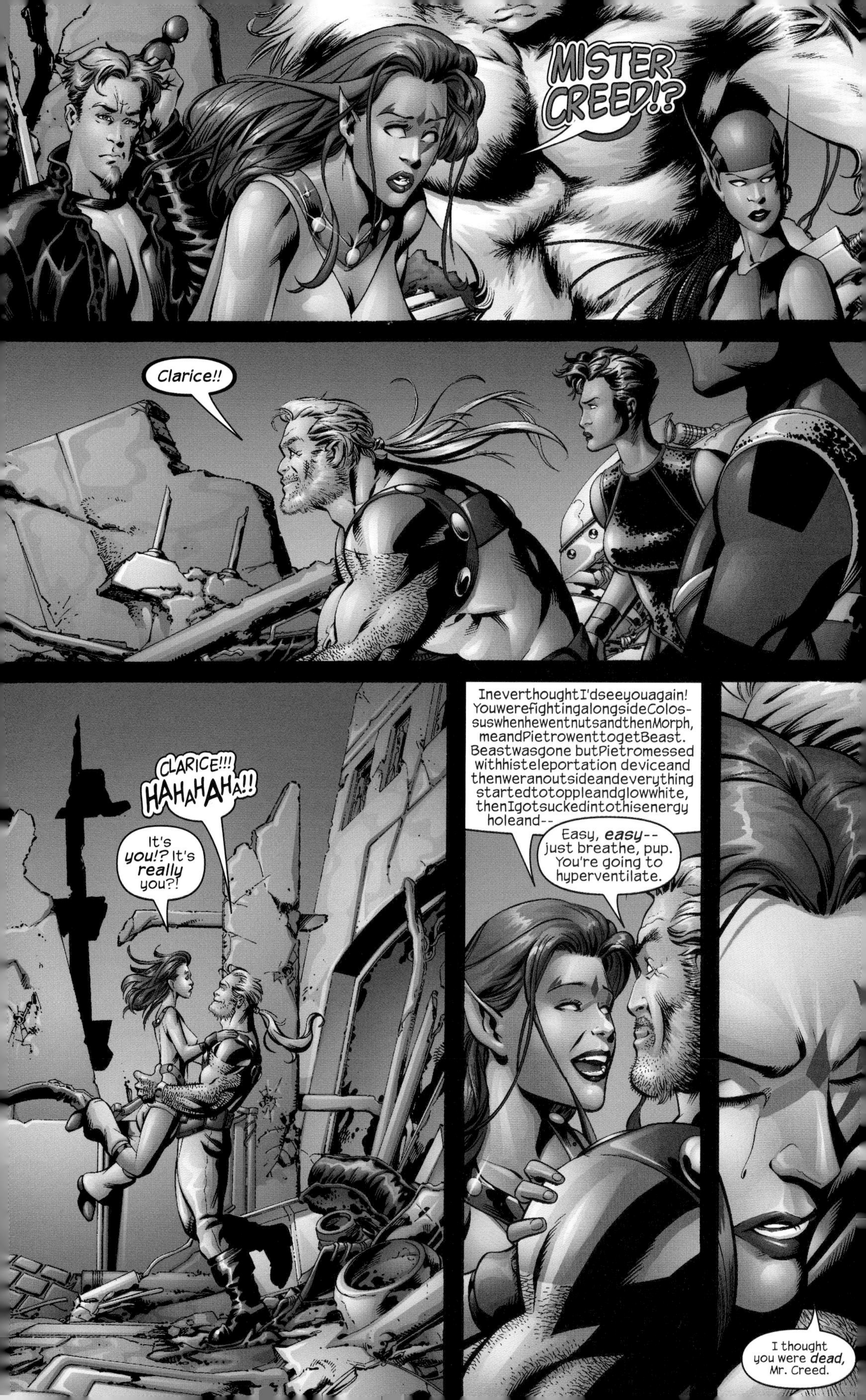
MISTER CREED!?
Clarice!!
CLARICE!!! HAHAHAHA!!
It's you!? It's really you?!
Ineverthought I'dseeyouagain! Youwerefightingalongside Colossuswhenhewentnutsandthen Morph, meand Pietrowenttoget Beast. Beastwasgone but Pietromessed withhisteleportation deviceand thenweranoutsideandeverything startedtotoppleandglowwhite, then Igotsuckedintothisenergy holeand--
Easy, easy-- just breathe, pup. You're going to hyperventilate.
I thought you were dead, Mr. Creed.

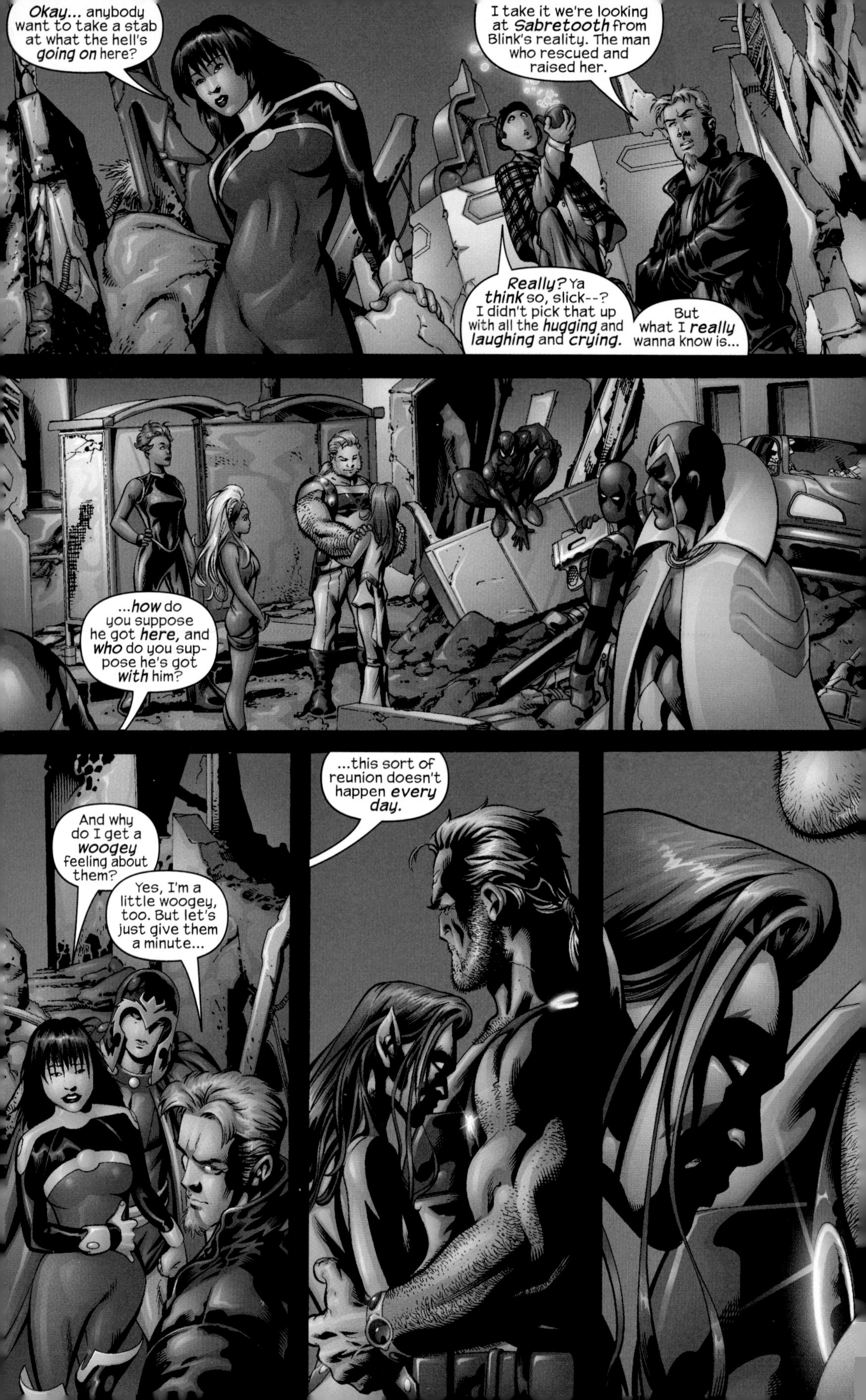
Okay... anybody want to take a stab at what the hell's going on here?
I take it we're looking at Sabretooth from Blink's reality. The man who rescued and raised her.
Really? Ya think so, slick--? I didn't pick that up with all the hugging and laughing and crying.
But what I really wanna know is...
...how do you suppose he got here, and who do you suppose he's got with him?
And why do I get a woogey feeling about them?
Yes, I'm a little woogey, too. But let's just give them a minute...
...this sort of reunion doesn't happen every day.

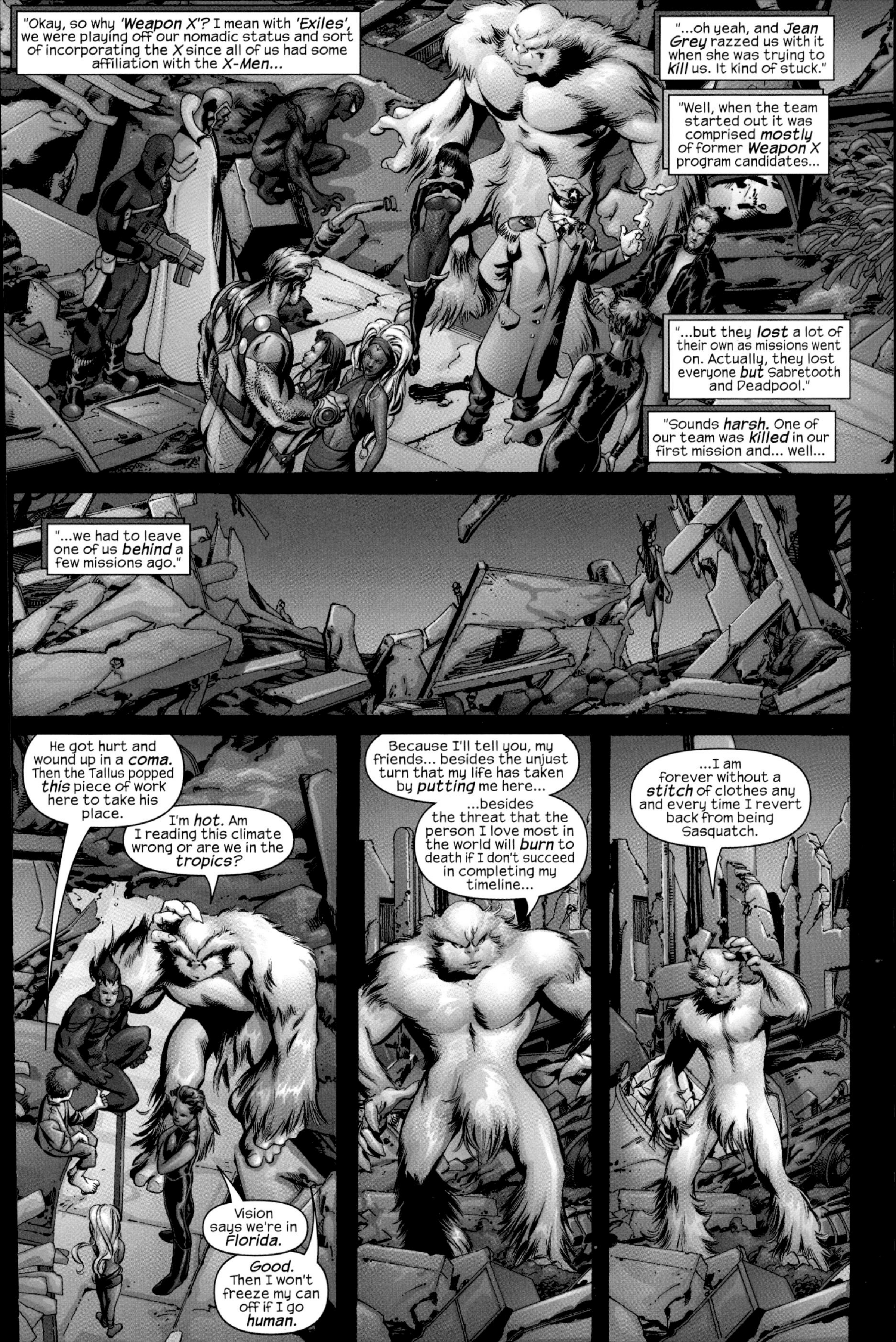
"Okay, so why 'Weapon X'? I mean with 'Exiles', we were playing off our nomadic status and sort of incorporating the X since all of us had some affiliation with the X-Men...
"...oh yeah, and Jean Grey razzed us with it when she was trying to kill us. It kind of stuck."
"Well, when the team started out it was comprised mostly of former Weapon X program candidates...
"...but they lost a lot of their own as missions went on. Actually, they lost everyone but Sabretooth and Deadpool."
"Sounds harsh. One of our team was killed in our first mission and... well...
"...we had to leave one of us behind a few missions ago."
He got hurt and wound up in a coma. Then the Tallus popped this piece of work here to take his place.
I'm hot. Am I reading this climate wrong or are we in the tropics?
Vision says we're in Florida.
Good. Then I won't freeze my can off if I go human.
Because I'll tell you, my friends... besides the unjust turn that my life has taken by putting me here...
...besides the threat that the person I love most in the world will burn to death if I don't succeed in completing my timeline...
...I am forever without a stitch of clothes any and every time I revert back from being Sasquatch.

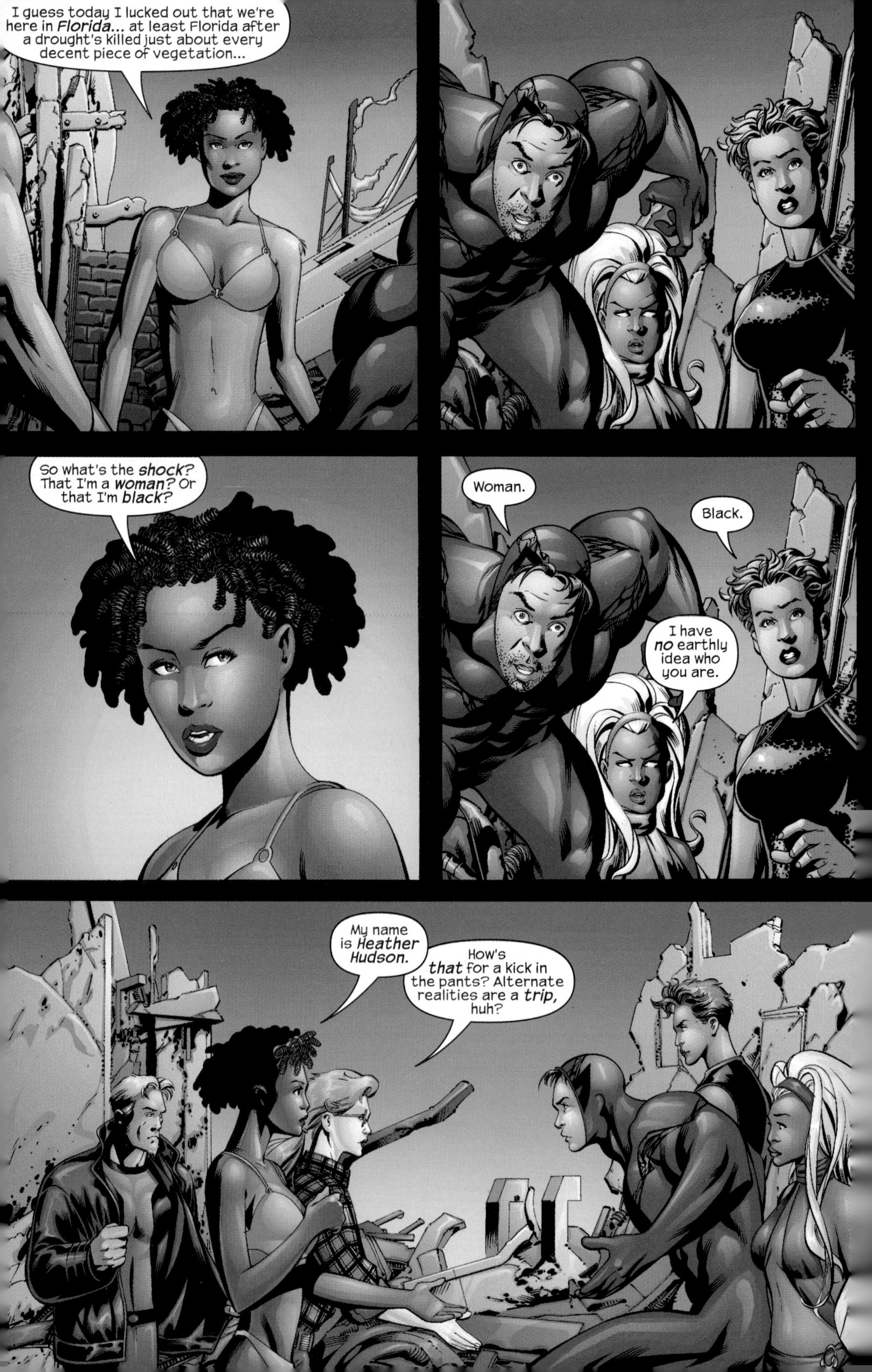
I guess today I lucked out that we're here in *Florida...* at least Florida after a drought's killed just about every decent piece of vegetation...
So what's the *shock?* That I'm a *woman?* Or that I'm *black?*
Woman.
Black.
I have *no* earthly idea who you are.
My name is *Heather Hudson.*
How's *that* for a kick in the pants? Alternate realities are a *trip,* huh?

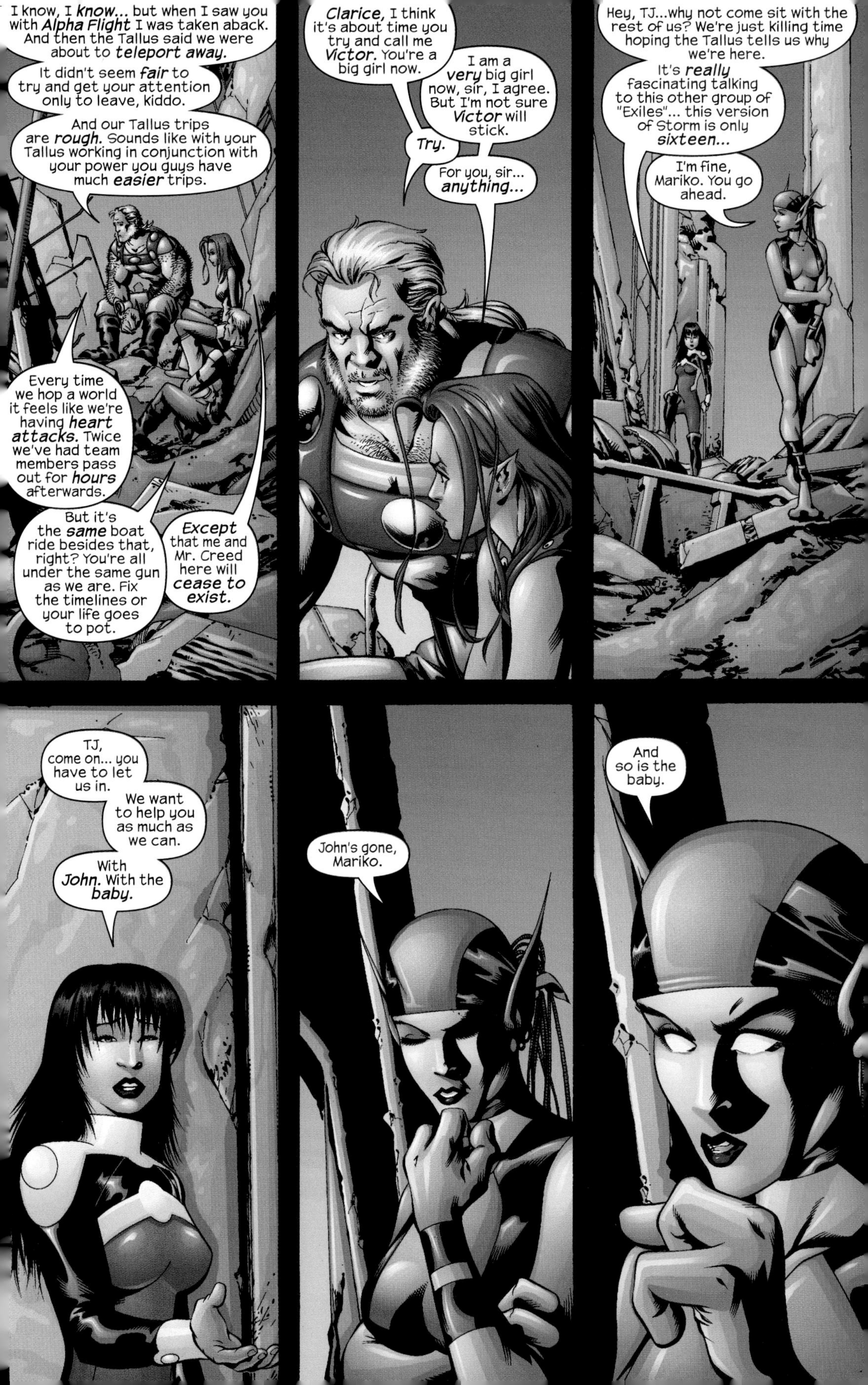
I know, I know... but when I saw you with Alpha Flight I was taken aback. And then the Tallus said we were about to teleport away.
It didn't seem fair to try and get your attention only to leave, kiddo.
And our Tallus trips are rough. Sounds like with your Tallus working in conjunction with your power you guys have much easier trips.
Every time we hop a world it feels like we're having heart attacks. Twice we've had team members pass out for hours afterwards.
But it's the same boat ride besides that, right? You're all under the same gun as we are. Fix the timelines or your life goes to pot.
Except that me and Mr. Creed here will cease to exist.
Clarice, I think it's about time you try and call me Victor. You're a big girl now.
I am a very big girl now, sir, I agree. But I'm not sure Victor will stick.
Try.
For you, sir... anything...
Hey, TJ...why not come sit with the rest of us? We're just killing time hoping the Tallus tells us why we're here.
It's really fascinating talking to this other group of "Exiles"... this version of Storm is only sixteen...
I'm fine, Mariko. You go ahead.
TJ, come on... you have to let us in.
We want to help you as much as we can.
With John. With the baby.
John's gone, Mariko.
And so is the baby.

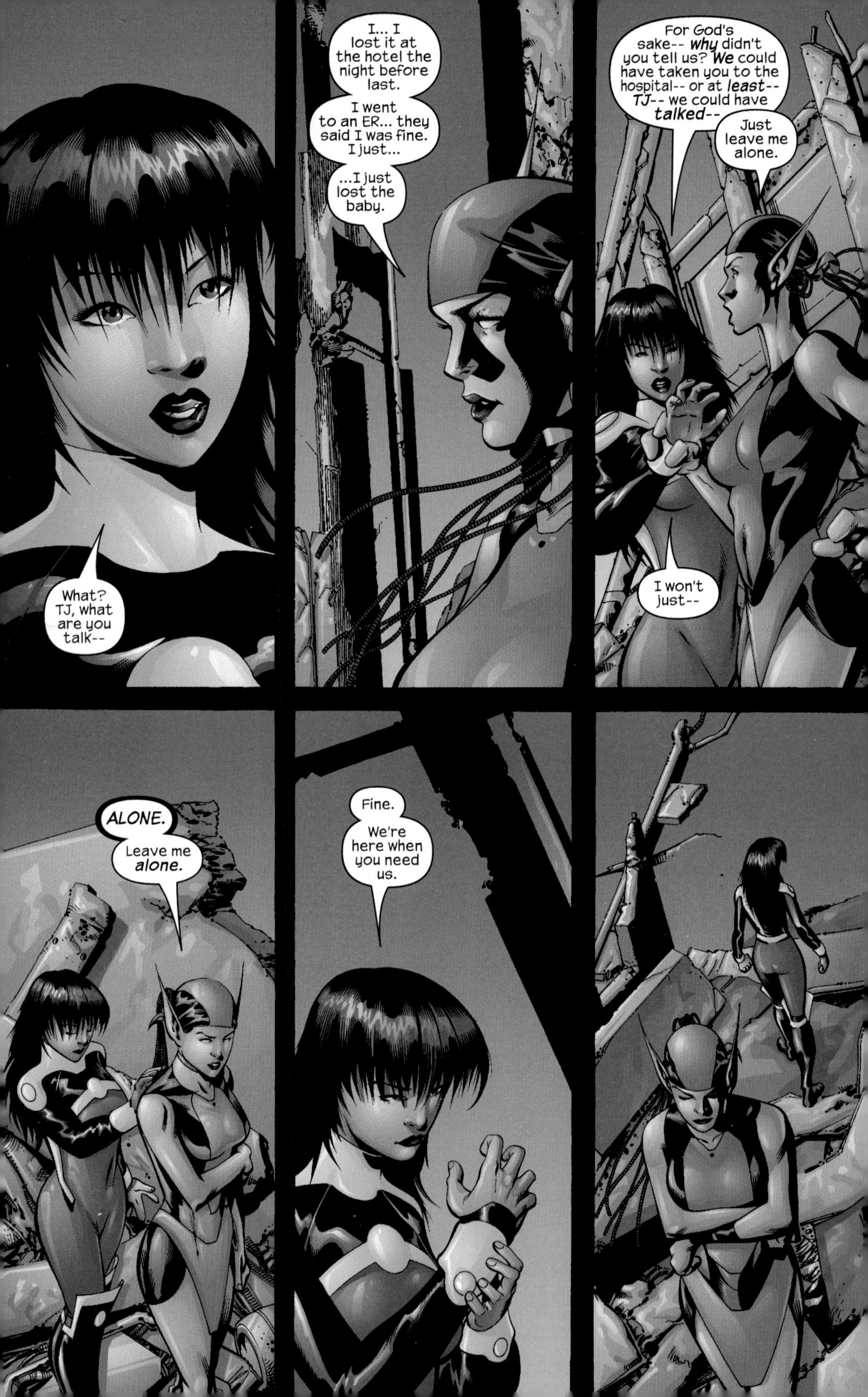
What? TJ, what are you talk--
I... I lost it at the hotel the night before last.
I went to an ER... they said I was fine. I just...
...I just lost the baby.
For God's sake-- *why* didn't you tell us? *We* could have taken you to the hospital-- or at *least*-- *TJ*-- we could have *talked*--
Just leave me alone.
I won't just--
ALONE.
Leave me *alone.*
Fine.
We're here when you need us.

"I don't like this. I don't like *them*."

"Hey, lady, you have *not* been around long enough to start whining about our predicament... 'sides...'"

...I *like* meeting up with another team. It's *hopeful*. It implies a *greater order* to this disaster we live in. Maybe there's a lot *more* of us out there.

Maybe this whole thing is incredibly *common* and we'll be back in our own beds before we know it.

I can agree with you on *that*... it's just that this crew makes me nervous. Have you *heard* the missions they had to complete to jump to their next worlds?

They *crippled* Doctor Strange. They threw Atlantis into *war* with the Inhumans.

They *blew up* Avengers mansion.

Laid waste to the Morlocks.

They *murdered* Tony Stark.

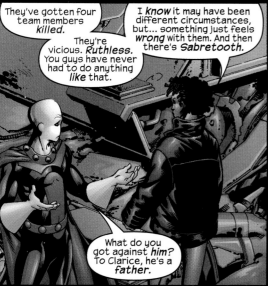

They've gotten four team members *killed.*

They're vicious. *Ruthless.* You guys have never had to do anything *like* that.

I *know* it may have been different circumstances, but... something just feels *wrong* with them. And then there's *Sabretooth.*

What do you got against *him*? To Clarice, he's a *father.*

Yes. But in *every one* of our realities-- he's the *coldest* of killers any of us has ever seen. He's a *monster...* not a "dad".

Hey, gang! Listen up!

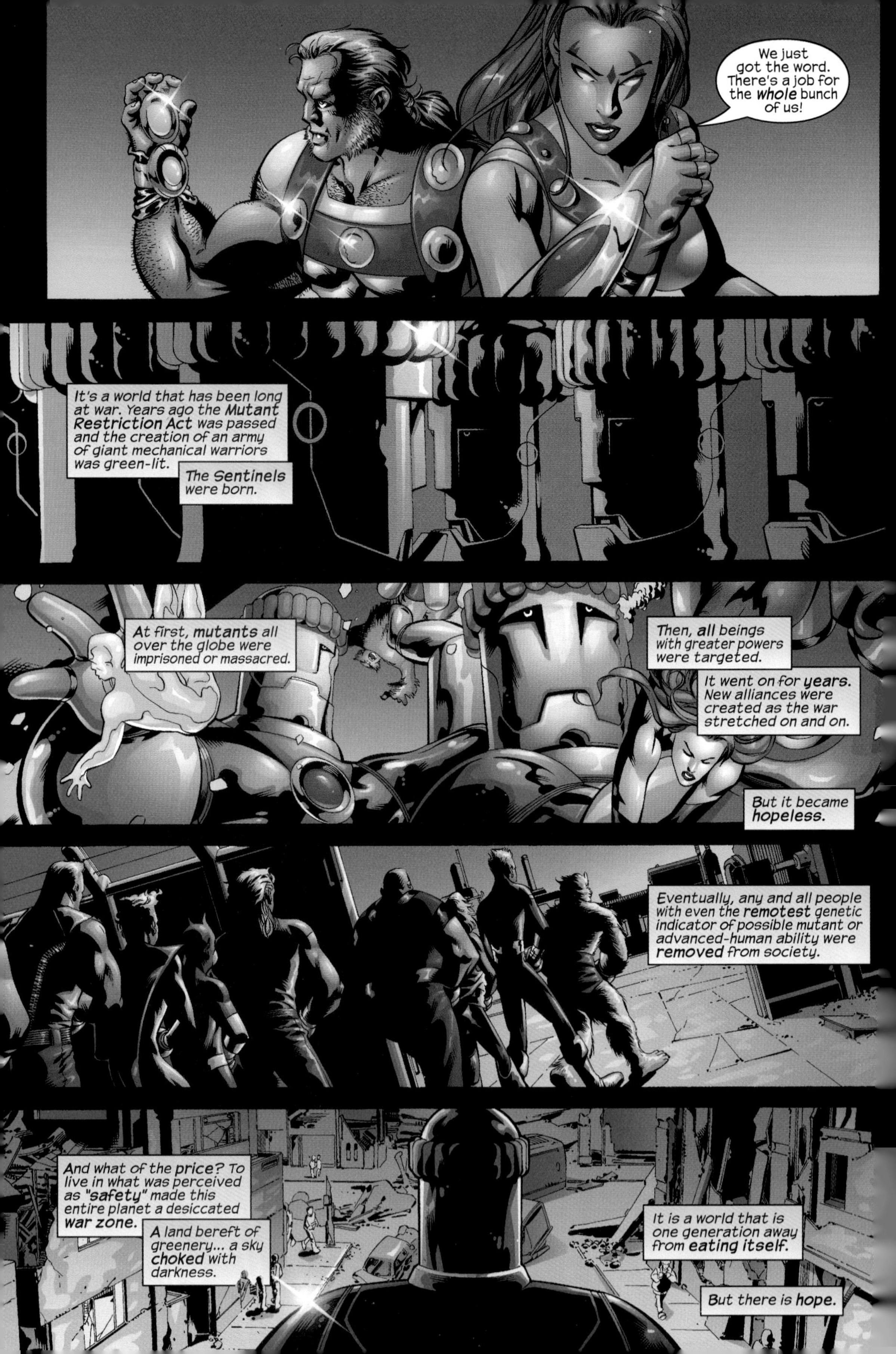

We just got the word. There's a job for the whole bunch of us!
It's a world that has been long at war. Years ago the Mutant Restriction Act was passed and the creation of an army of giant mechanical warriors was green-lit.
The Sentinels were born.
At first, mutants all over the globe were imprisoned or massacred.
Then, all beings with greater powers were targeted.
It went on for years. New alliances were created as the war stretched on and on.
But it became hopeless.
Eventually, any and all people with even the remotest genetic indicator of possible mutant or advanced-human ability were removed from society.
And what of the price? To live in what was perceived as "safety" made this entire planet a desiccated war zone.
A land bereft of greenery... a sky choked with darkness.
It is a world that is one generation away from eating itself.
But there is hope.

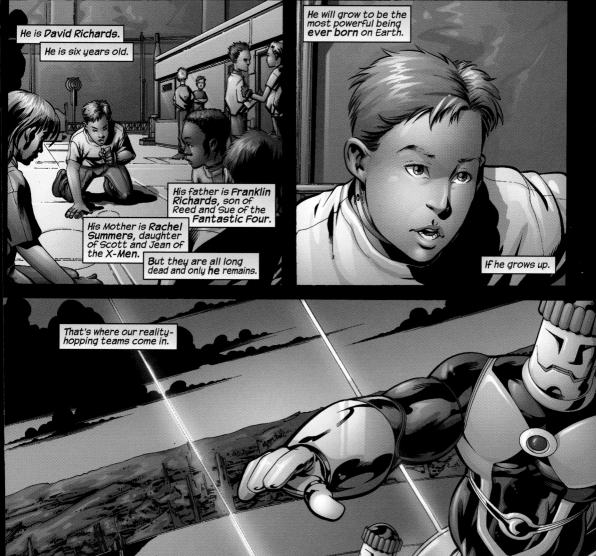

He is David Richards.

He is six years old.

He will grow to be the most powerful being ever born on Earth.

His father is Franklin Richards, son of Reed and Sue of the Fantastic Four.

His Mother is Rachel Summers, daughter of Scott and Jean of the X-Men.

But they are all long dead and only he remains.

If he grows up.

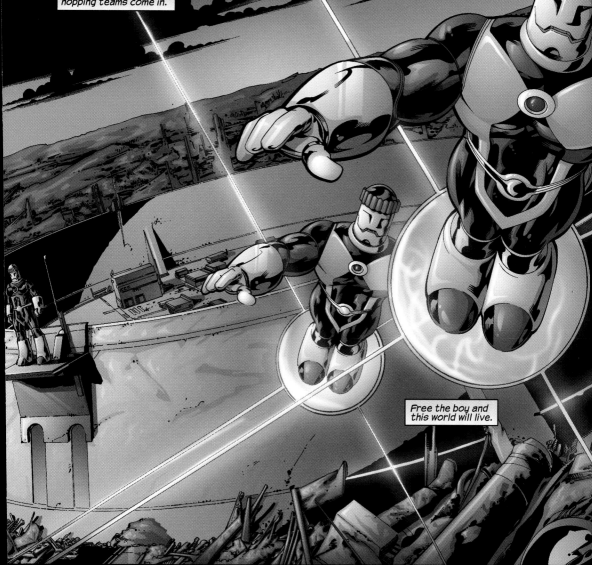

That's where our reality-hopping teams come in.

Free the boy and this world will live.

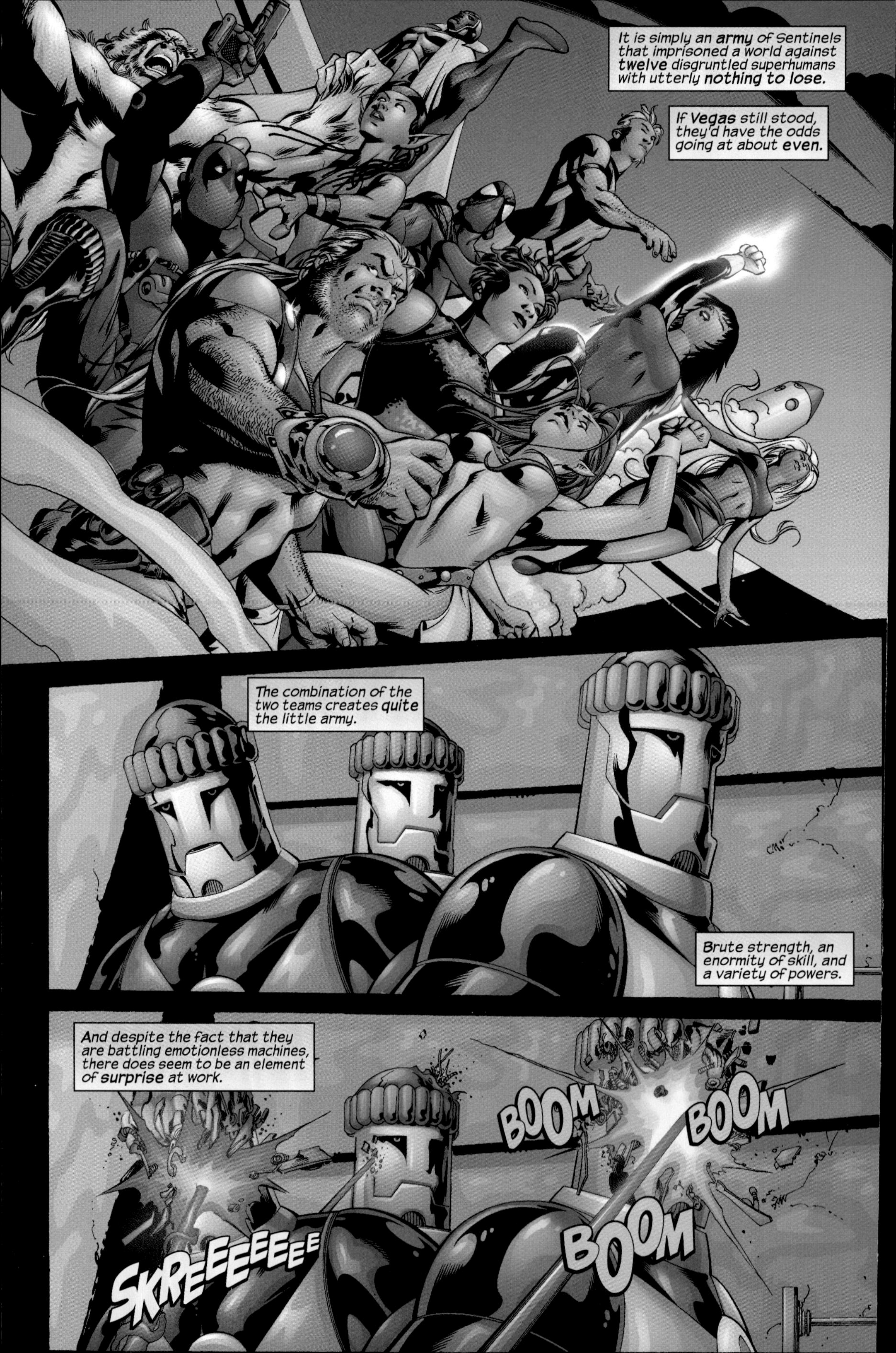
It is simply an army of Sentinels that imprisoned a world against twelve disgruntled superhumans with utterly nothing to lose.
If Vegas still stood, they'd have the odds going at about even.
The combination of the two teams creates quite the little army.
Brute strength, an enormity of skill, and a variety of powers.
And despite the fact that they are battling emotionless machines, there does seem to be an element of surprise at work.
BOOM
BOOM
SKREEEEEEEE
BOOM

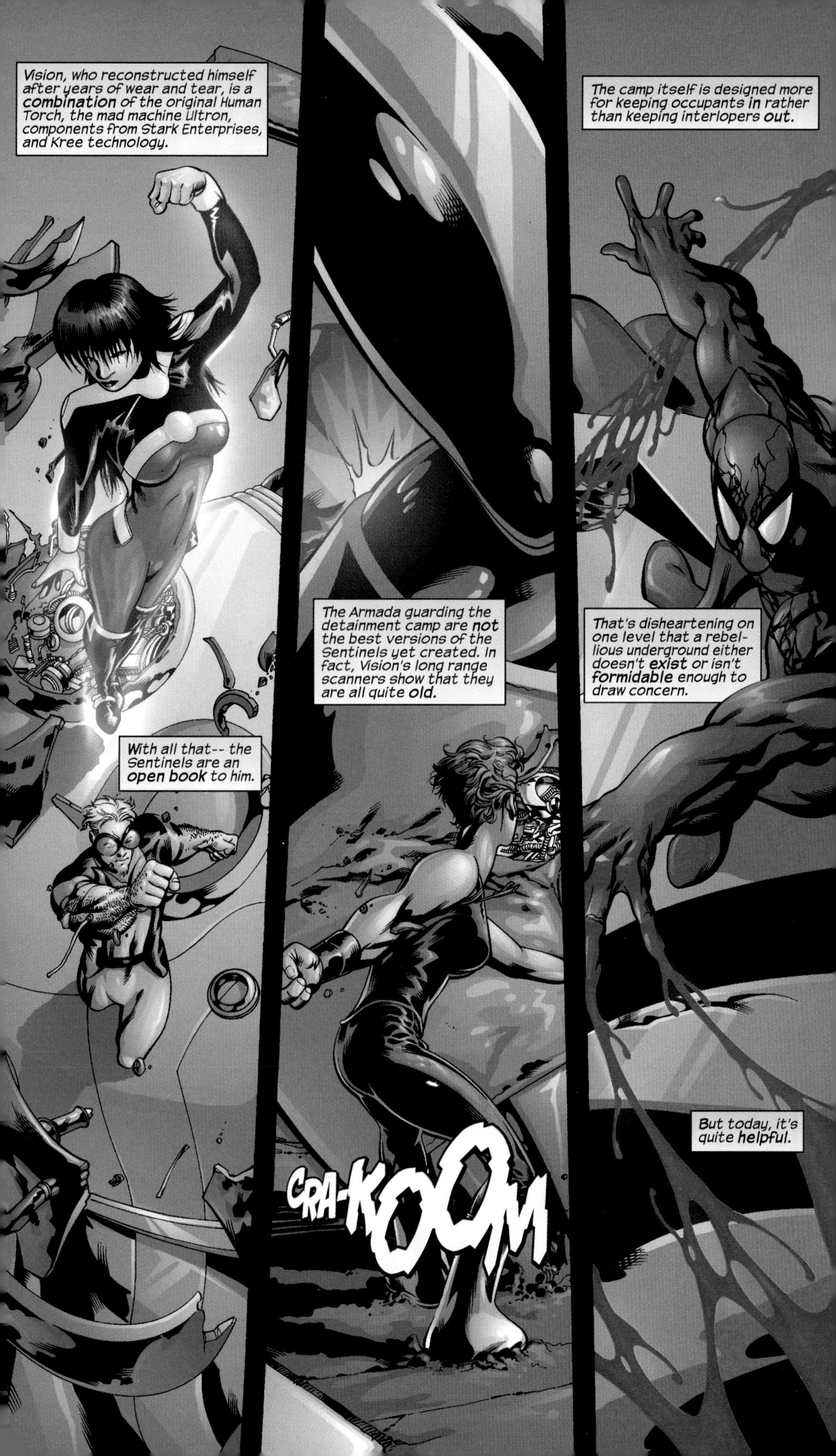
Vision, who reconstructed himself after years of wear and tear, is a combination of the original Human Torch, the mad machine Ultron, components from Stark Enterprises, and Kree technology.
With all that-- the Sentinels are an open book to him.
The Armada guarding the detainment camp are not the best versions of the Sentinels yet created. In fact, Vision's long range scanners show that they are all quite old.
GRA-KOOM
The camp itself is designed more for keeping occupants in rather than keeping interlopers out.
That's disheartening on one level that a rebellious underground either doesn't exist or isn't formidable enough to draw concern.
But today, it's quite helpful.

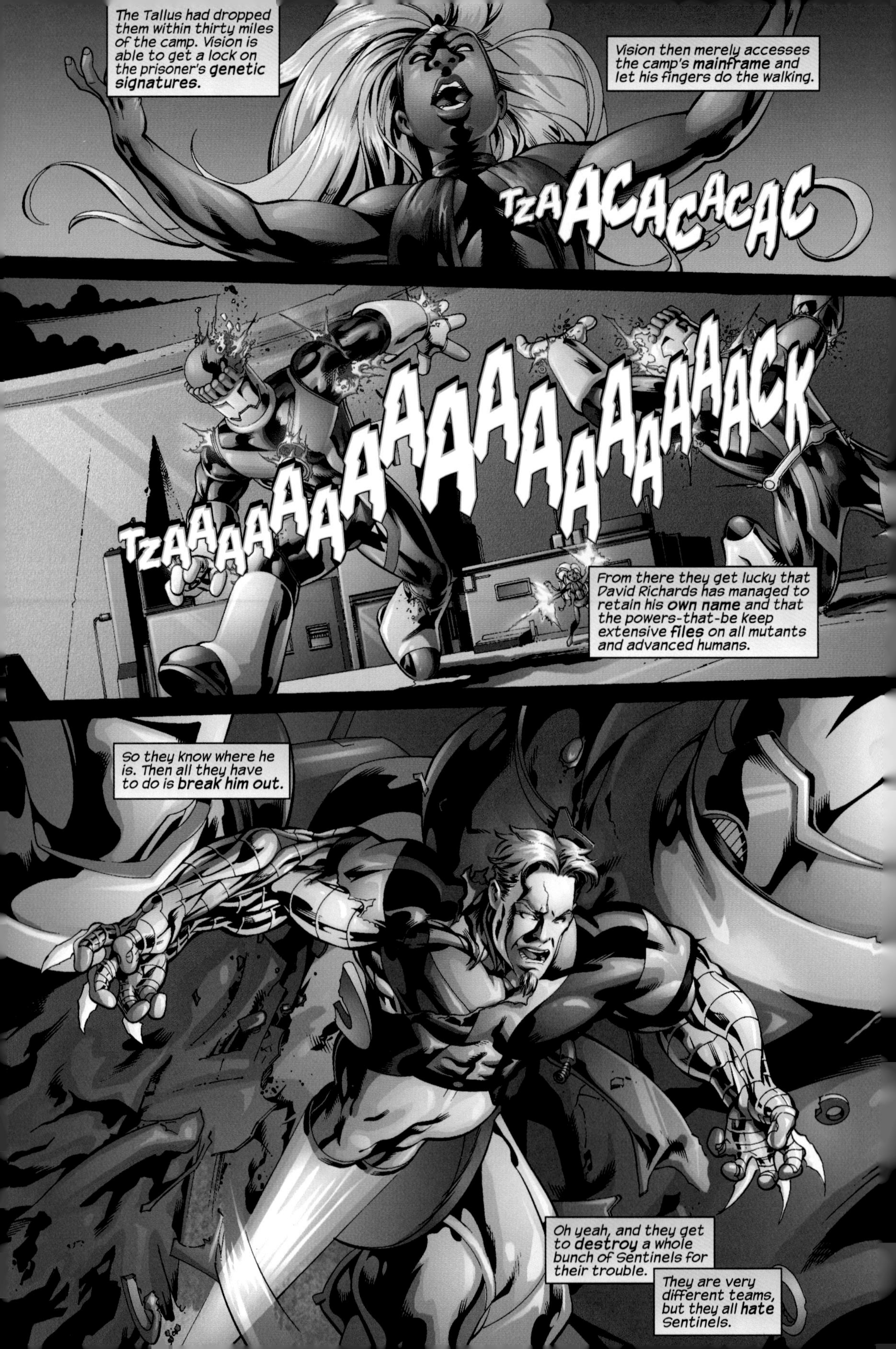
The Tallus had dropped them within thirty miles of the camp. Vision is able to get a lock on the prisoner's **genetic signatures.**
Vision then merely accesses the camp's **mainframe** and let his fingers do the walking.
TZAACACACACAC
TZAAAAAAAAAAAAAAAAACK
From there they get lucky that David Richards has managed to retain his **own name** and that the powers-that-be keep extensive **files** on all mutants and advanced humans.
So they know where he is. Then all they have to do is **break him out.**
Oh yeah, and they get to **destroy** a whole bunch of Sentinels for their trouble.
They are very different teams, but they all **hate** Sentinels.

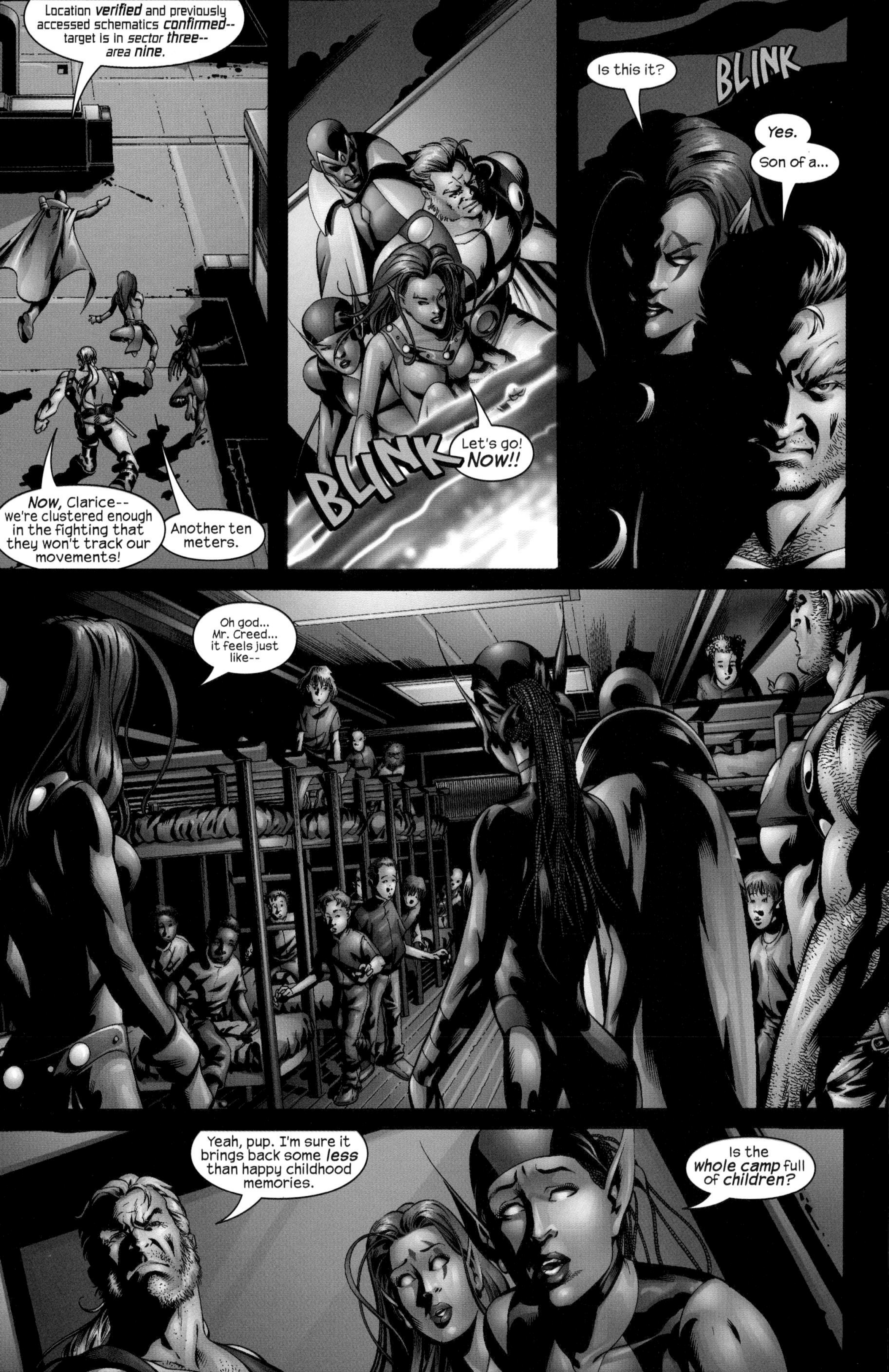
Location *verified* and previously accessed schematics *confirmed*-- target is in *sector three*-- *area nine*.
Now, Clarice-- we're clustered enough in the fighting that they won't track our movements!
Another ten meters.
BLINK
Let's go! *NOW!!*
Is this it?
BLINK
Yes.
Son of a...
Oh god... Mr. Creed... it feels just like--
Yeah, pup. I'm sure it brings back some *less* than happy childhood memories.
Is the *whole camp* full of *children?*

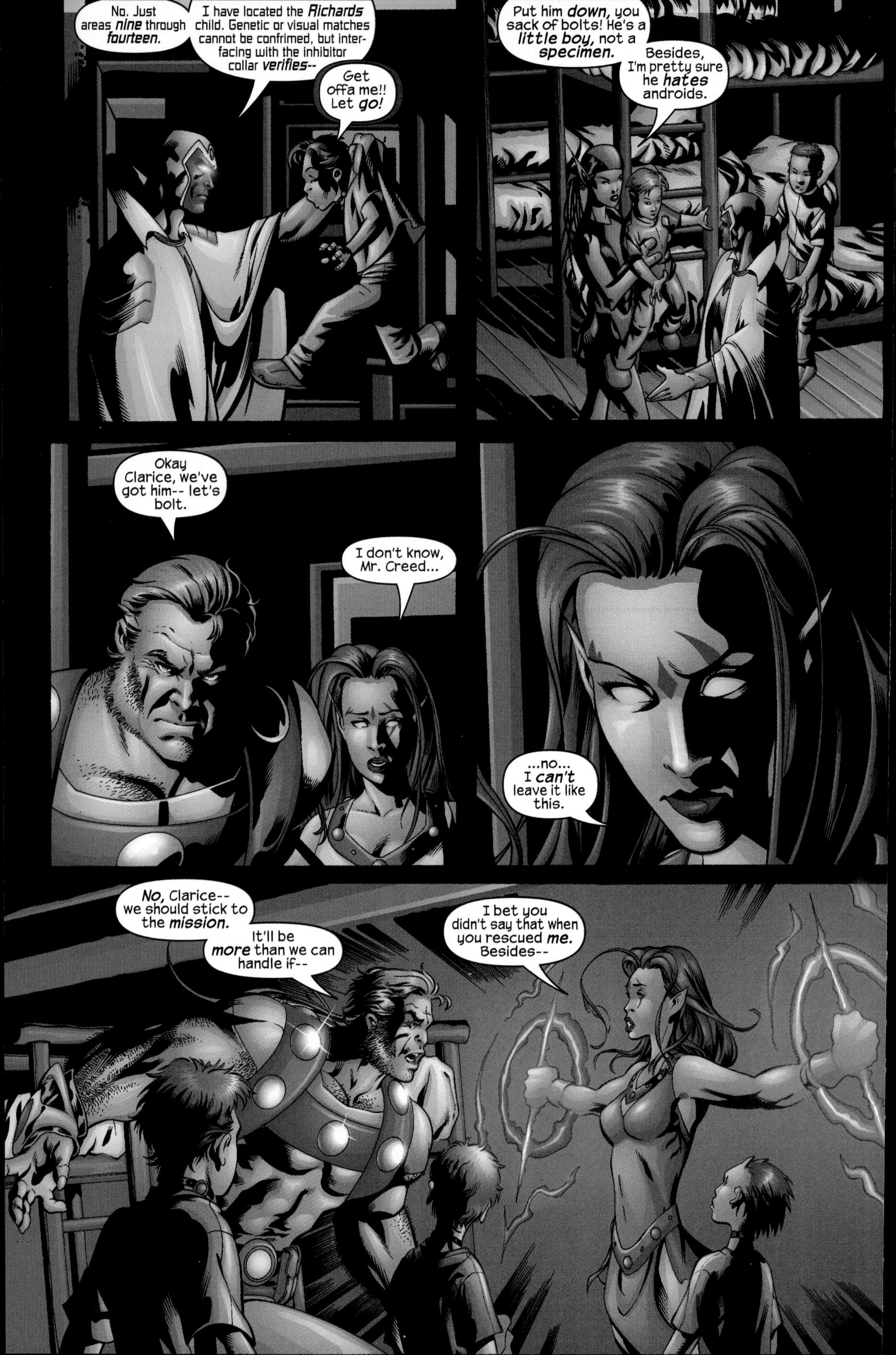
No. Just areas *nine* through *fourteen*.
I have located the *Richards* child. Genetic or visual matches cannot be confirmed, but interfacing with the inhibitor collar *verifies*--
Get offa me!! Let *go!*
Put him *down,* you sack of bolts! He's a *little boy,* not a *specimen.*
Besides, I'm pretty sure he *hates* androids.
Okay Clarice, we've got him-- let's bolt.
I don't know, Mr. Creed...
...no... I *can't* leave it like this.
No, Clarice-- we should stick to the *mission.*
It'll be *more* than we can handle if--
I bet you didn't say that when you rescued *me.* Besides--

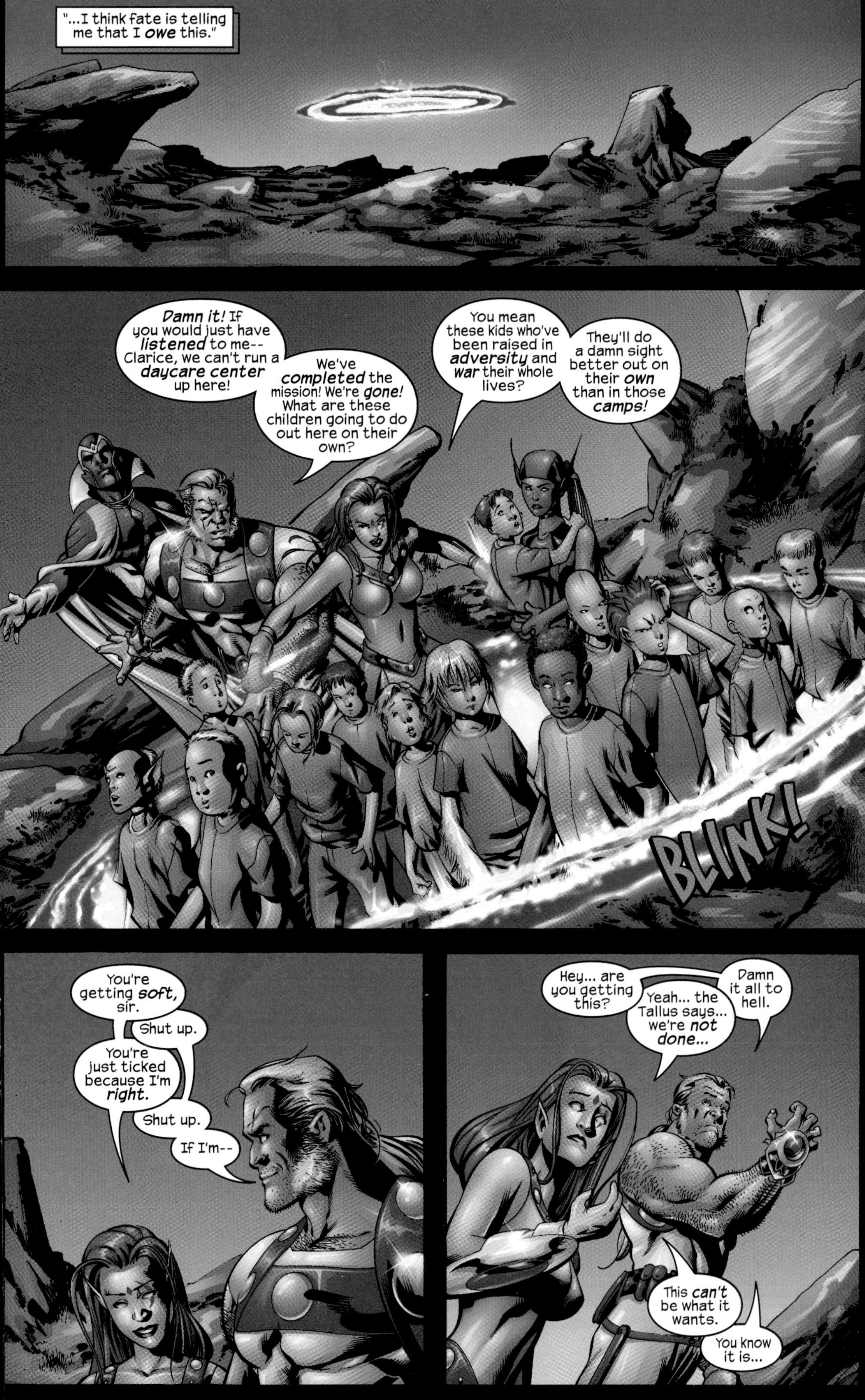
"...I think fate is telling me that I owe this."
Damn it! If you would just have listened to me-- Clarice, we can't run a daycare center up here!
We've completed the mission! We're gone! What are these children going to do out here on their own?
You mean these kids who've been raised in adversity and war their whole lives?
They'll do a damn sight better out on their own than in those camps!
BLINK!
You're getting soft, sir.
Shut up.
You're just ticked because I'm right.
Shut up.
If I'm--
Hey... are you getting this?
Yeah... the Tallus says... we're not done...
Damn it all to hell.
This can't be what it wants.
You know it is...

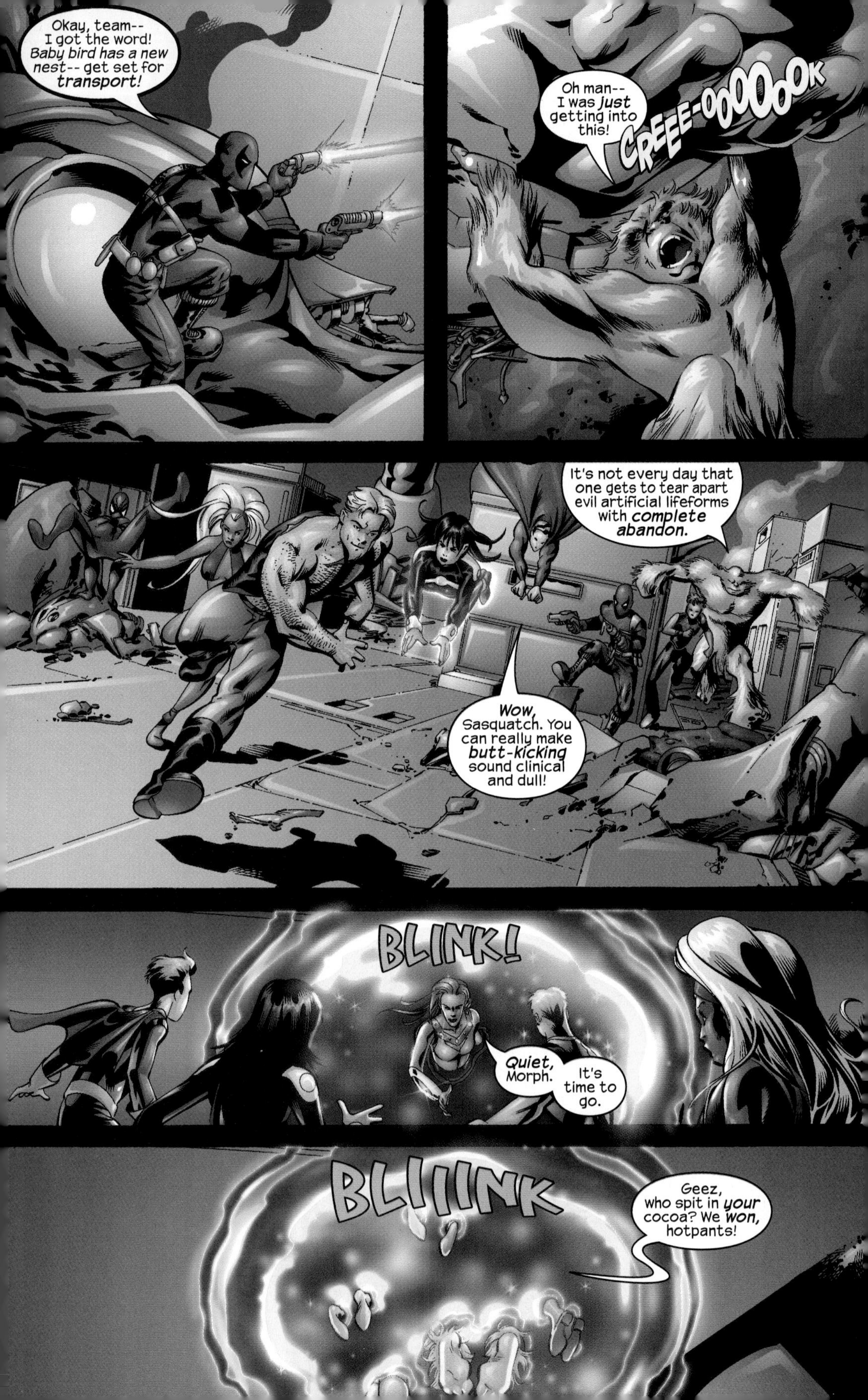
Okay, team-- I got the word! Baby bird has a new nest-- get set for transport!
Oh man-- I was just getting into this!
CREEE-OOOOOOK
It's not every day that one gets to tear apart evil artificial lifeforms with complete abandon.
Wow, Sasquatch. You can really make butt-kicking sound clinical and dull!
BLINK!
Quiet, Morph.
It's time to go.
BLIIINK
Geez, who spit in your cocoa? We won, hotpants!

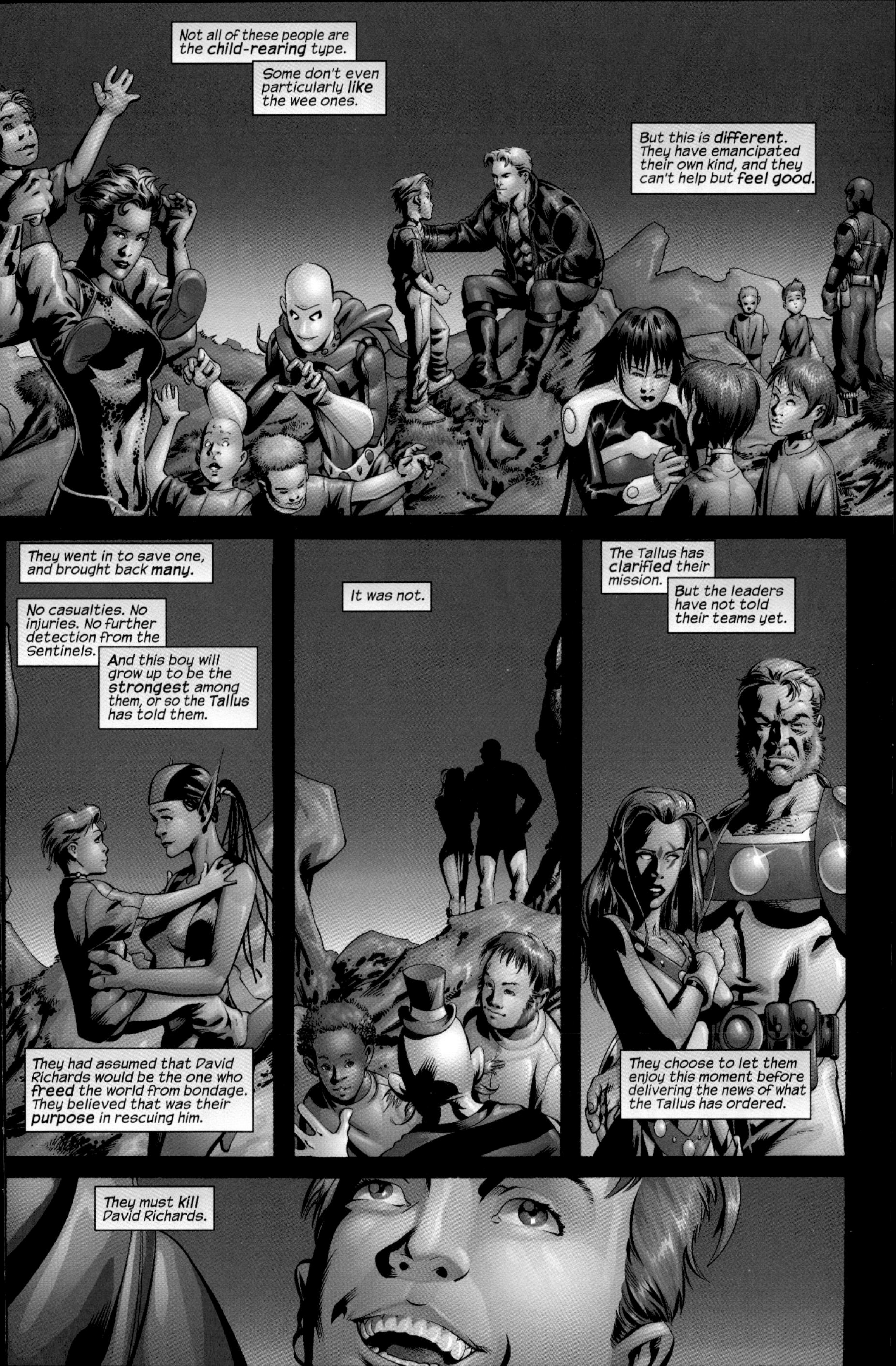
Not all of these people are the child-rearing type.
Some don't even particularly like the wee ones.
But this is different. They have emancipated their own kind, and they can't help but feel good.
They went in to save one, and brought back many.
No casualties. No injuries. No further detection from the Sentinels.
And this boy will grow up to be the strongest among them, or so the Tallus has told them.
They had assumed that David Richards would be the one who freed the world from bondage. They believed that was their purpose in rescuing him.
It was not.
The Tallus has clarified their mission.
But the leaders have not told their teams yet.
They choose to let them enjoy this moment before delivering the news of what the Tallus has ordered.
They must kill David Richards.

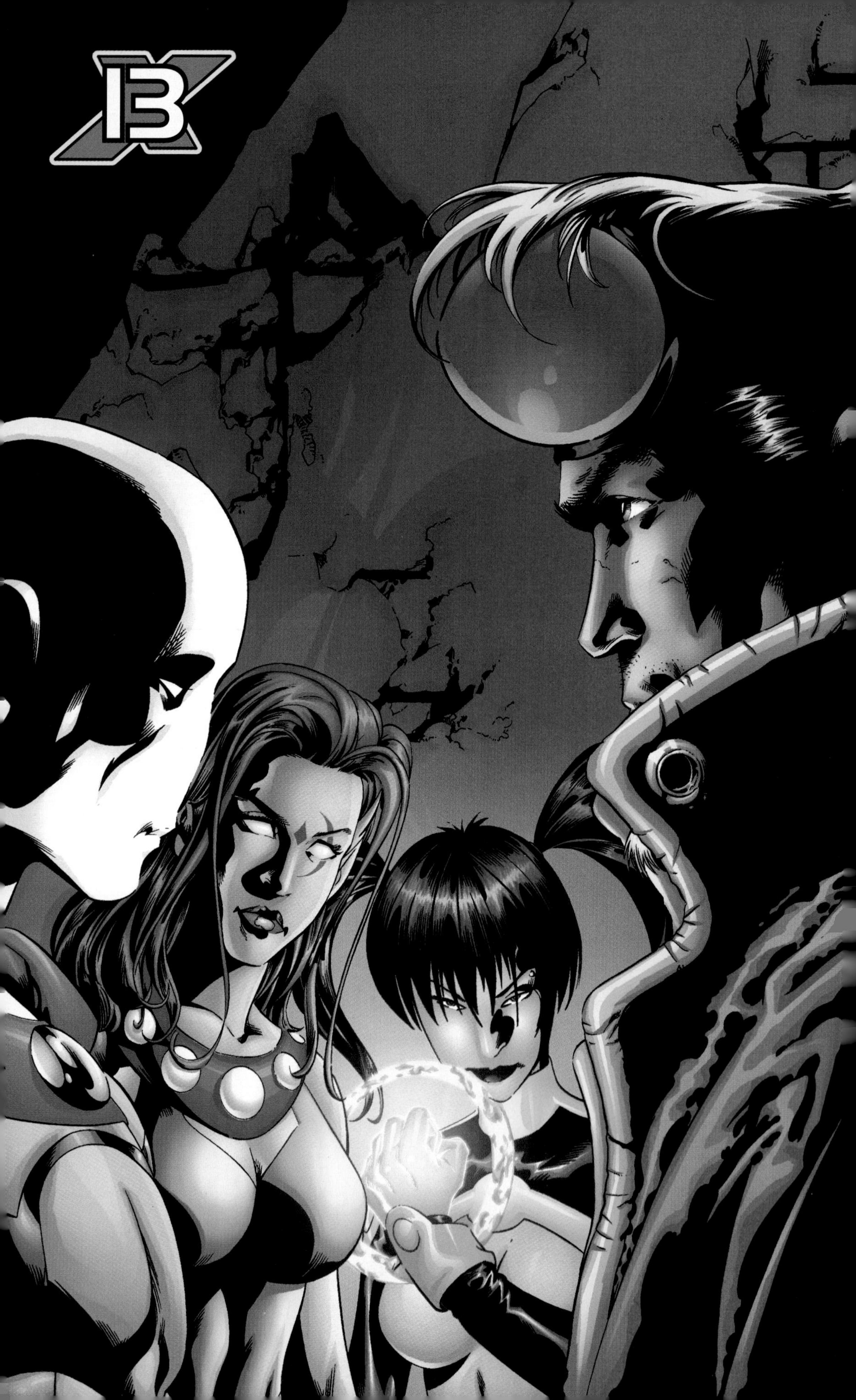

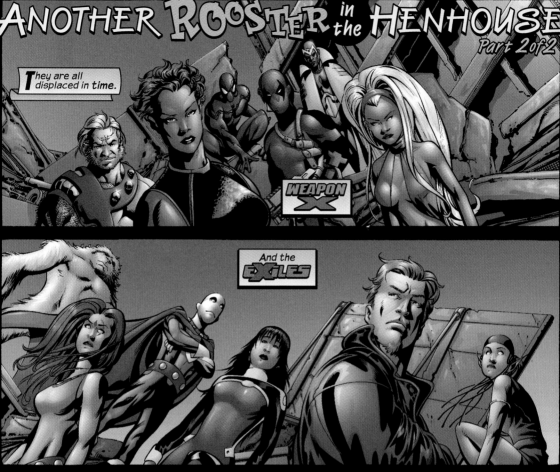

ANOTHER ROOSTER in the HENHOUSE
Part 2 of 2
They are all displaced in time.
WEAPON X
And the EXILES
All trying to right the wrongs in the timeline that will eventually return each of them to their own lives.
Both teams possessing a Tallus. A mysterious device that cryptically instructs them on what actions to take.
They are cast together here to free a child from bondage.
He lives in a world of crushing persecution. All mutants or manner of superhumans have either been exterminated or imprisoned.
Their jailers and executioners are one and the same.
The SENTINELS
But when David Richards grows, he will develop power so immense that he will set free the entire planet.

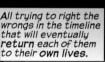

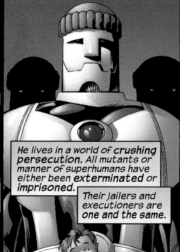

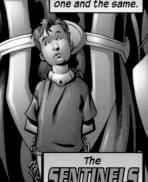

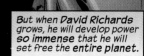

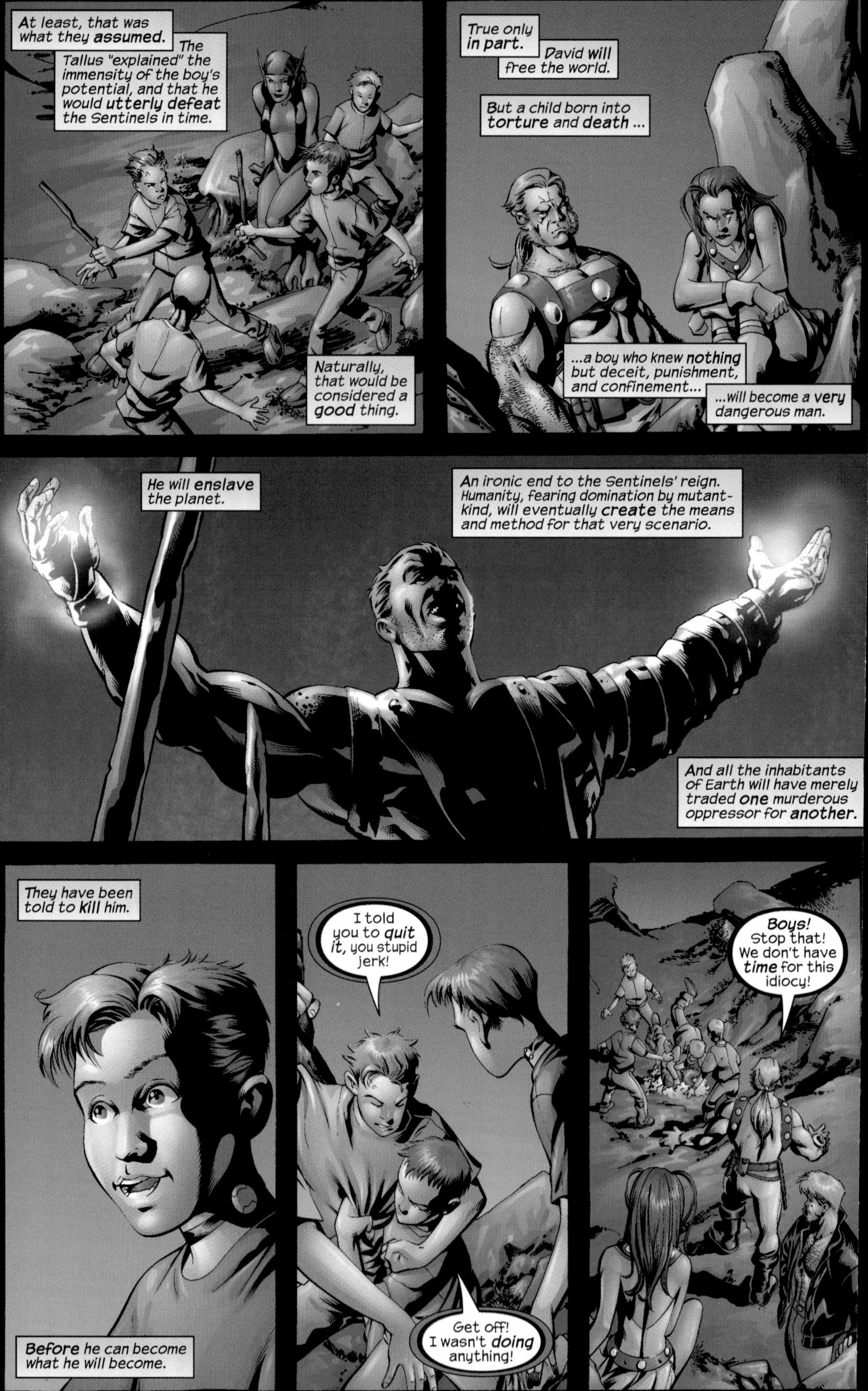
At least, that was what they assumed.
The Tallus "explained" the immensity of the boy's potential, and that he would utterly defeat the Sentinels in time.
Naturally, that would be considered a good thing.
True only in part.
David will free the world.
But a child born into torture and death ...
...a boy who knew nothing but deceit, punishment, and confinement...
...will become a very dangerous man.
He will enslave the planet.
An ironic end to the Sentinels' reign. Humanity, fearing domination by mutant-kind, will eventually create the means and method for that very scenario.
And all the inhabitants of Earth will have merely traded one murderous oppressor for another.
They have been told to kill him.
Before he can become what he will become.
I told you to quit it, you stupid jerk!
Get off! I wasn't doing anything!
Boys! Stop that! We don't have time for this idiocy!

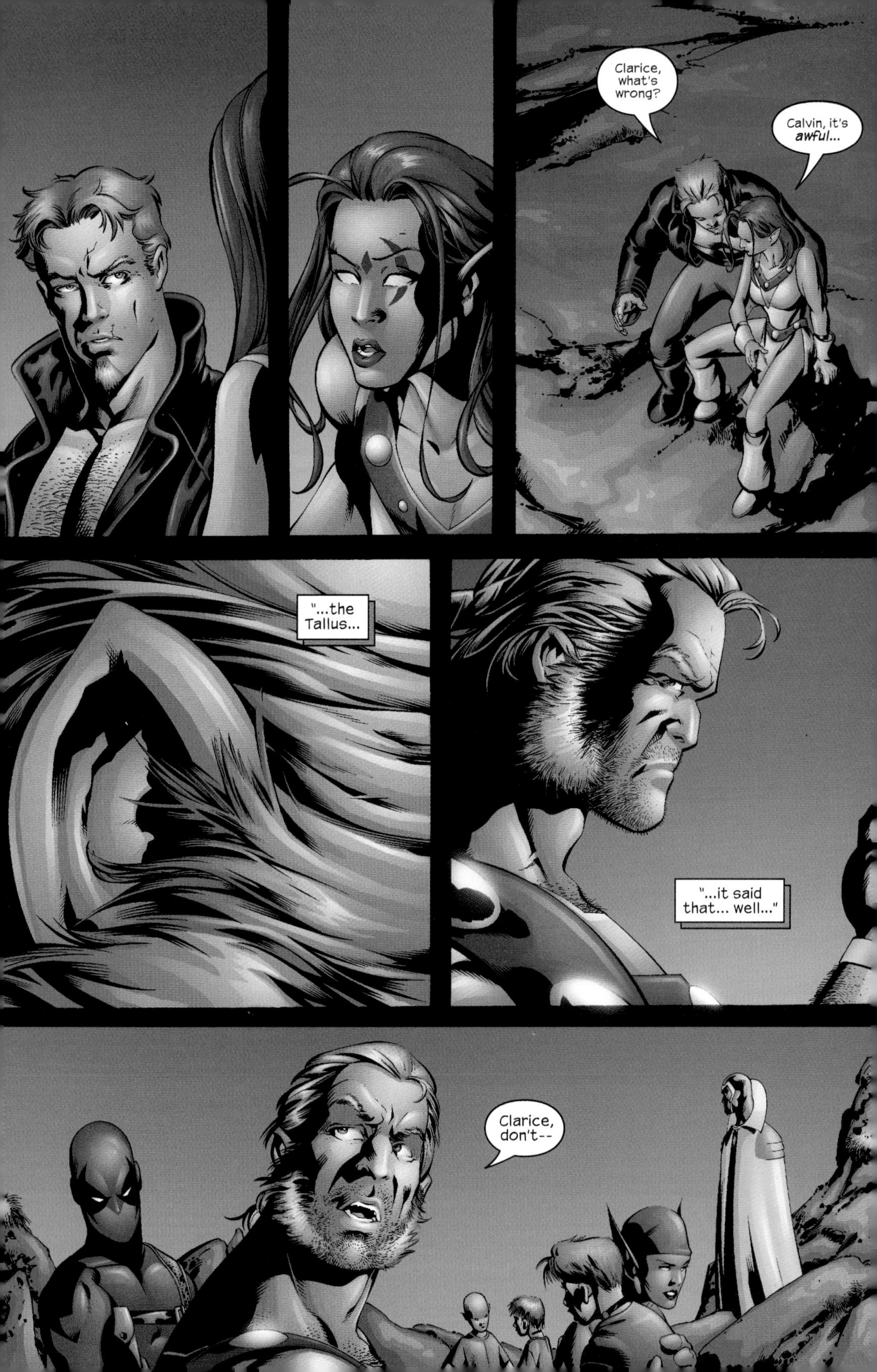

Clarice, what's wrong?
Calvin, it's *awful*...
"...the Tallus...
"...it said that... well..."
Clarice, don't--

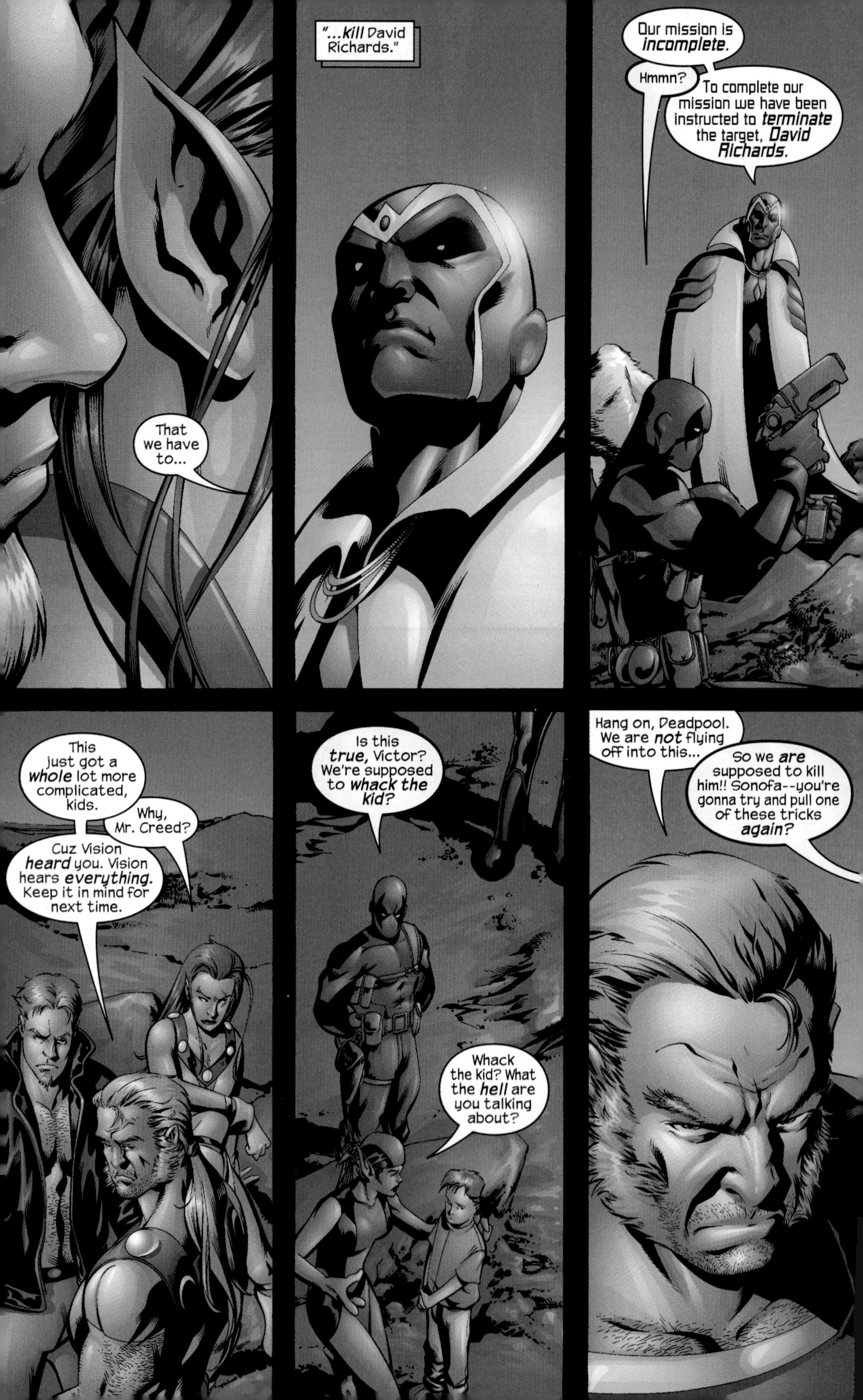
That we have to...
"...kill David Richards."
Our mission is incomplete.
Hmmn?
To complete our mission we have been instructed to terminate the target, David Richards.
This just got a whole lot more complicated, kids.
Why, Mr. Creed?
Cuz Vision heard you. Vision hears everything. Keep it in mind for next time.
Is this true, Victor? We're supposed to whack the kid?
Whack the kid? What the hell are you talking about?
Hang on, Deadpool. We are not flying off into this...
So we are supposed to kill him!! Sonofa--you're gonna try and pull one of these tricks again?

We are **not** going to murder a little boy.

What-- why **not**? What's the **matter** with you people?

I can't believe this...

Seriously. Gang, it's **him** or **us.** We don't hop forward if we don't finish the job.

How much longer did we have to stay on that godforsaken planet because **you** wouldn't let us kill **Gambit**?! **Months!**

And in the end we had to kill him **anyway.** Rogue, too!

I'm sorry, Nocturne... but he's right. This **has** to be the way.

You're @#$% **right**, I'm right.

No one move. Or it'll be a lot more than the **boy** who gets it, okay?

No! We are **not** going through this again! This ends now!

HEY! Lay off him, you **psychopath!** You are not--

CRACK!

Mr. Creed...?

Clarice... this isn't some damn **rabbit** hunt from home. Okay?

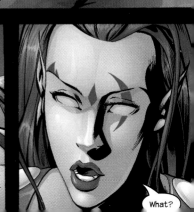

What?

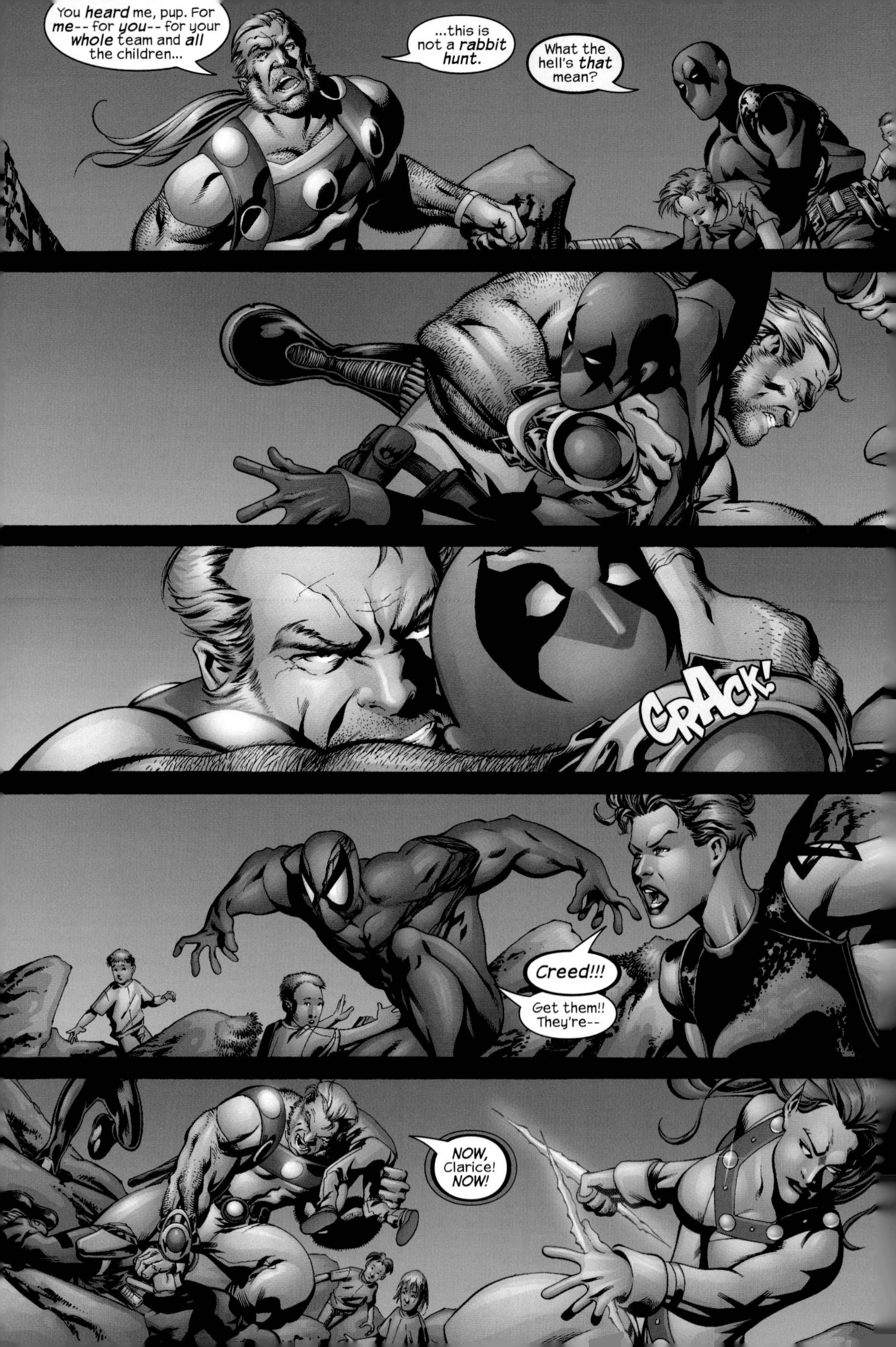
You heard me, pup. For me-- for you-- for your whole team and all the children...
...this is not a rabbit hunt.
What the hell's that mean?
CRACK!
Creed!!!
Get them!! They're--
NOW, Clarice! NOW!

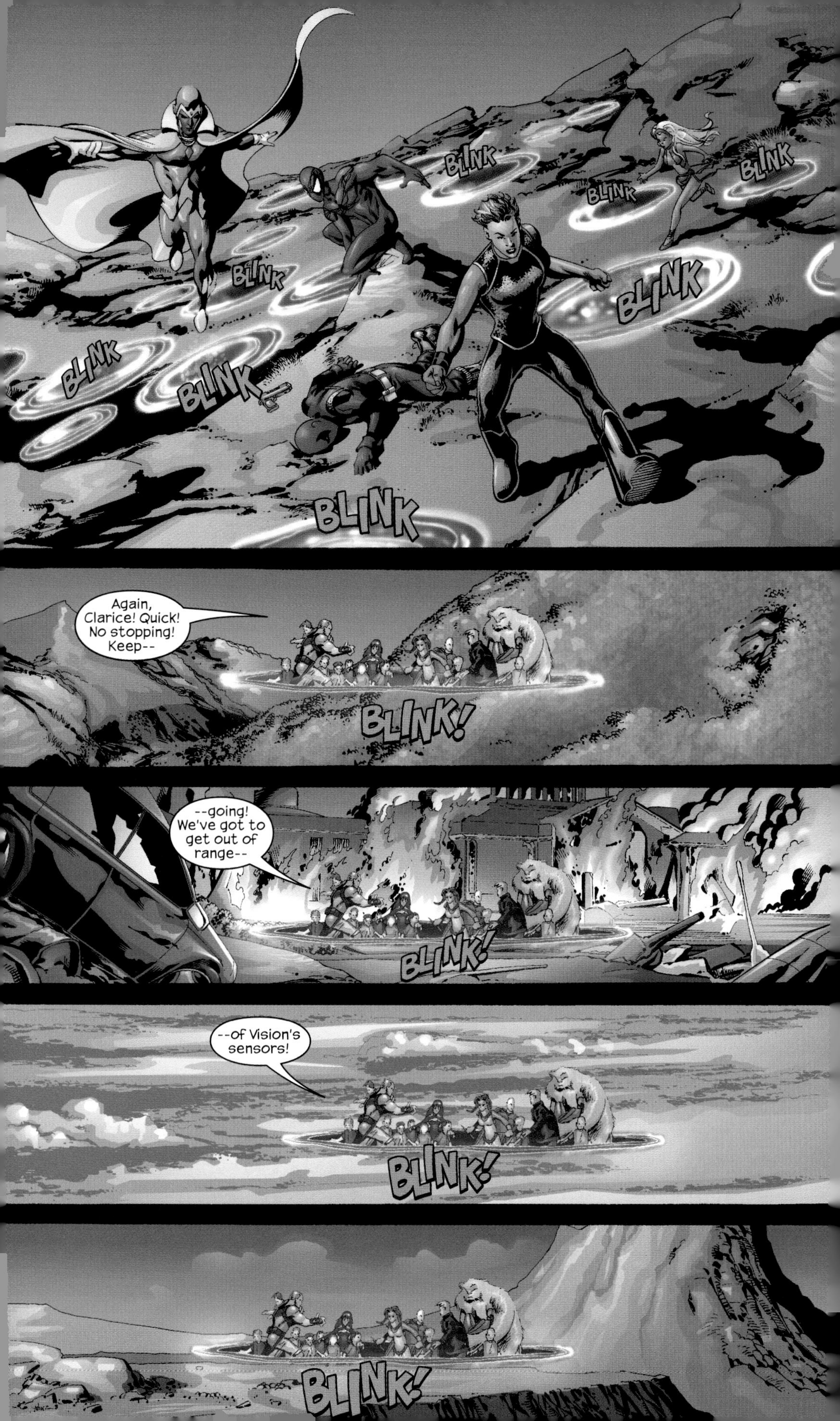

BLINK
BLINK
BLINK
BLINK
BLINK
BLINK
BLINK
BLINK
Again, Clarice! Quick! No stopping! Keep--
BLINK!
--going! We've got to get out of range--
BLINK!
--of Vision's sensors!
BLINK!
BLINK!

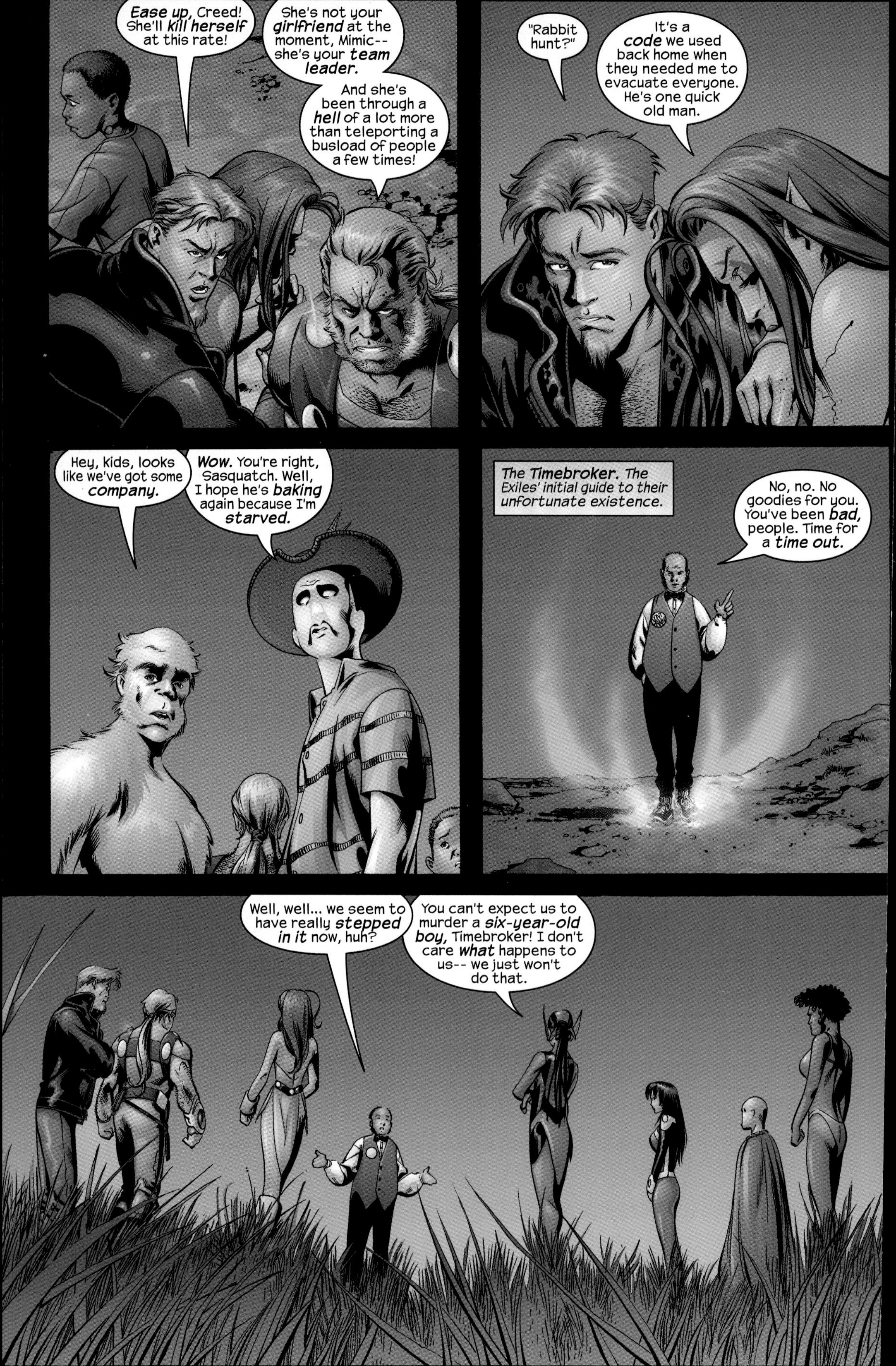

Ease up, Creed! She'll kill herself at this rate!
She's not your girlfriend at the moment, Mimic-- she's your team leader.
And she's been through a hell of a lot more than teleporting a busload of people a few times!
"Rabbit hunt?"
It's a code we used back home when they needed me to evacuate everyone. He's one quick old man.
Hey, kids, looks like we've got some company.
Wow. You're right, Sasquatch. Well, I hope he's baking again because I'm starved.
The Timebroker. The Exiles' initial guide to their unfortunate existence.
No, no. No goodies for you. You've been bad, people. Time for a time out.
Well, well... we seem to have really stepped in it now, huh?
You can't expect us to murder a six-year-old boy, Timebroker! I don't care what happens to us-- we just won't do that.

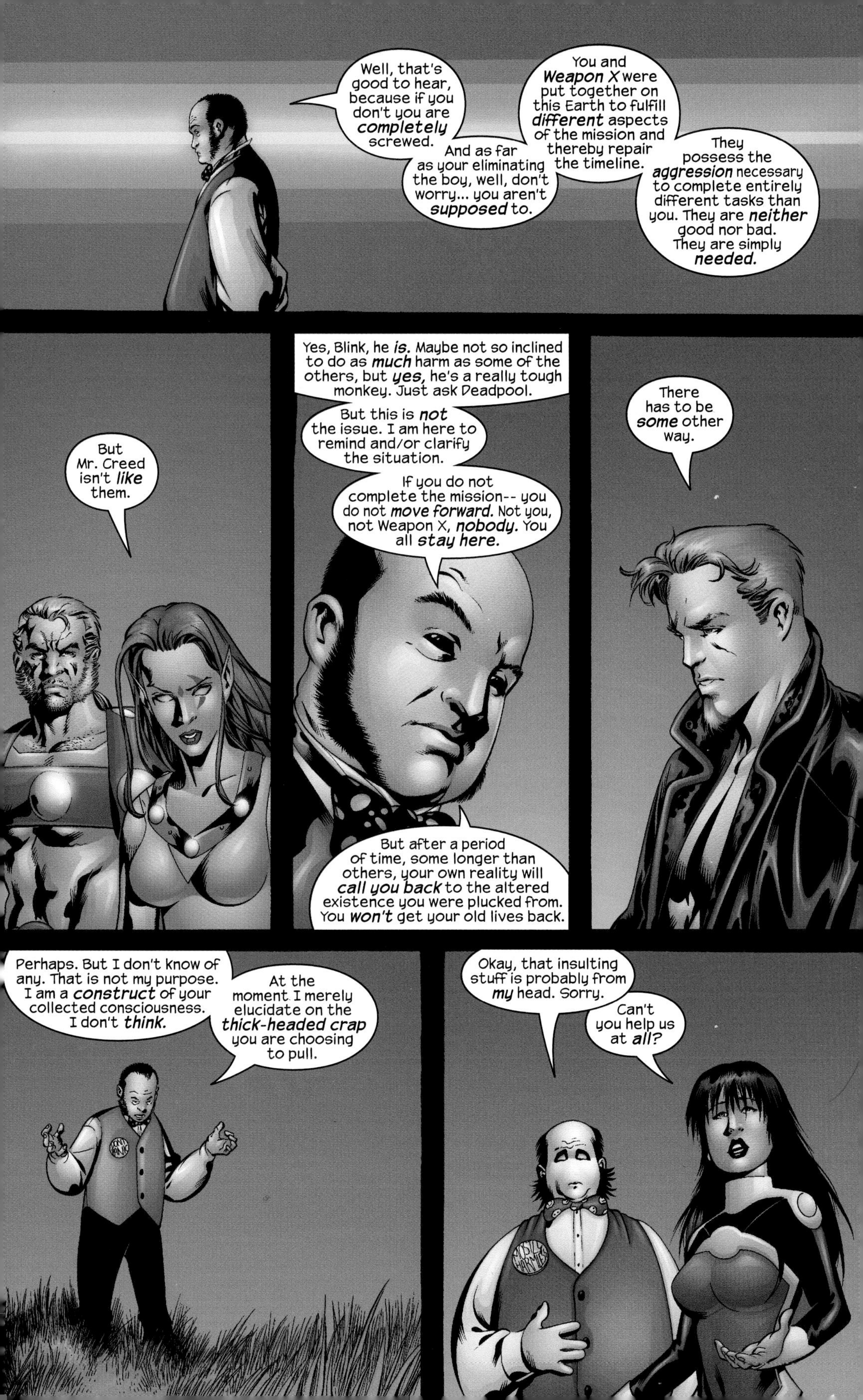

Well, that's good to hear, because if you don't you are completely screwed.
And as far as your eliminating the boy, well, don't worry... you aren't supposed to.
You and Weapon X were put together on this Earth to fulfill different aspects of the mission and thereby repair the timeline.
They possess the aggression necessary to complete entirely different tasks than you. They are neither good nor bad. They are simply needed.
But Mr. Creed isn't like them.
Yes, Blink, he is. Maybe not so inclined to do as much harm as some of the others, but yes, he's a really tough monkey. Just ask Deadpool.
But this is not the issue. I am here to remind and/or clarify the situation.
If you do not complete the mission-- you do not move forward. Not you, not Weapon X, nobody. You all stay here.
But after a period of time, some longer than others, your own reality will call you back to the altered existence you were plucked from. You won't get your old lives back.
There has to be some other way.
Perhaps. But I don't know of any. That is not my purpose. I am a construct of your collected consciousness. I don't think.
At the moment I merely elucidate on the thick-headed crap you are choosing to pull.
Okay, that insulting stuff is probably from my head. Sorry.
Can't you help us at all?

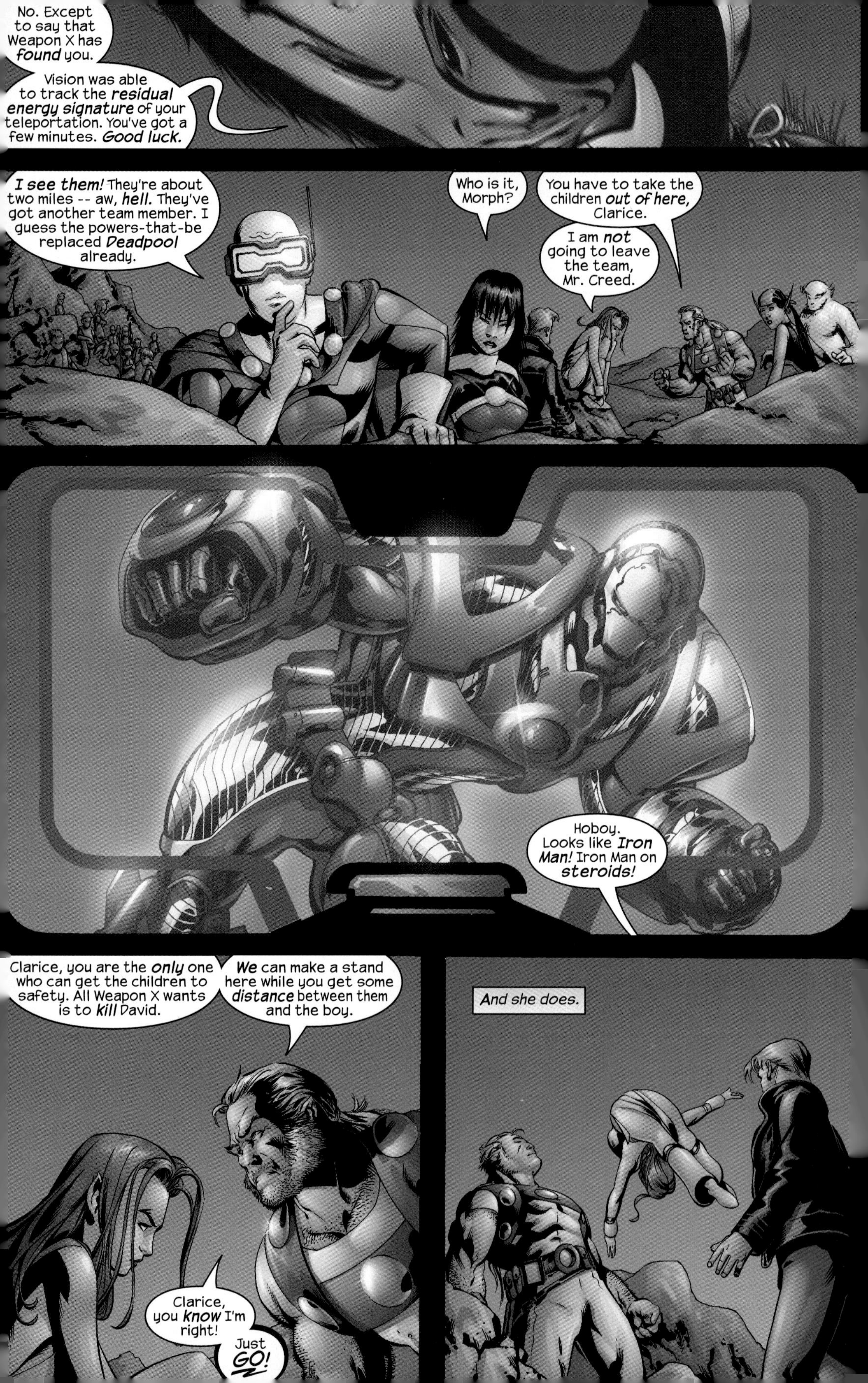
No. Except to say that Weapon X has found you.
Vision was able to track the residual energy signature of your teleportation. You've got a few minutes. Good luck.
I see them! They're about two miles -- aw, hell. They've got another team member. I guess the powers-that-be replaced Deadpool already.
Who is it, Morph?
You have to take the children out of here, Clarice.
I am not going to leave the team, Mr. Creed.
Hoboy. Looks like Iron Man! Iron Man on steroids!
Clarice, you are the only one who can get the children to safety. All Weapon X wants is to kill David.
We can make a stand here while you get some distance between them and the boy.
Clarice, you know I'm right!
Just GO!
And she does.

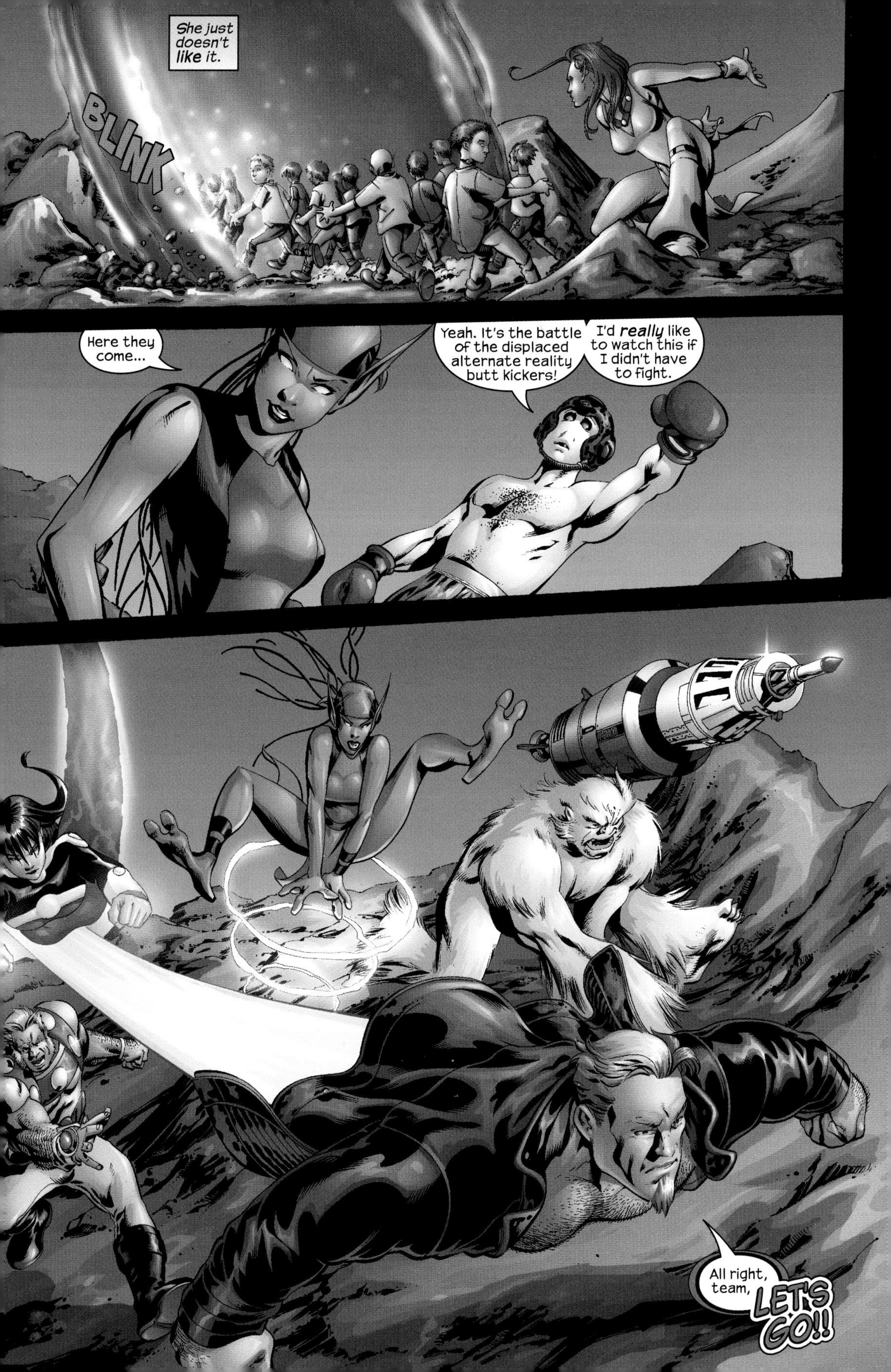
She just doesn't like it.
BLINK
Here they come...
Yeah. It's the battle of the displaced alternate reality butt kickers!
I'd really like to watch this if I didn't have to fight.
All right, team, LET'S GO!!

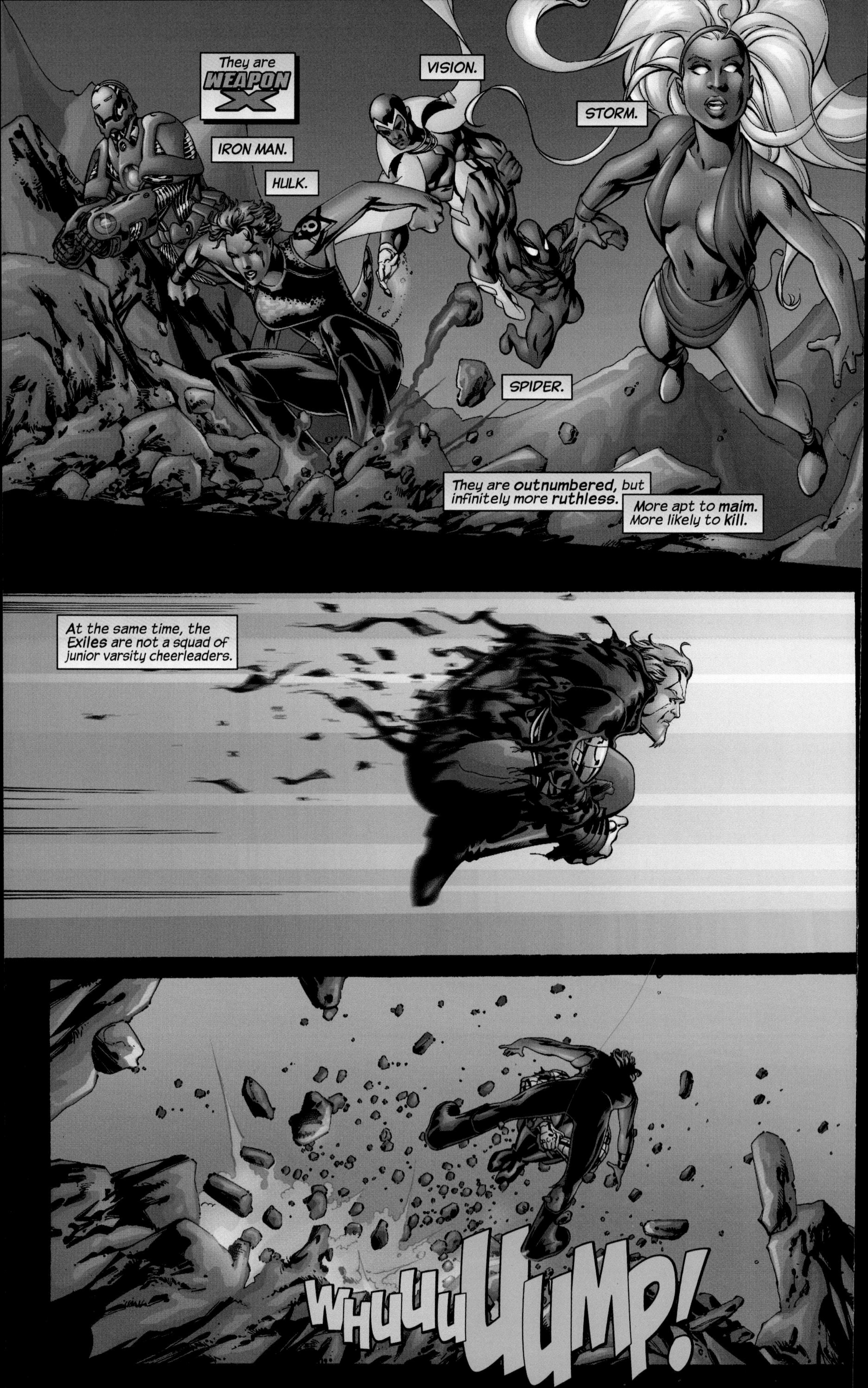
They are WEAPON X
IRON MAN.
HULK.
VISION.
STORM.
SPIDER.
They are outnumbered, but infinitely more ruthless.
More apt to maim. More likely to kill.
At the same time, the Exiles are not a squad of junior varsity cheerleaders.
WHUUUUUMP!

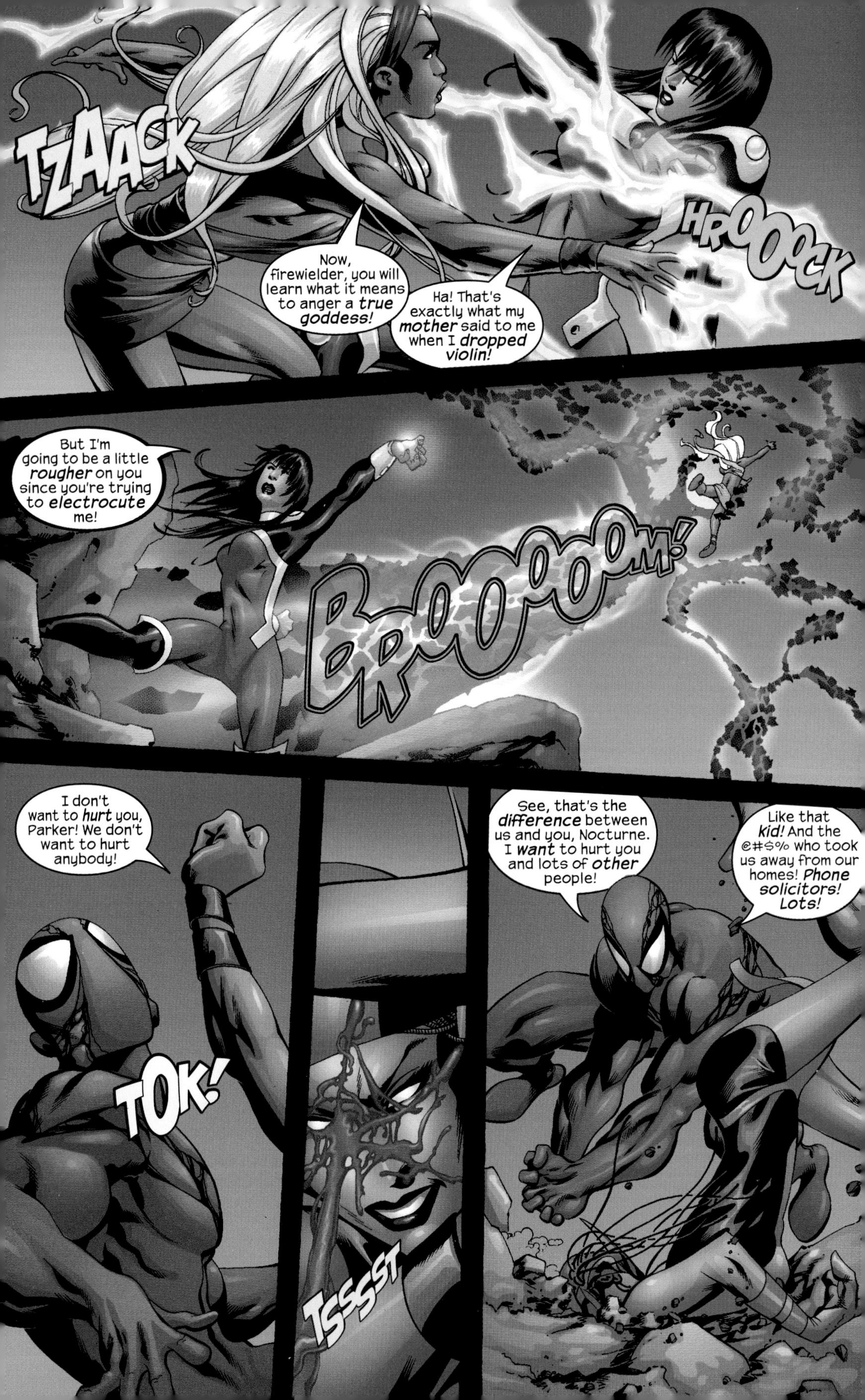
TZAACK
Now, firewielder, you will learn what it means to anger a *true goddess!*
HROOOOCK
Ha! That's exactly what my *mother* said to me when I *dropped* violin!
But I'm going to be a little *rougher* on you since you're trying to *electrocute* me!
BROOOOOOM!
I don't want to *hurt* you, Parker! We don't want to hurt anybody!
TOK!
TSSSST
See, that's the *difference* between us and you, Nocturne. I *want* to hurt you and lots of *other* people!
Like that *kid!* And the @#$% who took us away from our homes! *Phone solicitors! Lots!*

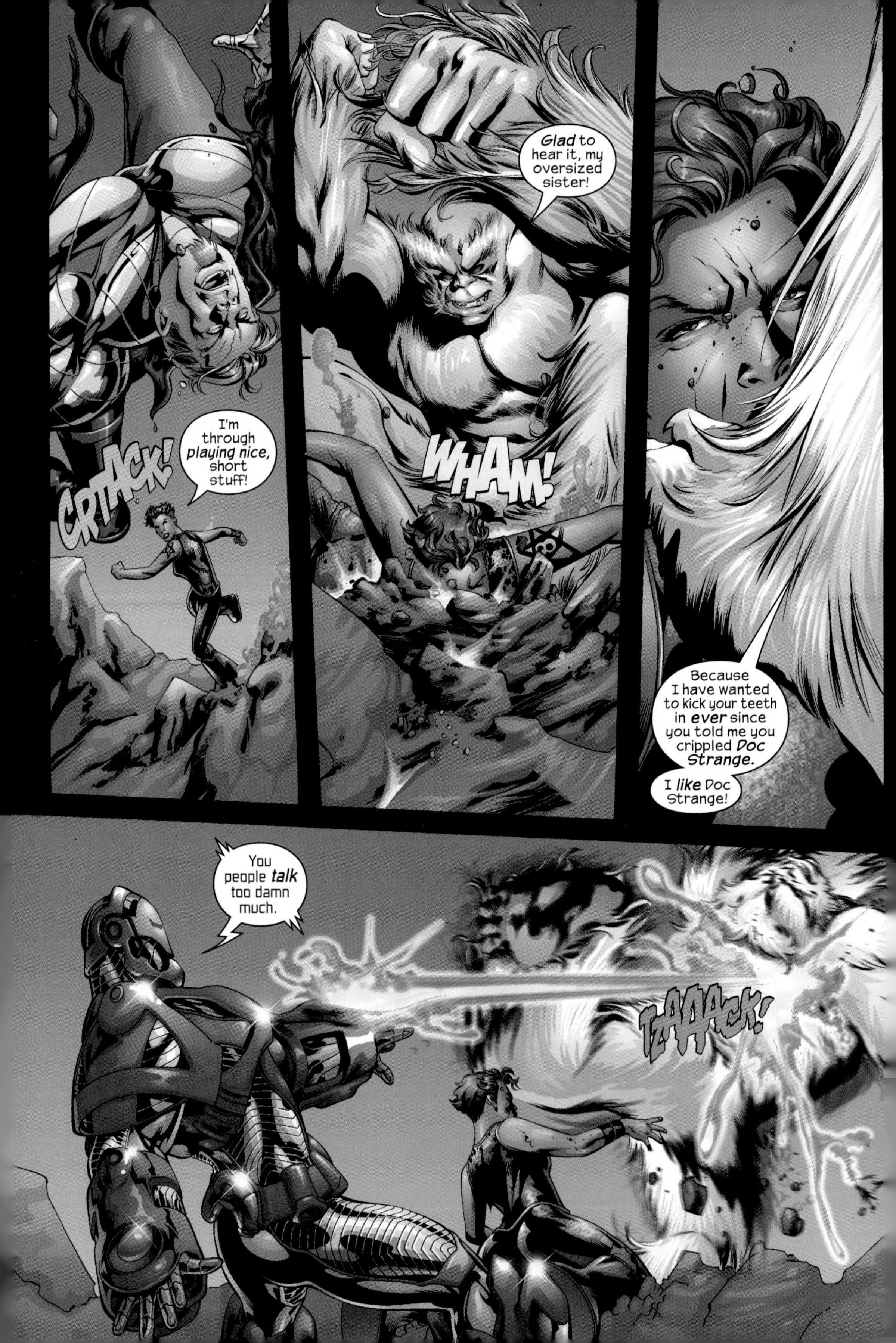

CRTACK!
I'm through playing nice, short stuff!
Glad to hear it, my oversized sister!
WHAM!
Because I have wanted to kick your teeth in ever since you told me you crippled Doc Strange.
I like Doc Strange!
You people talk too damn much.
TZAAACK!

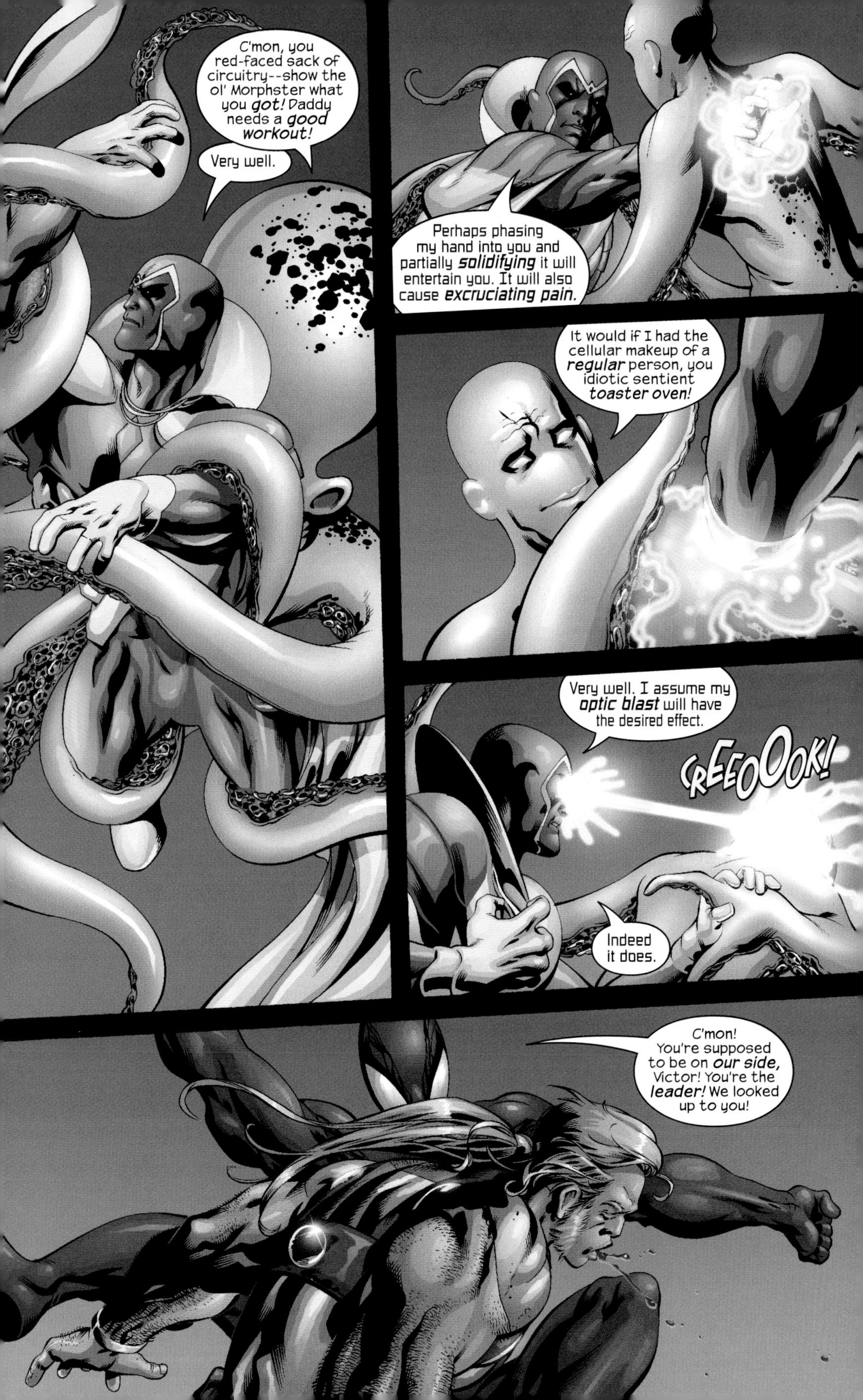
C'mon, you red-faced sack of circuitry--show the ol' Morphster what you *got!* Daddy needs a *good workout!*
Very well.
Perhaps phasing my hand into you and partially *solidifying* it will entertain you. It will also cause *excruciating pain.*
It would if I had the cellular makeup of a *regular* person, you idiotic sentient *toaster oven!*
Very well. I assume my *optic blast* will have the desired effect.
CREEOOOK!
Indeed it does.
C'mon! You're supposed to be on *our side,* Victor! You're the *leader!* We looked up to you!

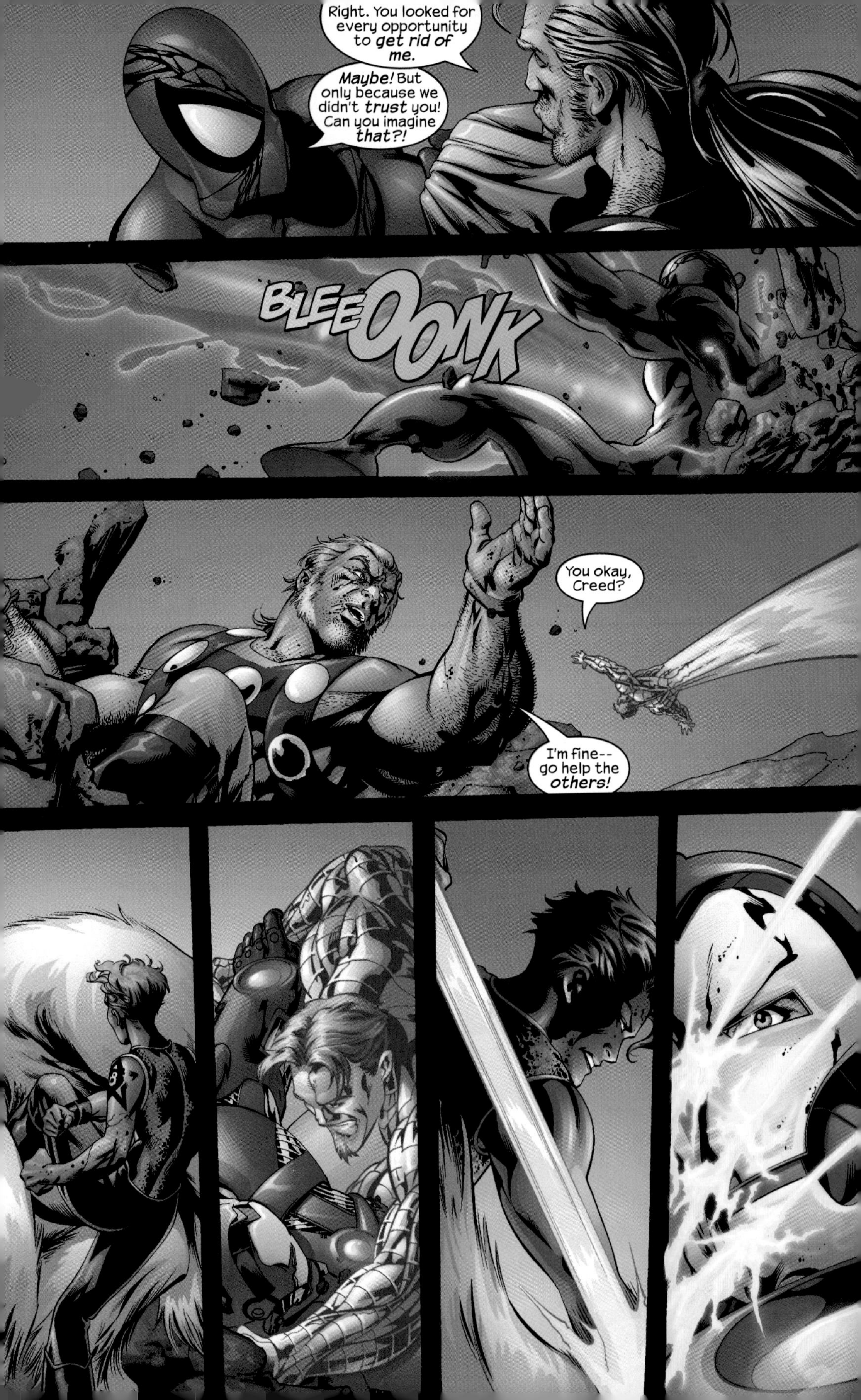
Right. You looked for every opportunity to *get rid of me.*
Maybe! But only because we didn't *trust* you! Can you imagine *that?!*
BLEEOONK
You okay, Creed?
I'm fine-- go help the *others!*

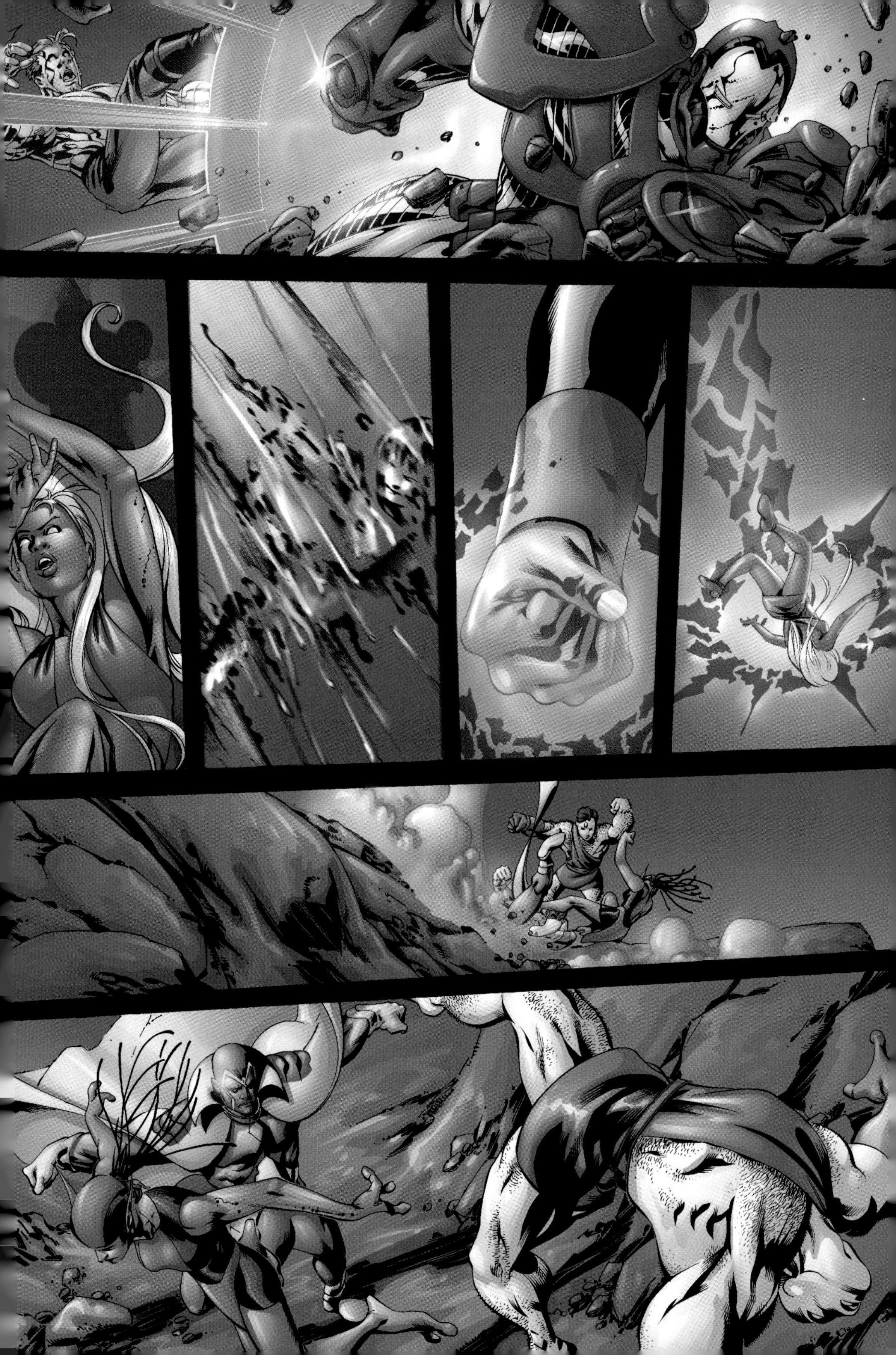

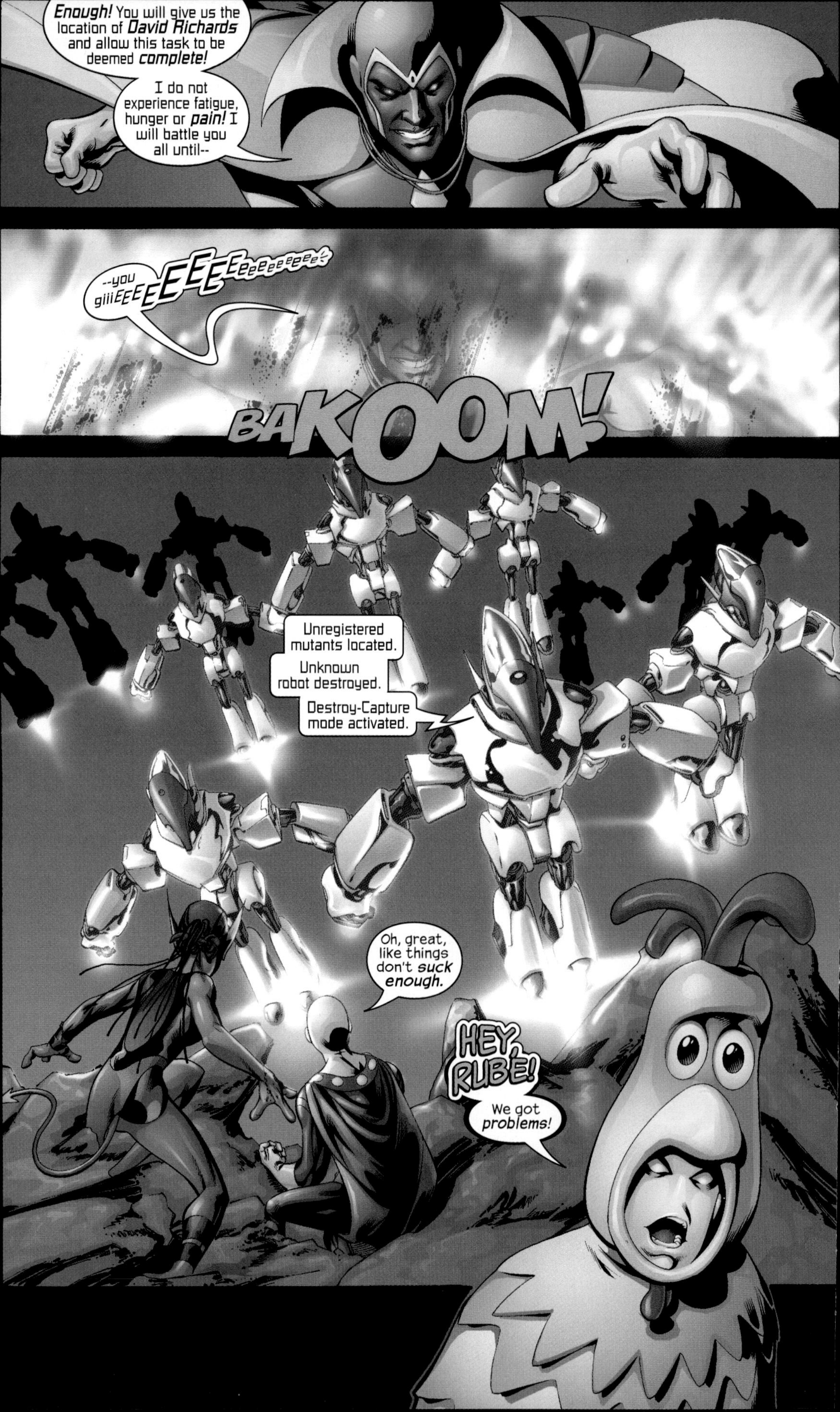

Enough! You will give us the location of David Richards and allow this task to be deemed complete!
I do not experience fatigue, hunger or pain! I will battle you all until--
--you giiiEEEEEEEeeeeeeeee!
BAKOOM!
Unregistered mutants located.
Unknown robot destroyed.
Destroy-Capture mode activated.
Oh, great, like things don't suck enough.
HEY, RUBE!
We got problems!

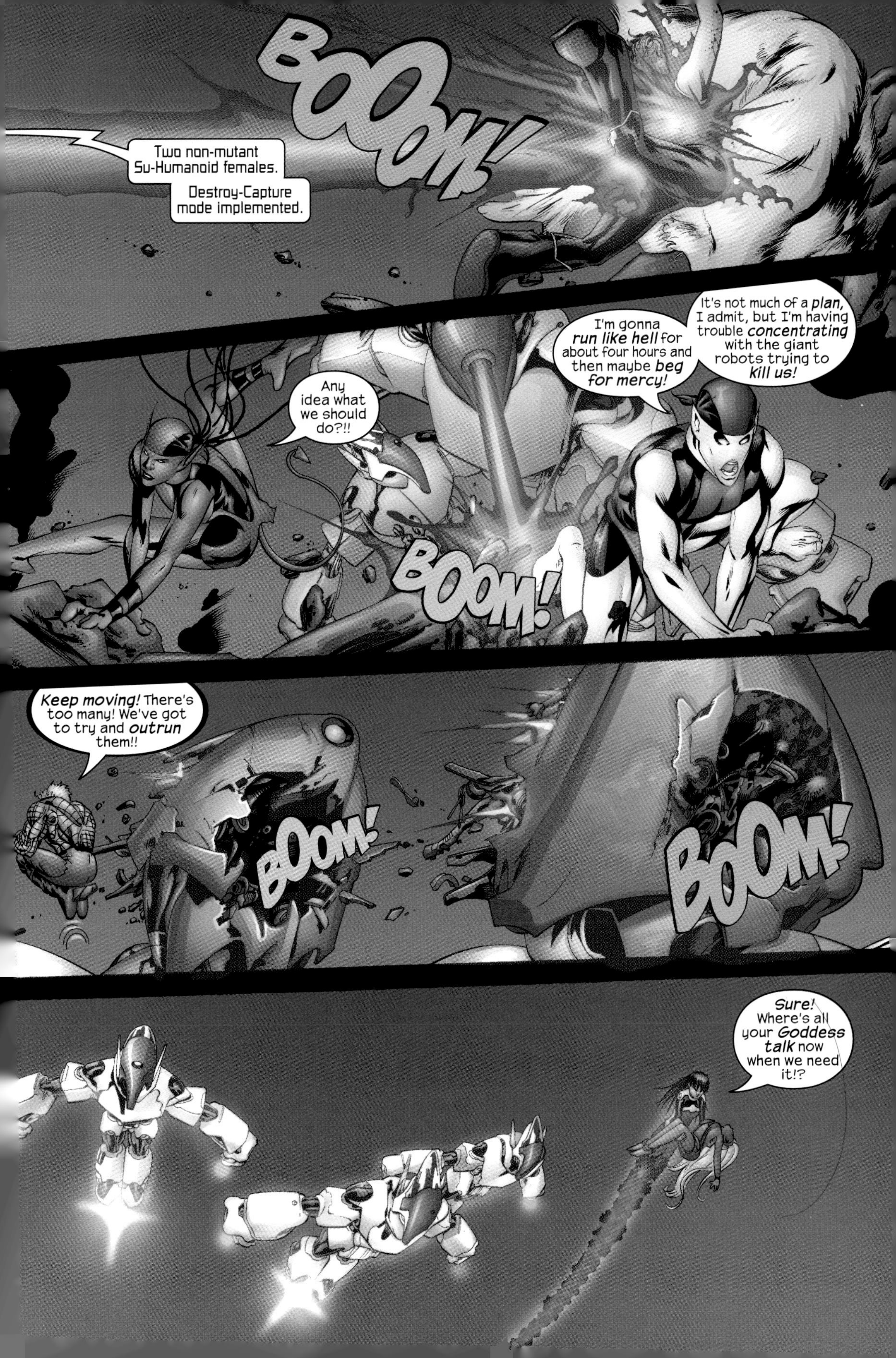
BOOOOM!
Two non-mutant Su-Humanoid females.
Destroy-Capture mode implemented.
Any idea what we should do?!!
I'm gonna run like hell for about four hours and then maybe beg for mercy!
It's not much of a plan, I admit, but I'm having trouble concentrating with the giant robots trying to kill us!
BOOM!
Keep moving! There's too many! We've got to try and outrun them!!
BOOM!
BOOM!
Sure! Where's all your Goddess talk now when we need it!?

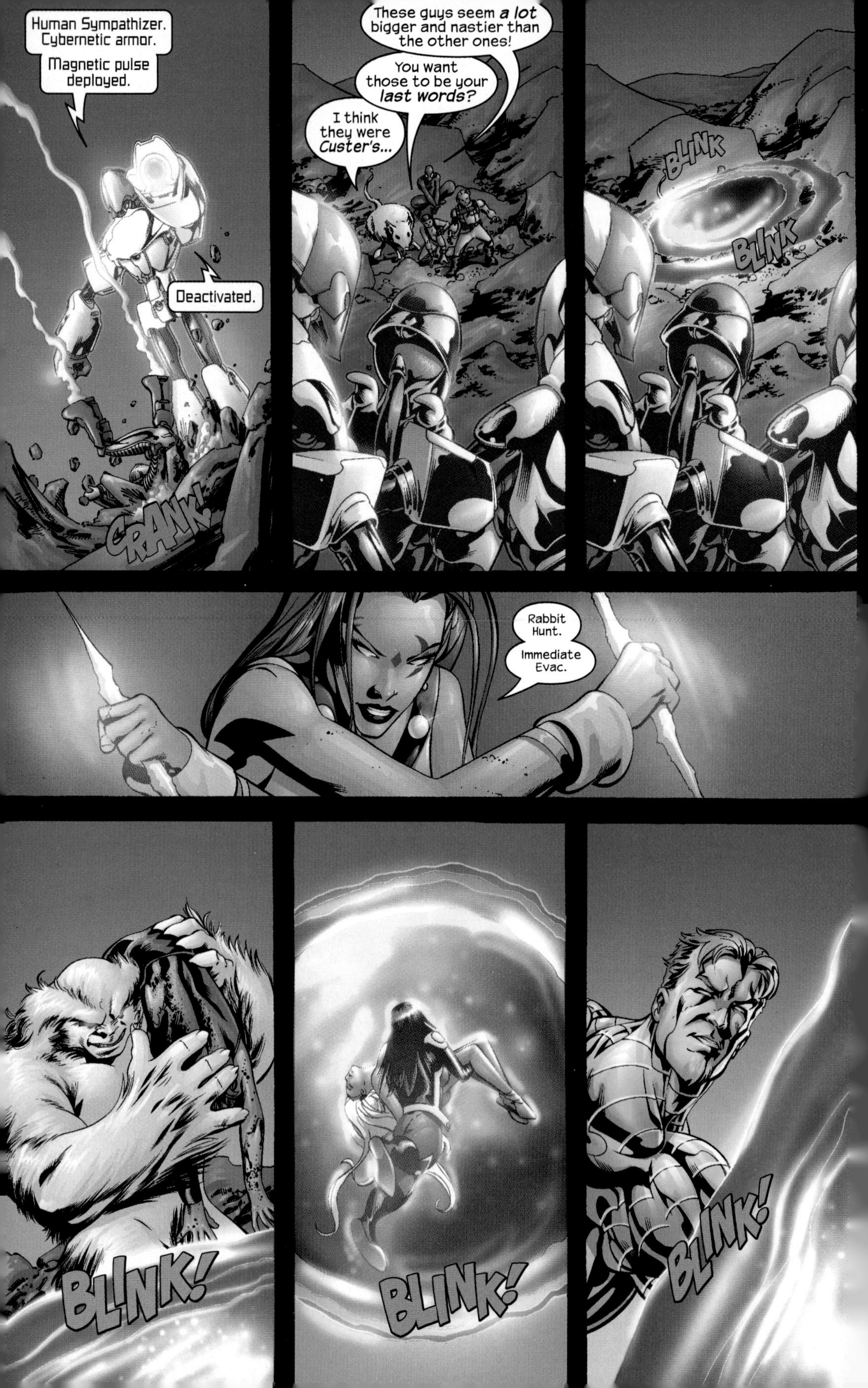
Human Sympathizer. Cybernetic armor.
Magnetic pulse deployed.
Deactivated.
CRANK!
These guys seem a lot bigger and nastier than the other ones!
You want those to be your last words?
I think they were Custer's...
BLINK
BLINK
Rabbit Hunt.
Immediate Evac.
BLINK!
BLINK!
BLINK!

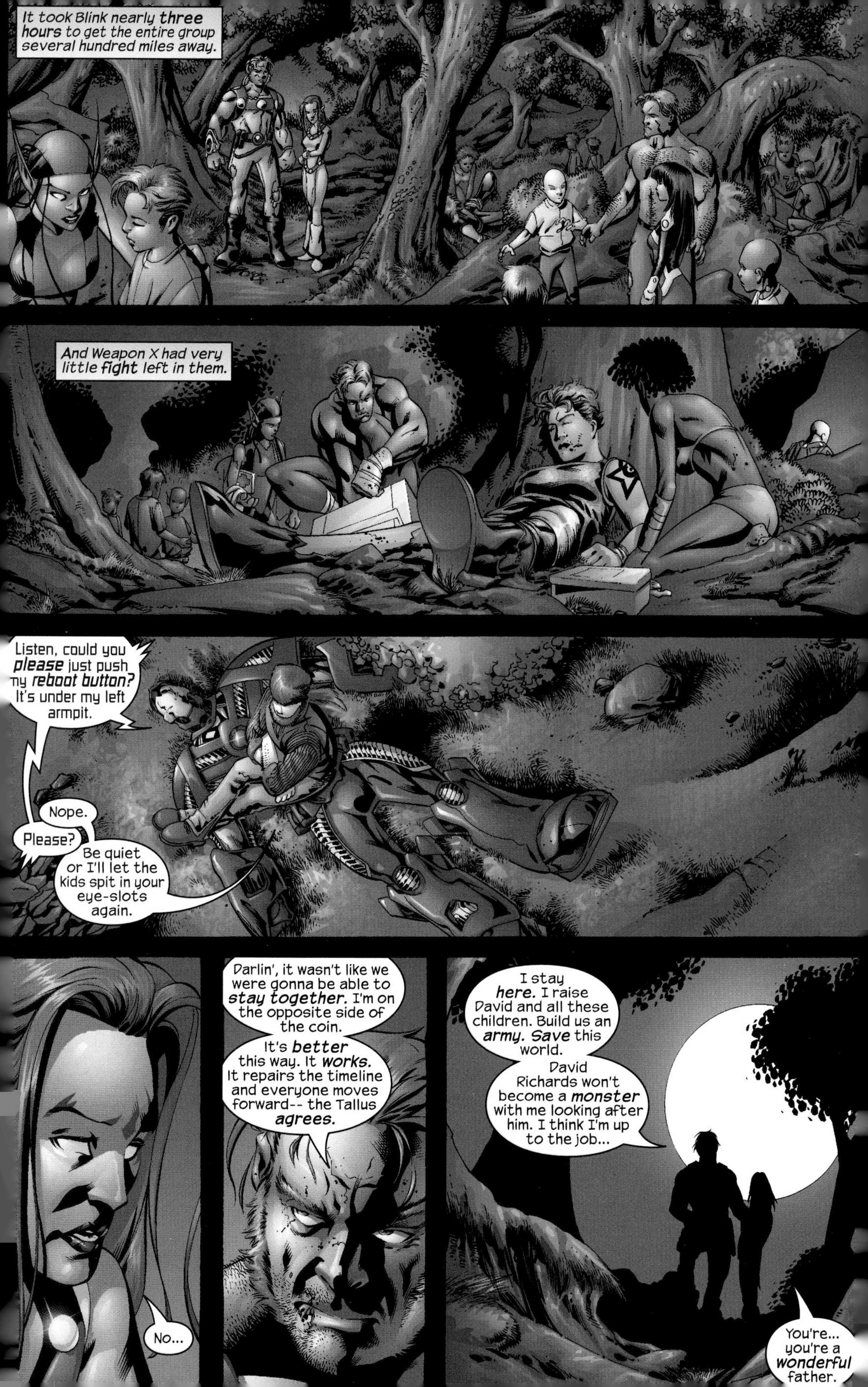

It took Blink nearly **three hours** to get the entire group several hundred miles away.
And Weapon X had very little **fight** left in them.
Listen, could you ***please*** just push my ***reboot button?*** It's under my left armpit.
Nope.
Please?
Be quiet or I'll let the kids spit in your eye-slots again.
Darlin', it wasn't like we were gonna be able to ***stay together.*** I'm on the opposite side of the coin.
It's ***better*** this way. It ***works.*** It repairs the timeline and everyone moves forward-- the Tallus ***agrees.***
No...
I stay ***here.*** I raise David and all these children. Build us an ***army. Save*** this world.
David Richards won't become a ***monster*** with me looking after him. I think I'm up to the job...
You're... you're a ***wonderful*** father.

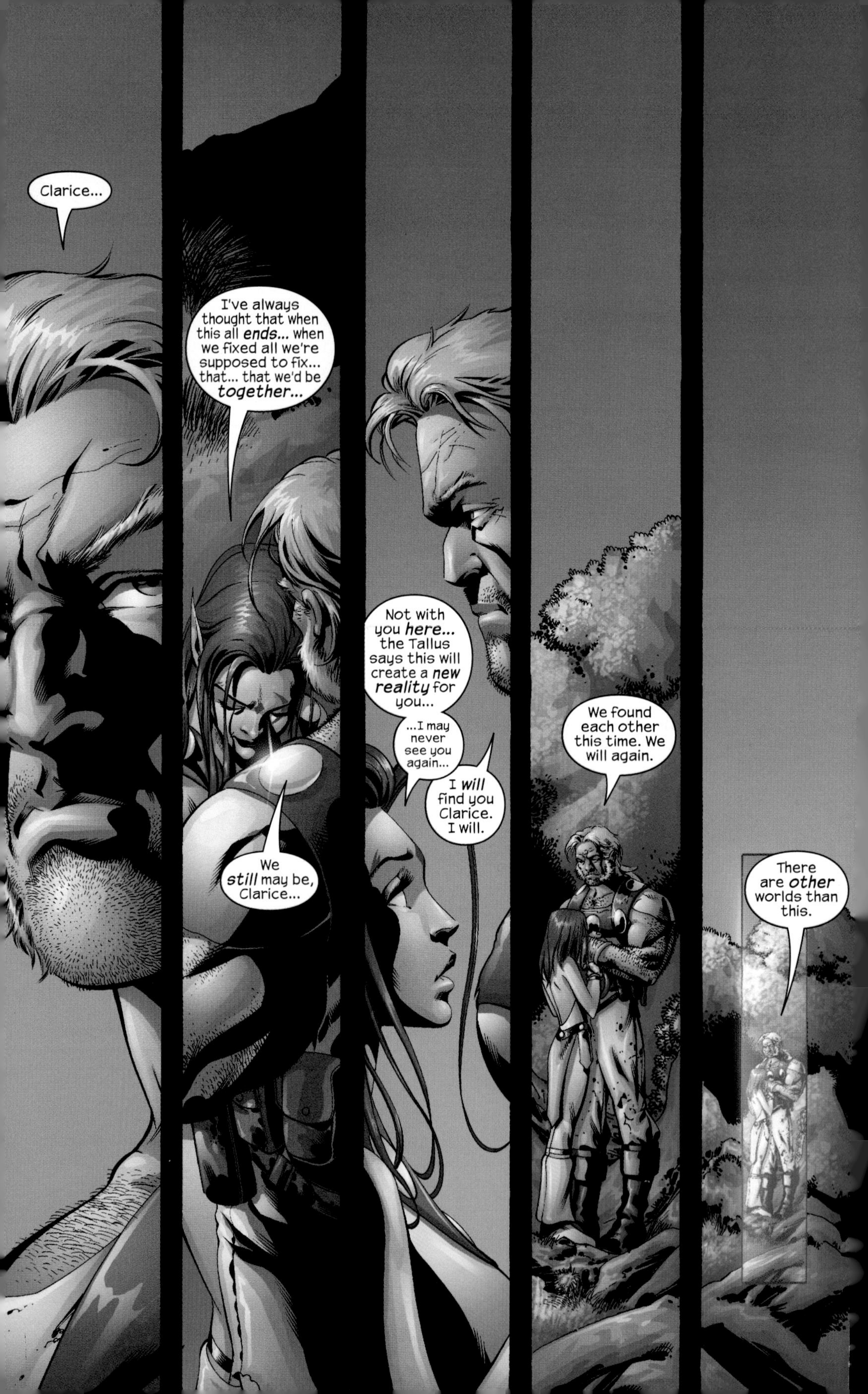
Clarice...
I've always thought that when this all ends... when we fixed all we're supposed to fix... that... that we'd be together...
We still may be, Clarice...
Not with you here... the Tallus says this will create a new reality for you...
...I may never see you again...
I will find you Clarice. I will.
We found each other this time. We will again.
There are other worlds than this.

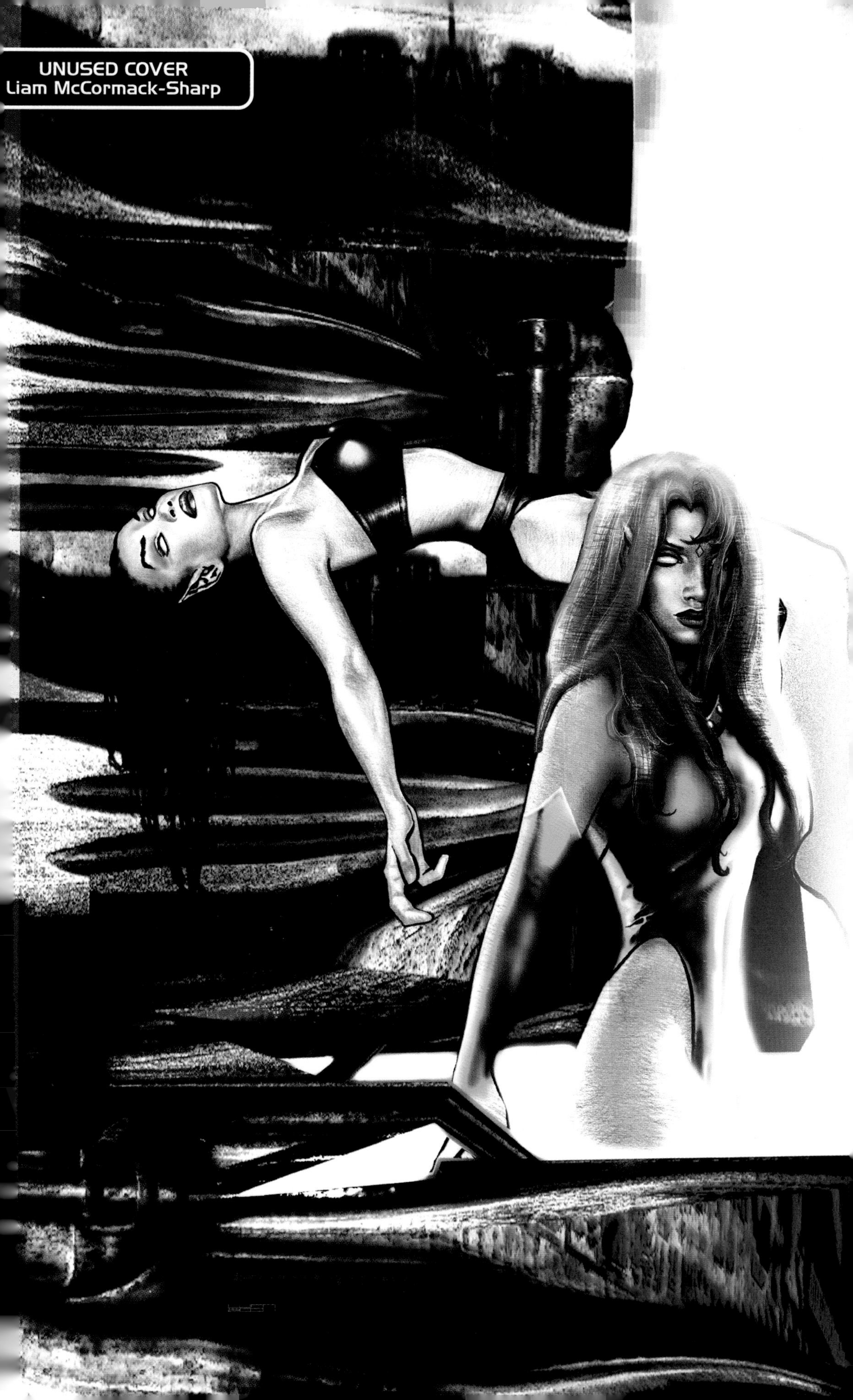
UNUSED COVER
Liam McCormack-Sharp

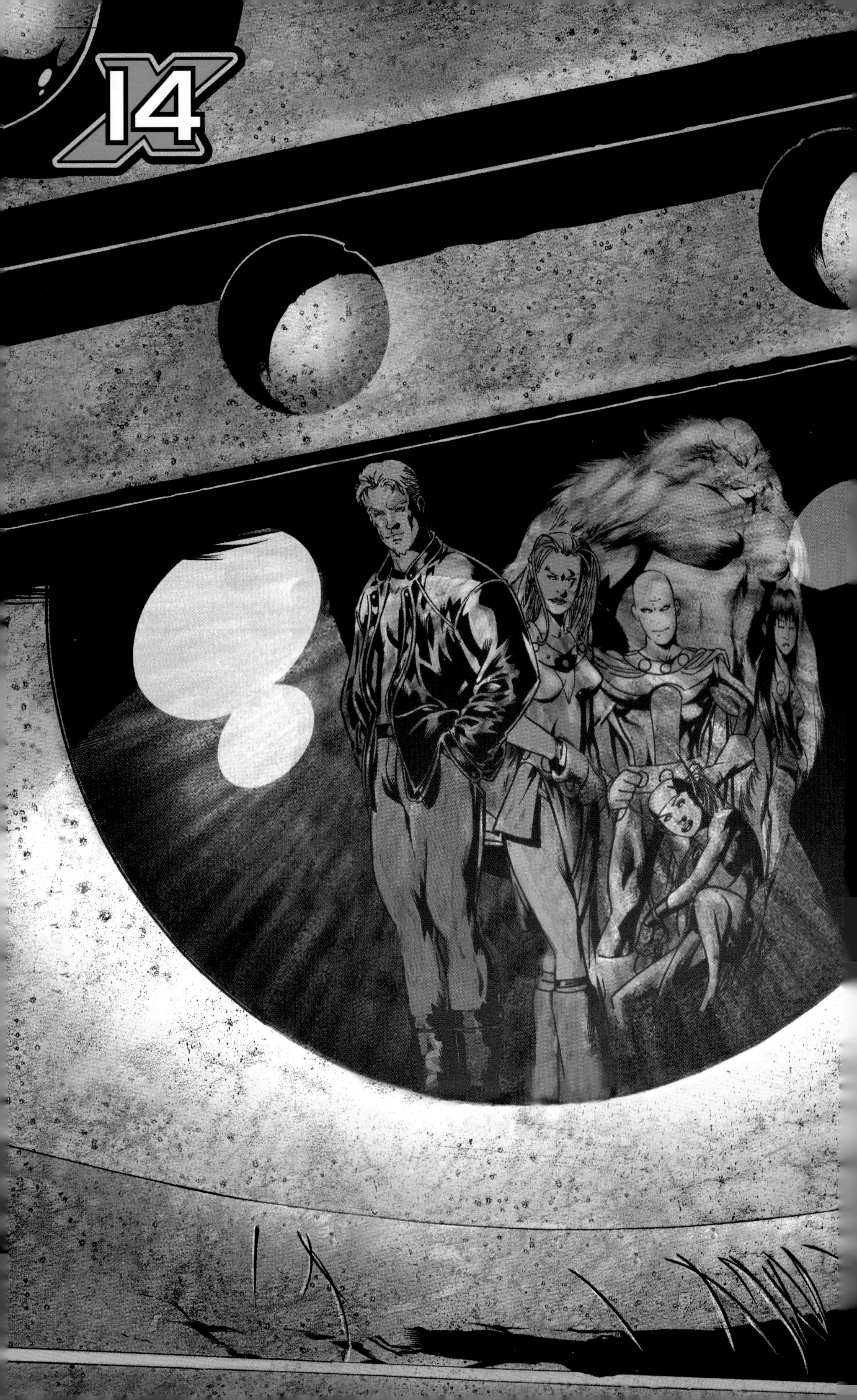
14

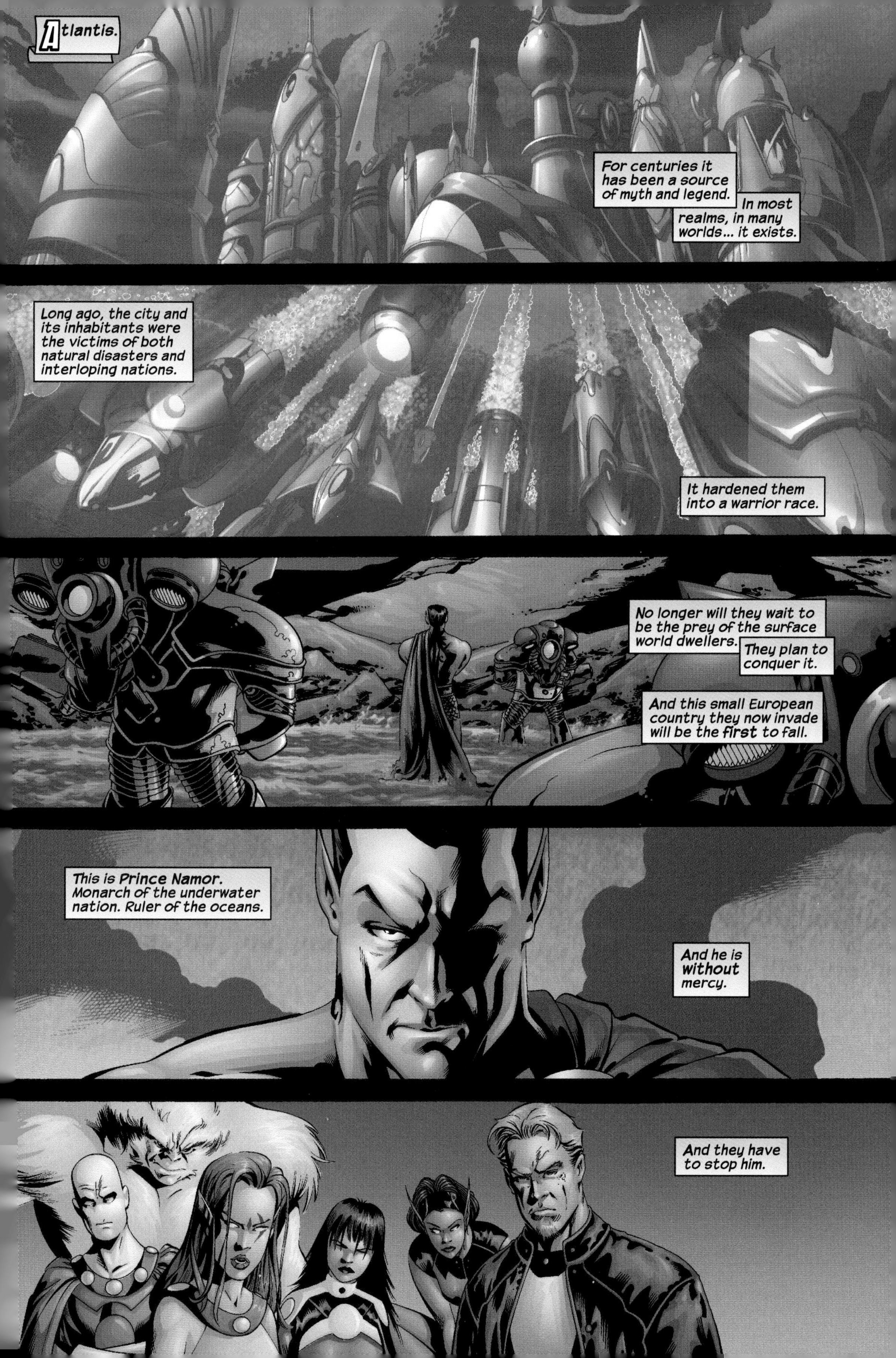
Atlantis.
For centuries it has been a source of myth and legend.
In most realms, in many worlds... it exists.
Long ago, the city and its inhabitants were the victims of both natural disasters and interloping nations.
It hardened them into a warrior race.
No longer will they wait to be the prey of the surface world dwellers.
They plan to conquer it.
And this small European country they now invade will be the first to fall.
This is Prince Namor. Monarch of the underwater nation. Ruler of the oceans.
And he is without mercy.
And they have to stop him.

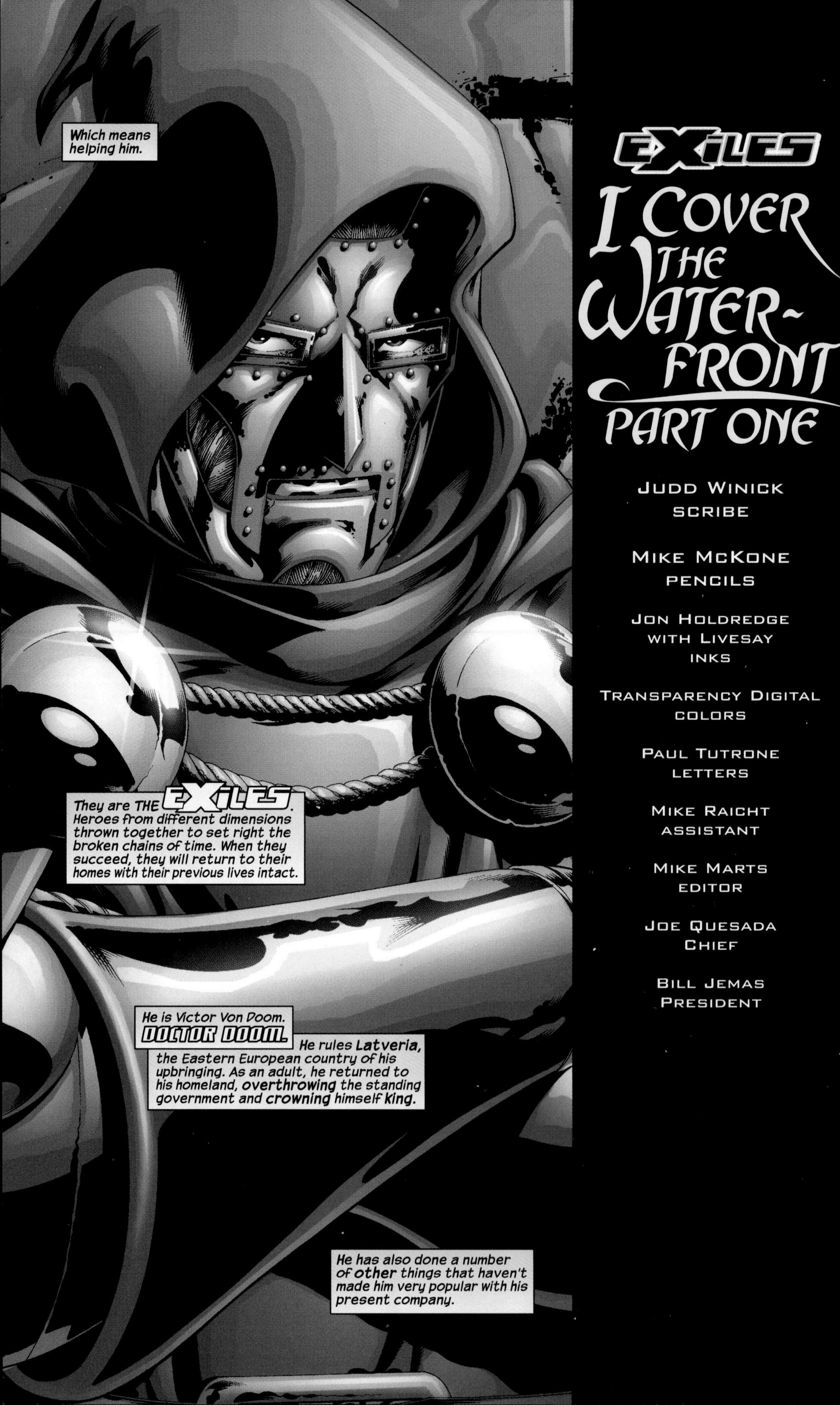
Which means helping him.
EXILES
I COVER THE WATER-FRONT
PART ONE
JUDD WINICK SCRIBE
MIKE McKONE PENCILS
JON HOLDREDGE WITH LIVESAY INKS
TRANSPARENCY DIGITAL COLORS
PAUL TUTRONE LETTERS
MIKE RAICHT ASSISTANT
MIKE MARTS EDITOR
JOE QUESADA CHIEF
BILL JEMAS PRESIDENT
They are THE EXILES. Heroes from different dimensions thrown together to set right the broken chains of time. When they succeed, they will return to their homes with their previous lives intact.
He is Victor Von Doom. DOCTOR DOOM.
He rules Latveria, the Eastern European country of his upbringing. As an adult, he returned to his homeland, overthrowing the standing government and crowning himself king.
He has also done a number of other things that haven't made him very popular with his present company.

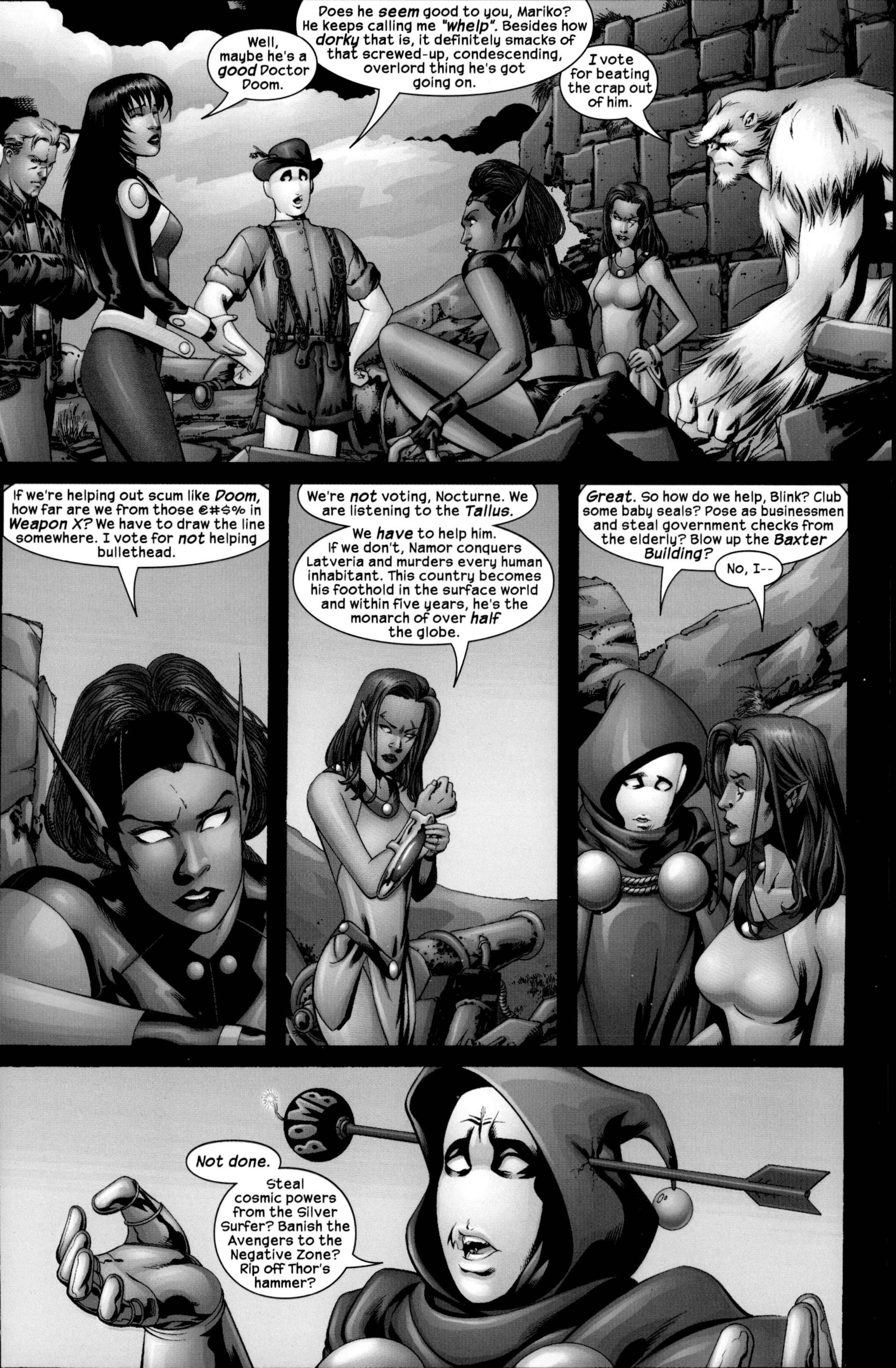
Well, maybe he's a *good* Doctor Doom.
Does he *seem* good to you, Mariko? He keeps calling me *"whelp"*. Besides how *dorky* that is, it definitely smacks of that screwed-up, condescending, overlord thing he's got going on.
I vote for beating the crap out of him.
If we're helping out scum like *Doom*, how far are we from those @#$% in *Weapon X?* We have to draw the line somewhere. I vote for *not* helping bullethead.
We're *not* voting, Nocturne. We are listening to the *Tallus*.
We *have* to help him. If we don't, Namor conquers Latveria and murders every human inhabitant. This country becomes his foothold in the surface world and within five years, he's the monarch of over *half* the globe.
Great. So how do we help, Blink? Club some baby seals? Pose as businessmen and steal government checks from the elderly? Blow up the *Baxter Building?*
No, I--
BOMB
Not done.
Steal cosmic powers from the Silver Surfer? Banish the Avengers to the Negative Zone? Rip off Thor's hammer?

In your reality he stole Thor's hammer?

No, but don't act like he ain't *thinking* about it. Go ahead-- *ask* him.

Stop this. We all *know* what we have to do. So let's do it.

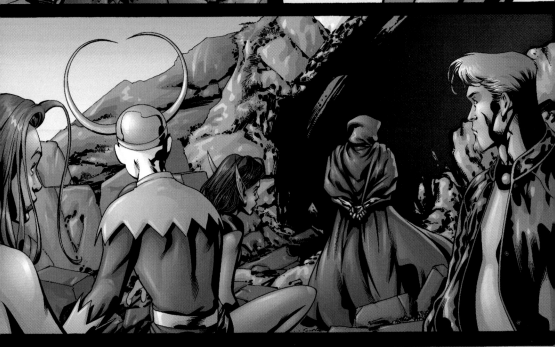

What are *you* looking at, steel britches? You got a *problem!?!*

Chill, Morph.

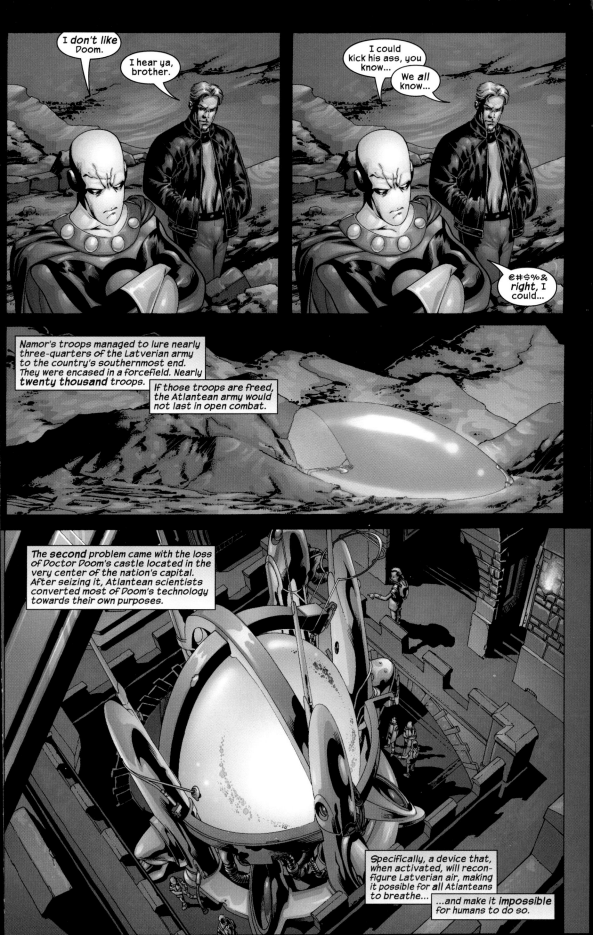

I don't like Doom.

I hear ya, brother.

I could kick his ass, you know... We all know...

@#$%& right, I could...

Namor's troops managed to lure nearly three-quarters of the Latverian army to the country's southernmost end. They were encased in a forcefield. Nearly twenty thousand troops.

If those troops are freed, the Atlantean army would not last in open combat.

The second problem came with the loss of Doctor Doom's castle located in the very center of the nation's capital. After seizing it, Atlantean scientists converted most of Doom's technology towards their own purposes.

Specifically, a device that, when activated, will reconfigure Latverian air, making it possible for all Atlanteans to breathe... ...and make it impossible for humans to do so.

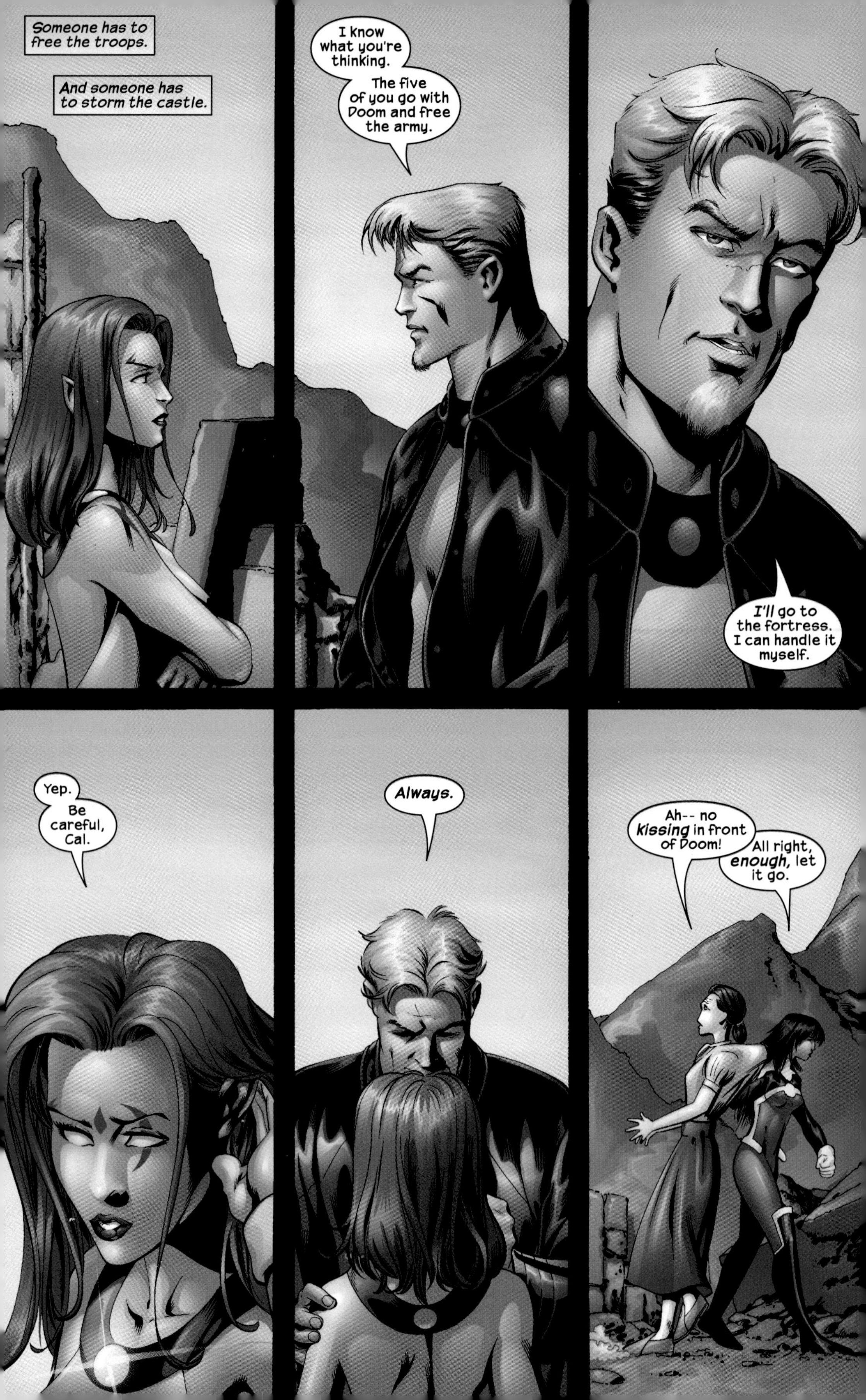
Someone has to free the troops.
And someone has to storm the castle.
I know what you're thinking.
The five of you go with Doom and free the army.
I'll go to the fortress. I can handle it myself.
Yep.
Be careful, Cal.
Always.
Ah-- no kissing in front of Doom!
All right, enough, let it go.

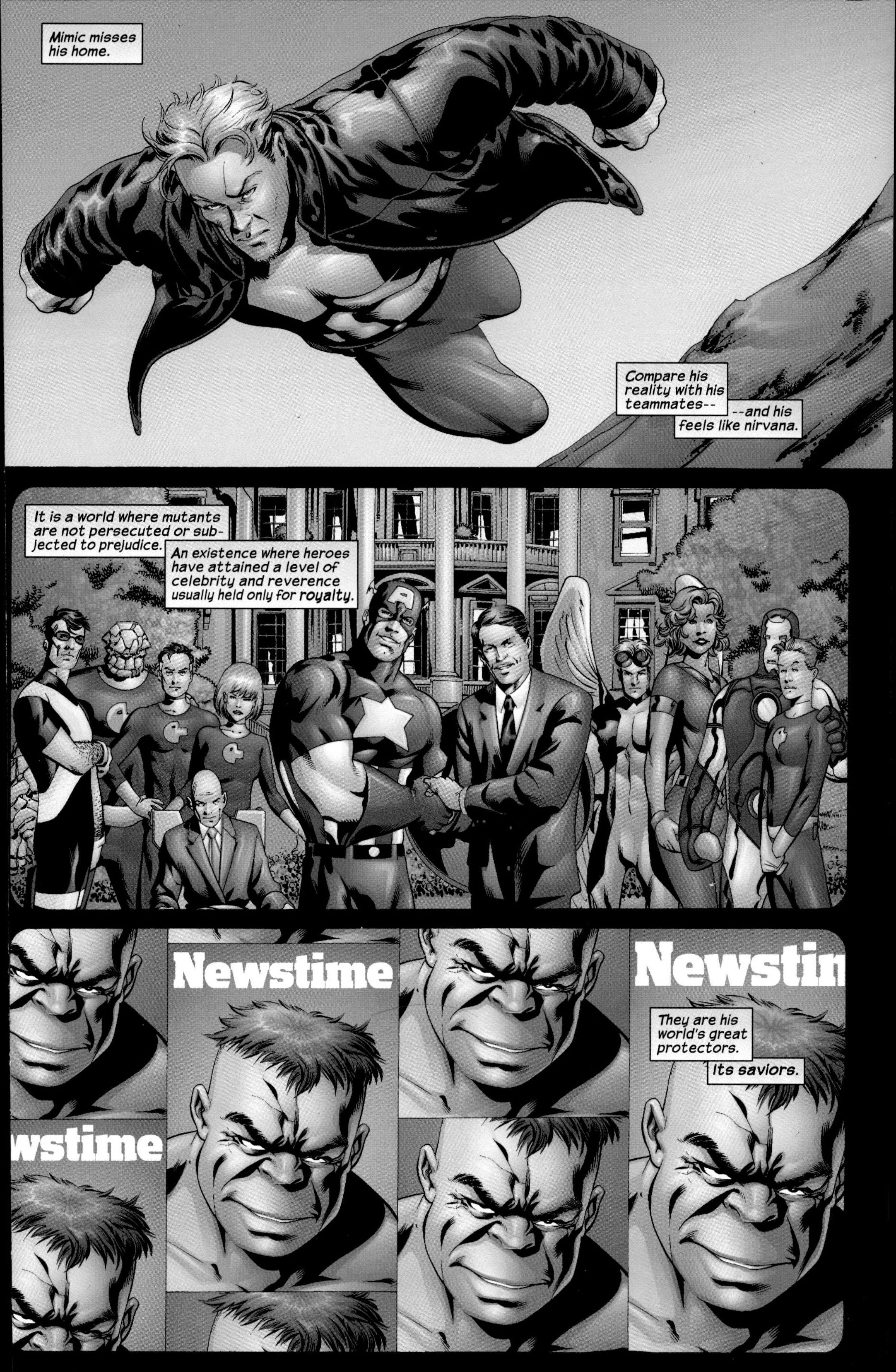
Mimic misses his home.
Compare his reality with his teammates--
--and his feels like nirvana.
It is a world where mutants are not persecuted or subjected to prejudice.
An existence where heroes have attained a level of celebrity and reverence usually held only for royalty.
Newstime
Newstim
wstime
They are his world's great protectors.
Its saviors.

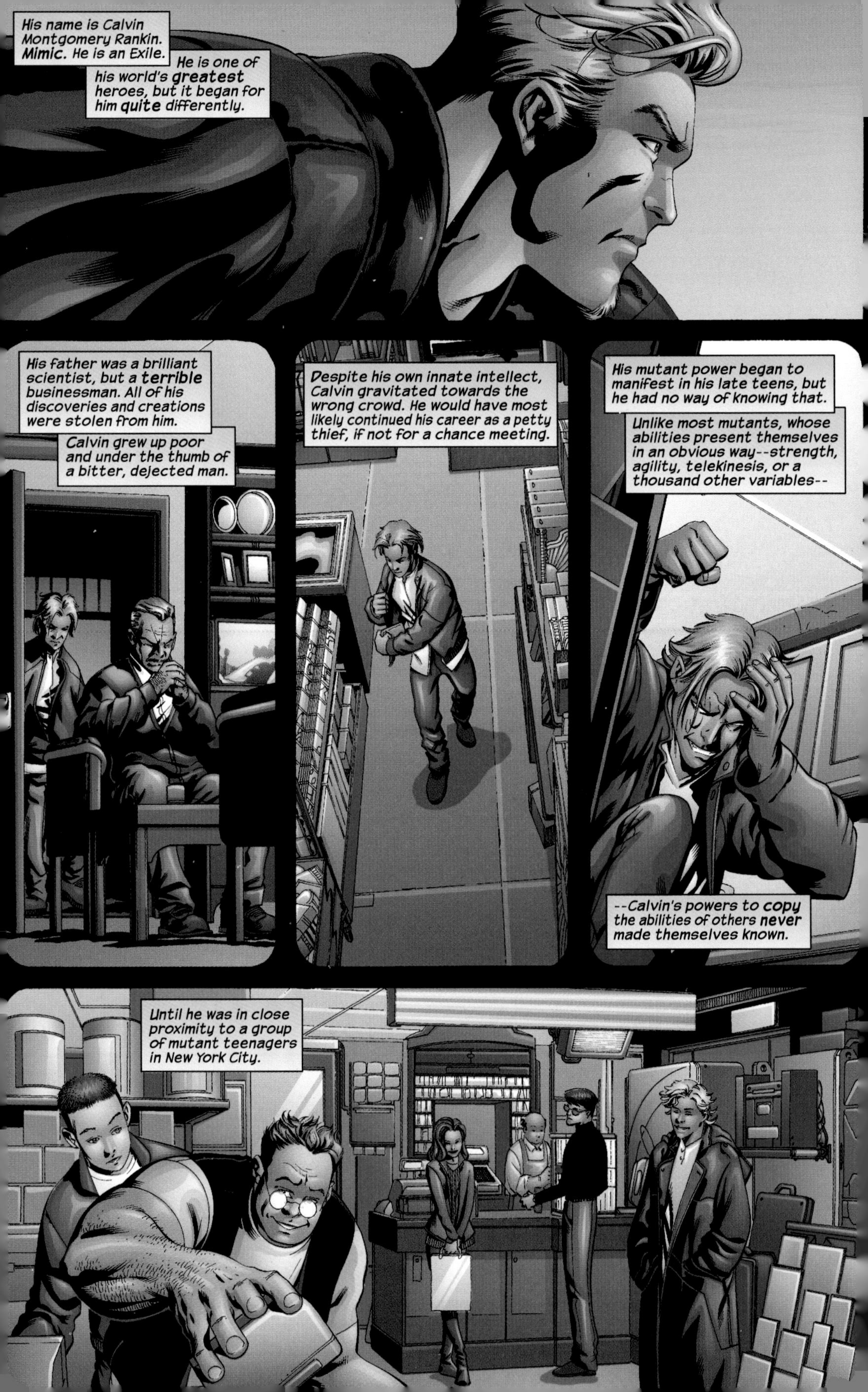
His name is Calvin Montgomery Rankin. Mimic. He is an Exile.
He is one of his world's greatest heroes, but it began for him quite differently.
His father was a brilliant scientist, but a terrible businessman. All of his discoveries and creations were stolen from him.
Calvin grew up poor and under the thumb of a bitter, dejected man.
Despite his own innate intellect, Calvin gravitated towards the wrong crowd. He would have most likely continued his career as a petty thief, if not for a chance meeting.
His mutant power began to manifest in his late teens, but he had no way of knowing that.
Unlike most mutants, whose abilities present themselves in an obvious way--strength, agility, telekinesis, or a thousand other variables--
--Calvin's powers to copy the abilities of others never made themselves known.
Until he was in close proximity to a group of mutant teenagers in New York City.

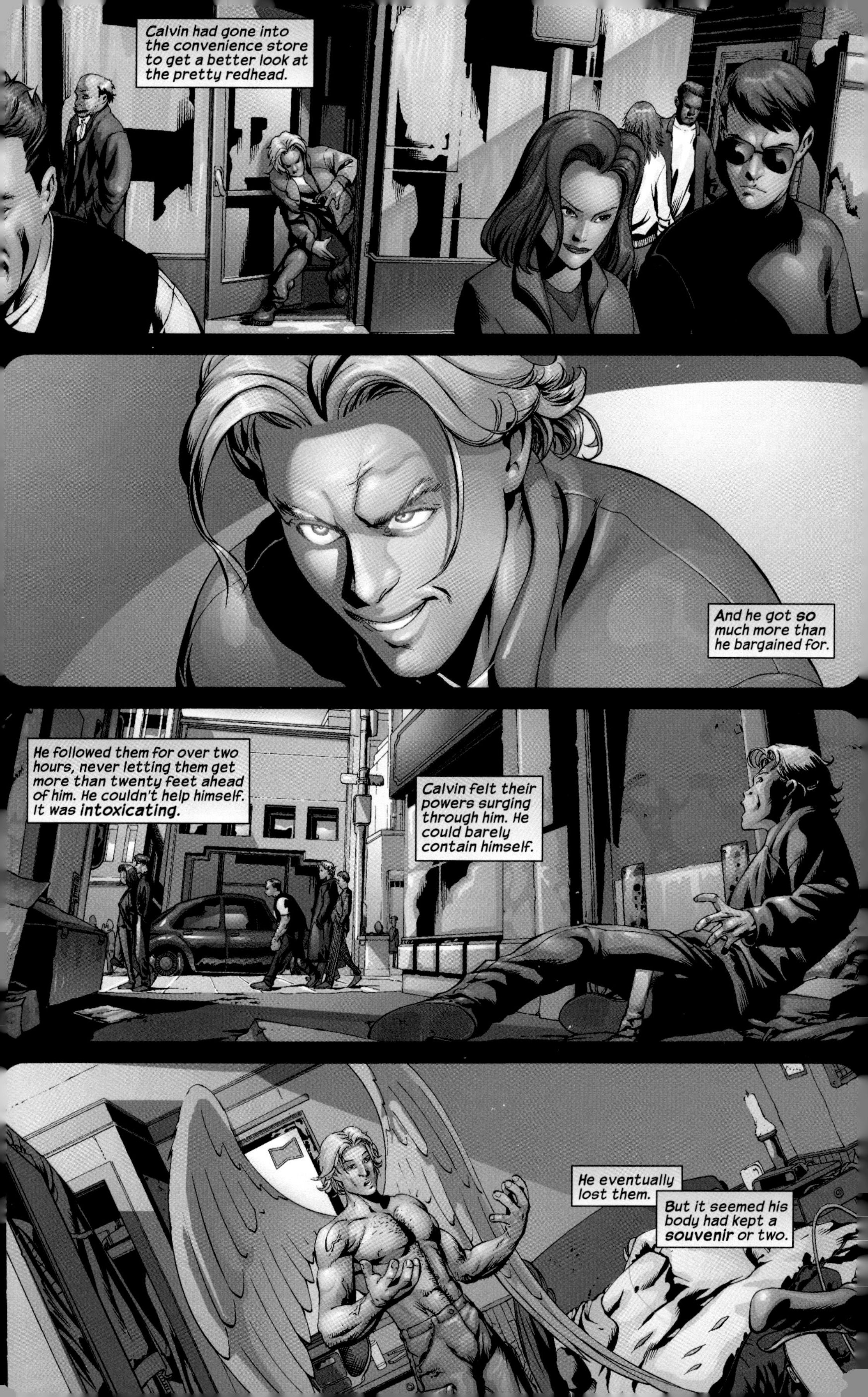
Calvin had gone into the convenience store to get a better look at the pretty redhead.
And he got **so** much more than he bargained for.
He followed them for over two hours, never letting them get more than twenty feet ahead of him. He couldn't help himself. It was **intoxicating.**
Calvin felt their powers surging through him. He could barely contain himself.
He eventually lost them.
But it seemed his body had kept a **souvenir** or two.

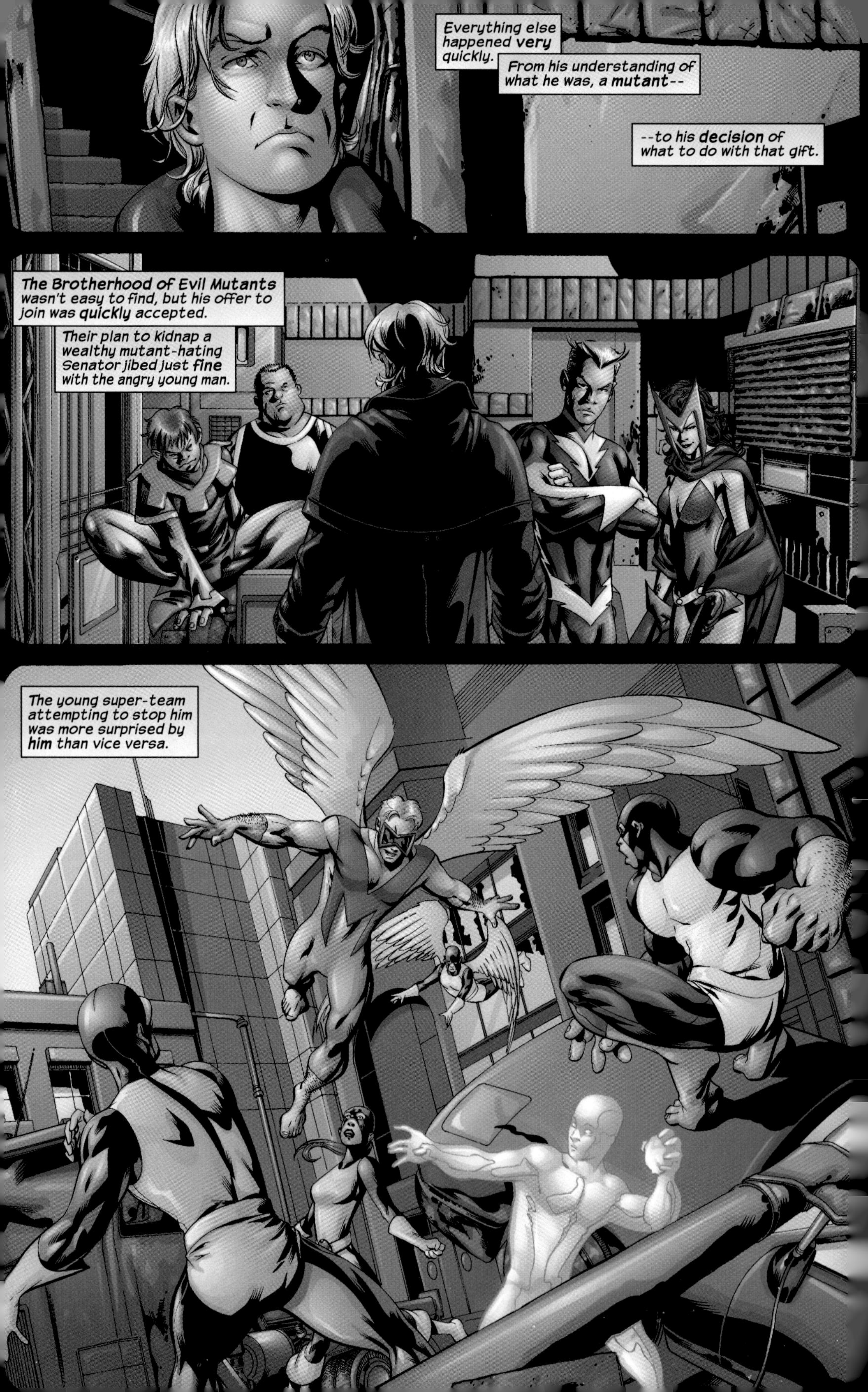
Everything else happened very quickly.
From his understanding of what he was, a mutant--
--to his decision of what to do with that gift.
The Brotherhood of Evil Mutants wasn't easy to find, but his offer to join was quickly accepted.
Their plan to kidnap a wealthy mutant-hating Senator jibed just fine with the angry young man.
The young super-team attempting to stop him was more surprised by him than vice versa.

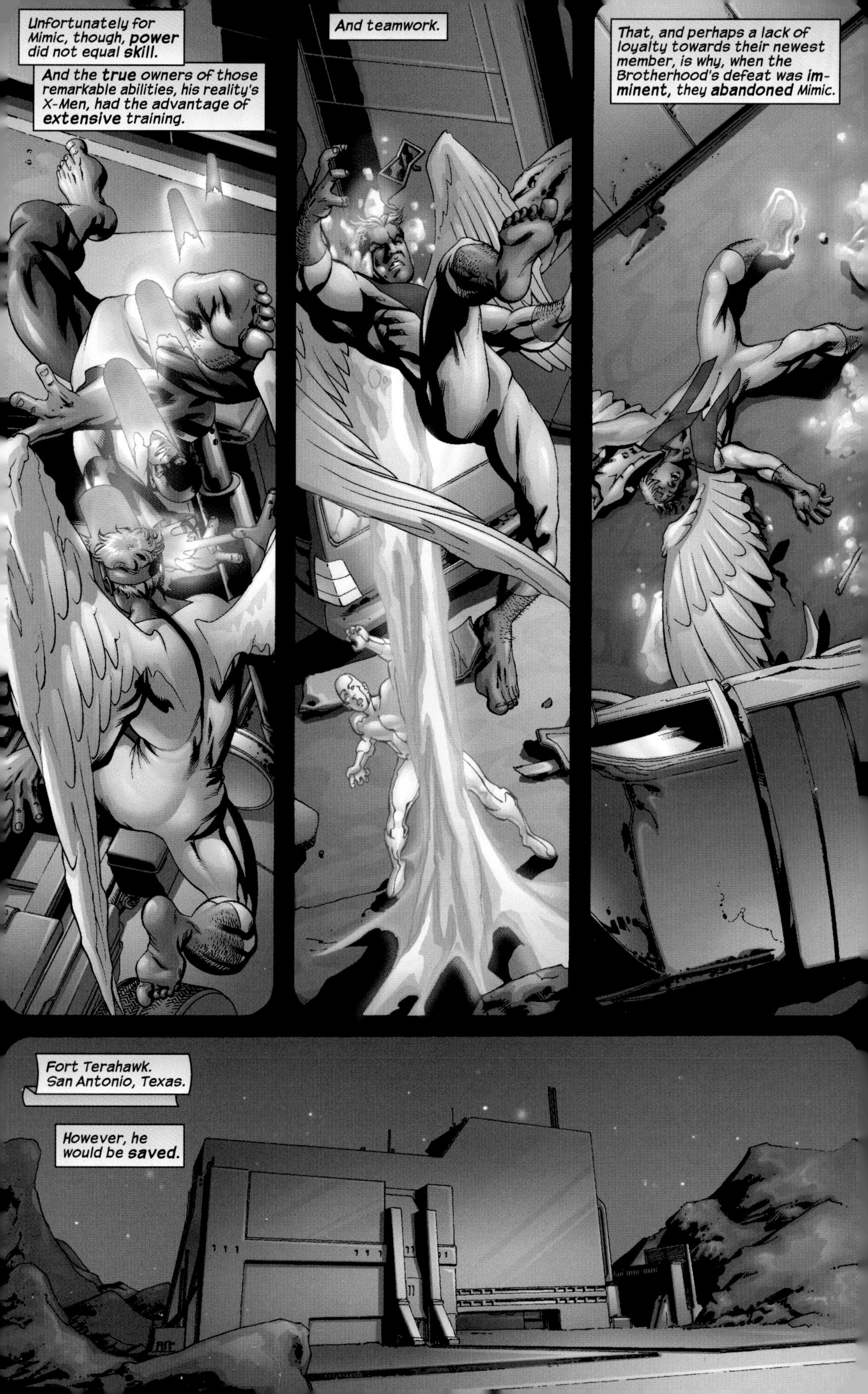

Unfortunately for Mimic, though, power did not equal skill.
And the true owners of those remarkable abilities, his reality's X-Men, had the advantage of extensive training.
And teamwork.
That, and perhaps a lack of loyalty towards their newest member, is why, when the Brotherhood's defeat was imminent, they abandoned Mimic.
Fort Terahawk.
San Antonio, Texas.
However, he would be saved.

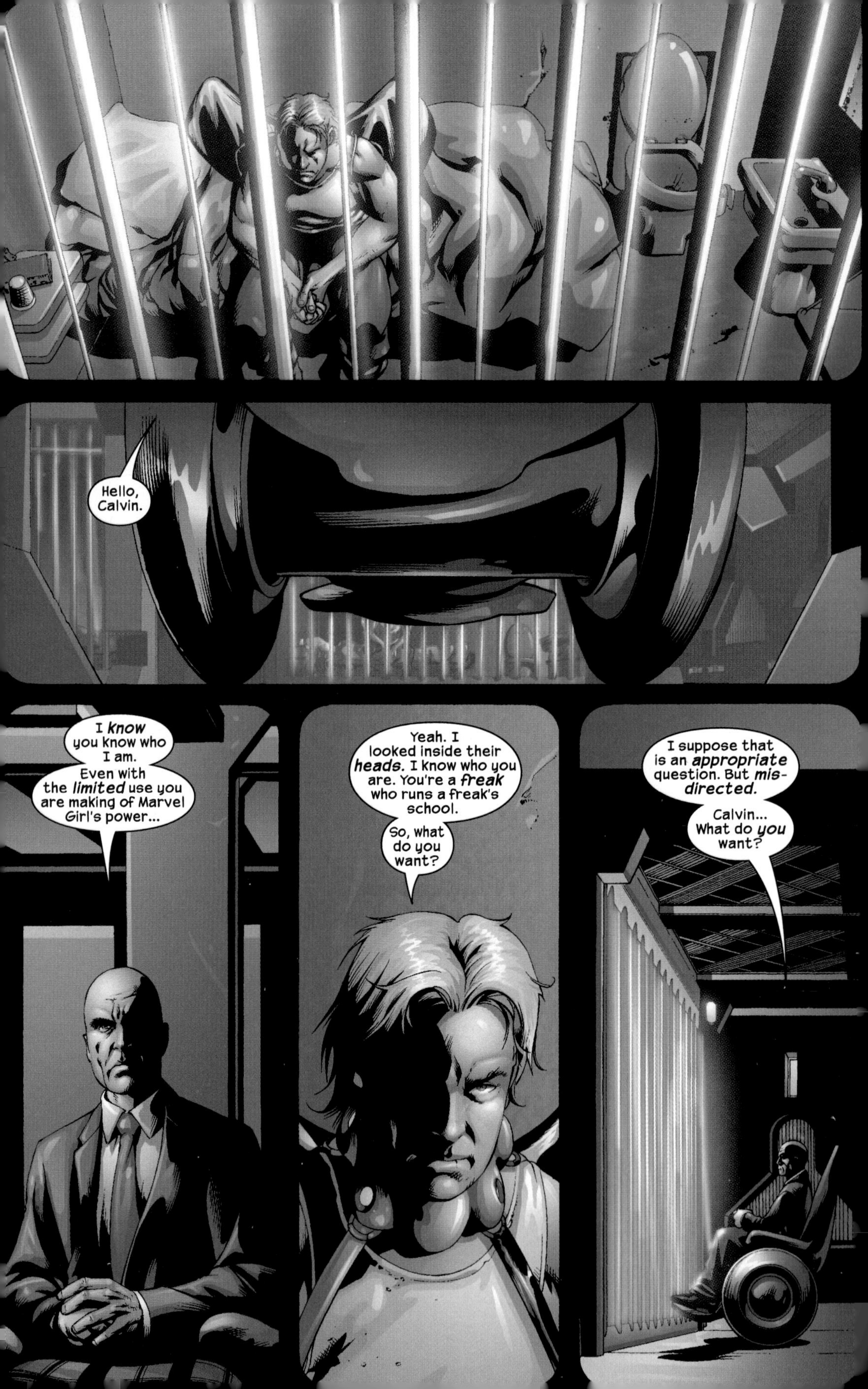

Hello, Calvin.
I know you know who I am. Even with the limited use you are making of Marvel Girl's power...
Yeah. I looked inside their heads. I know who you are. You're a freak who runs a freak's school.
So, what do you want?
I suppose that is an appropriate question. But misdirected.
Calvin... What do you want?

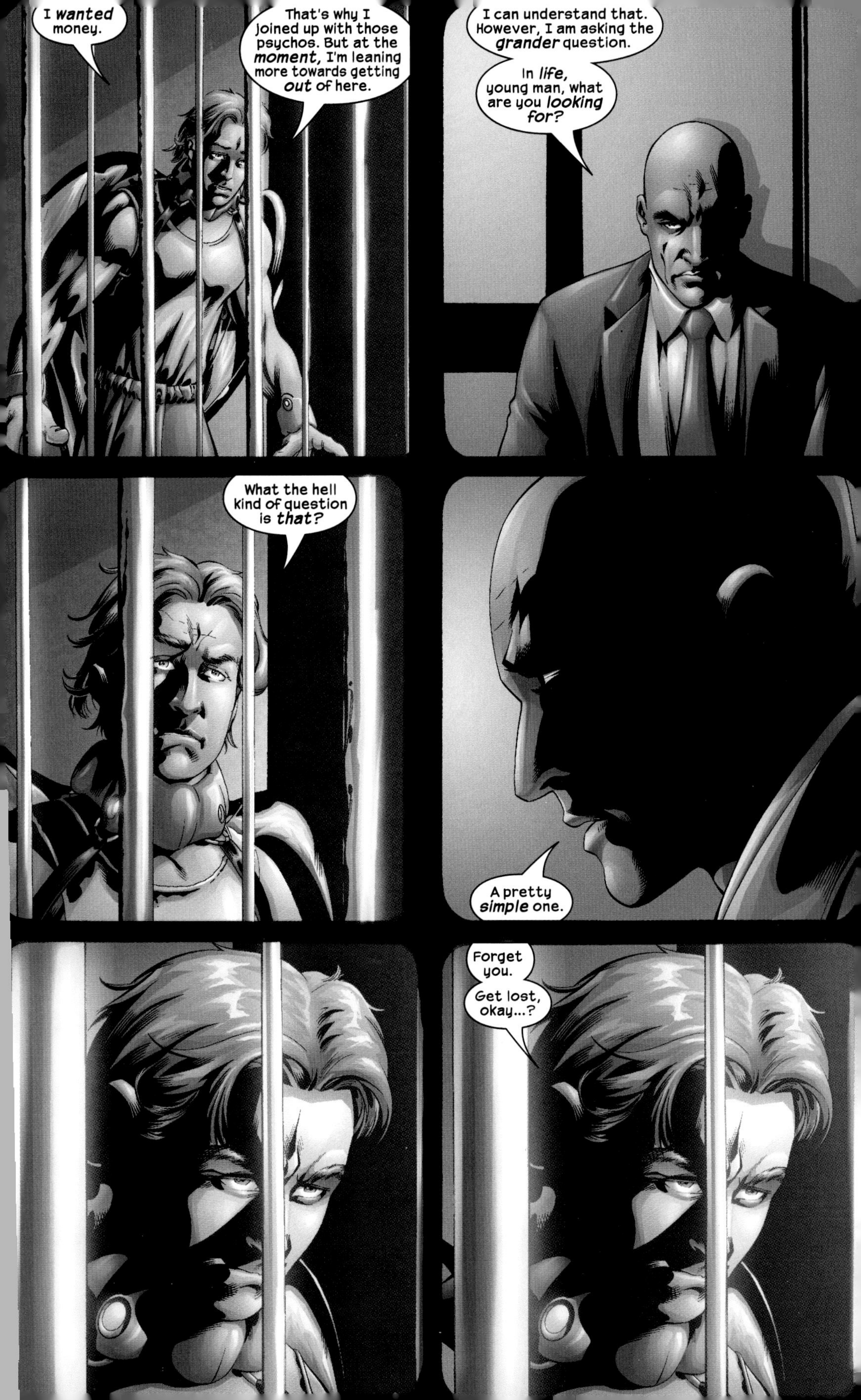
I *wanted* money.
That's why I joined up with those psychos. But at the *moment,* I'm leaning more towards getting *out* of here.
I can understand that. However, I am asking the *grander* question.
In *life,* young man, what are you *looking for?*
What the hell kind of question is *that?*
A pretty *simple* one.
Forget you.
Get lost, okay...?

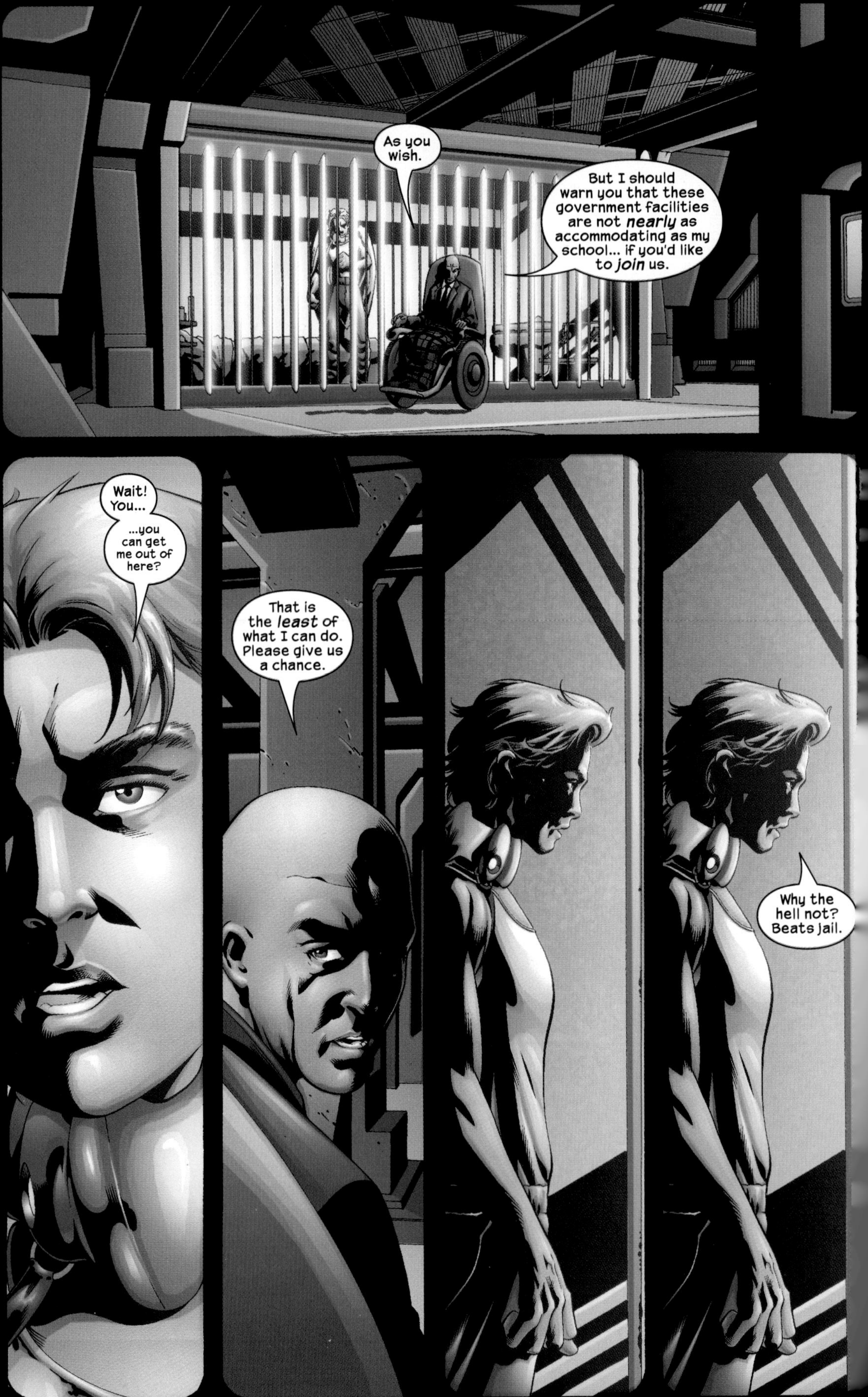
As you wish.
But I should warn you that these government facilities are not *nearly* as accommodating as my school... if you'd like to *join* us.
Wait! You...
...you can get me out of here?
That is the *least* of what I can do. Please give us a chance.
Why the hell not? Beats jail.

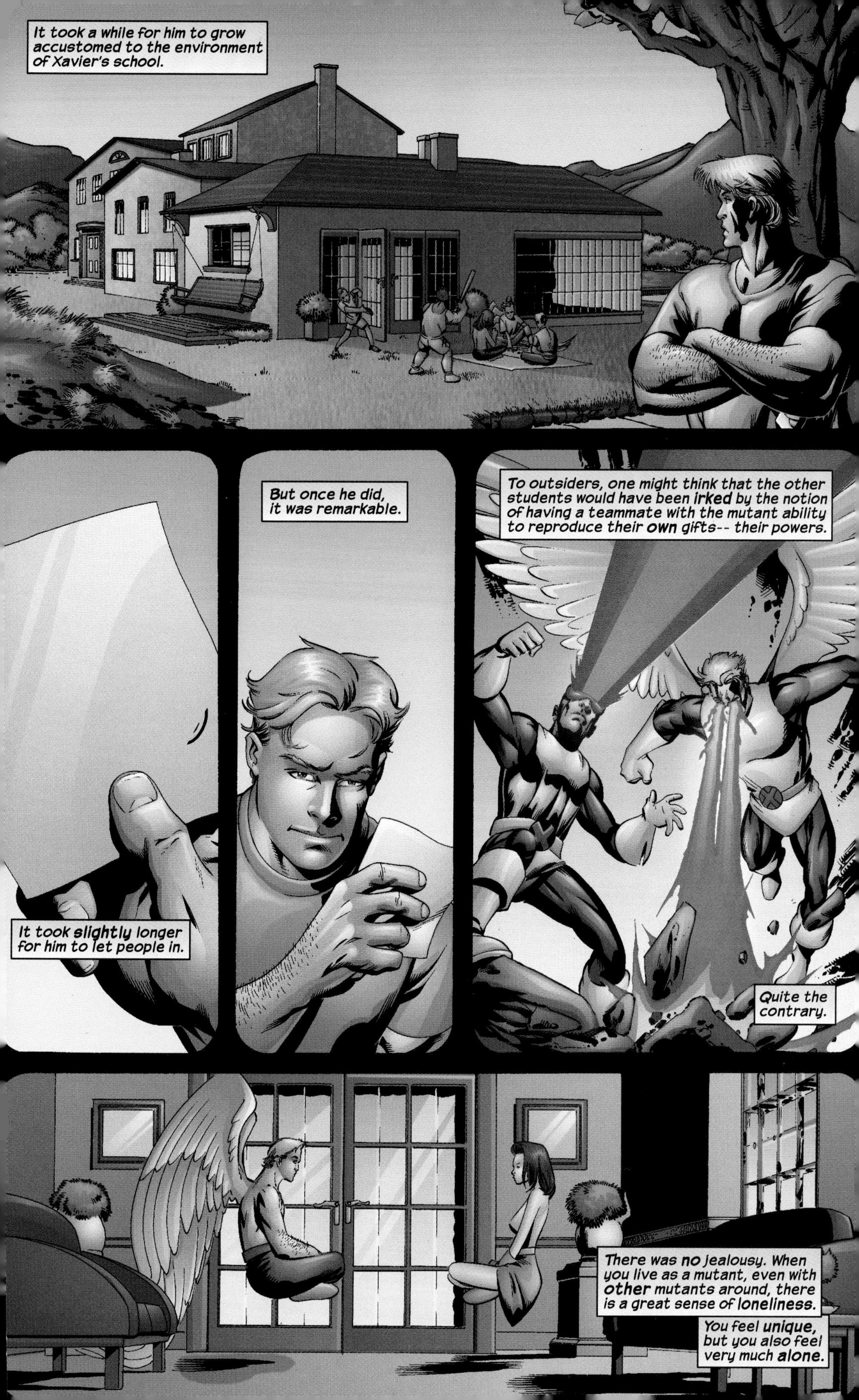
It took a while for him to grow accustomed to the environment of Xavier's school.
It took slightly longer for him to let people in.
But once he did, it was remarkable.
To outsiders, one might think that the other students would have been irked by the notion of having a teammate with the mutant ability to reproduce their own gifts-- their powers.
Quite the contrary.
There was no jealousy. When you live as a mutant, even with other mutants around, there is a great sense of loneliness.
You feel unique, but you also feel very much alone.

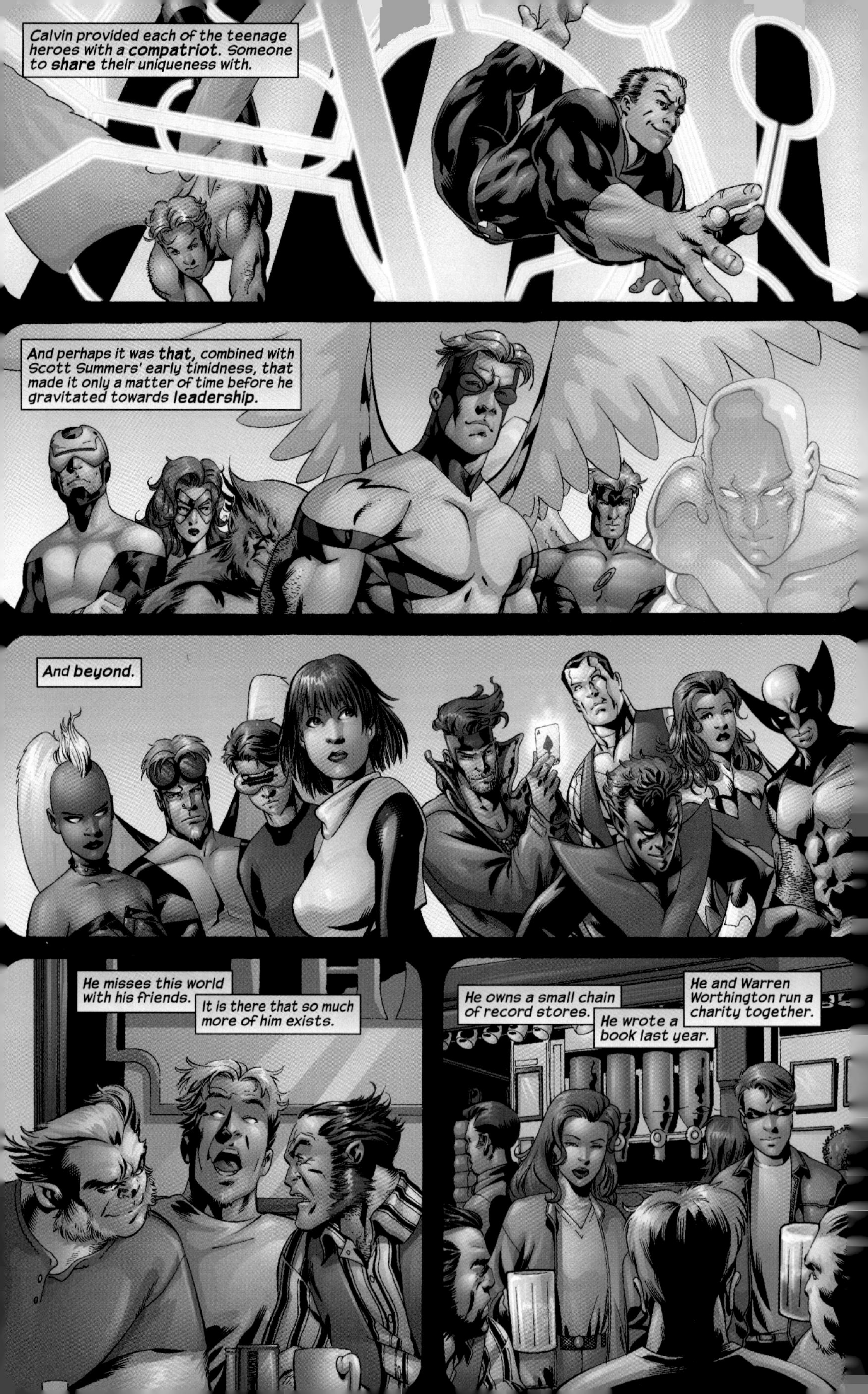
Calvin provided each of the teenage heroes with a compatriot. Someone to share their uniqueness with.
And perhaps it was that, combined with Scott Summers' early timidness, that made it only a matter of time before he gravitated towards leadership.
And beyond.
He misses this world with his friends.
It is there that so much more of him exists.
He owns a small chain of record stores.
He wrote a book last year.
He and Warren Worthington run a charity together.

Things. *Things that make up a life.*

Now he is a cog in a wheel.

And he fights to get his life back.

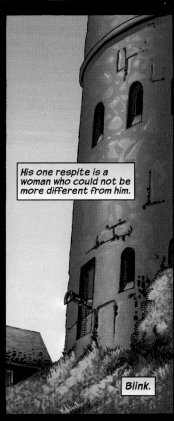

His one respite is a woman who could not be more different from him.

Blink.

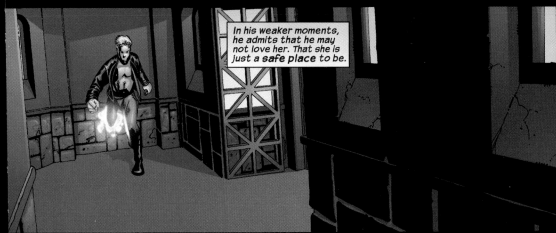

In his weaker moments, he admits that he may not love her. That she is just a safe place to be.

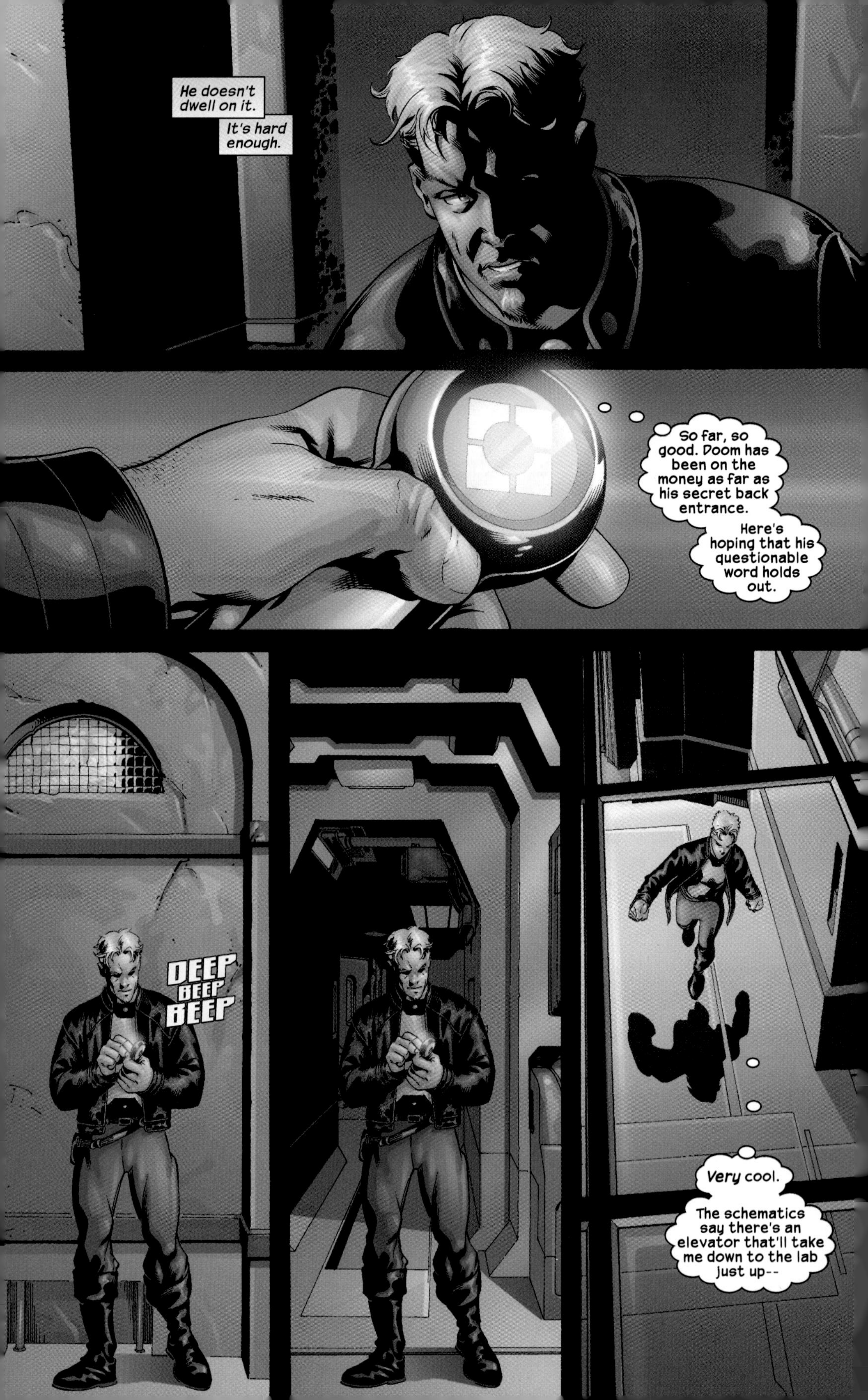
He doesn't dwell on it.
It's hard enough.
So far, so good. Doom has been on the money as far as his secret back entrance.
Here's hoping that his questionable word holds out.
DEEP BEEP BEEP
Very cool.
The schematics say there's an elevator that'll take me down to the lab just up--

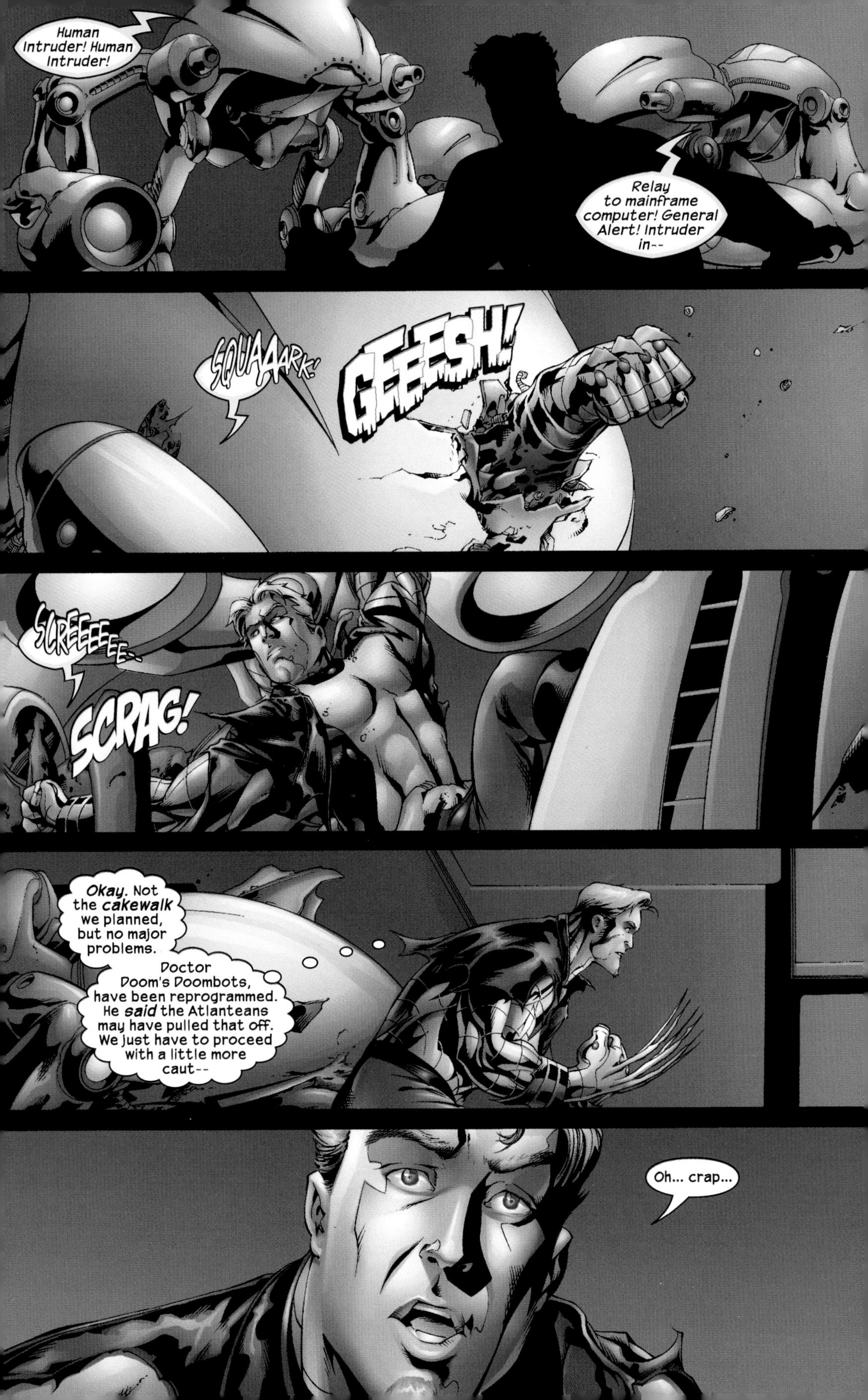

Human Intruder! Human Intruder!
Relay to mainframe computer! General Alert! Intruder in--
SQUAAARK!
GEEESH!
SCREEEEEEE--
SCRAG!
Okay. Not the cakewalk we planned, but no major problems.
Doctor Doom's Doombots, have been reprogrammed. He said the Atlanteans may have pulled that off. We just have to proceed with a little more caut--
Oh... crap...

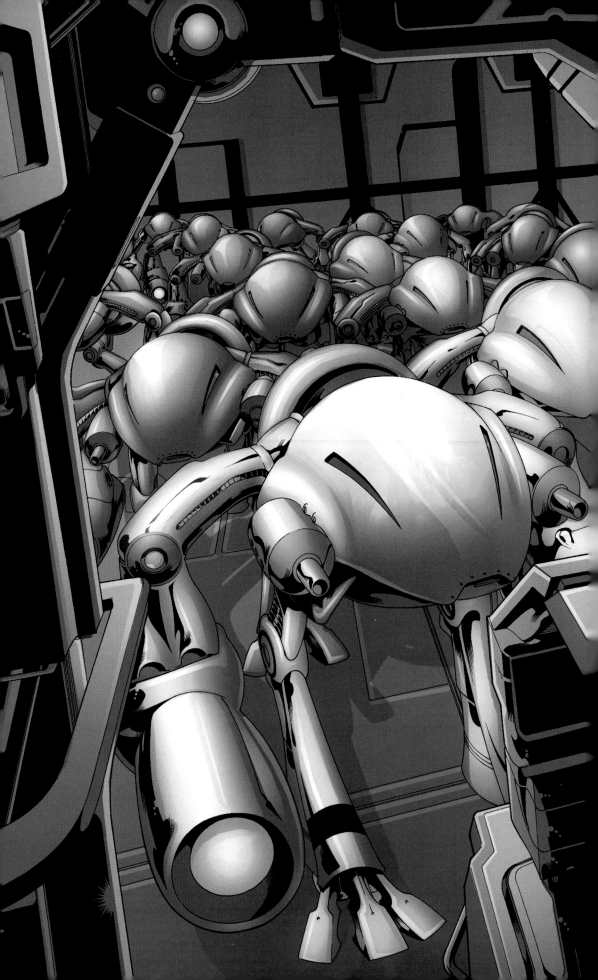

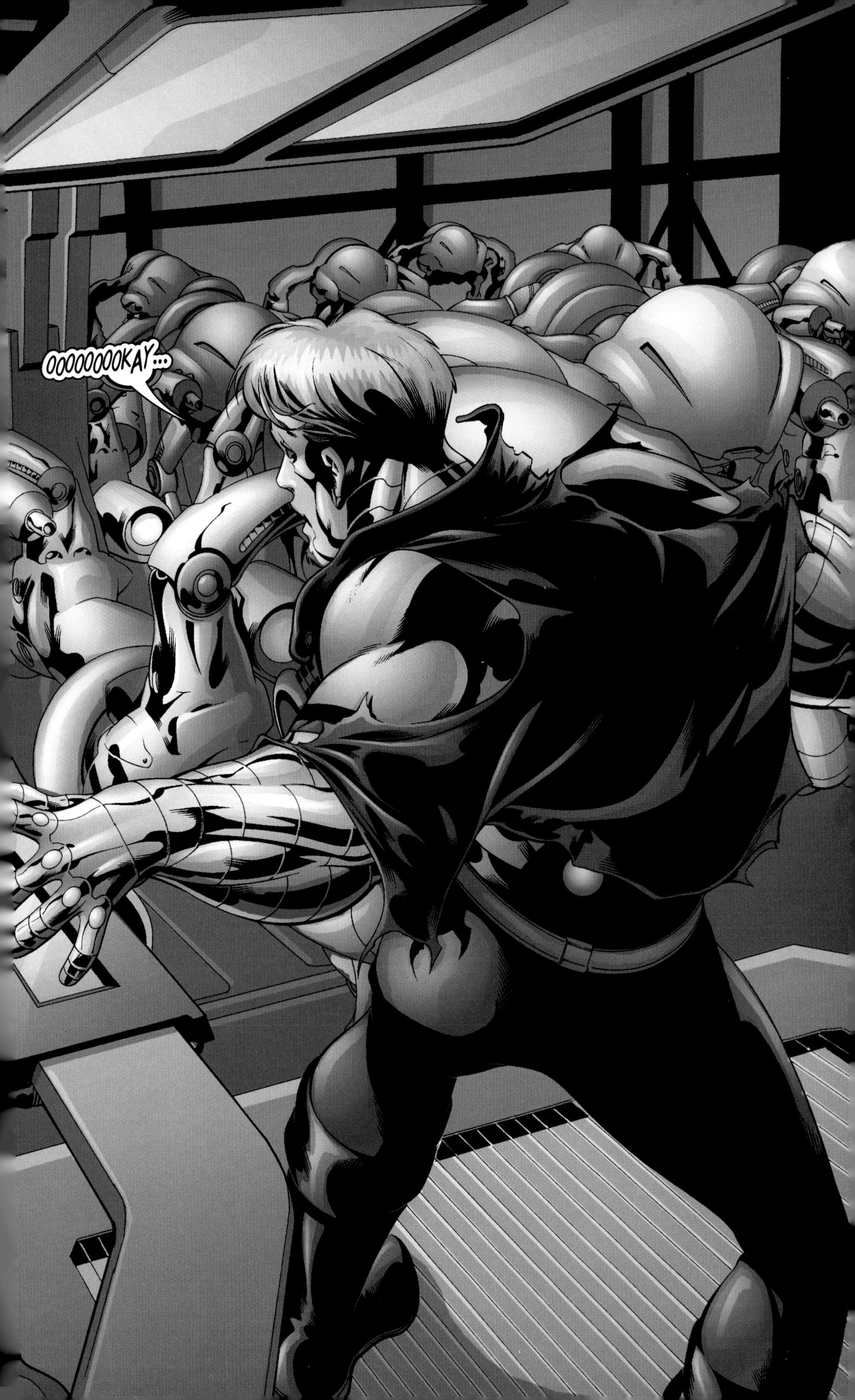
OOOOOOOOKAY...

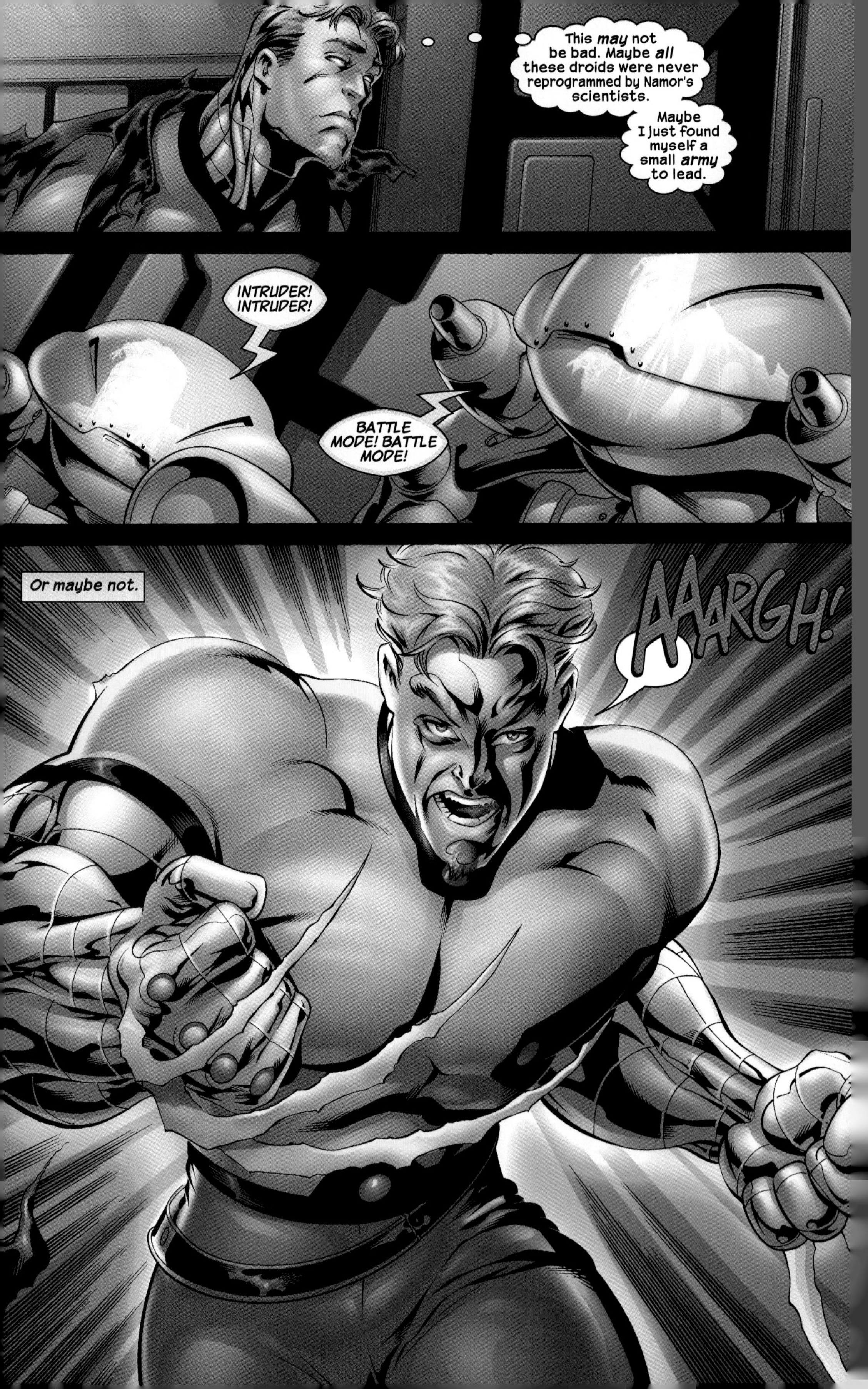
This *may* not be bad. Maybe *all* these droids were never reprogrammed by Namor's scientists.
Maybe I just found myself a small *army* to lead.
INTRUDER! INTRUDER!
BATTLE MODE! BATTLE MODE!
Or maybe not.
AAARGH!

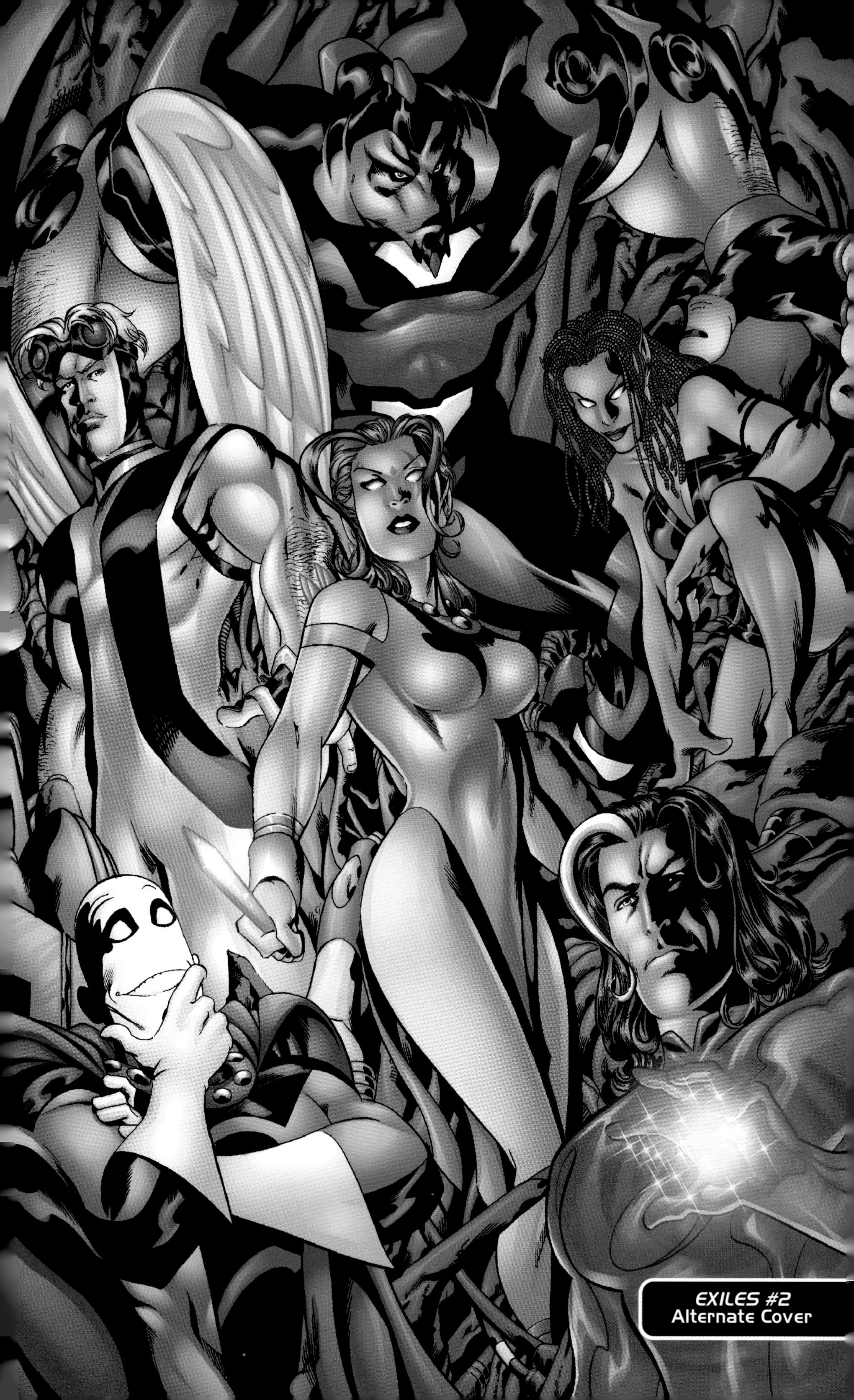

EXILES #2
Alternate Cover

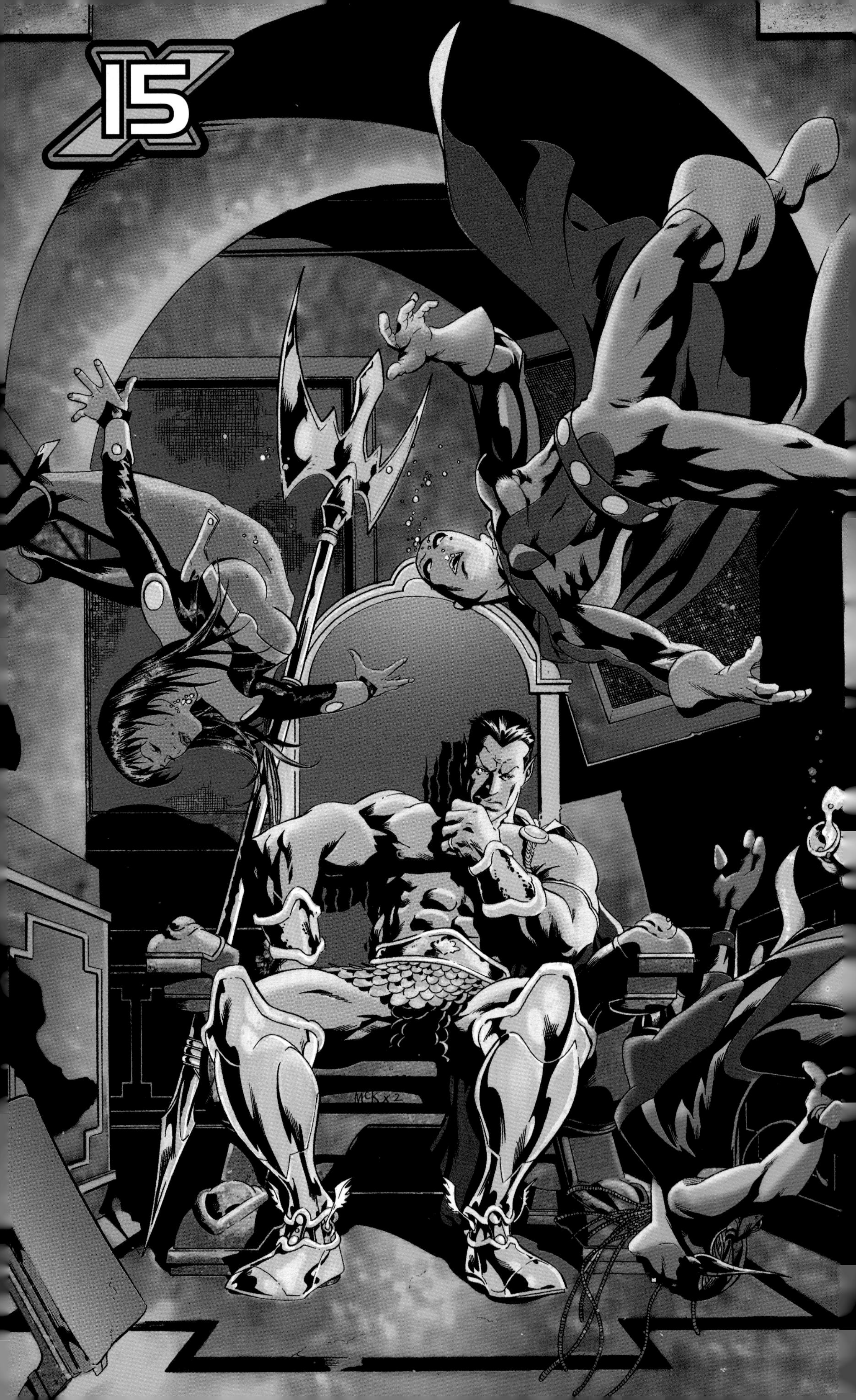

15
McK x 2

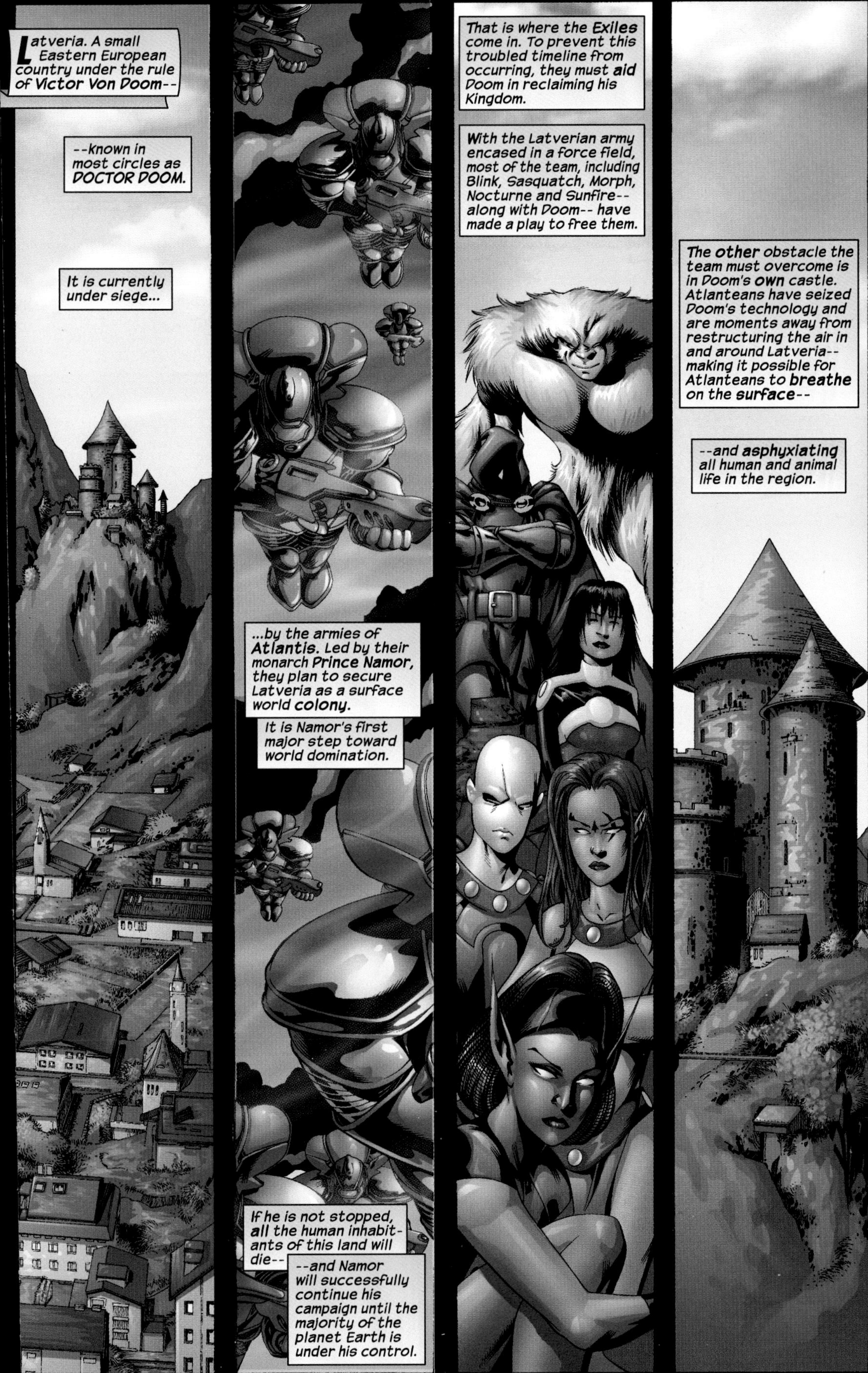
Latveria. A small Eastern European country under the rule of Victor Von Doom--
--known in most circles as DOCTOR DOOM.
It is currently under siege...
...by the armies of Atlantis. Led by their monarch Prince Namor, they plan to secure Latveria as a surface world colony.
It is Namor's first major step toward world domination.
If he is not stopped, all the human inhabitants of this land will die--
--and Namor will successfully continue his campaign until the majority of the planet Earth is under his control.
That is where the Exiles come in. To prevent this troubled timeline from occurring, they must aid Doom in reclaiming his Kingdom.
With the Latverian army encased in a force field, most of the team, including Blink, Sasquatch, Morph, Nocturne and Sunfire--along with Doom-- have made a play to free them.
The other obstacle the team must overcome is in Doom's own castle. Atlanteans have seized Doom's technology and are moments away from restructuring the air in and around Latveria--making it possible for Atlanteans to breathe on the surface--
--and asphyxiating all human and animal life in the region.

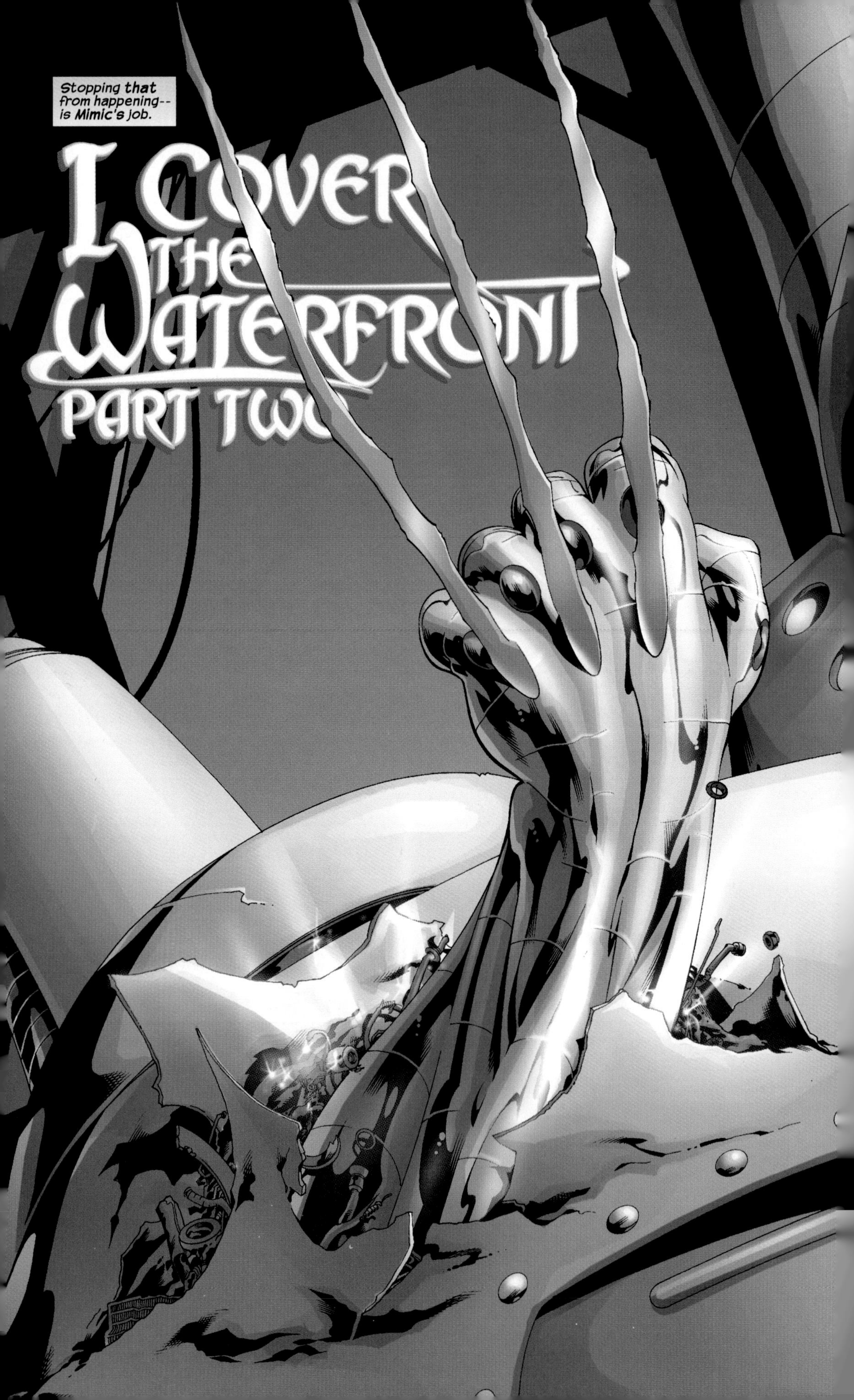
Stopping that from happening-- is Mimic's job.
I COVER THE WATERFRONT
PART TWO

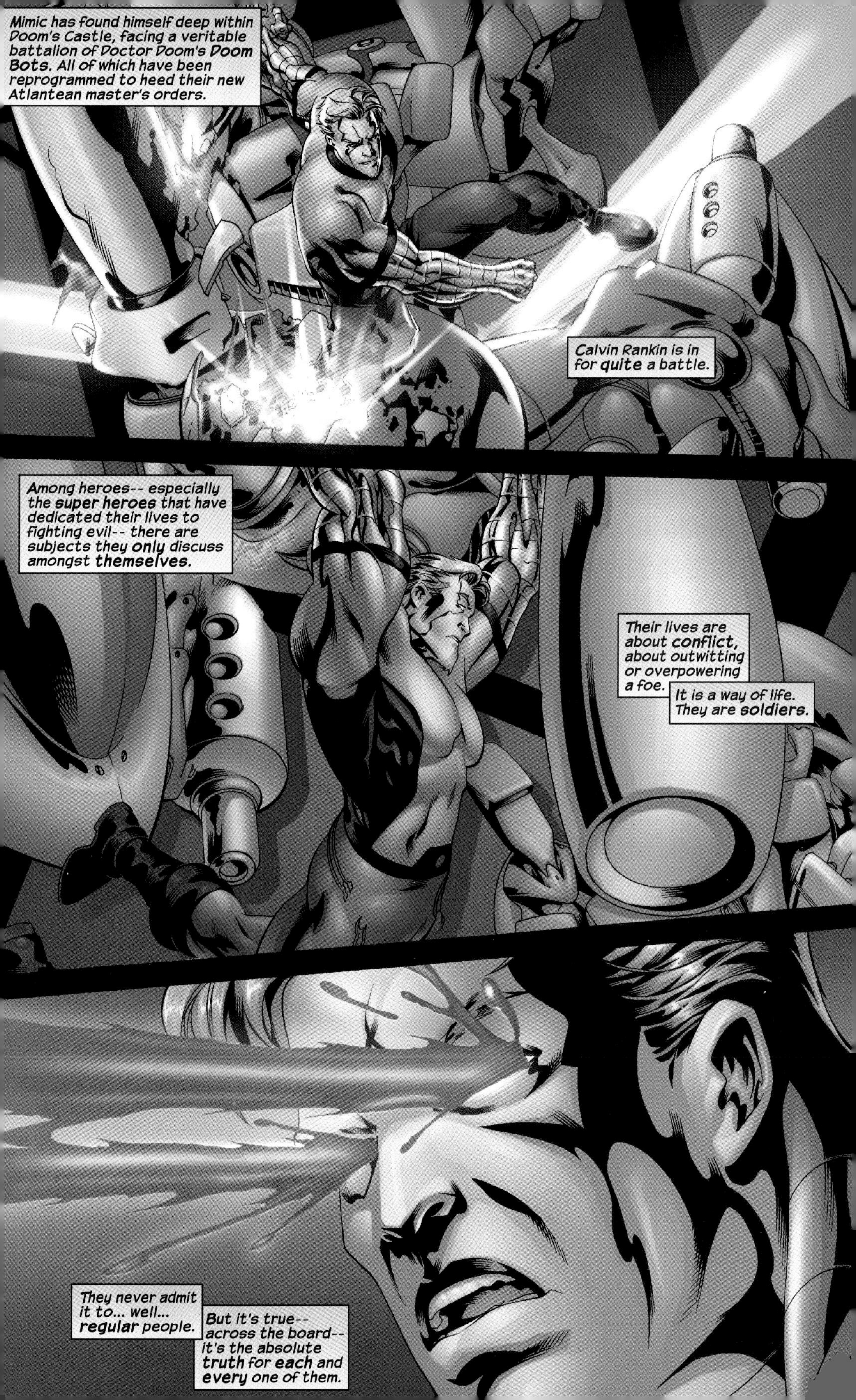
Mimic has found himself deep within Doom's Castle, facing a veritable battalion of Doctor Doom's Doom Bots. All of which have been reprogrammed to heed their new Atlantean master's orders.
Calvin Rankin is in for quite a battle.
Among heroes-- especially the super heroes that have dedicated their lives to fighting evil-- there are subjects they only discuss amongst themselves.
Their lives are about conflict, about outwitting or overpowering a foe.
It is a way of life. They are soldiers.
They never admit it to... well... regular people.
But it's true-- across the board-- it's the absolute truth for each and every one of them.

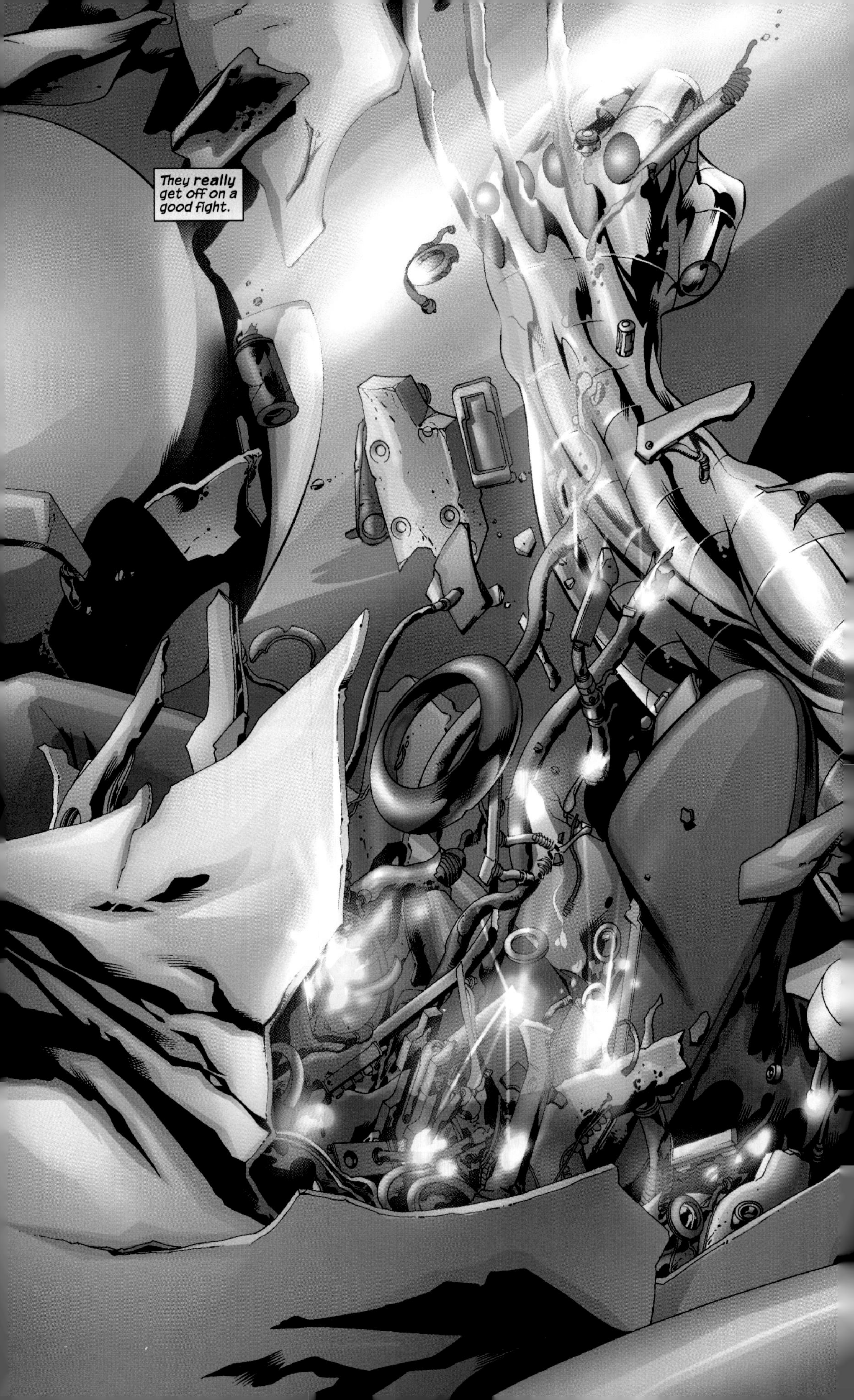
They really get off on a good fight.

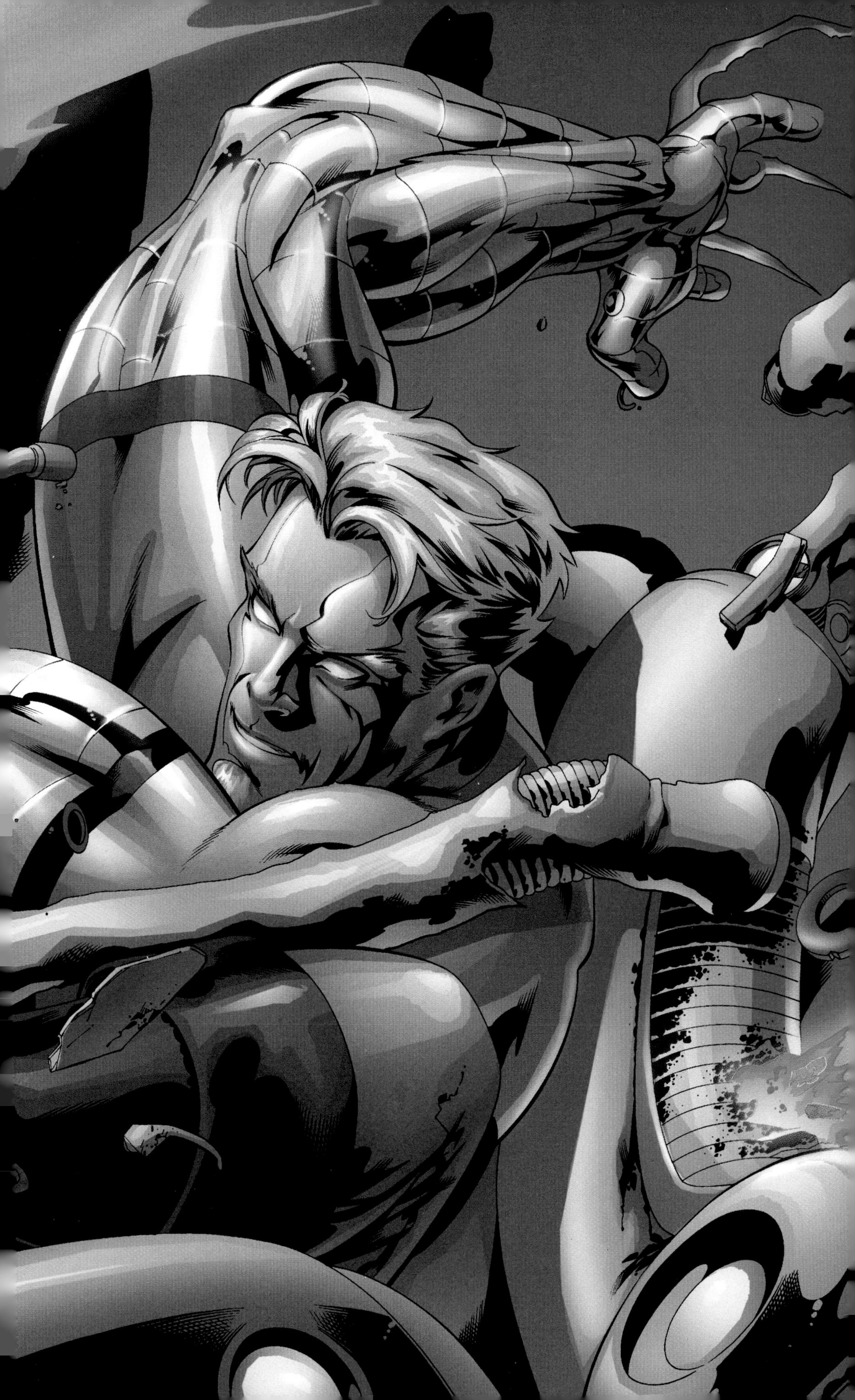

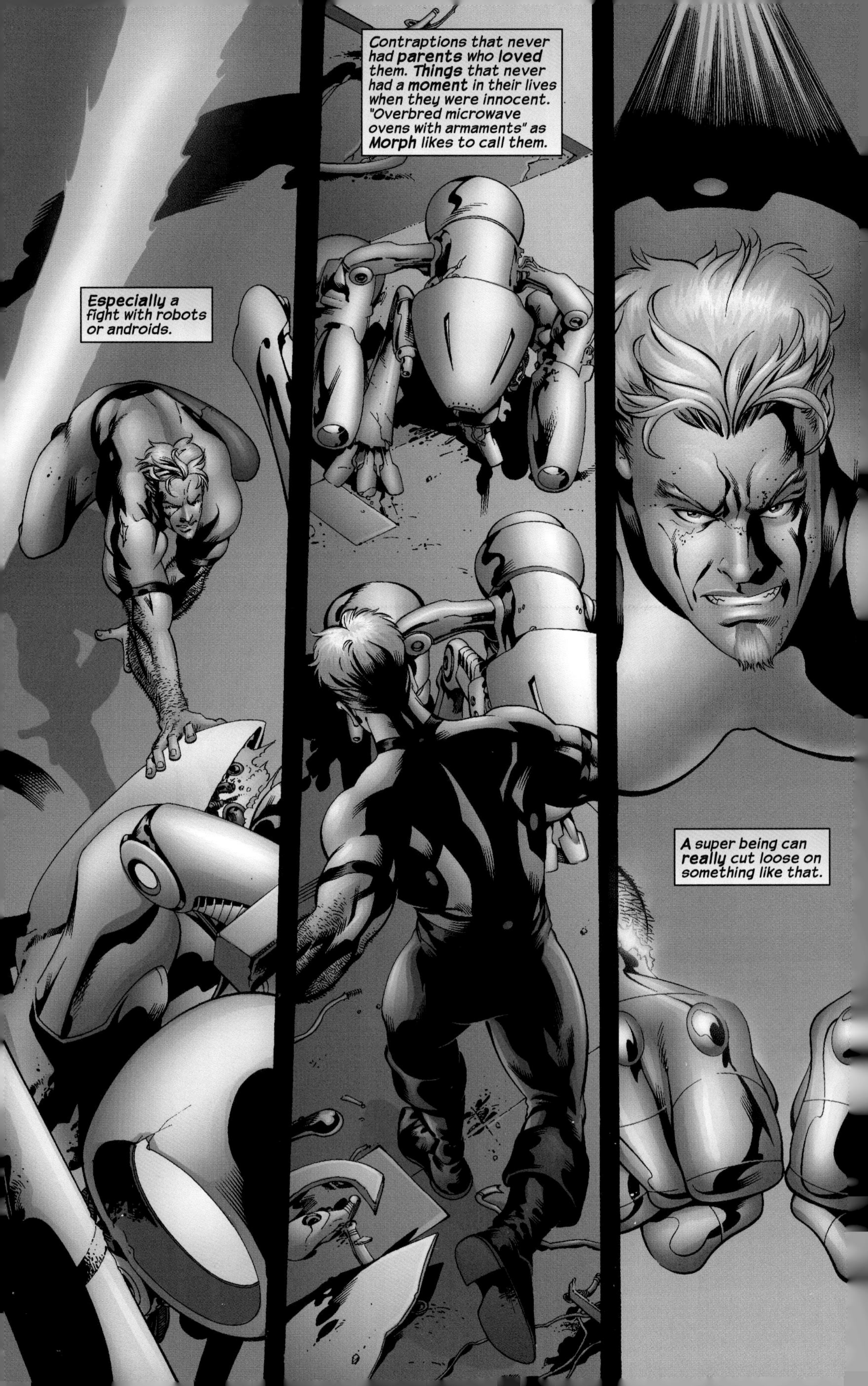
Especially a fight with robots or androids.
Contraptions that never had parents who loved them. Things that never had a moment in their lives when they were innocent. "Overbred microwave ovens with armaments" as Morph likes to call them.
A super being can really cut loose on something like that.

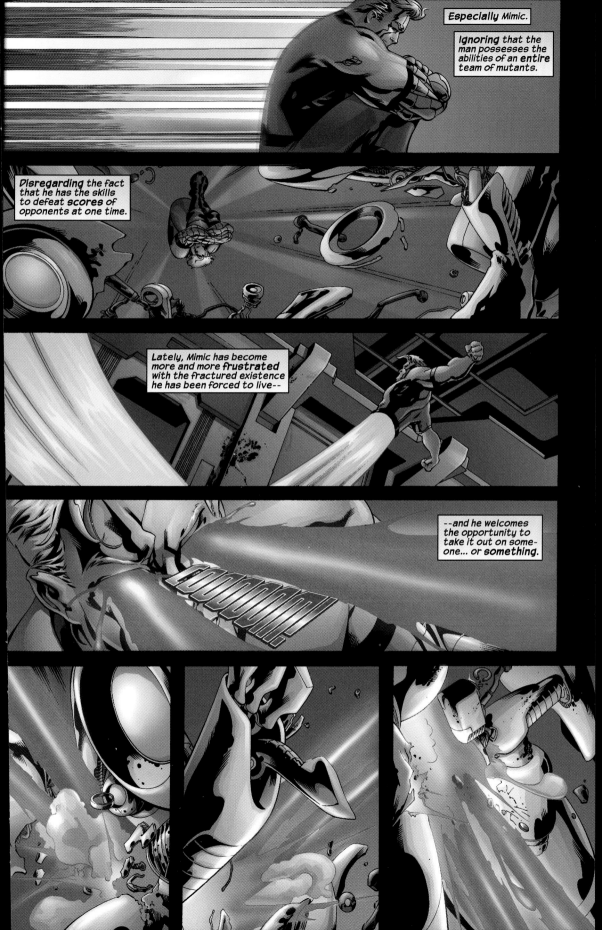

Especially Mimic.

Ignoring that the man possesses the abilities of an entire team of mutants.

Disregarding the fact that he has the skills to defeat scores of opponents at one time.

Lately, Mimic has become more and more frustrated with the fractured existence he has been forced to live--

--and he welcomes the opportunity to take it out on someone... or something.

FOOOOOOM!

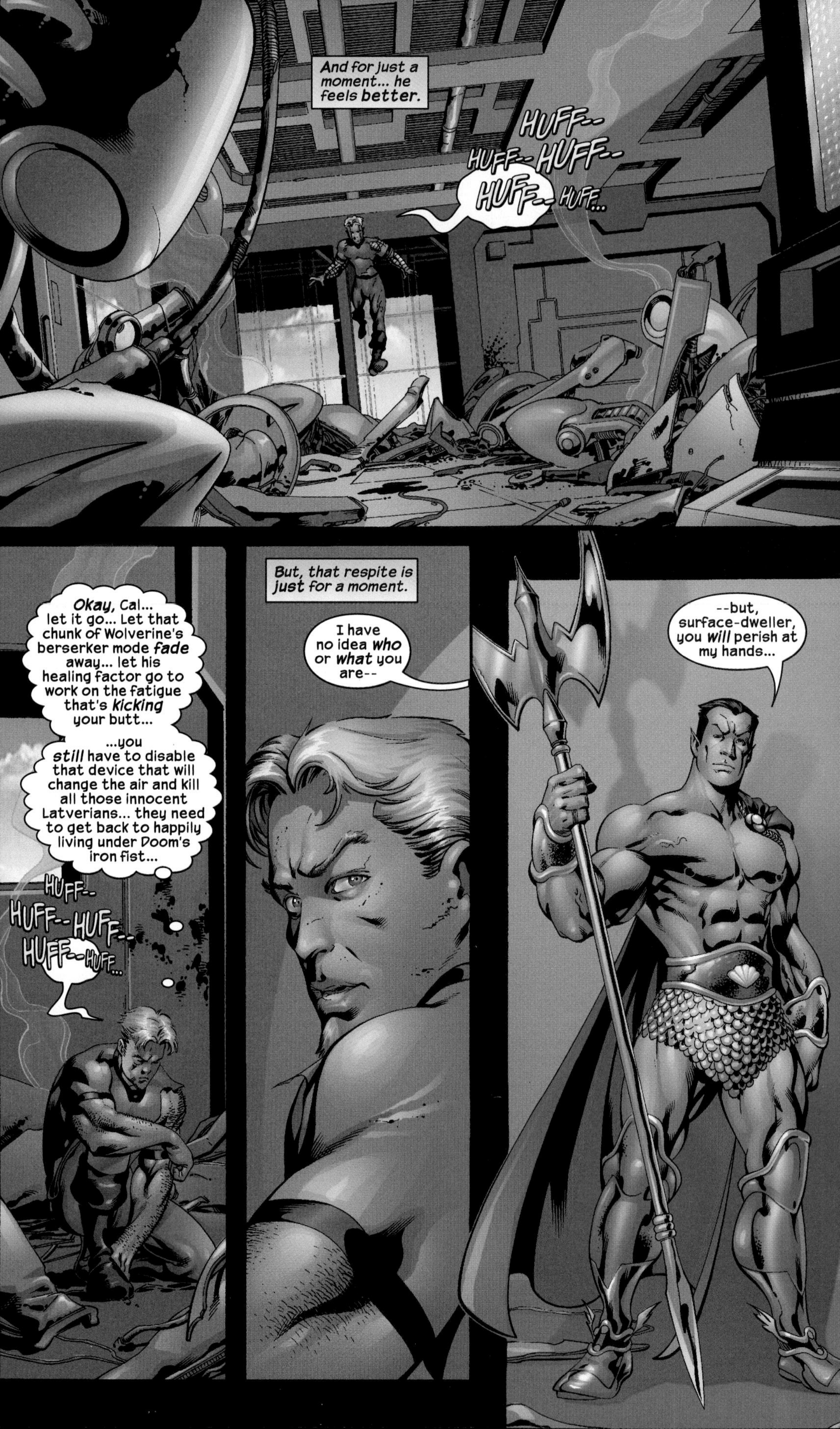
And for just a moment... he feels better.
HUFF-- HUFF-- HUFF-- HUFF-- HUFF...
Okay, Cal... let it go... Let that chunk of Wolverine's berserker mode fade away... let his healing factor go to work on the fatigue that's kicking your butt...
...you still have to disable that device that will change the air and kill all those innocent Latverians... they need to get back to happily living under Doom's iron fist...
HUFF-- HUFF-- HUFF-- HUFF-- HUFF...
But, that respite is just for a moment.
I have no idea who or what you are--
--but, surface-dweller, you will perish at my hands...

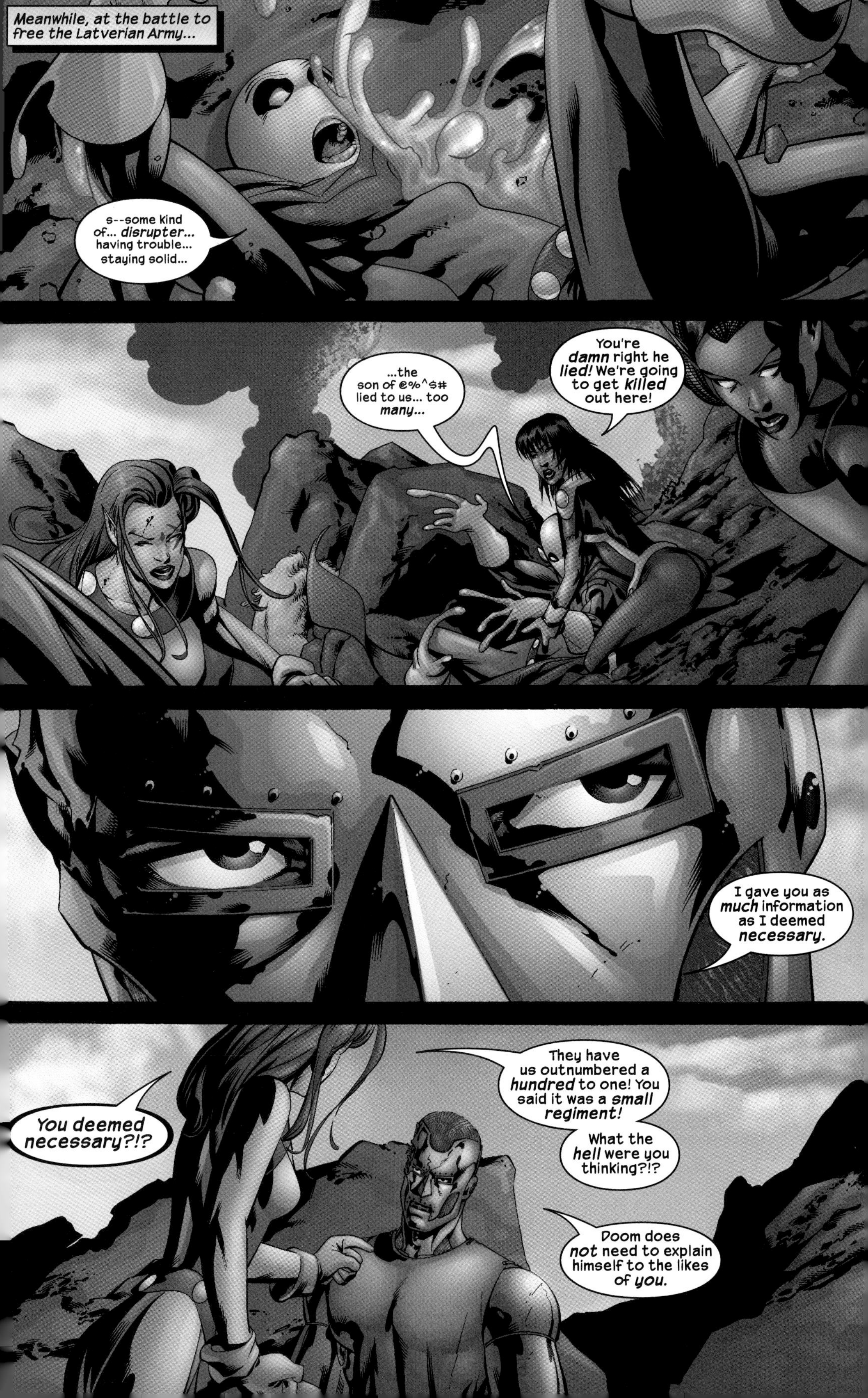
Meanwhile, at the battle to free the Latverian Army...
s--some kind of... disrupter... having trouble... staying solid...
...the son of @%^$# lied to us... too many...
You're damn right he lied! We're going to get killed out here!
I gave you as much information as I deemed necessary.
You deemed necessary?!?
They have us outnumbered a hundred to one! You said it was a small regiment!
What the hell were you thinking?!?
Doom does not need to explain himself to the likes of you.

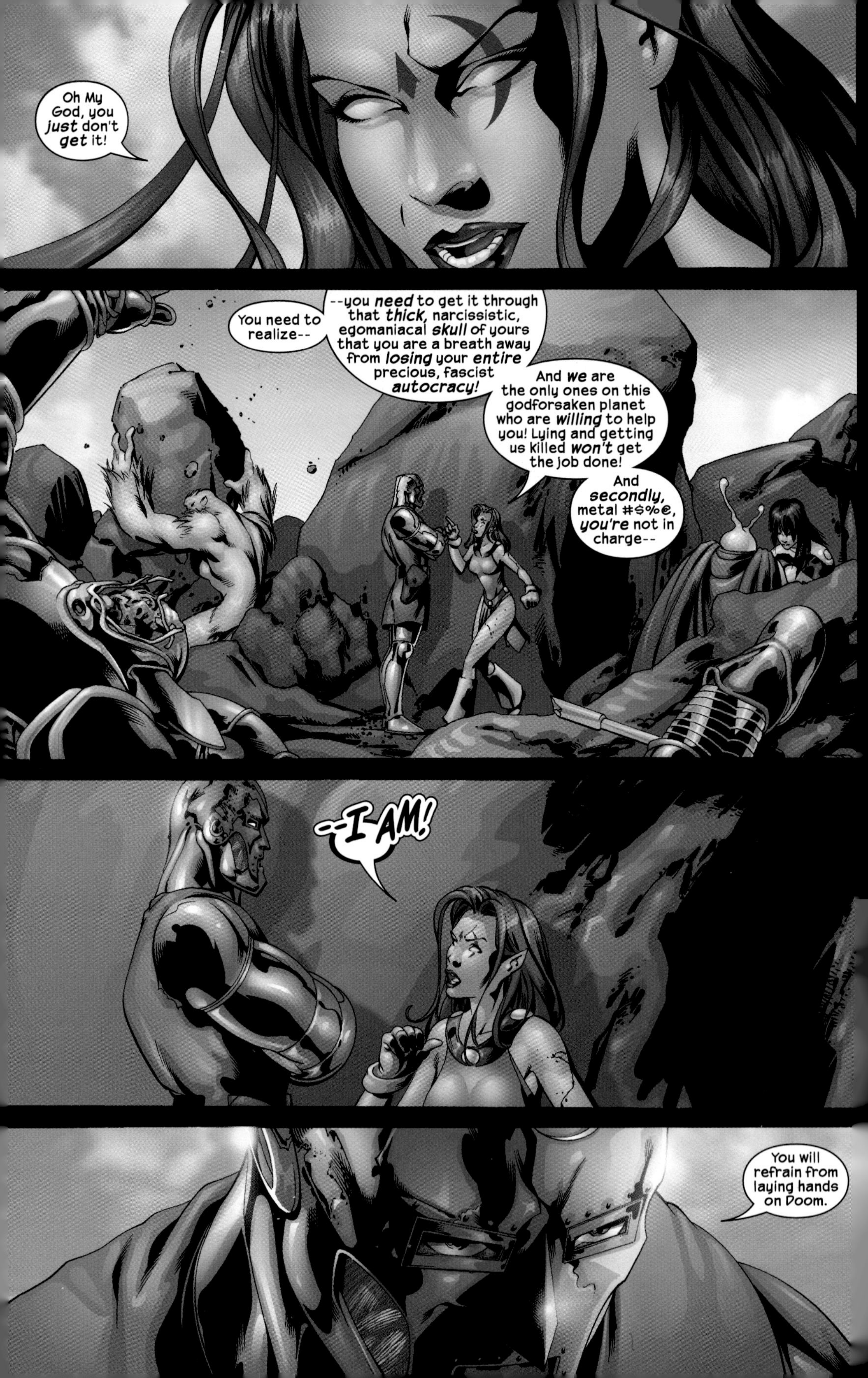

Oh My God, you just don't get it!
You need to realize--
--you need to get it through that thick, narcissistic, egomaniacal skull of yours that you are a breath away from losing your entire precious, fascist autocracy!
And we are the only ones on this godforsaken planet who are willing to help you! Lying and getting us killed won't get the job done!
And secondly, metal #$%€, you're not in charge--
--I AM!
You will refrain from laying hands on Doom.

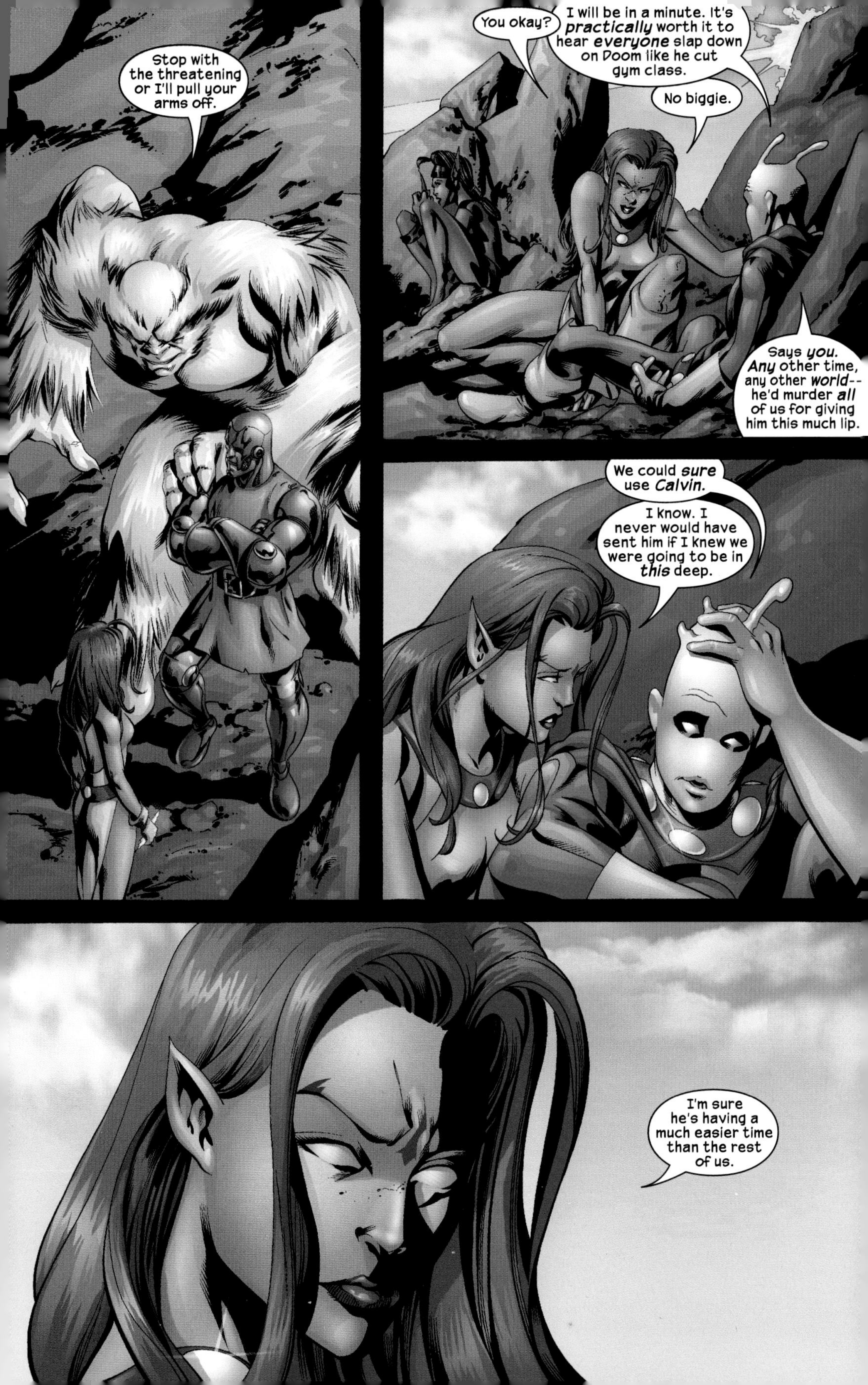
Stop with the threatening or I'll pull your arms off.
You okay?
I will be in a minute. It's *practically* worth it to hear *everyone* slap down on Doom like he cut gym class.
No biggie.
Says *you*. *Any* other time, any other *world*-- he'd murder *all* of us for giving him this much lip.
We could *sure* use *Calvin*.
I know. I never would have sent him if I knew we were going to be in *this* deep.
I'm sure he's having a much easier time than the rest of us.

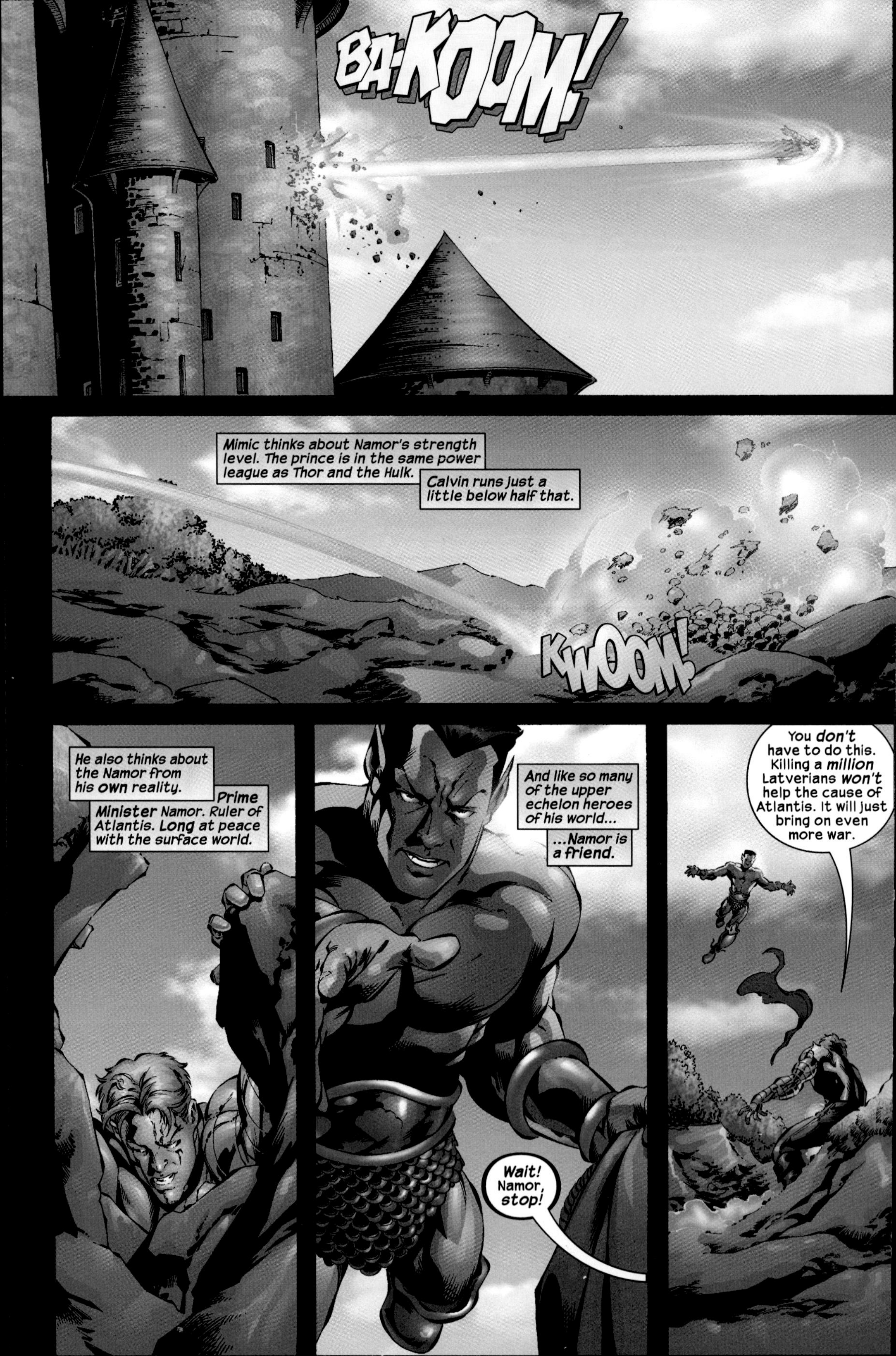
BA-KOOM!
Mimic thinks about Namor's strength level. The prince is in the same power league as Thor and the Hulk.
Calvin runs just a little below half that.
KWOOM!
He also thinks about the Namor from his own reality.
Prime Minister Namor. Ruler of Atlantis. Long at peace with the surface world.
And like so many of the upper echelon heroes of his world...
...Namor is a friend.
Wait! Namor, stop!
You don't have to do this. Killing a million Latverians won't help the cause of Atlantis. It will just bring on even more war.

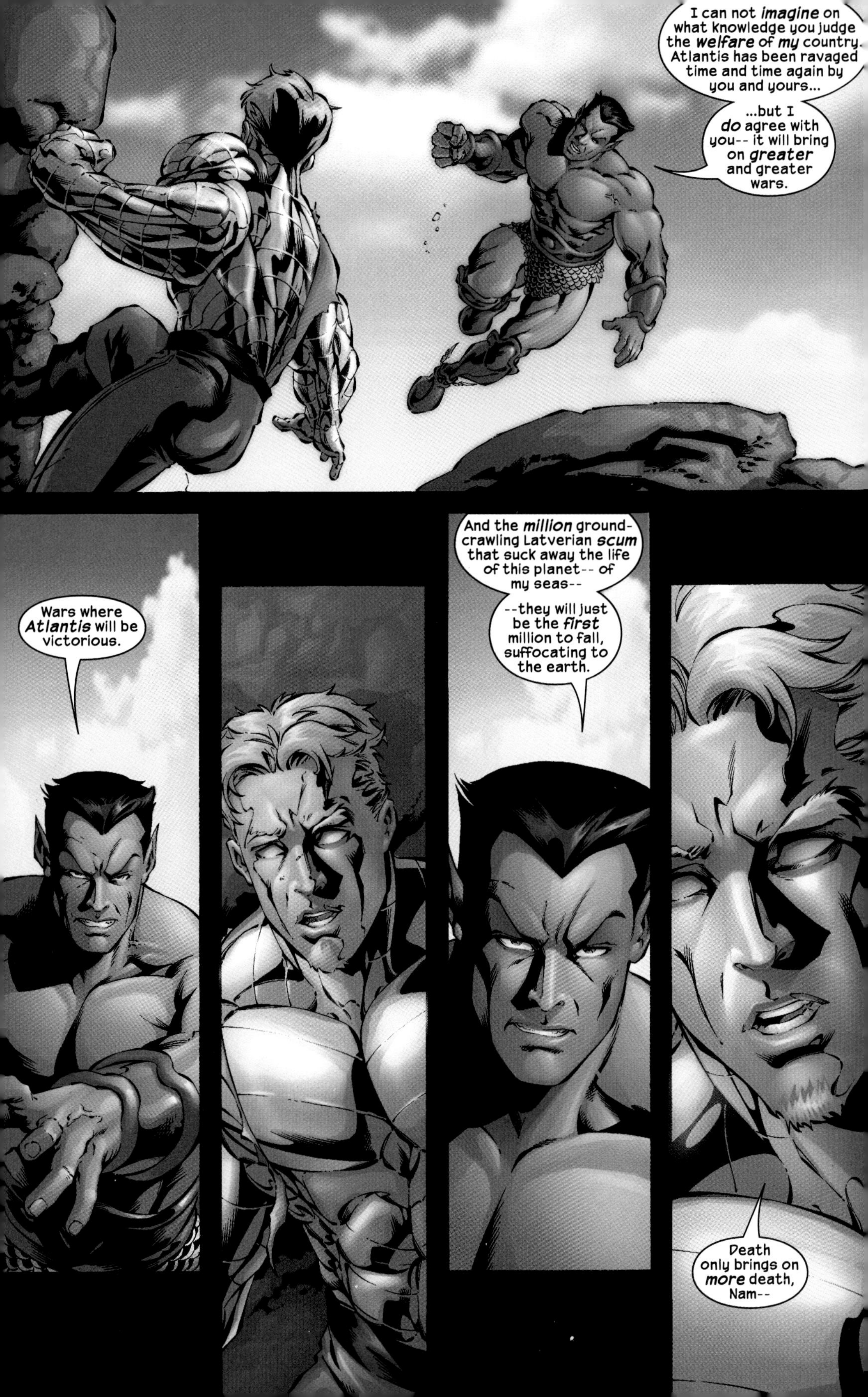
I can not *imagine* on what knowledge you judge the *welfare* of *my* country. Atlantis has been ravaged time and time again by you and yours...
...but I *do* agree with you-- it will bring on *greater* and greater wars.
Wars where *Atlantis* will be victorious.
And the *million* ground-crawling Latverian *scum* that suck away the life of this planet-- of my seas--
--they will just be the *first* million to fall, suffocating to the earth.
Death only brings on *more* death, Nam--

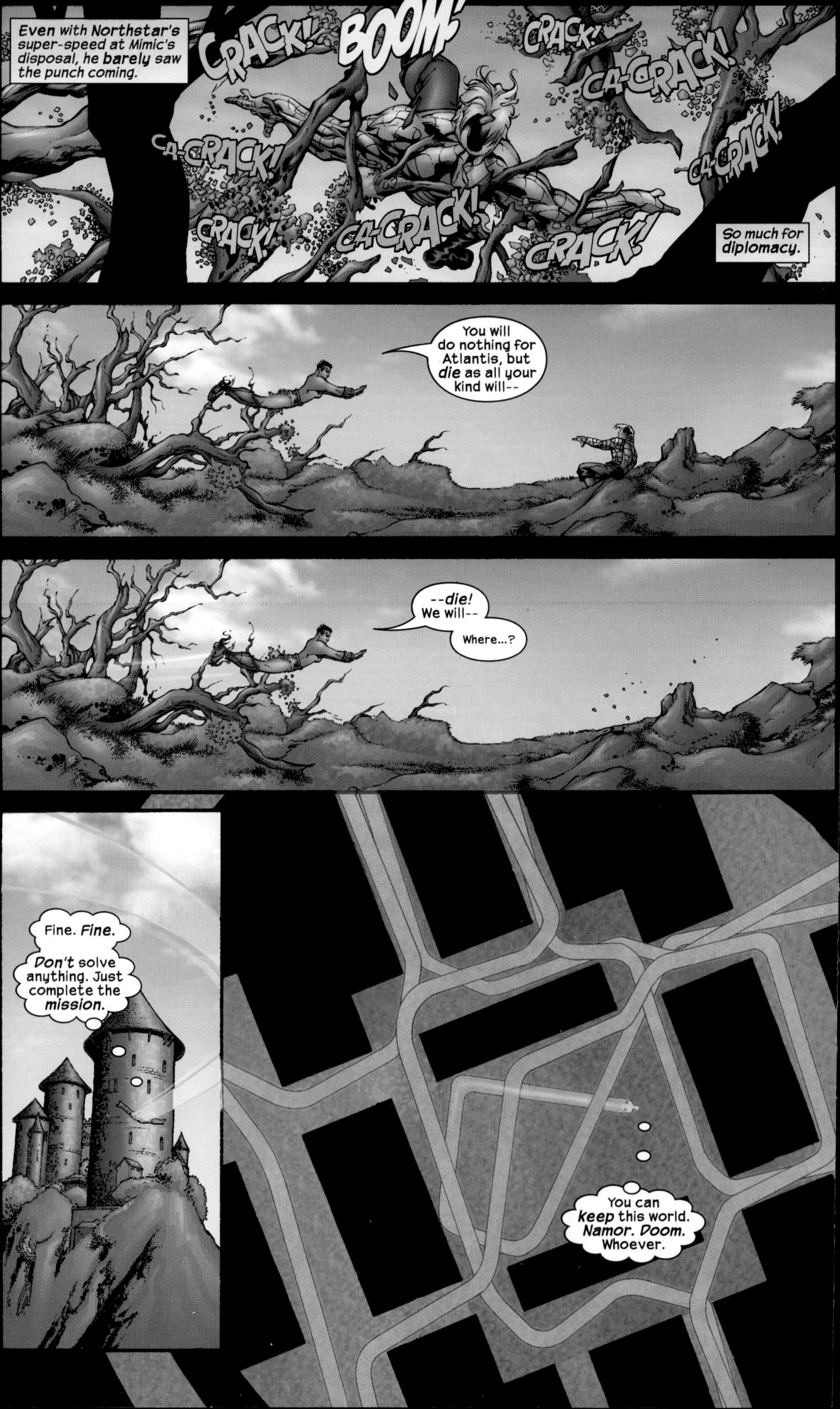
Even with Northstar's super-speed at Mimic's disposal, he barely saw the punch coming.
CRACK!
BOOM!
CRACK!
CA-CRACK!
CA-CRACK!
CA-CRACK!
CRACK!
CA-CRACK!
CRACK!
So much for diplomacy.
You will do nothing for Atlantis, but die as all your kind will--
--die! We will--
Where...?
Fine. Fine.
Don't solve anything. Just complete the mission.
You can keep this world. Namor. Doom. Whoever.

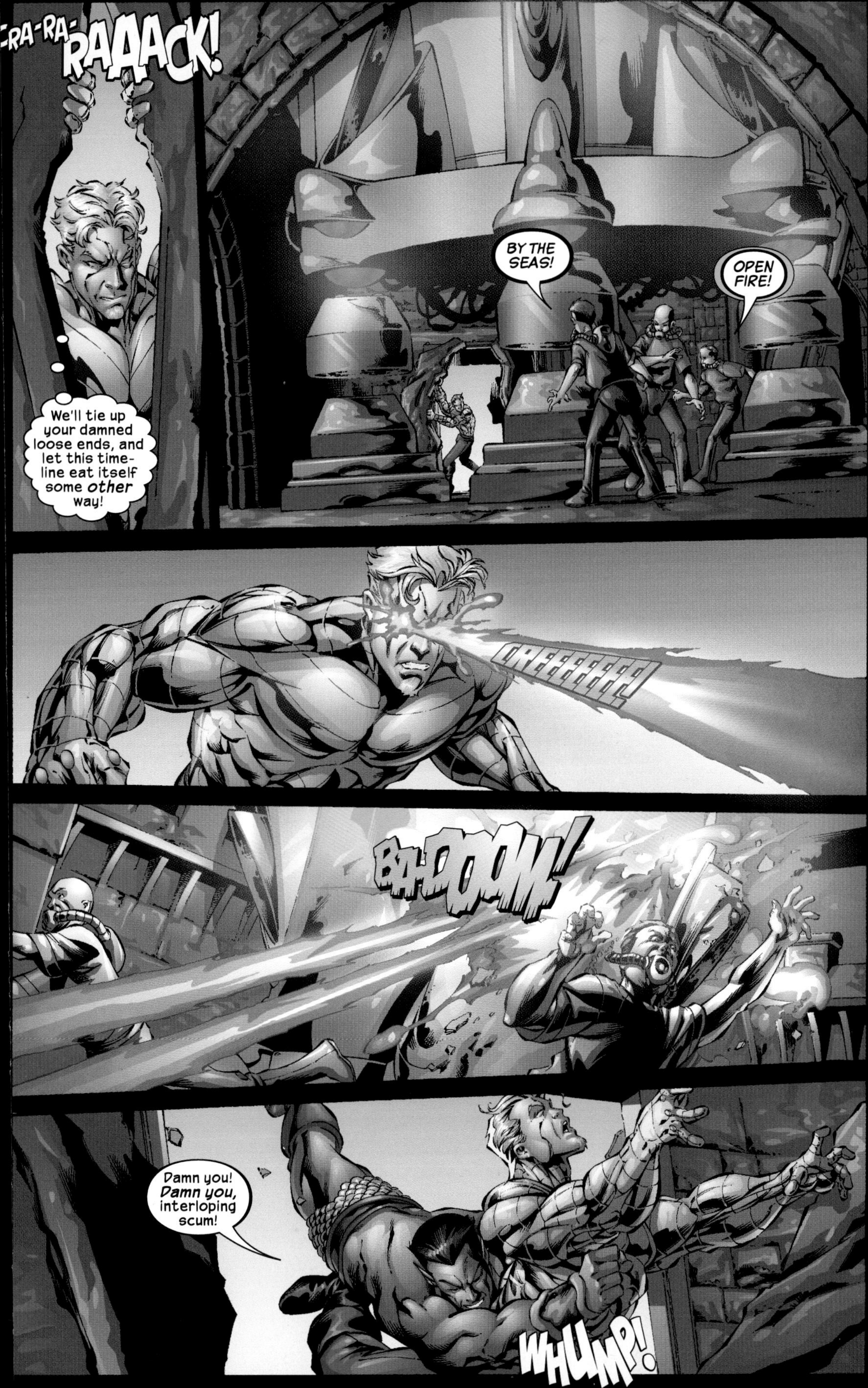
CRA-RA-RAAACK!
We'll tie up your damned loose ends, and let this time-line eat itself some *other* way!
BY THE SEAS!
OPEN FIRE!
BA-DOOOM!
Damn you! *Damn you,* interloping scum!
WHUMP!

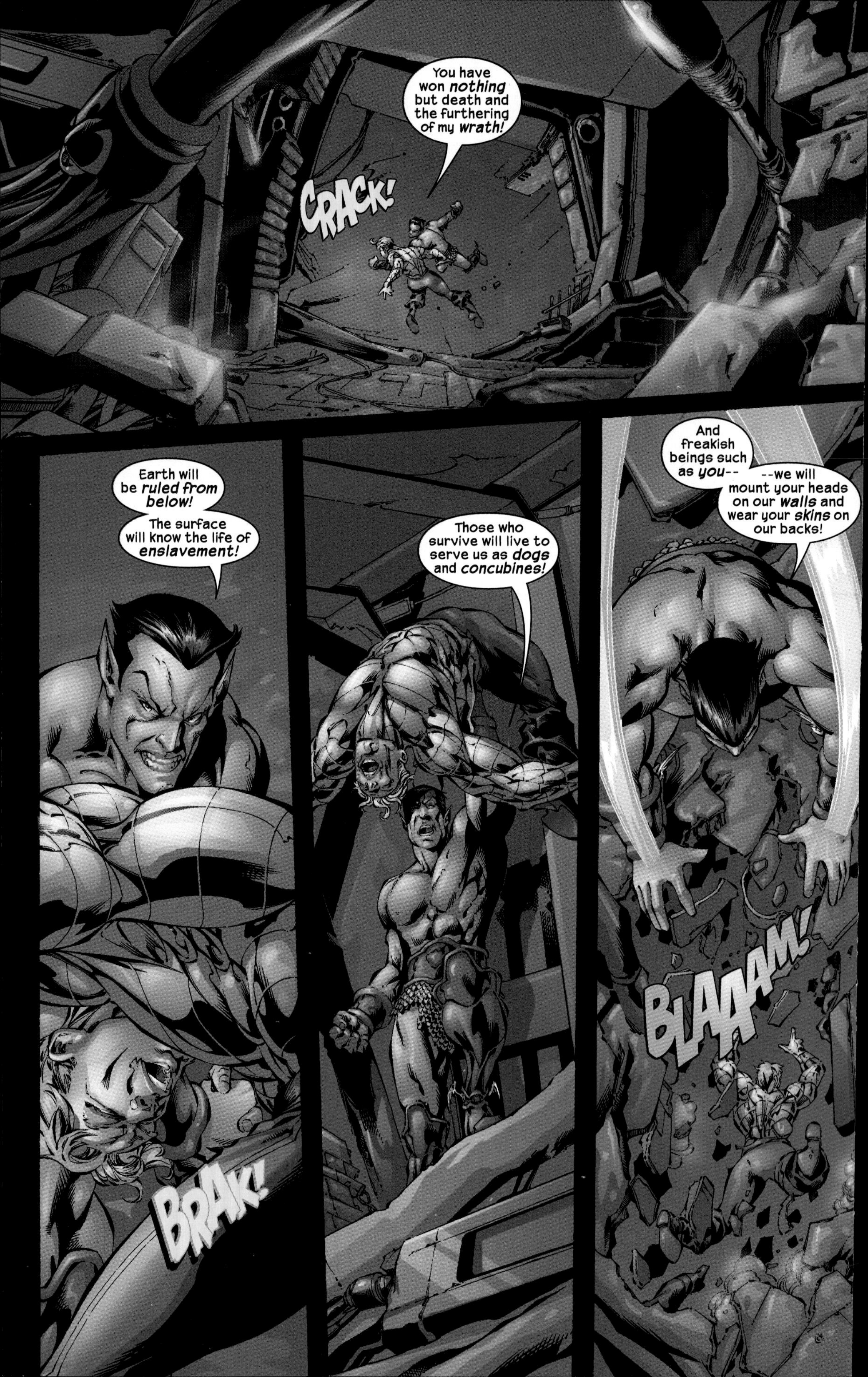
You have won *nothing* but death and the furthering of my *wrath!*
CRACK!
Earth will be *ruled from below!*
The surface will know the life of *enslavement!*
BRAK!
Those who survive will live to serve us as *dogs* and *concubines!*
And freakish beings such as *you*--
--we will mount your heads on our *walls* and wear your *skins* on our backs!
BLAAAM!

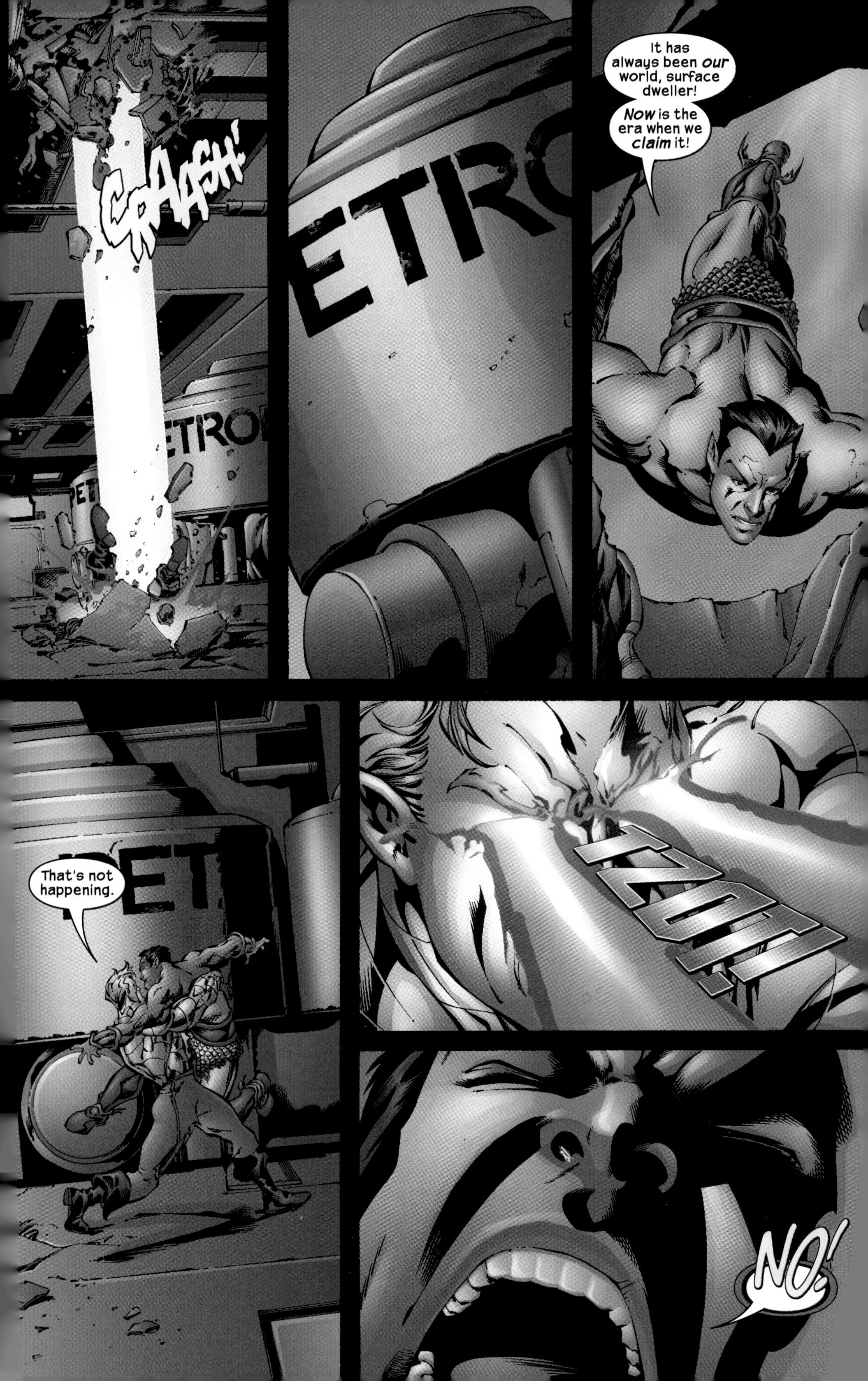
CRAASH!
PETROL
It has always been our world, surface dweller!
Now is the era when we claim it!
That's not happening.
TZOT!
NO!

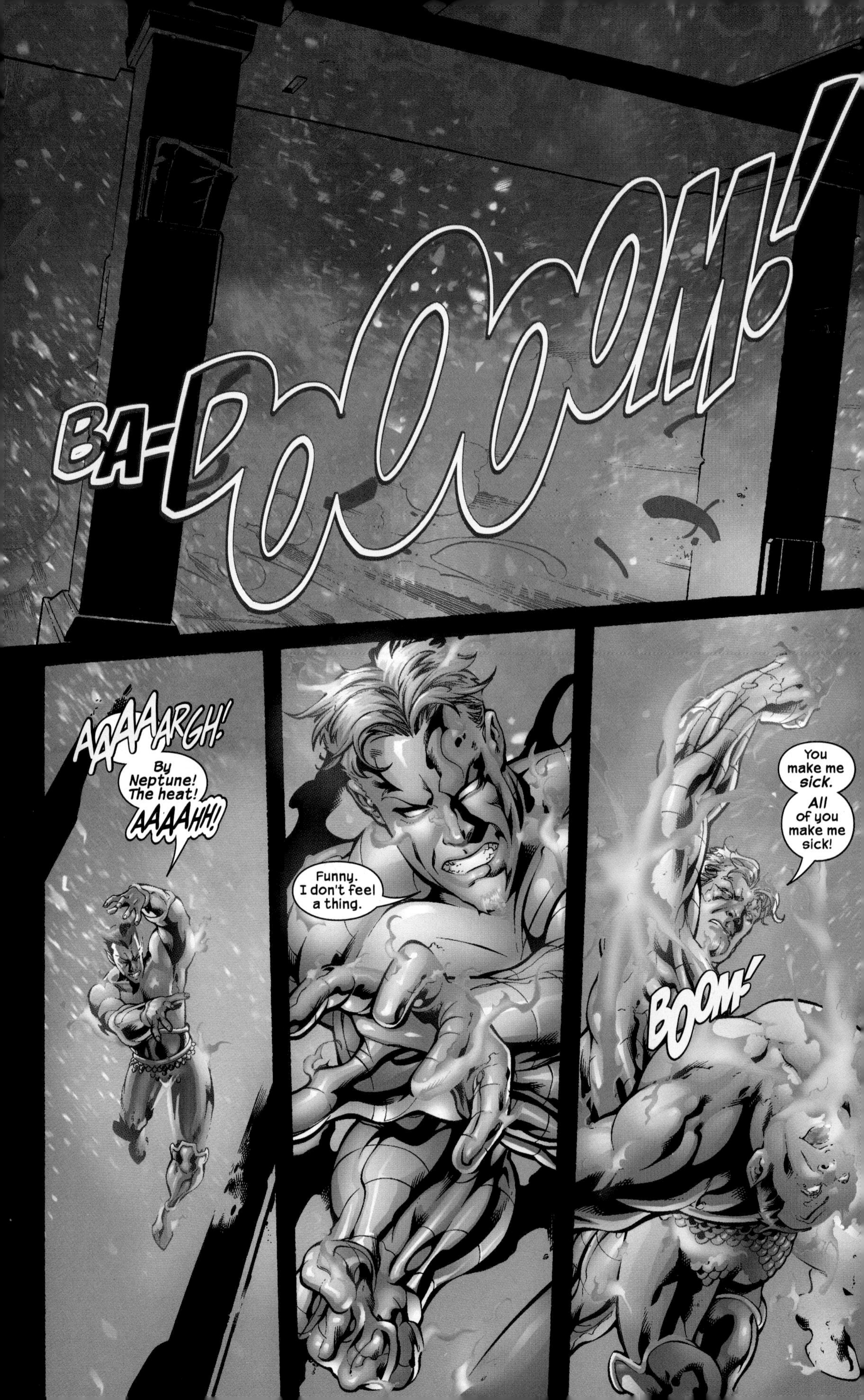
BA-DOOOOM!
AAAAARGH!
By Neptune! The heat! AAAAHH!
Funny. I don't feel a thing.
You make me sick. All of you make me sick!
BOOM!

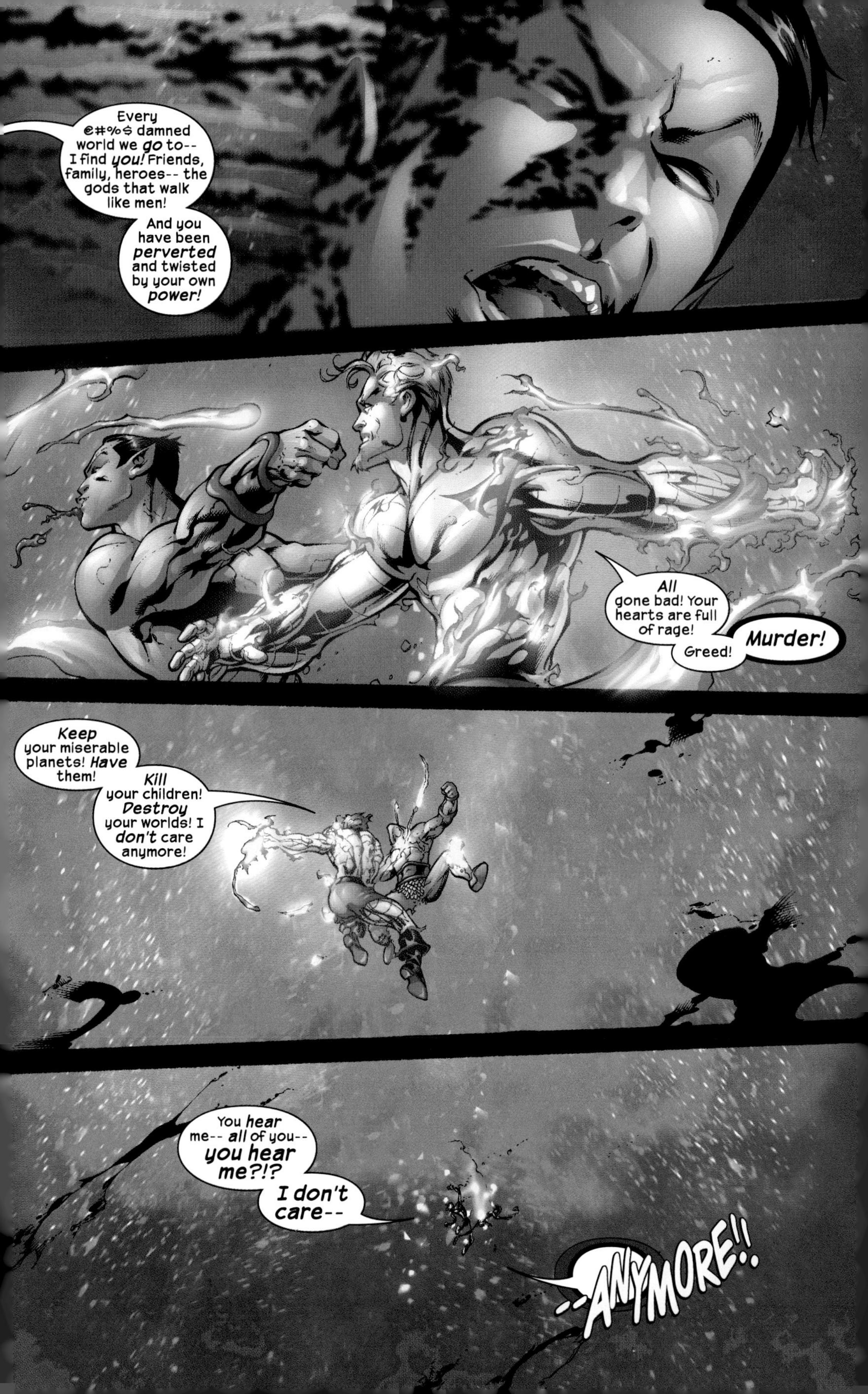

Every @#%$ damned world we *go* to-- I find *you!* Friends, family, heroes-- the gods that walk like men!
And you have been *perverted* and twisted by your own *power!*
All gone bad! Your hearts are full of rage!
Greed!
Murder!
Keep your miserable planets! *Have* them!
Kill your children! *Destroy* your worlds! I *don't* care anymore!
You *hear* me-- *all* of you-- you hear me?!?
I don't care--
--ANYMORE!!

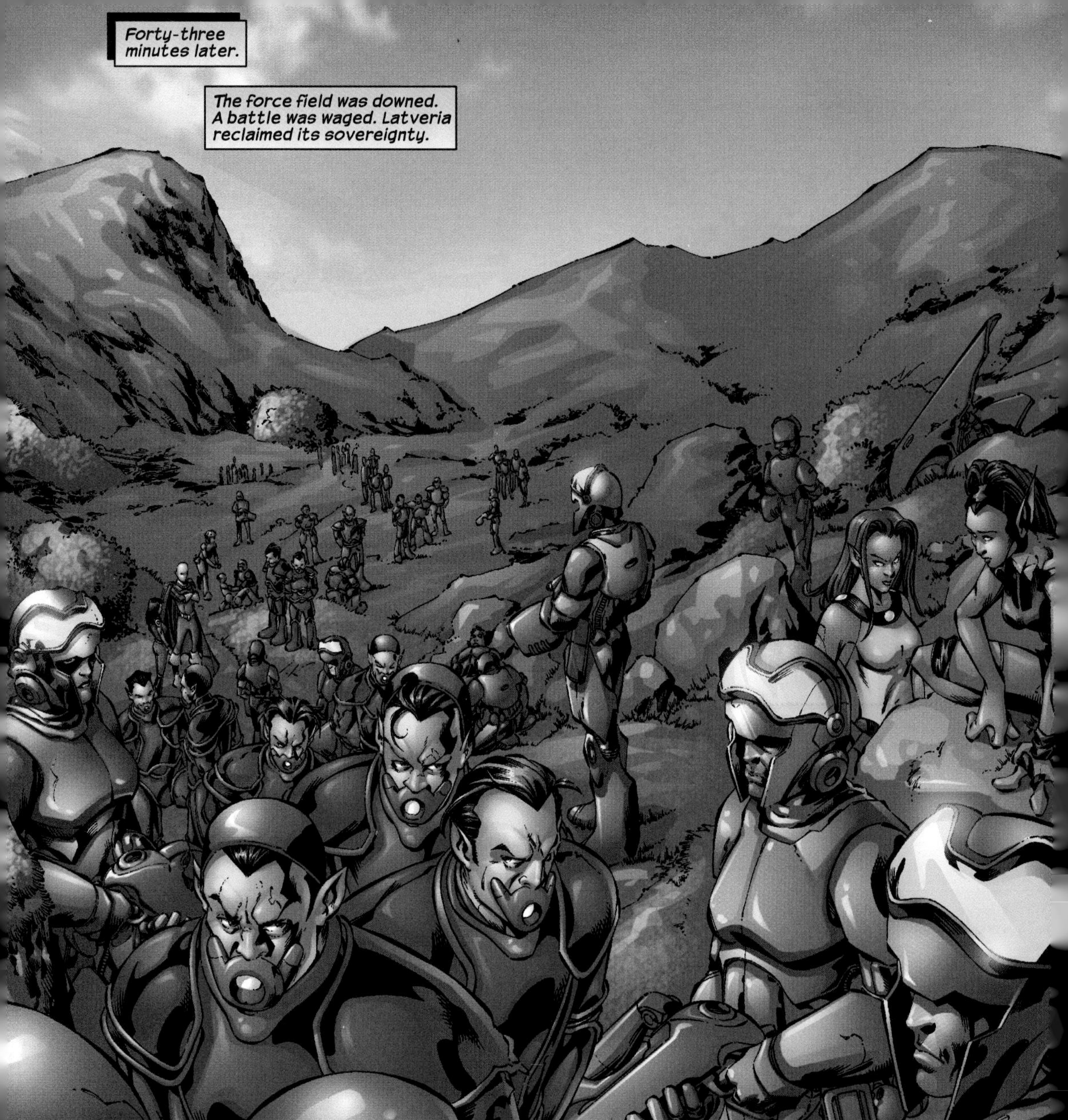
Forty-three minutes later.
The force field was downed. A battle was waged. Latveria reclaimed its sovereignty.

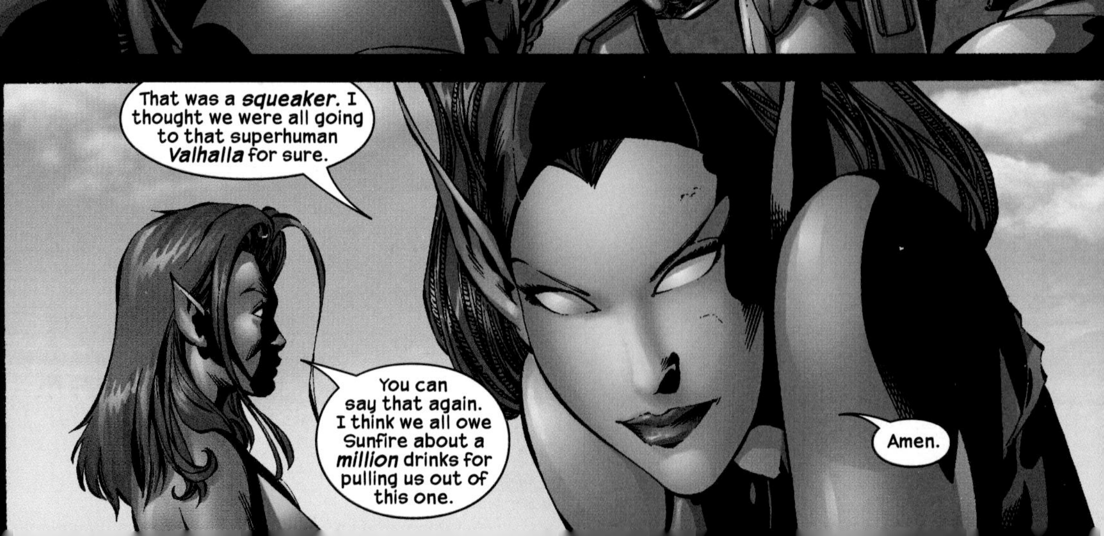
That was a *squeaker*. I thought we were all going to that superhuman *Valhalla* for sure.
You can say that again. I think we all owe Sunfire about a *million* drinks for pulling us out of this one.
Amen.

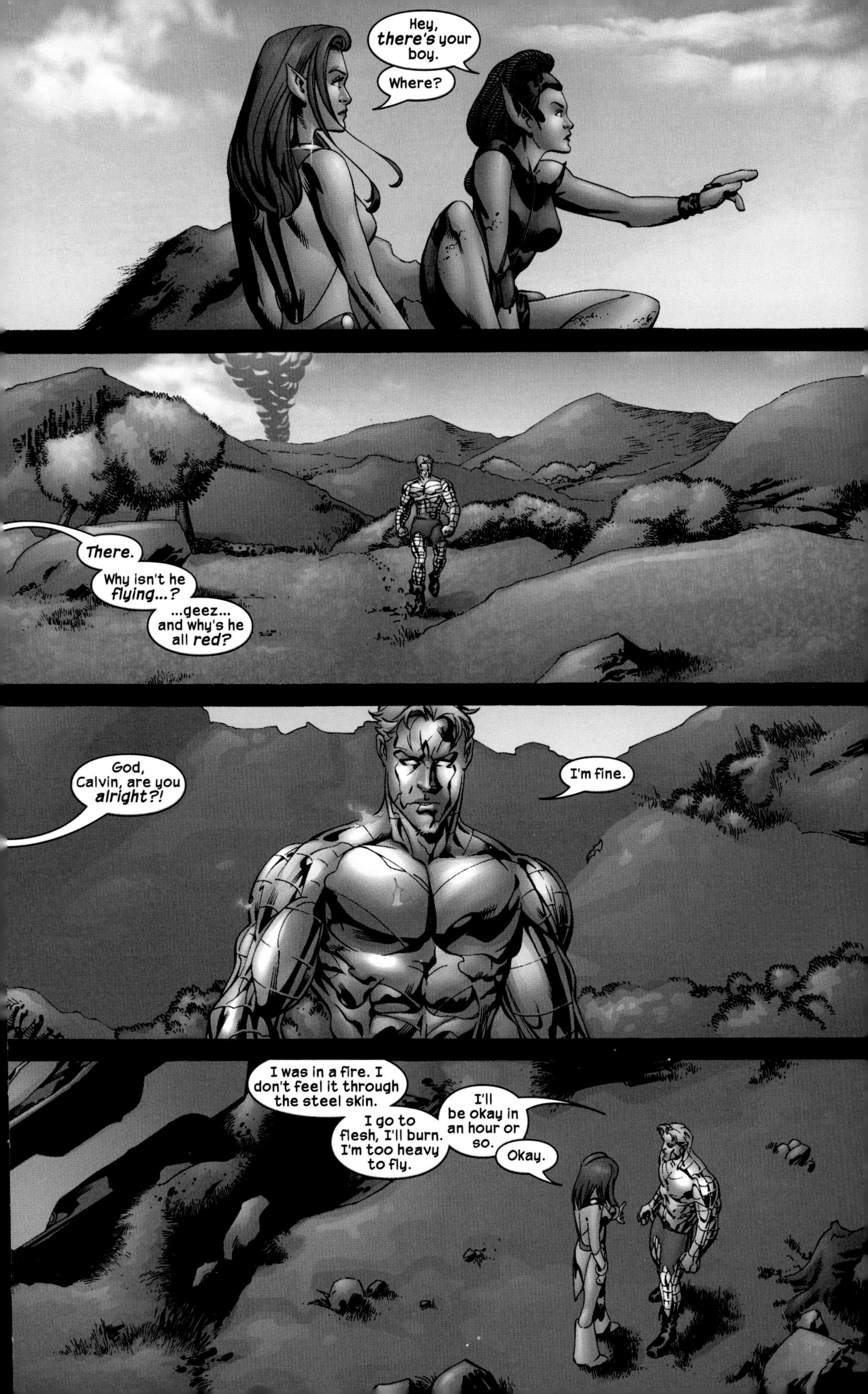

Hey, there's your boy.
Where?
There.
Why isn't he flying...?
...geez... and why's he all red?
God, Calvin, are you alright?!
I'm fine.
I was in a fire. I don't feel it through the steel skin.
I go to flesh, I'll burn. I'm too heavy to fly.
I'll be okay in an hour or so.
Okay.

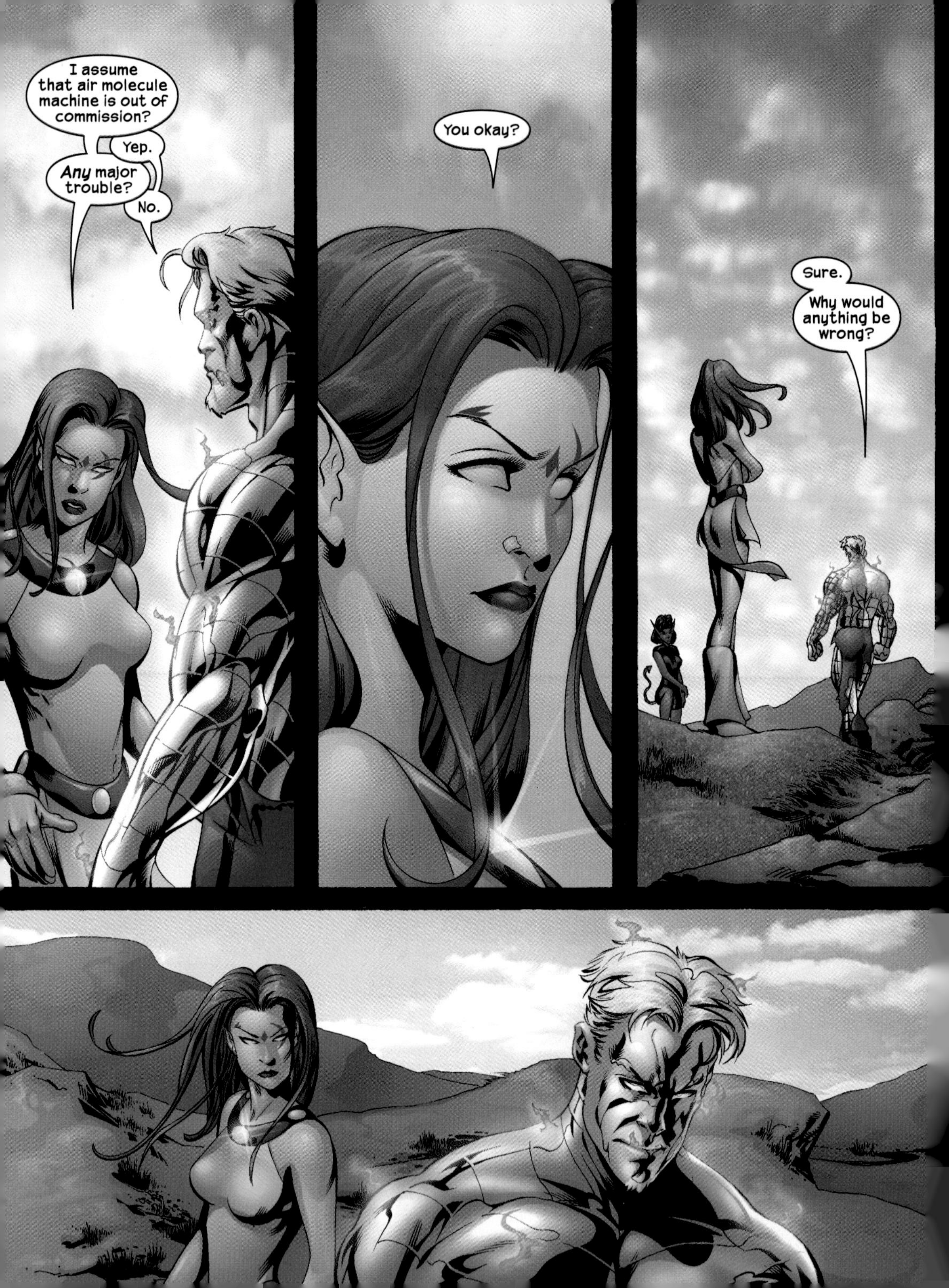
I assume that air molecule machine is out of commission?
Yep.
Any major trouble?
No.
You okay?
Sure.
Why would anything be wrong?

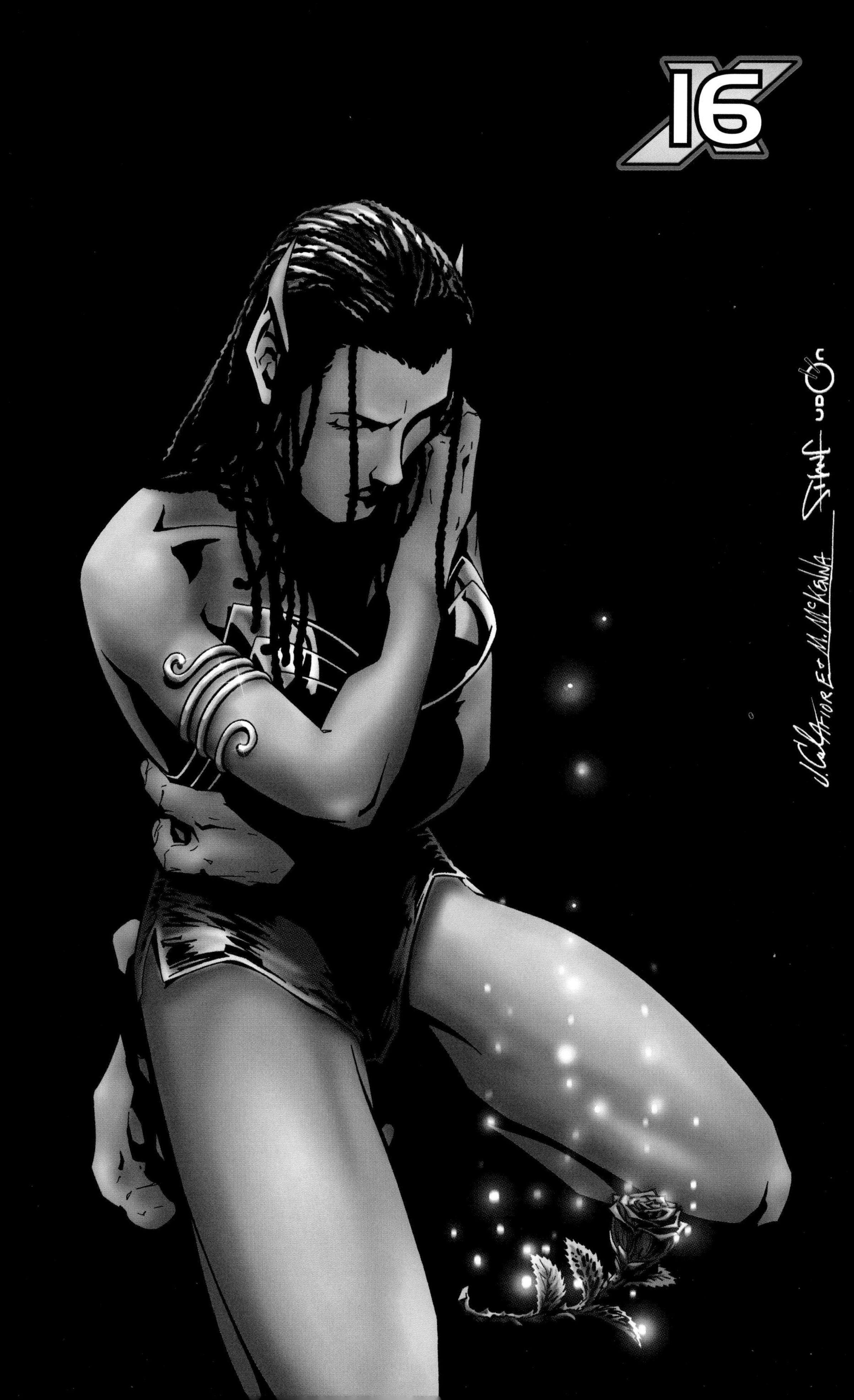
16

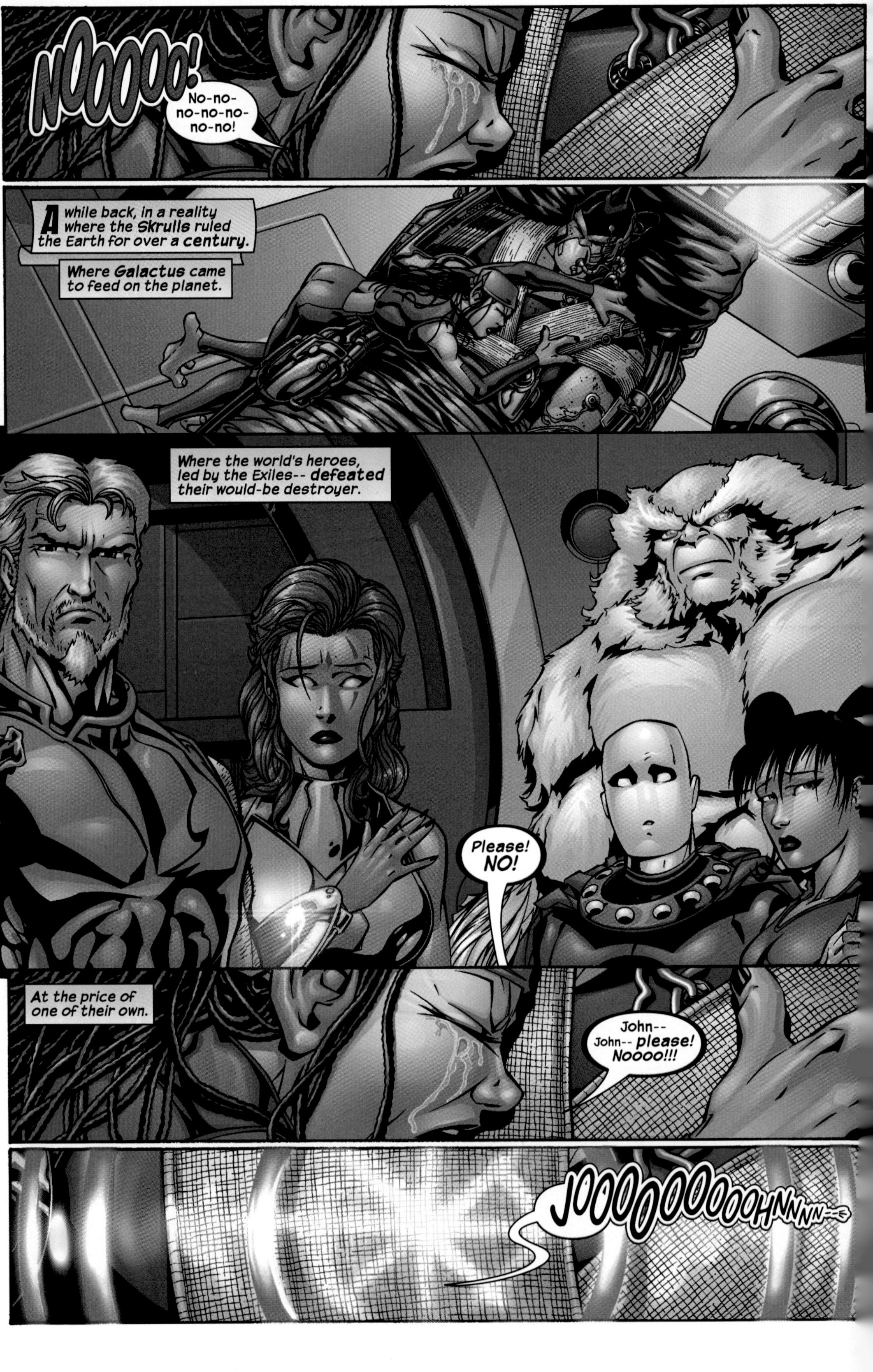
NOOOOO!
No-no-no-no-no-no-no-no!
A while back, in a reality where the Skrulls ruled the Earth for over a century.
Where Galactus came to feed on the planet.
Where the world's heroes, led by the Exiles-- defeated their would-be destroyer.
Please! NO!
At the price of one of their own.
John-- John-- please! Noooo!!!
JOOOOOOOOOHNNNN--

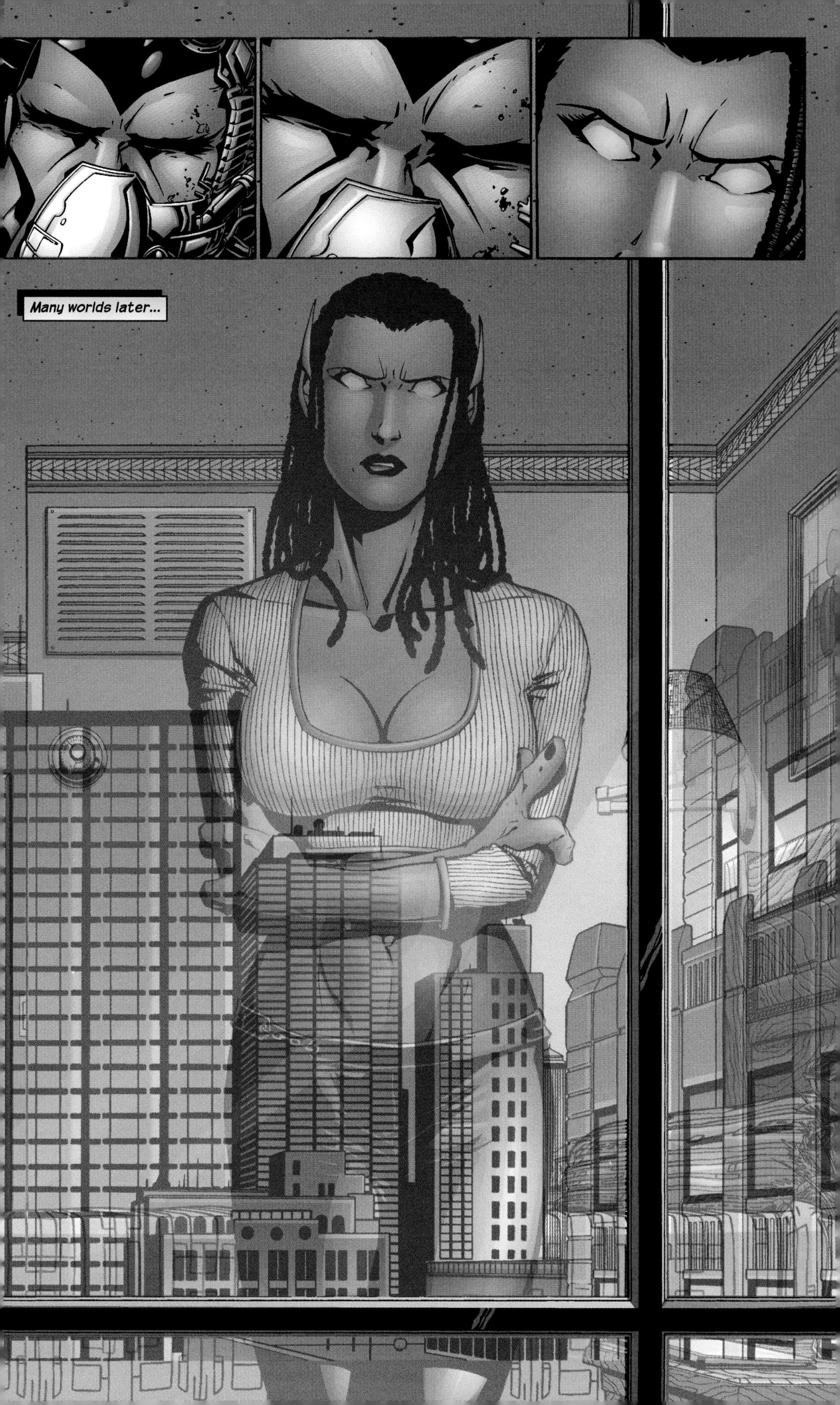
Many worlds later...

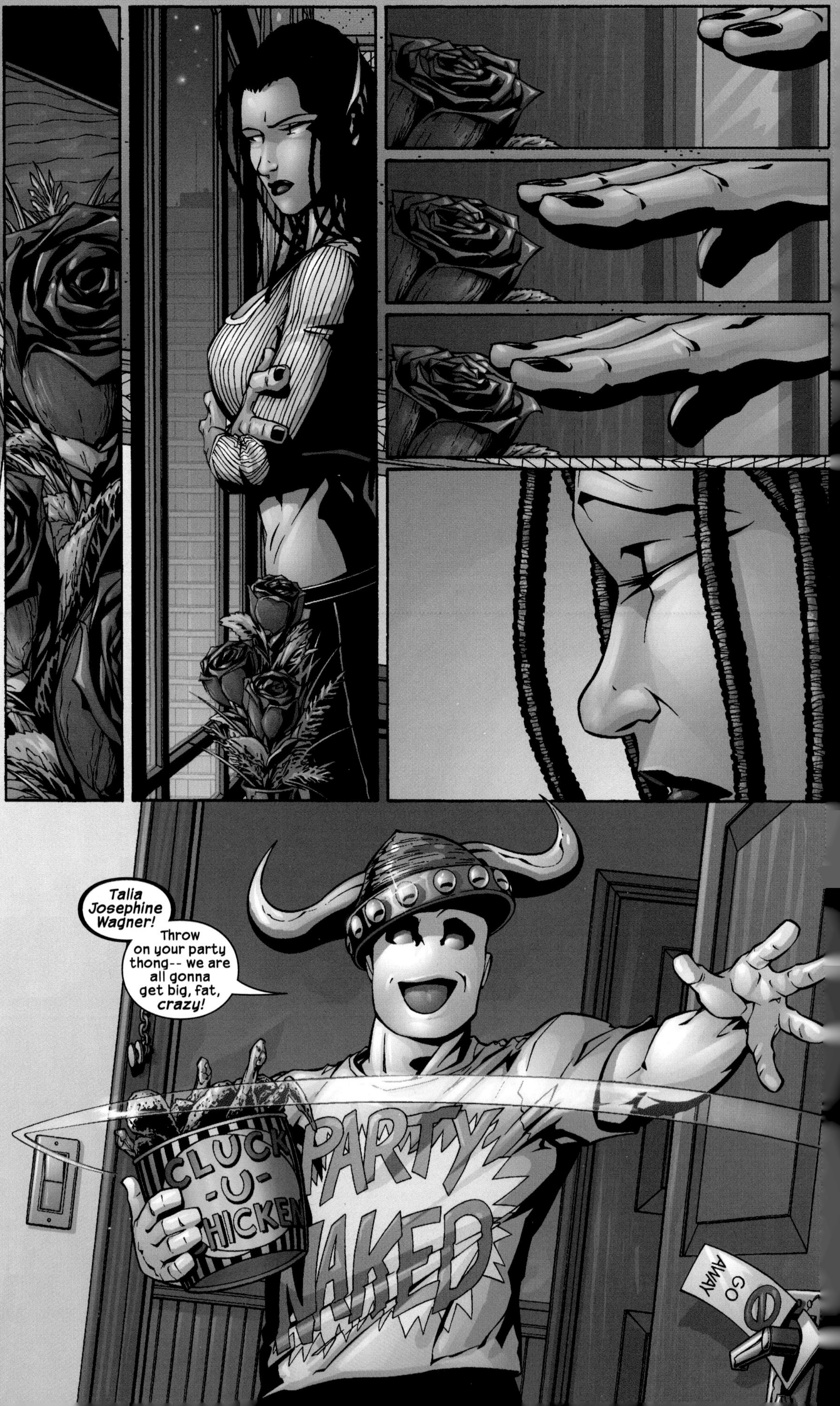

Talia Josephine Wagner!
Throw on your party thong-- we are all gonna get big, fat, crazy!
CLUCK -U- CHICKEN
PARTY NAKED
GO AWAY

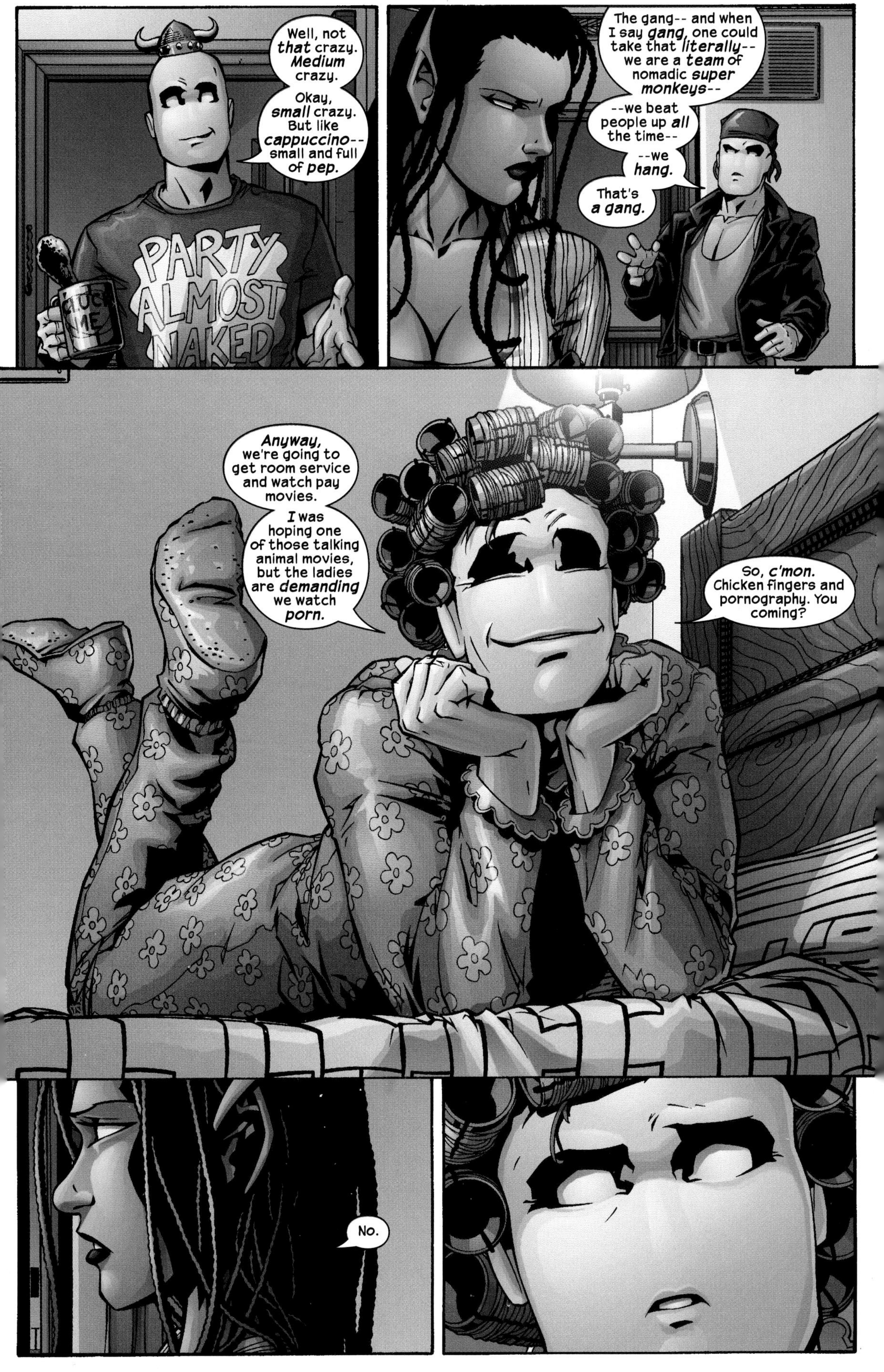
Well, not that crazy. Medium crazy.
Okay, small crazy. But like cappuccino-- small and full of pep.
PARTY ALMOST NAKED
CLUCK ME
The gang-- and when I say gang, one could take that literally-- we are a team of nomadic super monkeys--
--we beat people up all the time--
--we hang.
That's a gang.
Anyway, we're going to get room service and watch pay movies.
I was hoping one of those talking animal movies, but the ladies are demanding we watch porn.
So, c'mon. Chicken fingers and pornography. You coming?
No.

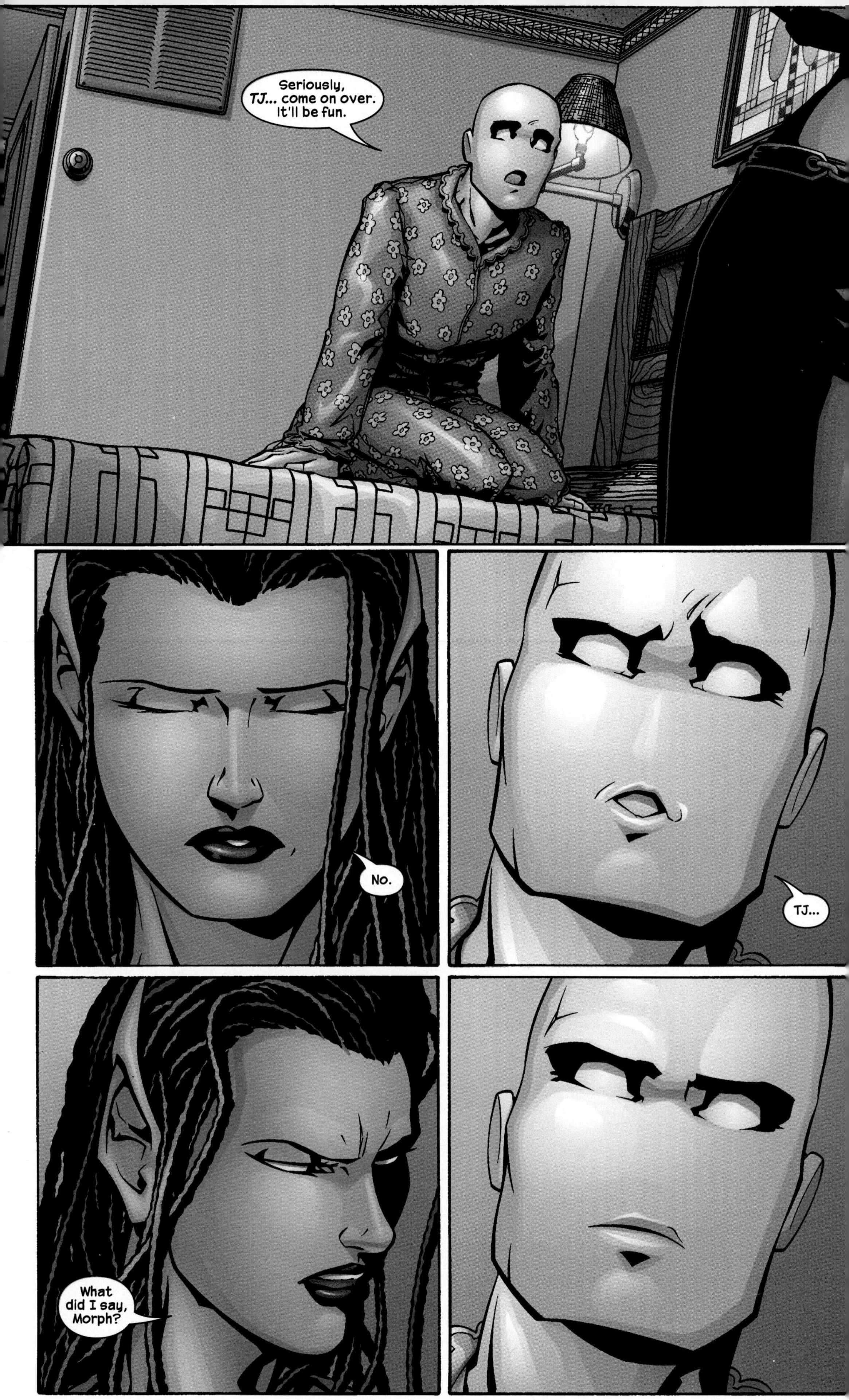
Seriously, TJ... come on over. It'll be fun.
No.
TJ...
What did I say, Morph?

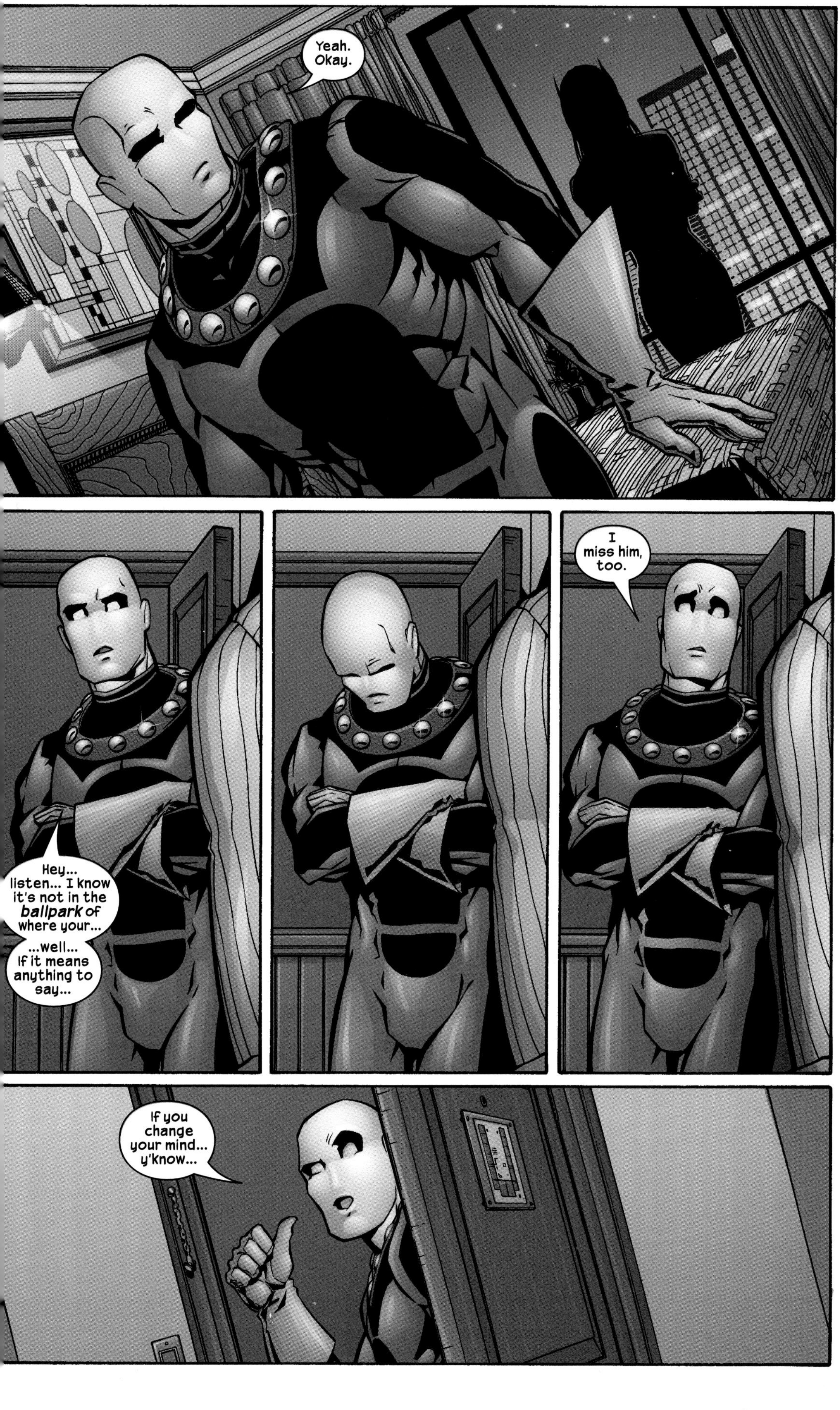
Yeah. Okay.
Hey... listen... I know it's not in the *ballpark* of where your...
...well... If it means anything to say...
I miss him, too.
If you change your mind... y'know...

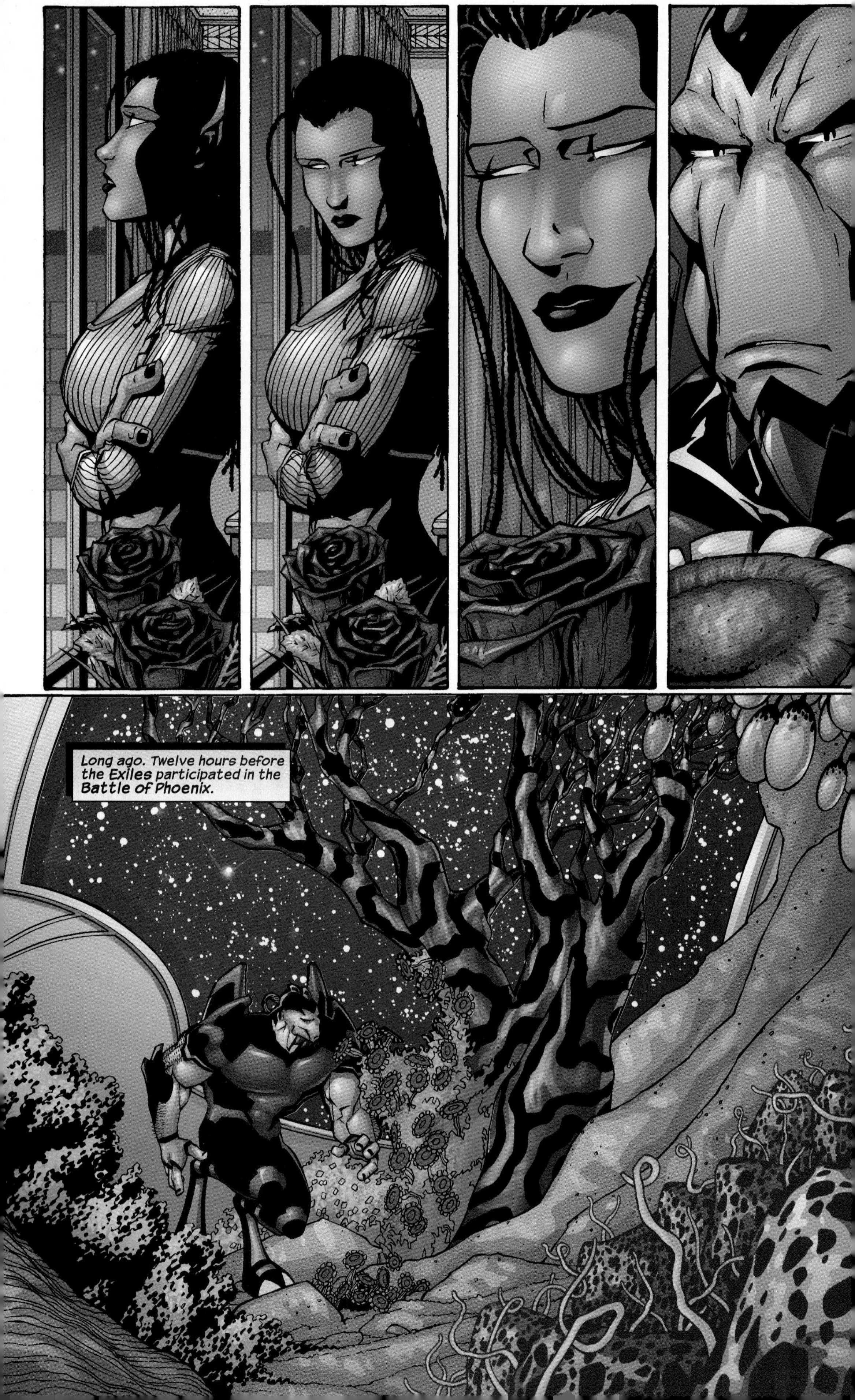
Long ago. Twelve hours before the Exiles participated in the Battle of Phoenix.

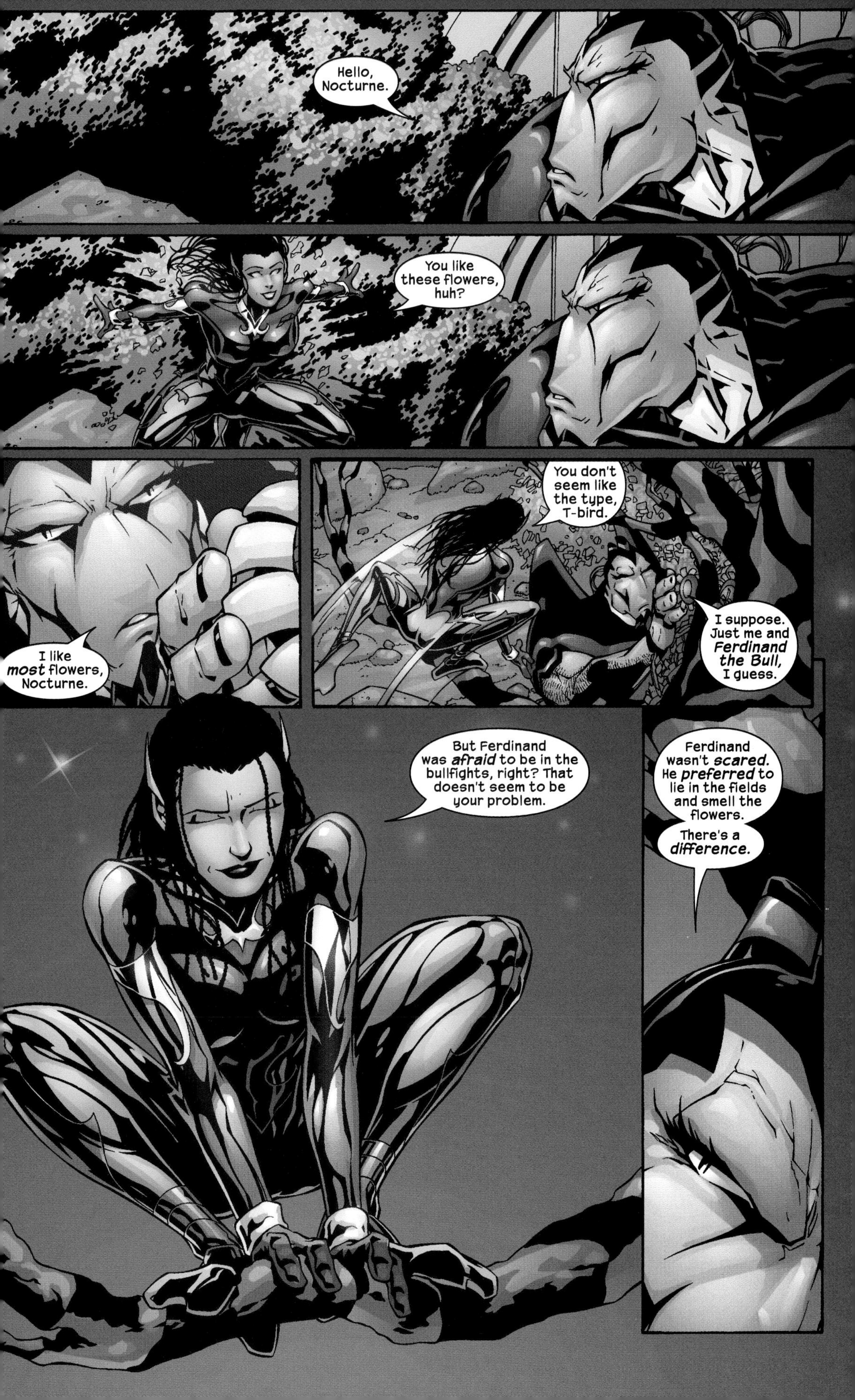
Hello, Nocturne.
You like these flowers, huh?
I like *most* flowers, Nocturne.
You don't seem like the type, T-bird.
I suppose. Just me and *Ferdinand the Bull,* I guess.
But Ferdinand was *afraid* to be in the bullfights, right? That doesn't seem to be your problem.
Ferdinand wasn't *scared.* He *preferred* to lie in the fields and smell the flowers.
There's a *difference.*

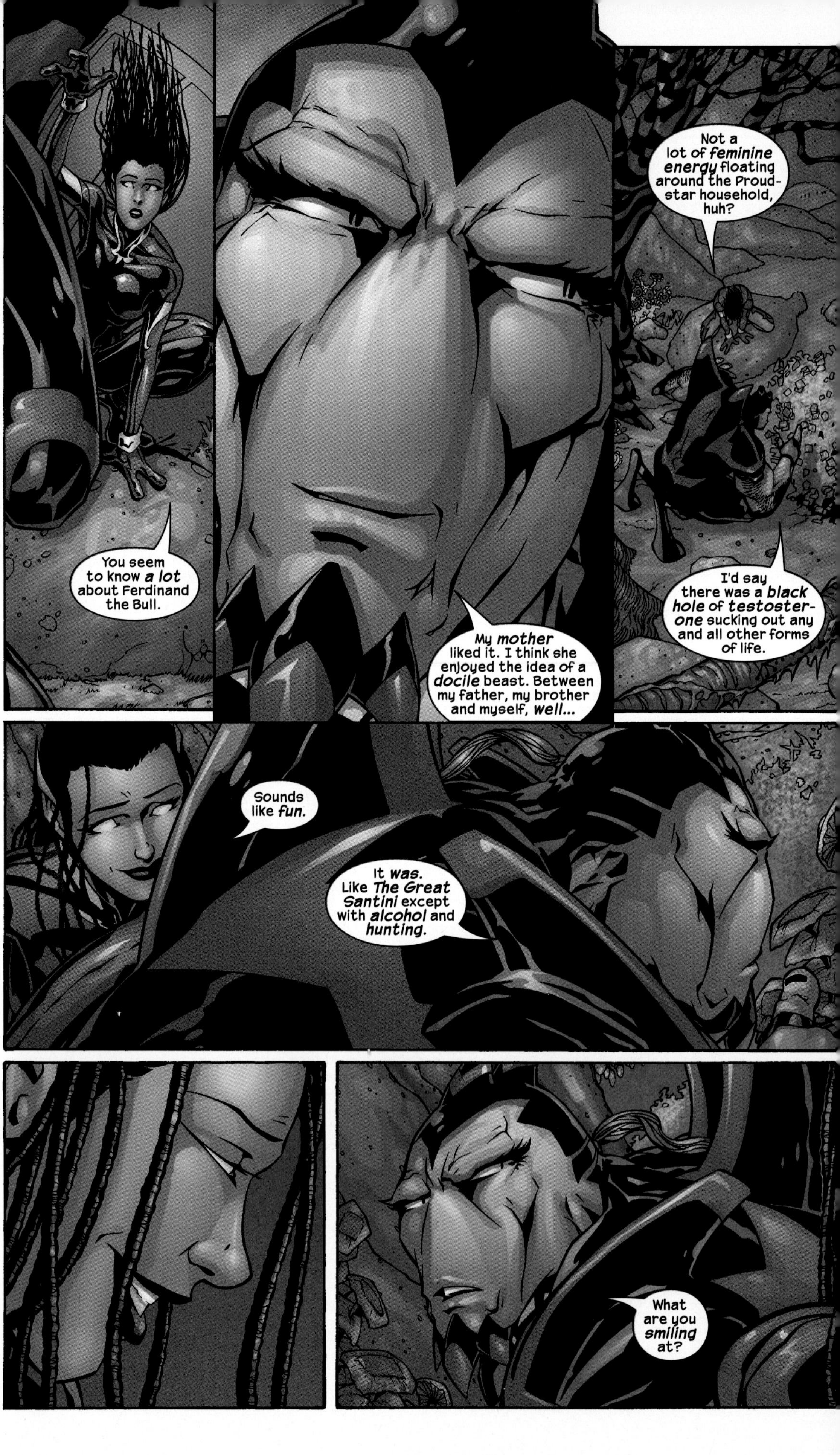
You seem to know *a lot* about Ferdinand the Bull.
My *mother* liked it. I think she enjoyed the idea of a *docile* beast. Between my father, my brother and myself, *well...*
Not a lot of *feminine energy* floating around the Proud-star household, huh?
I'd say there was a *black hole* of *testoster-one* sucking out any and all other forms of life.
Sounds like *fun.*
It *was.* Like *The Great Santini* except with *alcohol* and *hunting.*
What are you *smiling* at?

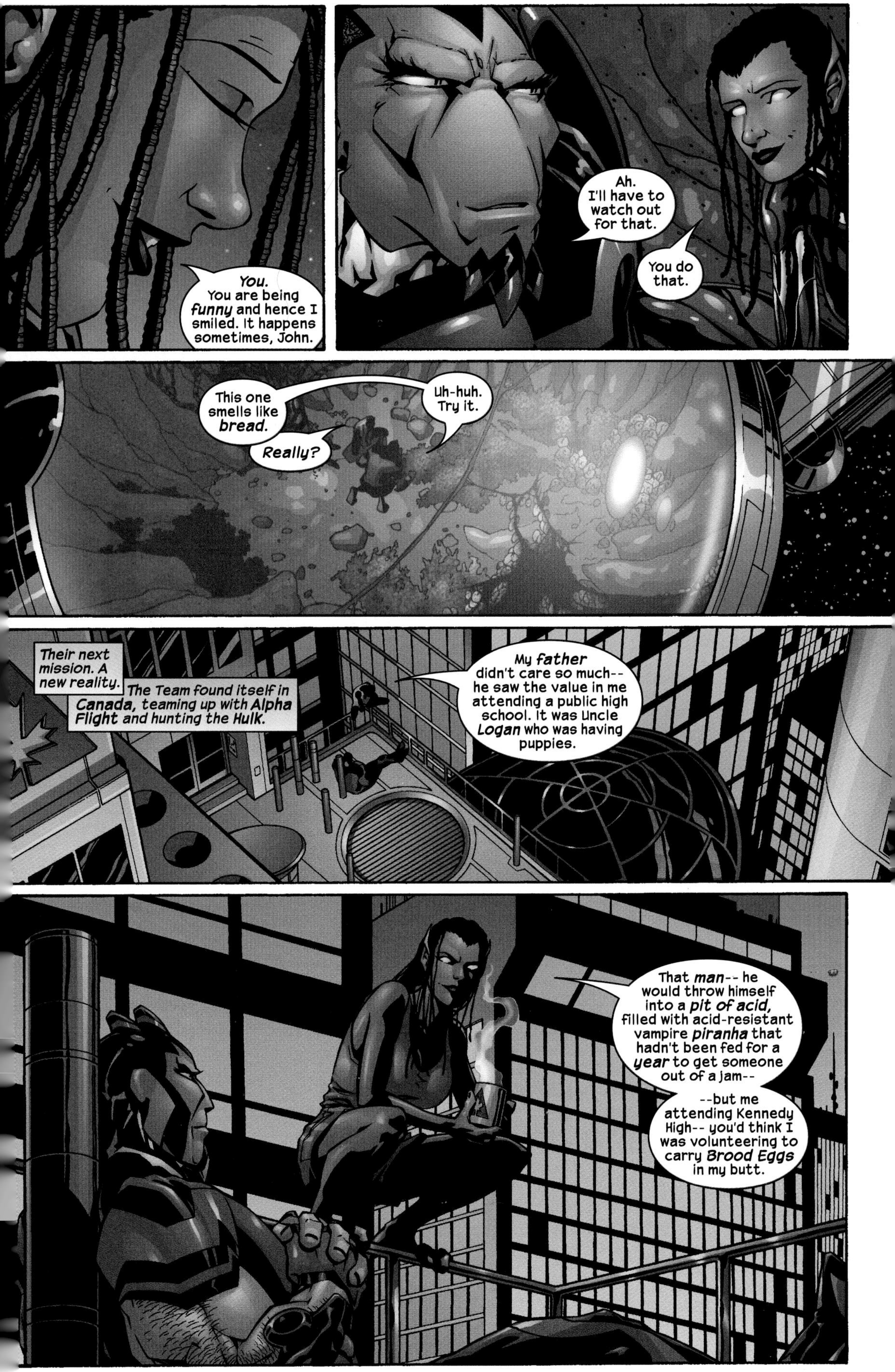
You.
You are being funny and hence I smiled. It happens sometimes, John.
Ah.
I'll have to watch out for that.
You do that.
This one smells like bread.
Uh-huh. Try it.
Really?
Their next mission. A new reality.
The Team found itself in Canada, teaming up with Alpha Flight and hunting the Hulk.
My father didn't care so much-- he saw the value in me attending a public high school. It was Uncle Logan who was having puppies.
That man-- he would throw himself into a pit of acid, filled with acid-resistant vampire piranha that hadn't been fed for a year to get someone out of a jam--
--but me attending Kennedy High-- you'd think I was volunteering to carry Brood Eggs in my butt.

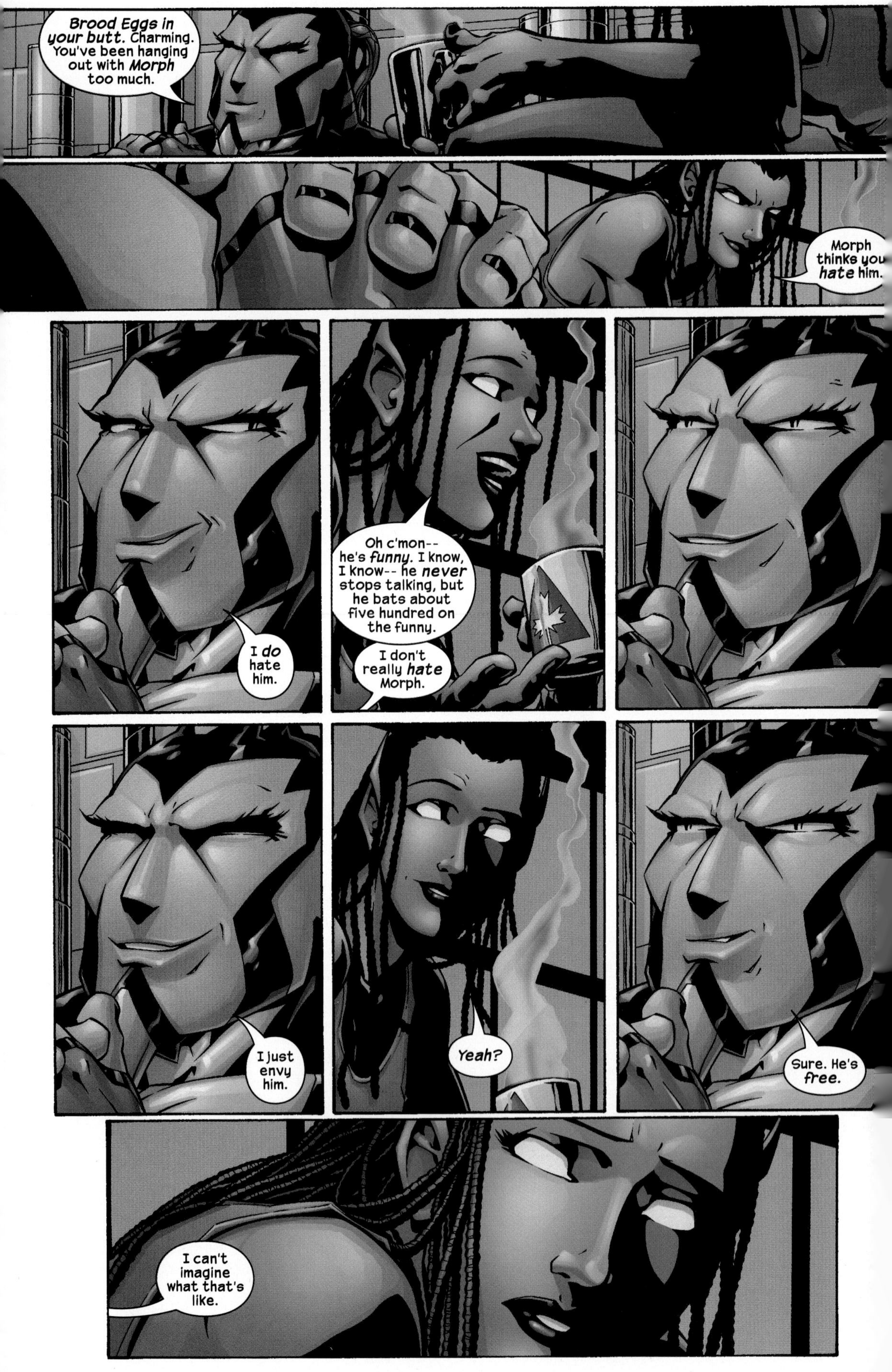
Brood Eggs in your butt. Charming. You've been hanging out with Morph too much.
Morph thinks you hate him.
I do hate him.
Oh c'mon-- he's funny. I know, I know-- he never stops talking, but he bats about five hundred on the funny.
I don't really hate Morph.
I just envy him.
Yeah?
Sure. He's free.
I can't imagine what that's like.

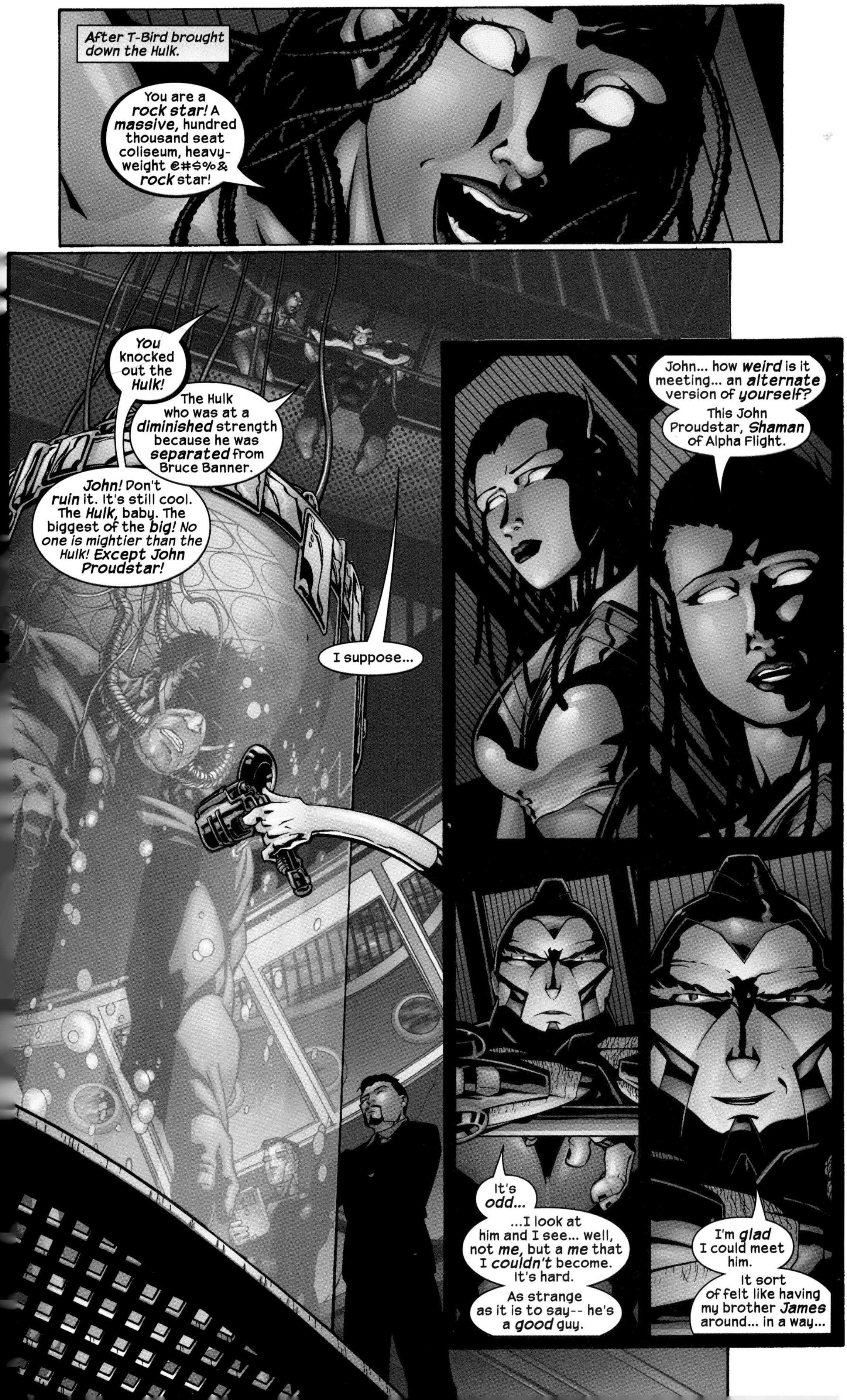

After T-Bird brought down the Hulk.
You are a rock star! A massive, hundred thousand seat coliseum, heavy-weight @#$%& rock star!
You knocked out the Hulk!
The Hulk who was at a diminished strength because he was separated from Bruce Banner.
John! Don't ruin it. It's still cool. The Hulk, baby. The biggest of the big! No one is mightier than the Hulk! Except John Proudstar!
I suppose...
John... how weird is it meeting... an alternate version of yourself?
This John Proudstar, Shaman of Alpha Flight.
It's odd...
...I look at him and I see... well, not me, but a me that I couldn't become. It's hard.
As strange as it is to say-- he's a good guy.
I'm glad I could meet him.
It sort of felt like having my brother James around... in a way...

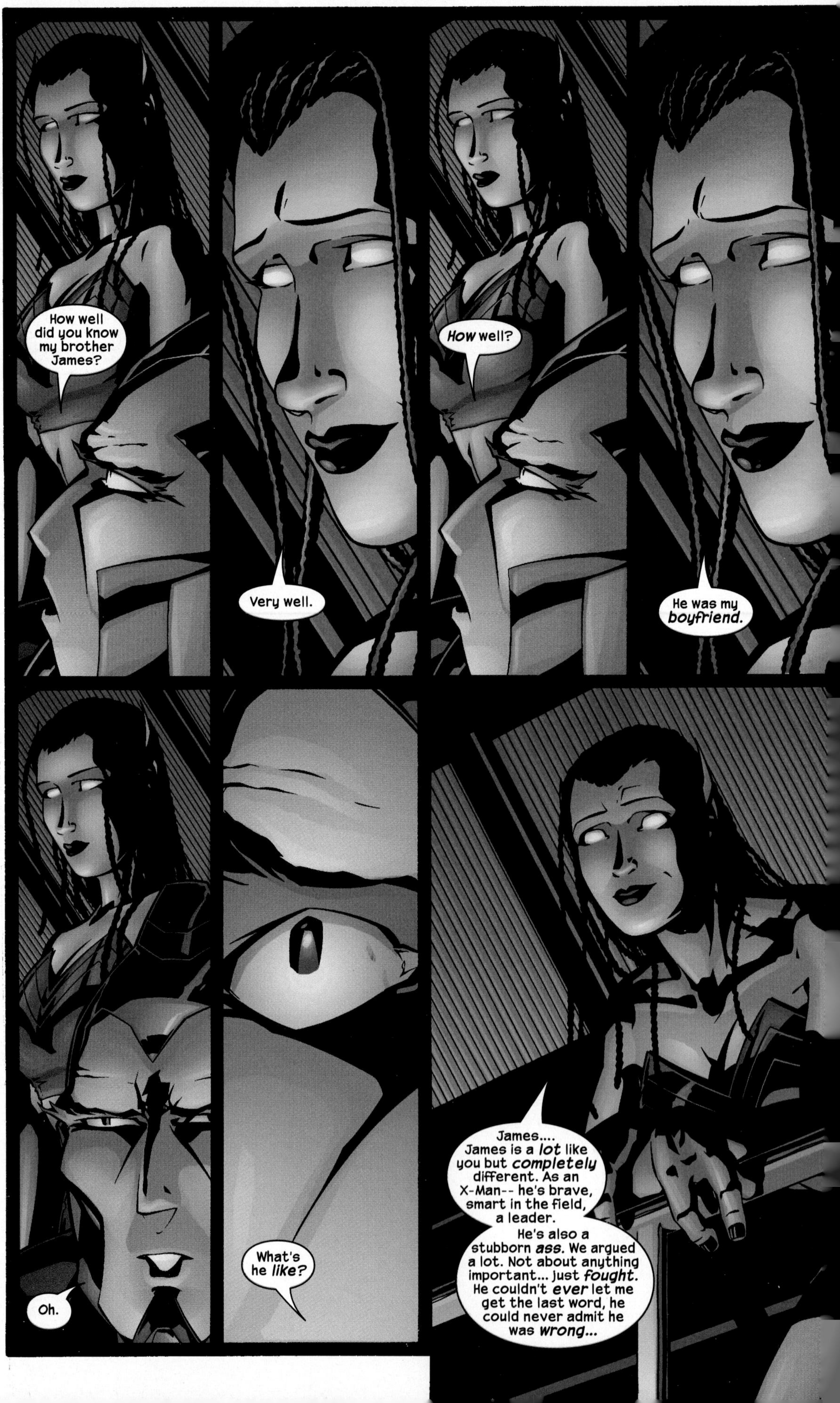
How well did you know my brother James?
Very well.
How well?
He was my *boyfriend*.
Oh.
What's he *like*?
James.... James is a *lot* like you but *completely* different. As an X-Man-- he's brave, smart in the field, a leader.
He's also a stubborn *ass*. We argued a lot. Not about anything important... just *fought*. He couldn't *ever* let me get the last word, he could never admit he was *wrong*...

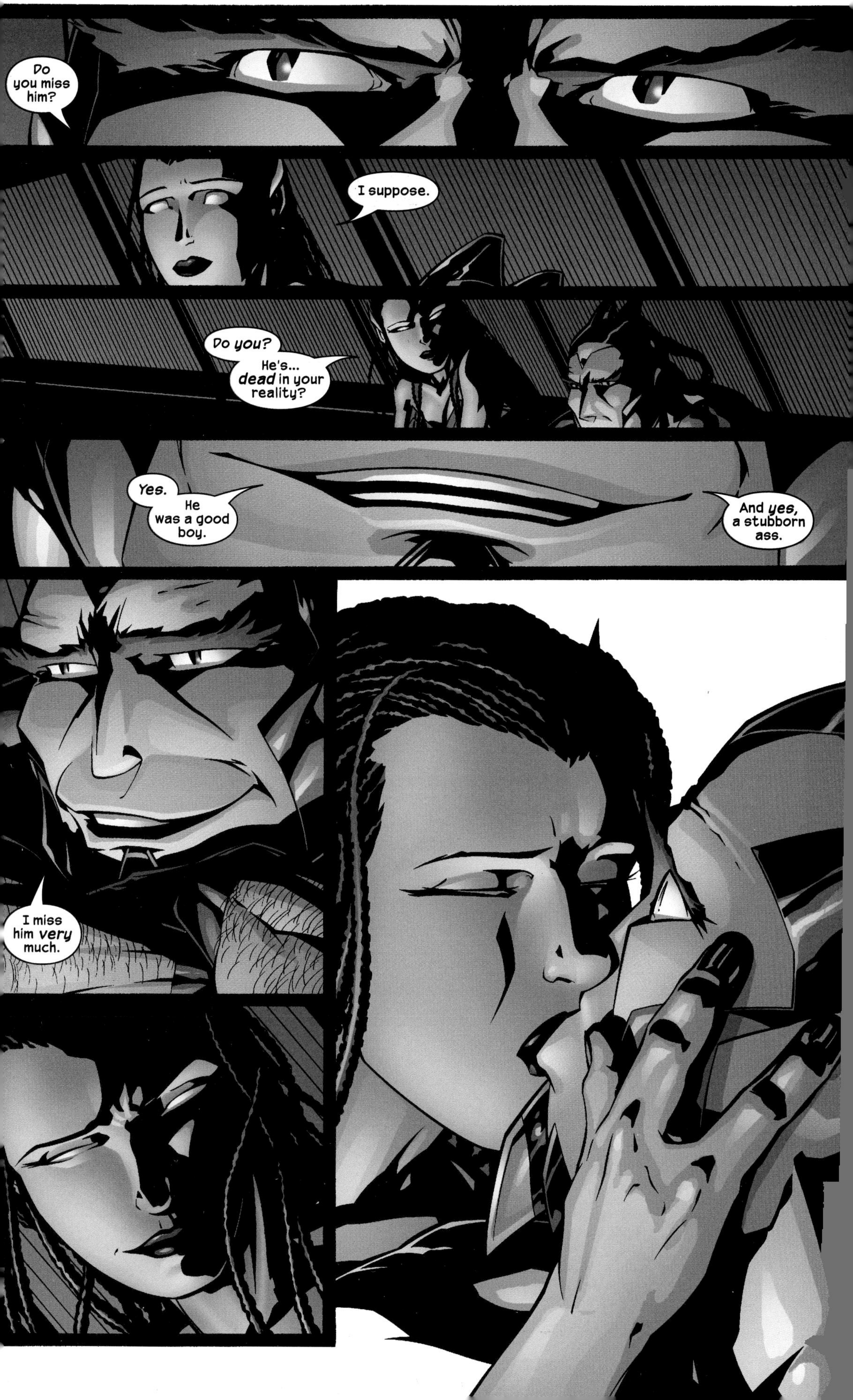
Do you miss him?
I suppose.
Do you?
He's... dead in your reality?
Yes. He was a good boy.
And yes, a stubborn ass.
I miss him very much.

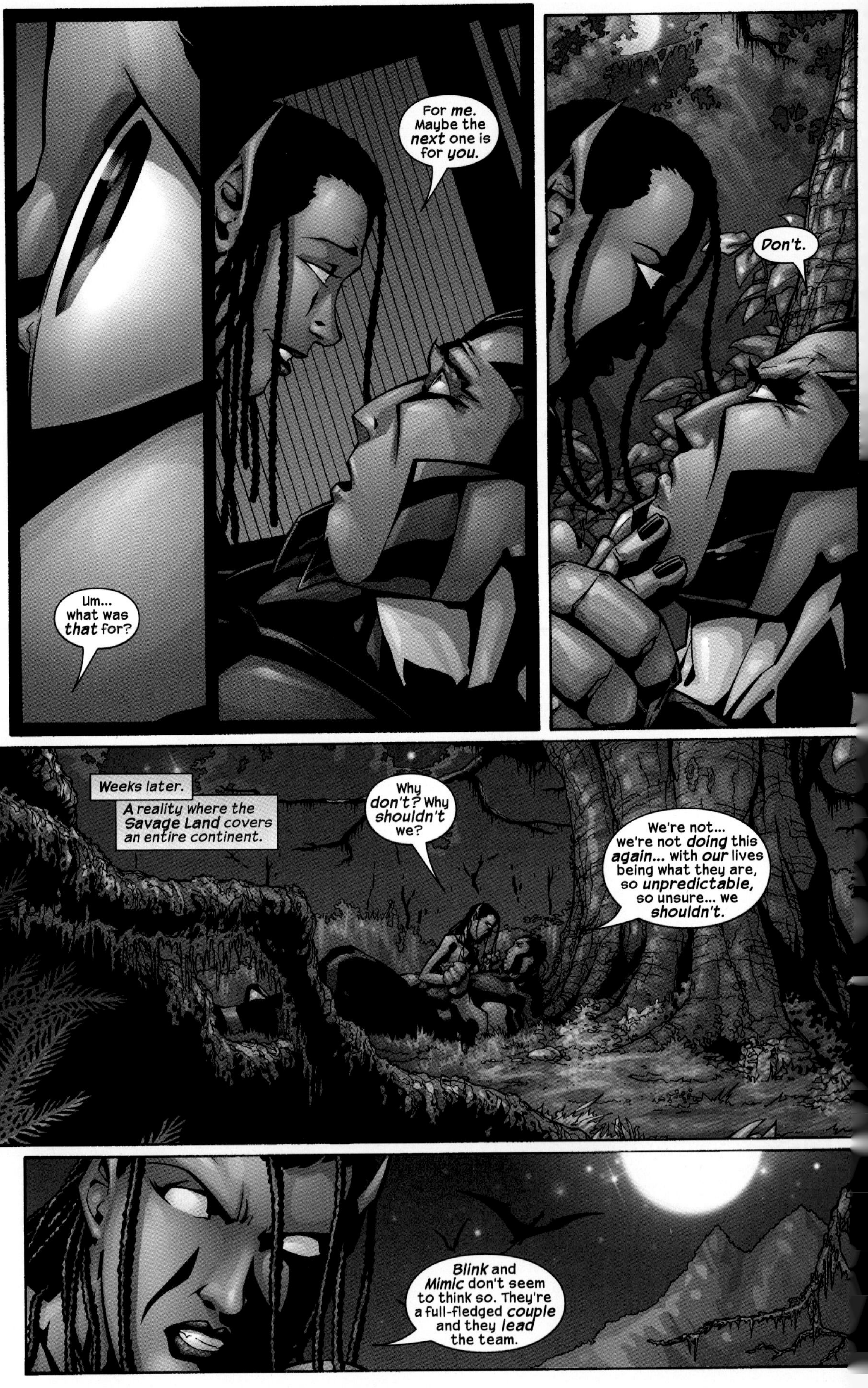

Um... what was that for?
For me. Maybe the next one is for you.
Don't.
Weeks later.
A reality where the Savage Land covers an entire continent.
Why don't? Why shouldn't we?
We're not... we're not doing this again... with our lives being what they are, so unpredictable, so unsure... we shouldn't.
Blink and Mimic don't seem to think so. They're a full-fledged couple and they lead the team.

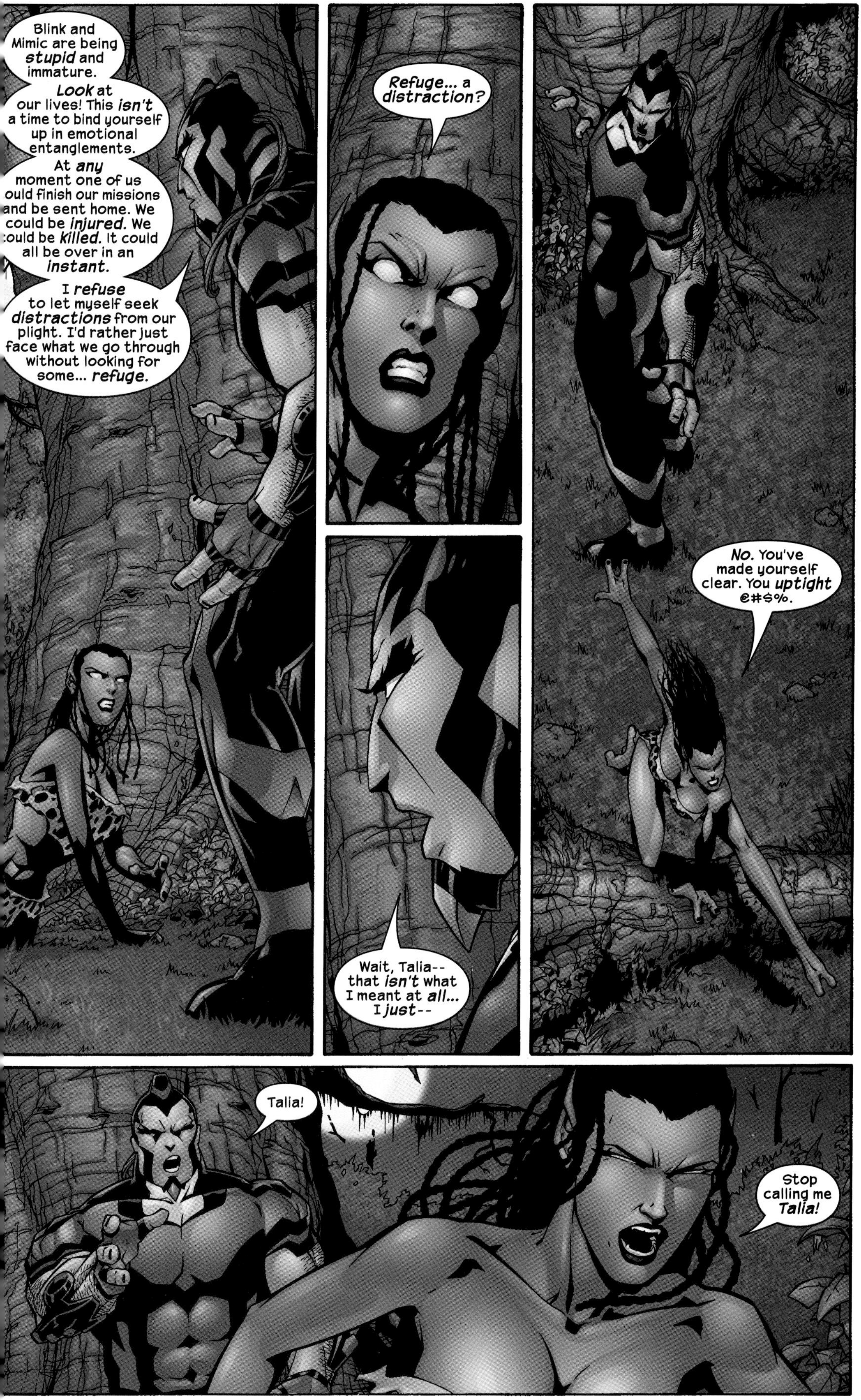
Blink and Mimic are being stupid and immature.
Look at our lives! This isn't a time to bind yourself up in emotional entanglements.
At any moment one of us ould finish our missions and be sent home. We could be injured. We ould be killed. It could all be over in an instant.
I refuse to let myself seek distractions from our plight. I'd rather just face what we go through without looking for some... refuge.
Refuge... a distraction?
Wait, Talia-- that isn't what I meant at all... I just--
No. You've made yourself clear. You uptight @#$%.
Talia!
Stop calling me Talia!

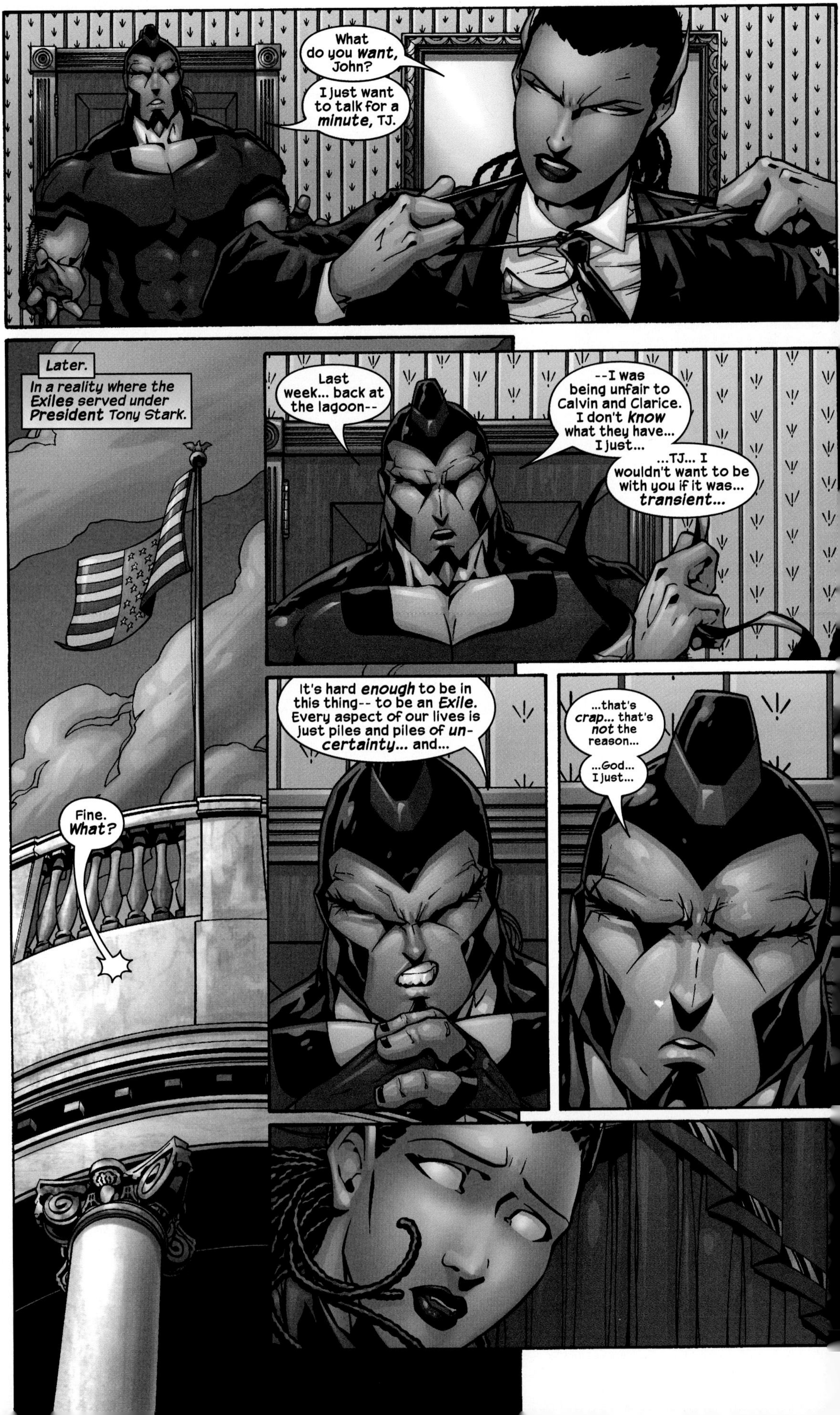
What do you want, John?
I just want to talk for a minute, TJ.
Later.
In a reality where the Exiles served under President Tony Stark.
Fine. What?
Last week... back at the lagoon--
--I was being unfair to Calvin and Clarice. I don't know what they have... I just...
...TJ... I wouldn't want to be with you if it was... transient...
It's hard enough to be in this thing-- to be an Exile. Every aspect of our lives is just piles and piles of un-certainty... and...
...that's crap... that's not the reason...
...God... I just...

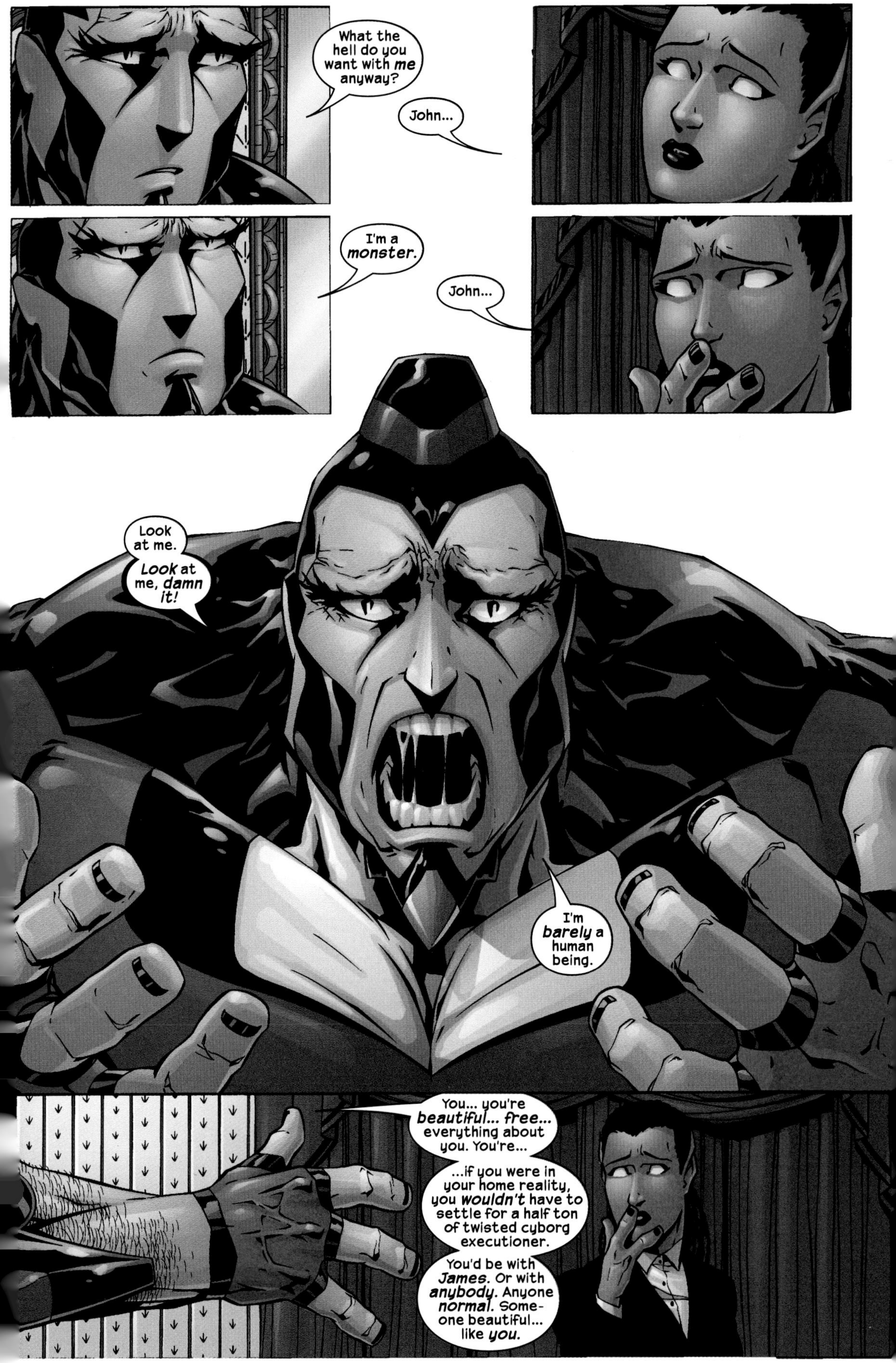
What the hell do you want with me anyway?
John...
I'm a monster.
John...
Look at me.
Look at me, damn it!
I'm barely a human being.
You... you're beautiful... free... everything about you. You're...
...if you were in your home reality, you wouldn't have to settle for a half ton of twisted cyborg executioner.
You'd be with James. Or with anybody. Anyone normal. Some-one beautiful... like you.

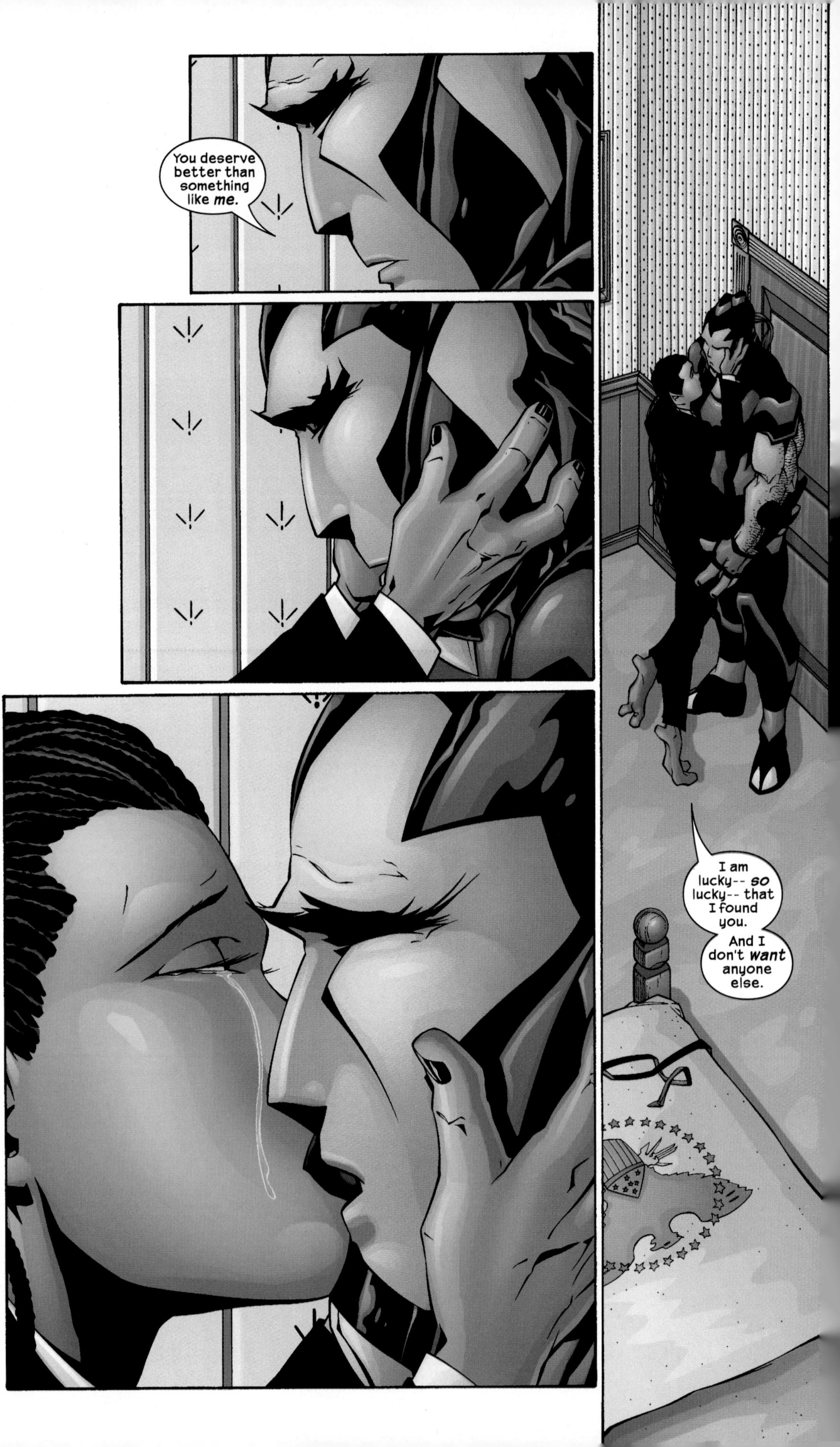
You deserve better than something like *me*.
I am lucky-- *so* lucky-- that I found you.
And I don't *want* anyone else.

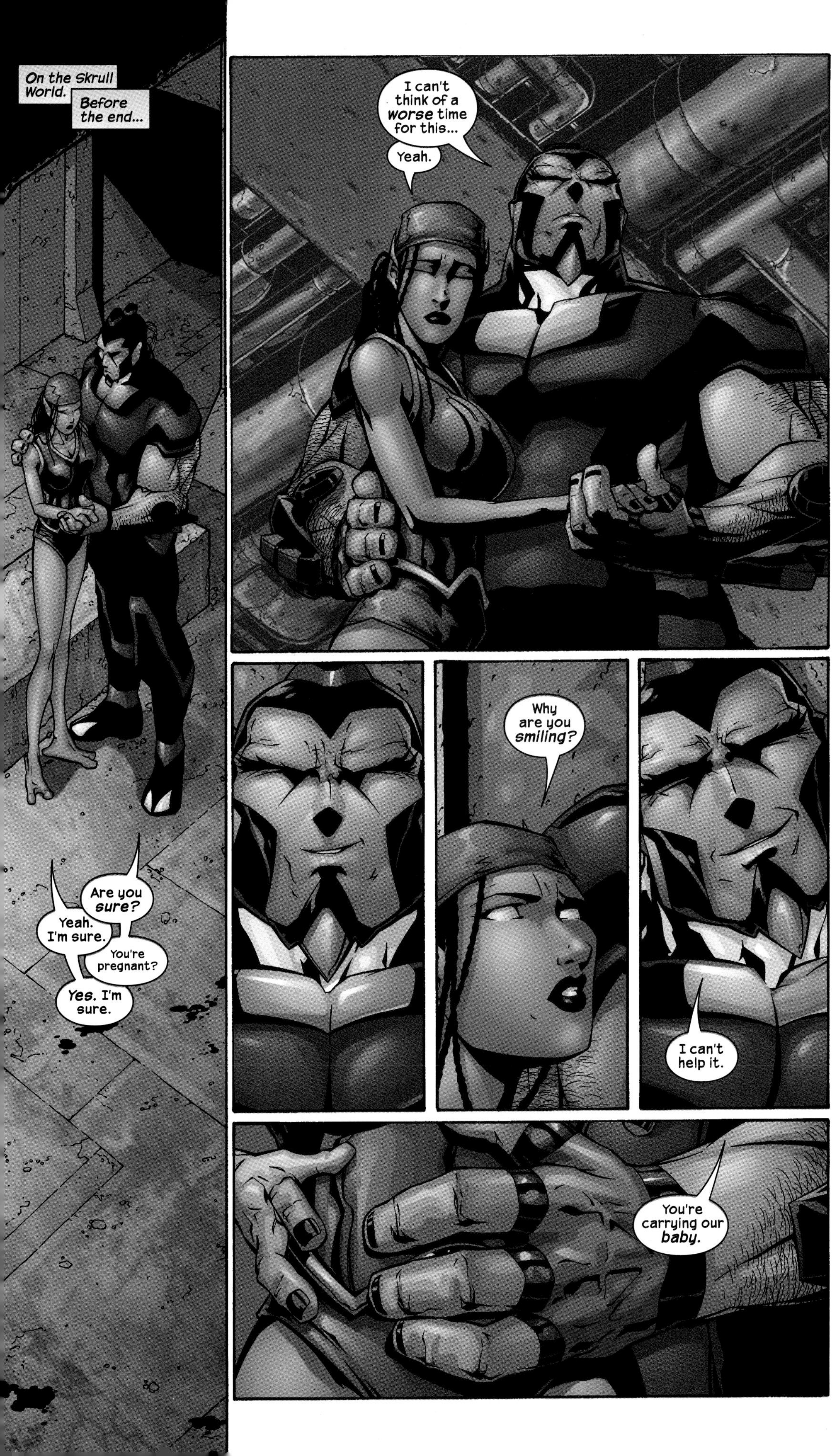
On the Skrull World.
Before the end...
Are you sure?
Yeah. I'm sure.
You're pregnant?
Yes. I'm sure.
I can't think of a worse time for this...
Yeah.
Why are you smiling?
I can't help it.
You're carrying our baby.

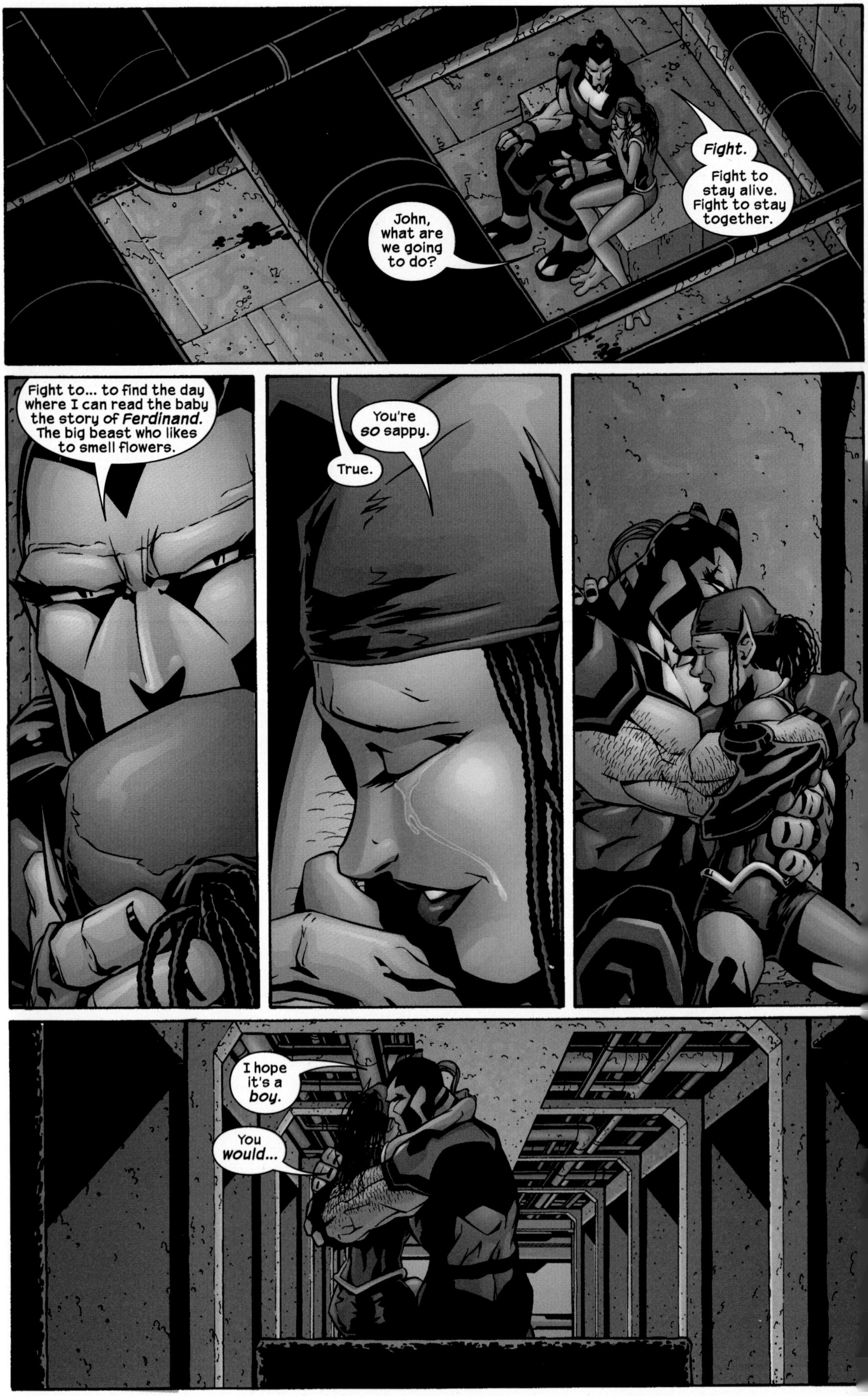
John, what are we going to do?
Fight.
Fight to stay alive. Fight to stay together.
Fight to... to find the day where I can read the baby the story of Ferdinand. The big beast who likes to smell flowers.
You're so sappy.
True.
I hope it's a boy.
You would...

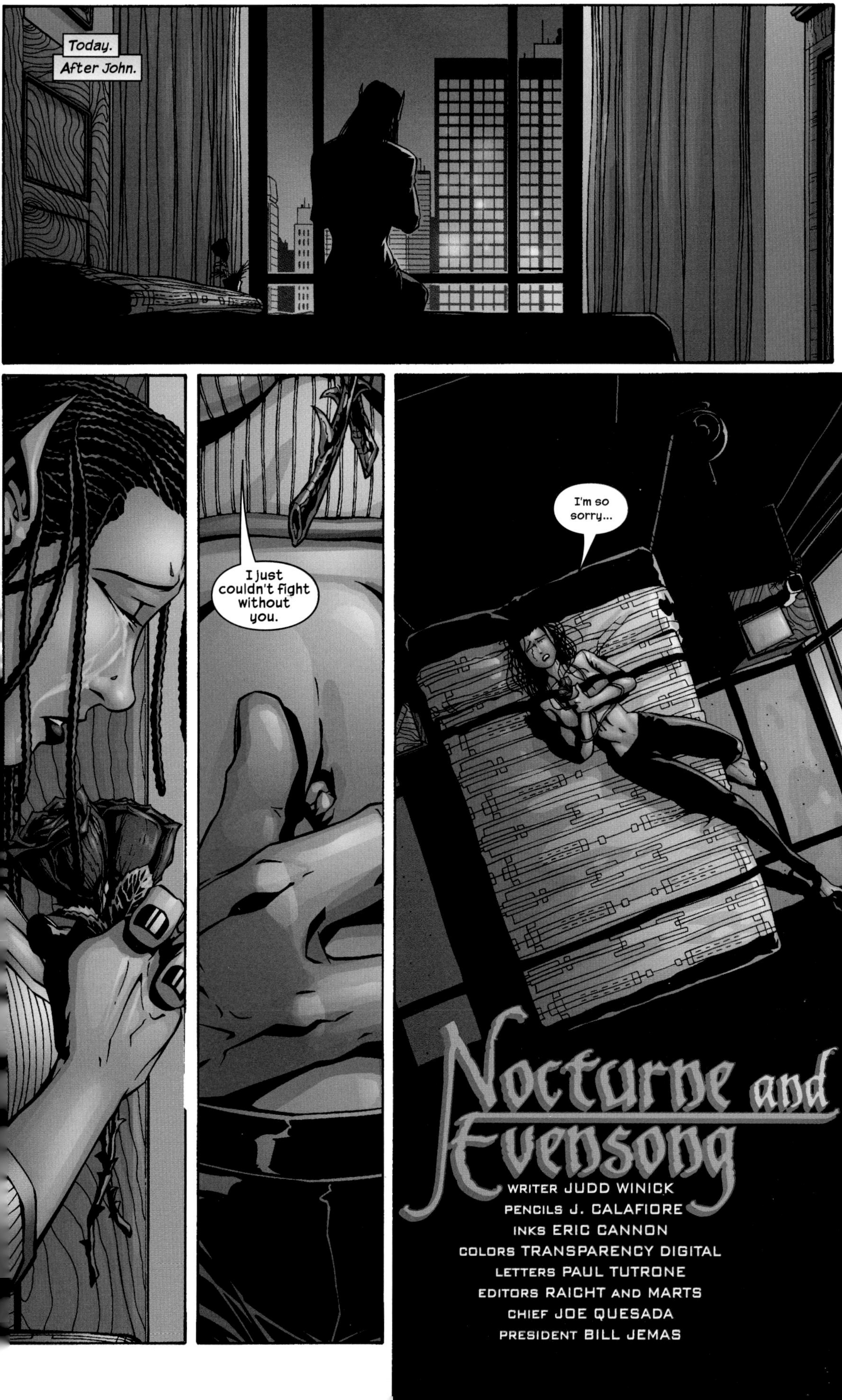
Today.
After John.
I just couldn't fight without you.
I'm so sorry...
Nocturne and Evensong
WRITER JUDD WINICK
PENCILS J. CALAFIORE
INKS ERIC CANNON
COLORS TRANSPARENCY DIGITAL
LETTERS PAUL TUTRONE
EDITORS RAICHT AND MARTS
CHIEF JOE QUESADA
PRESIDENT BILL JEMAS

17

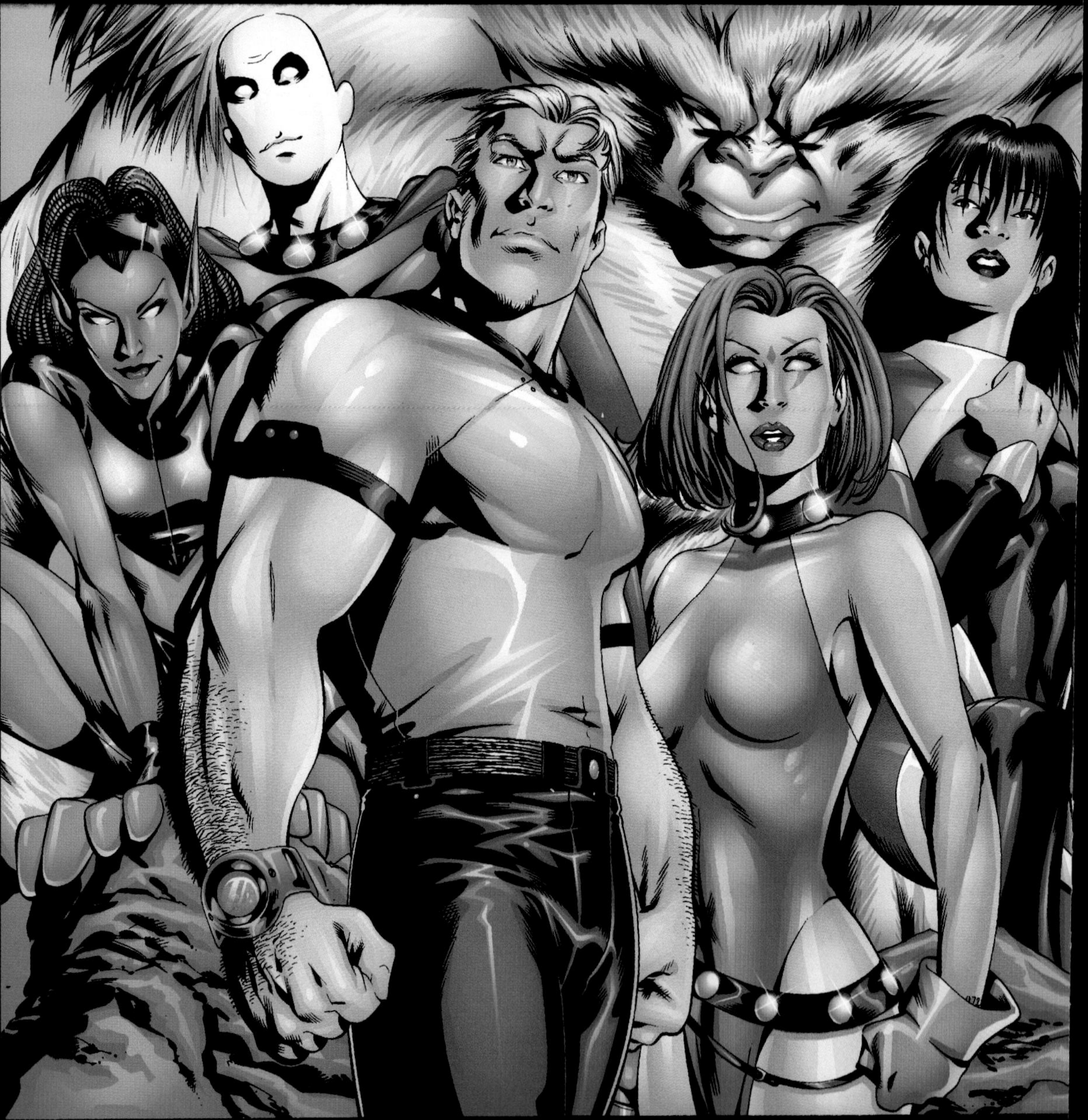

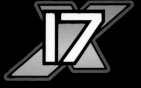

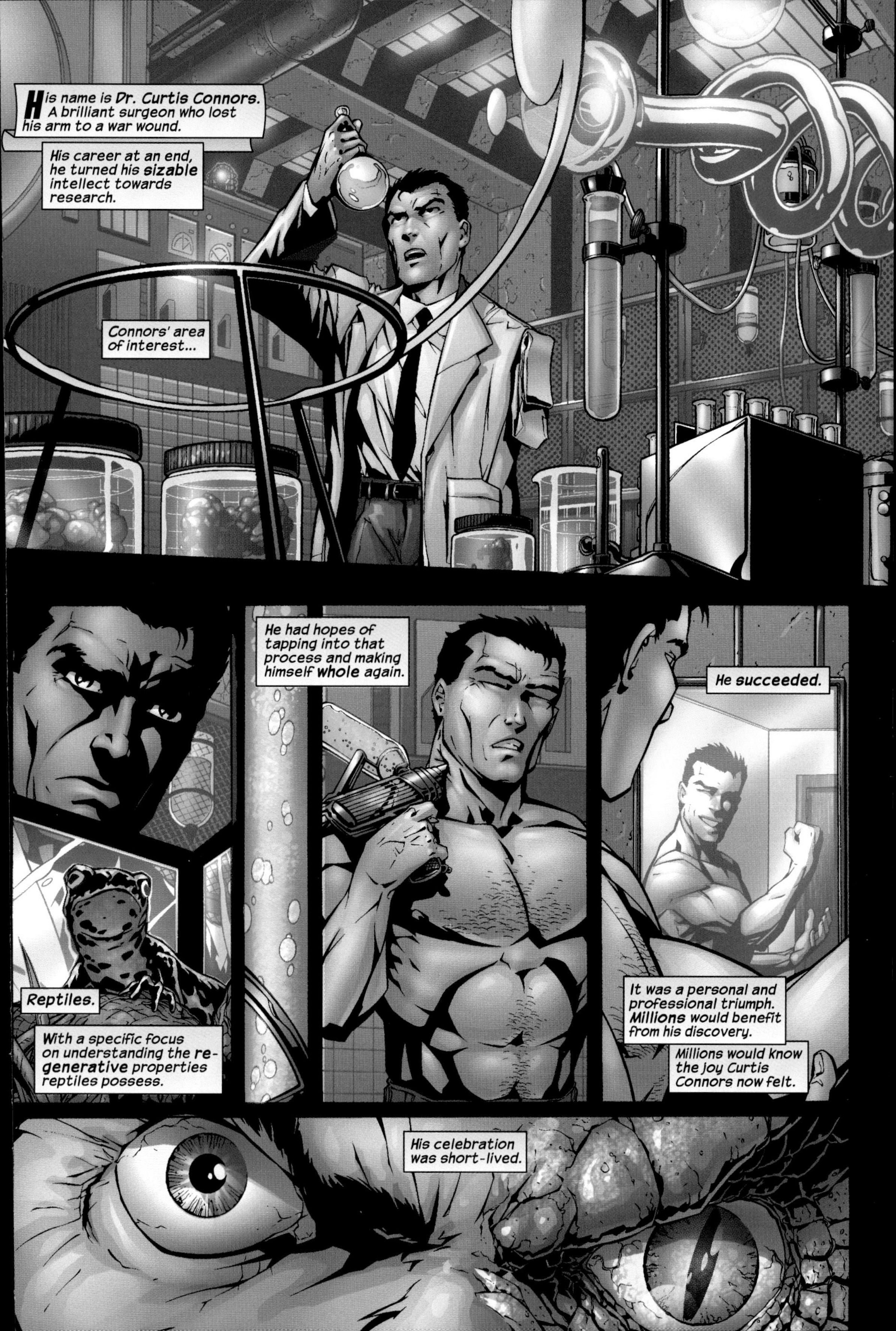
His name is Dr. Curtis Connors. A brilliant surgeon who lost his arm to a war wound.
His career at an end, he turned his sizable intellect towards research.
Connors' area of interest...
Reptiles.
With a specific focus on understanding the regenerative properties reptiles possess.
He had hopes of tapping into that process and making himself whole again.
He succeeded.
It was a personal and professional triumph. Millions would benefit from his discovery.
Millions would know the joy Curtis Connors now felt.
His celebration was short-lived.

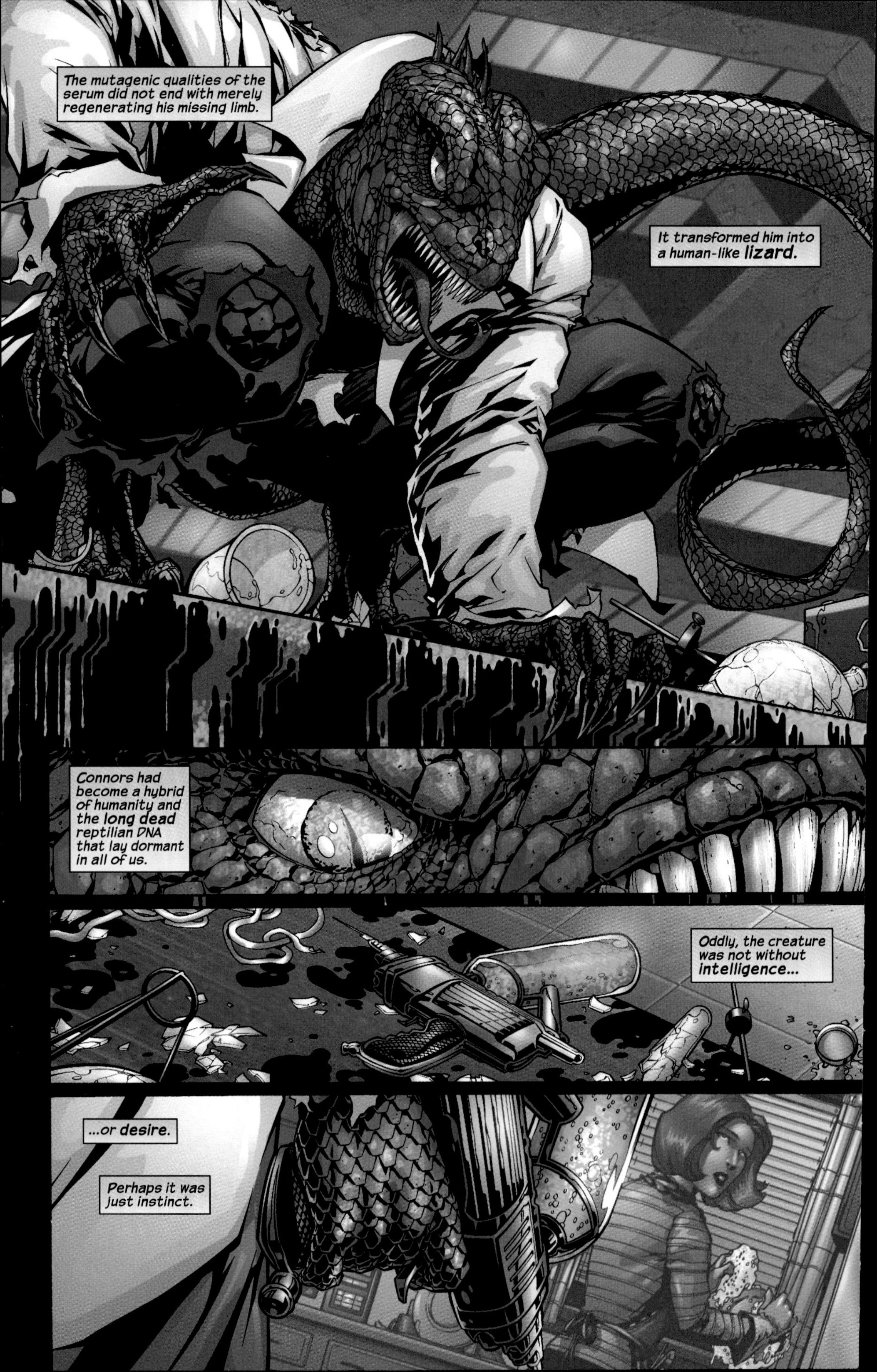
The mutagenic qualities of the serum did not end with merely regenerating his missing limb.
It transformed him into a human-like lizard.
Connors had become a hybrid of humanity and the long dead reptilian DNA that lay dormant in all of us.
Oddly, the creature was not without intelligence...
...or desire.
Perhaps it was just instinct.

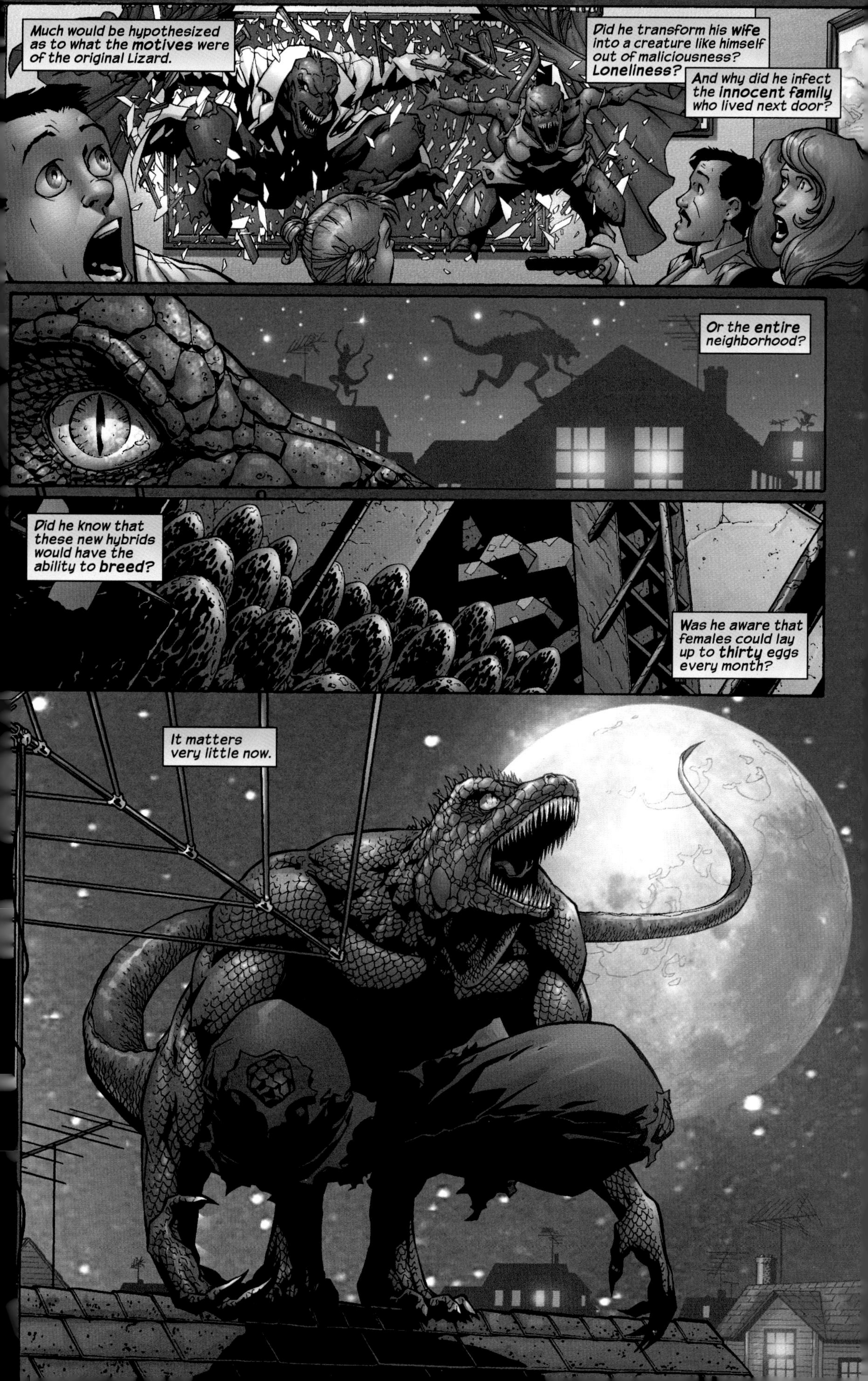
Much would be hypothesized as to what the motives were of the original Lizard.
Did he transform his wife into a creature like himself out of maliciousness? Loneliness?
And why did he infect the innocent family who lived next door?
Or the entire neighborhood?
Did he know that these new hybrids would have the ability to breed?
Was he aware that females could lay up to thirty eggs every month?
It matters very little now.

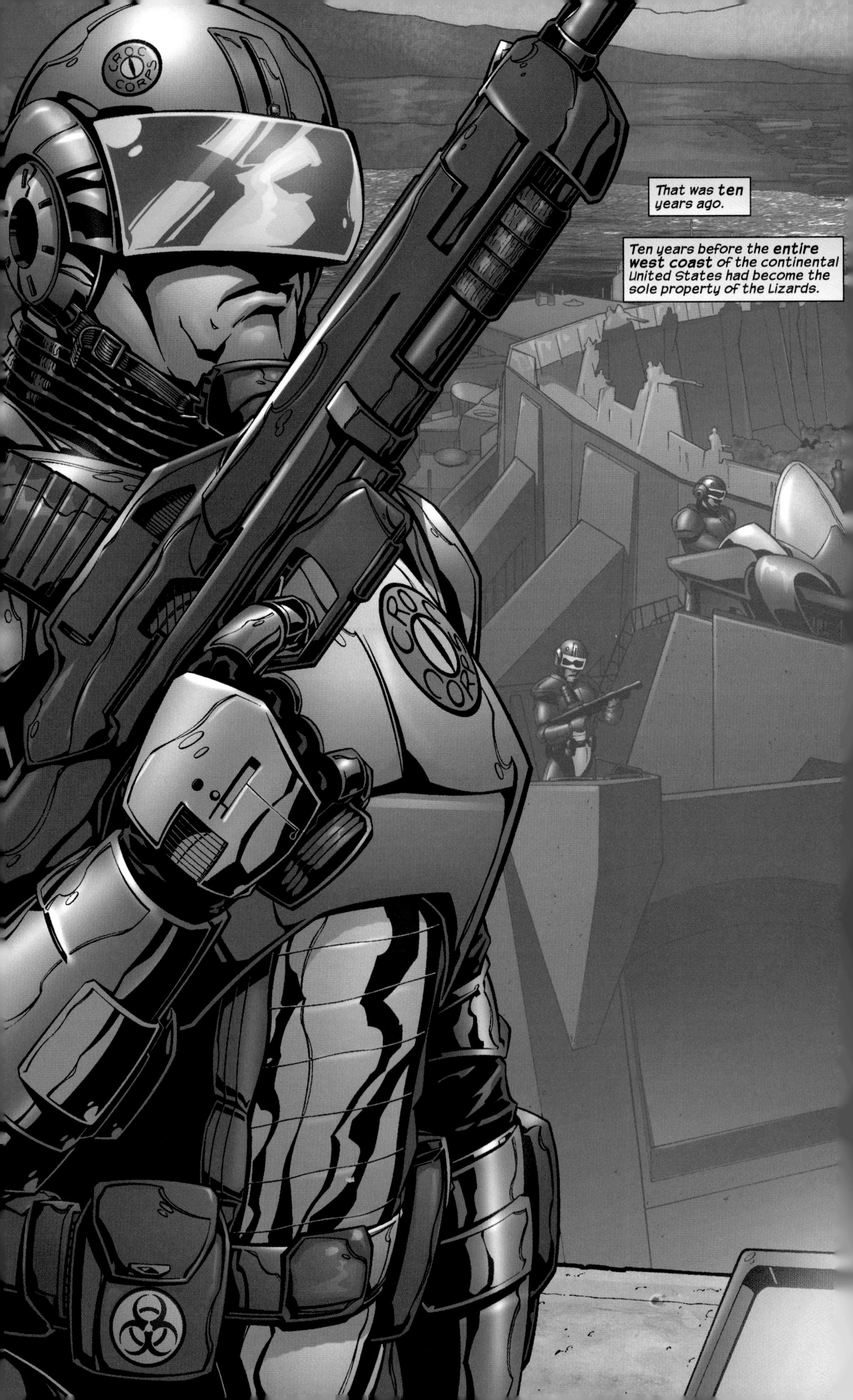

CROC CORPS
That was ten years ago.
Ten years before the entire west coast of the continental United States had become the sole property of the Lizards.
CROC CORPS

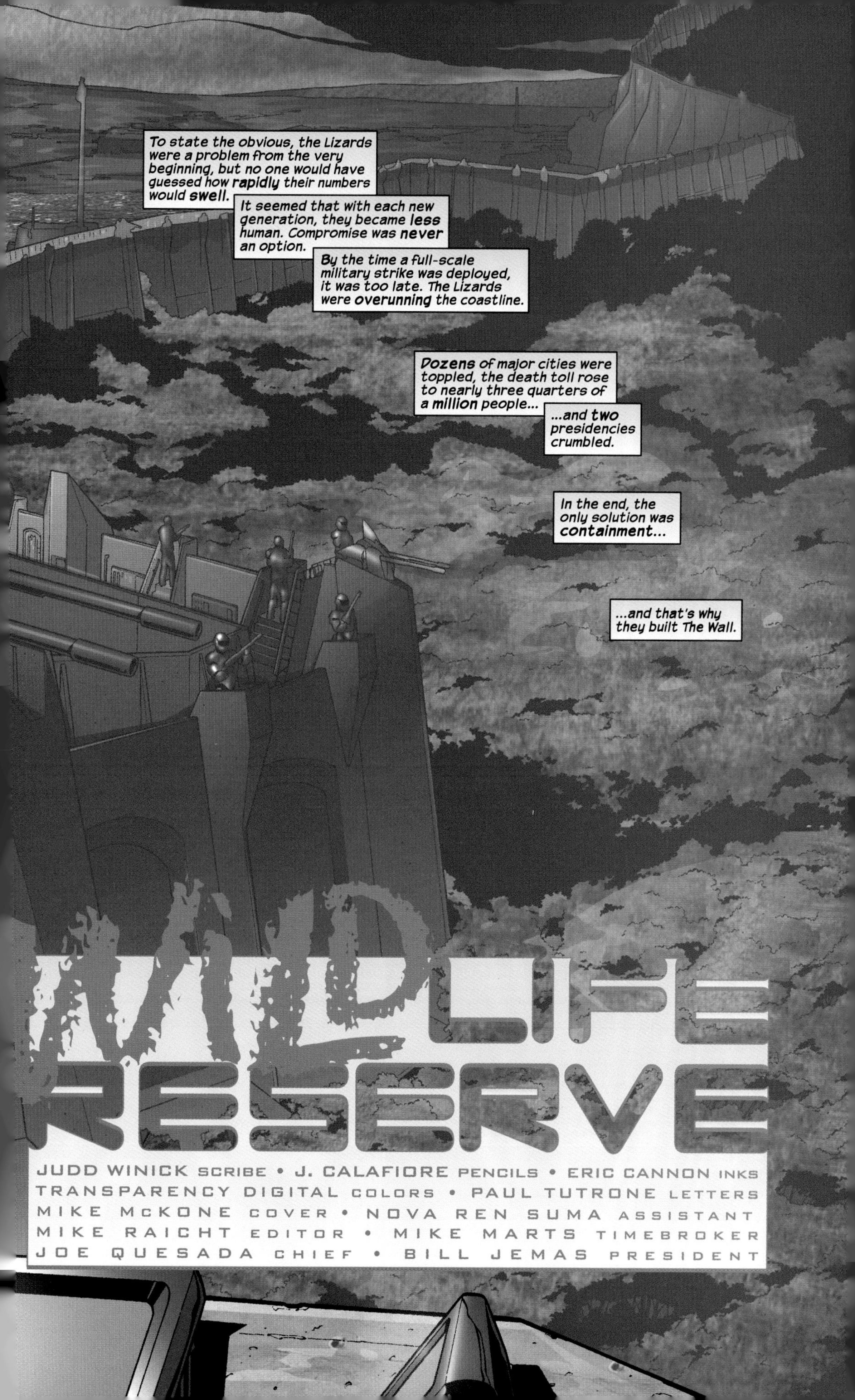
To state the obvious, the Lizards were a problem from the very beginning, but no one would have guessed how rapidly their numbers would swell.
It seemed that with each new generation, they became less human. Compromise was never an option.
By the time a full-scale military strike was deployed, it was too late. The Lizards were overrunning the coastline.
Dozens of major cities were toppled, the death toll rose to nearly three quarters of a million people...
...and two presidencies crumbled.
In the end, the only solution was containment...
...and that's why they built The Wall.
WILD LIFE RESERVE
JUDD WINICK SCRIBE • J. CALAFIORE PENCILS • ERIC CANNON INKS
TRANSPARENCY DIGITAL COLORS • PAUL TUTRONE LETTERS
MIKE McKONE COVER • NOVA REN SUMA ASSISTANT
MIKE RAICHT EDITOR • MIKE MARTS TIMEBROKER
JOE QUESADA CHIEF • BILL JEMAS PRESIDENT

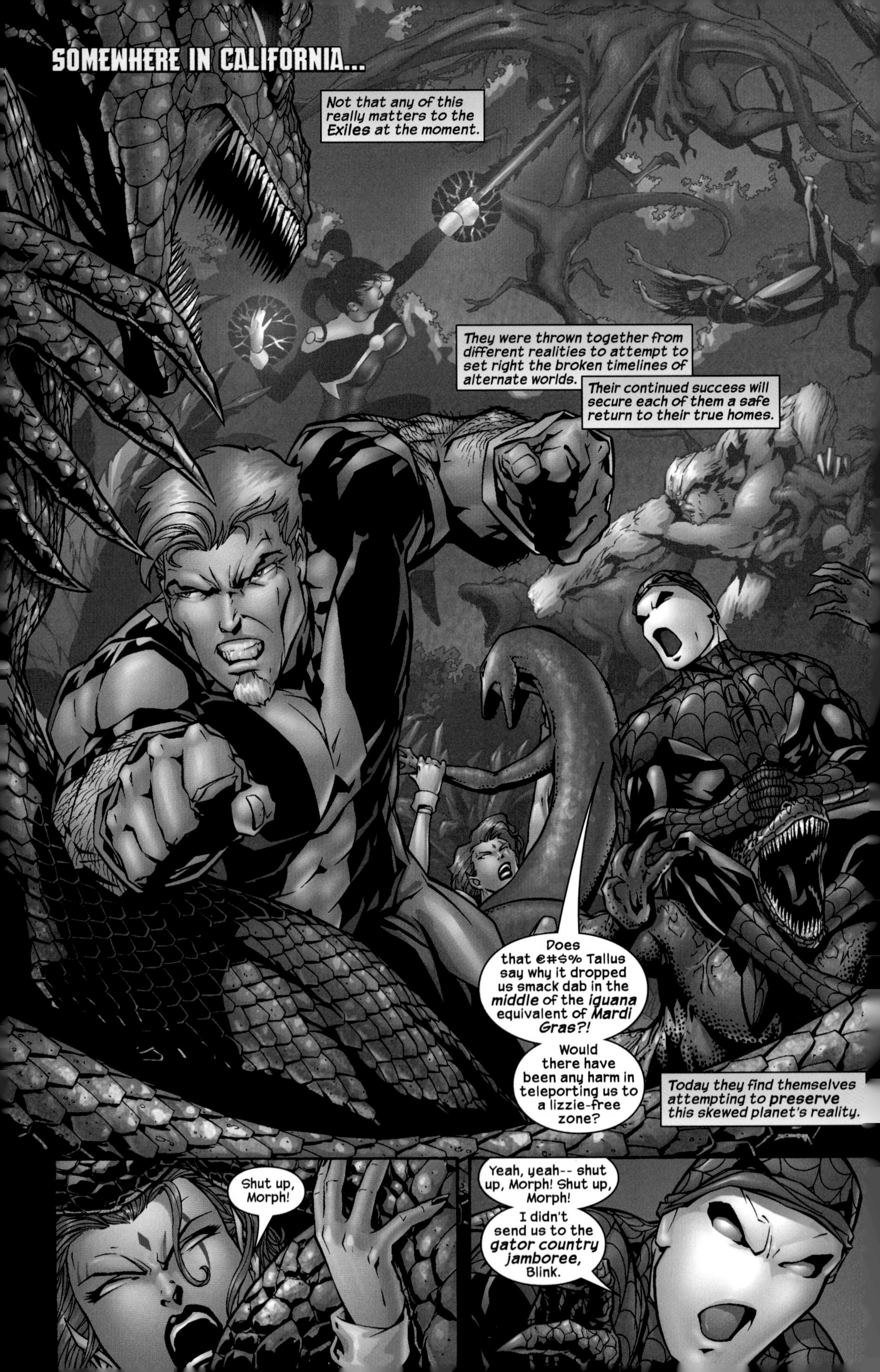
SOMEWHERE IN CALIFORNIA...
Not that any of this really matters to the Exiles at the moment.
They were thrown together from different realities to attempt to set right the broken timelines of alternate worlds.
Their continued success will secure each of them a safe return to their true homes.
Does that @#$% Tallus say why it dropped us smack dab in the middle of the iguana equivalent of Mardi Gras?!
Would there have been any harm in teleporting us to a lizzie-free zone?
Today they find themselves attempting to preserve this skewed planet's reality.
Shut up, Morph!
Yeah, yeah-- shut up, Morph! Shut up, Morph!
I didn't send us to the gator country jamboree, Blink.

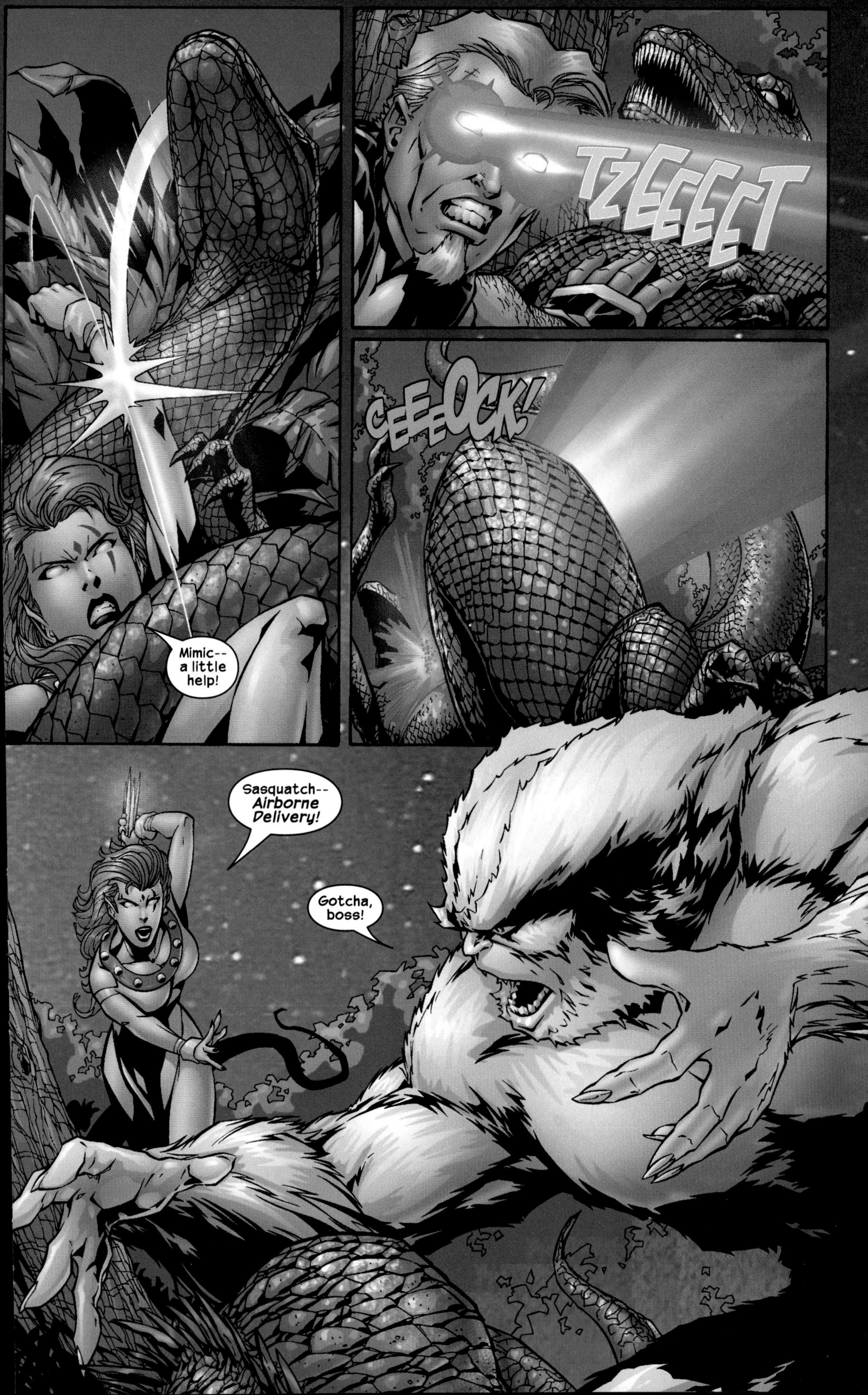
TZEEEECT
Mimic-- a little help!
CEEEOCK!
Sasquatch-- Airborne Delivery!
Gotcha, boss!

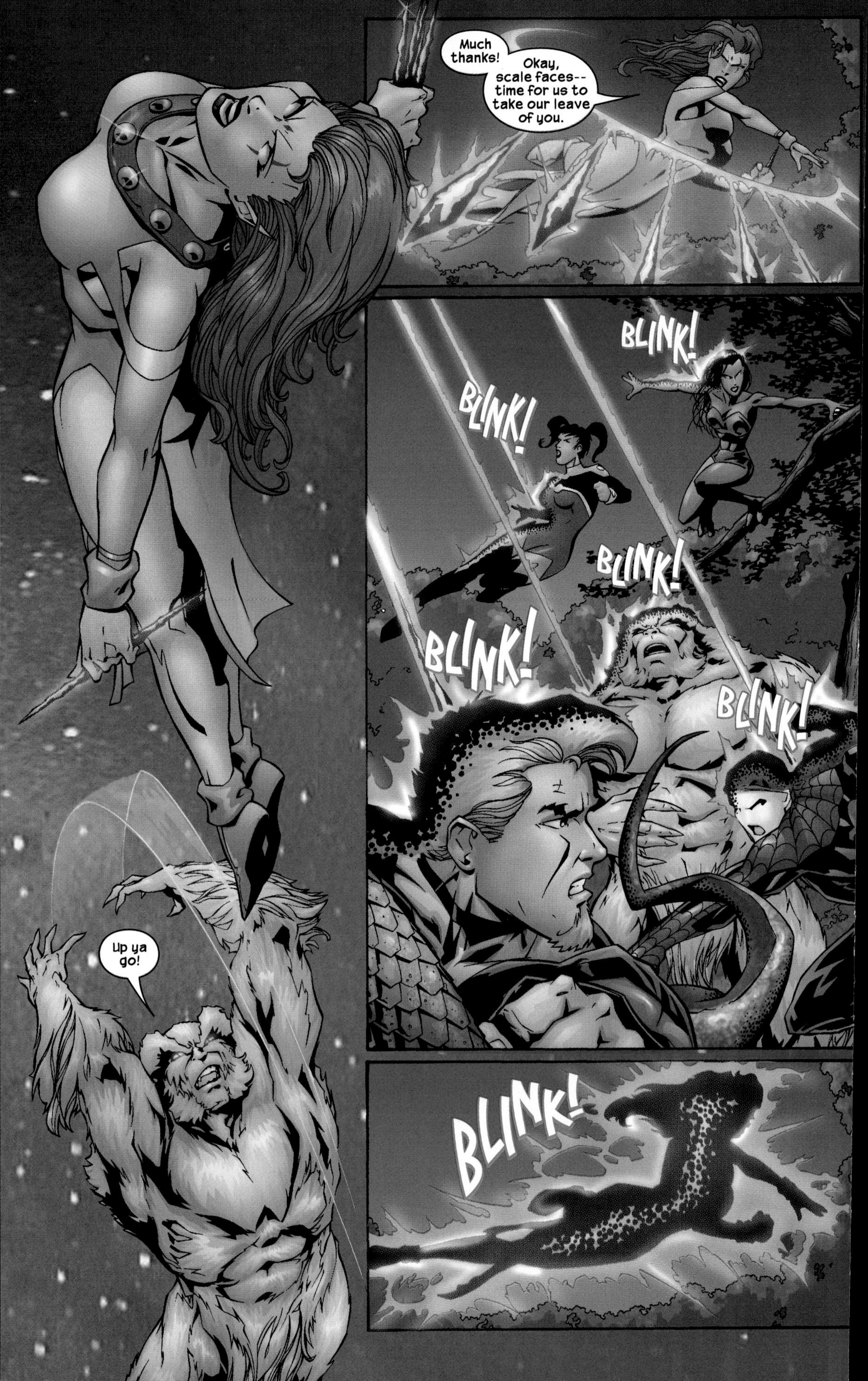
Up ya go!
Much thanks!
Okay, scale faces-- time for us to take our leave of you.
BLINK!
BLINK!
BLINK!
BLINK!
BLINK!
BLINK!

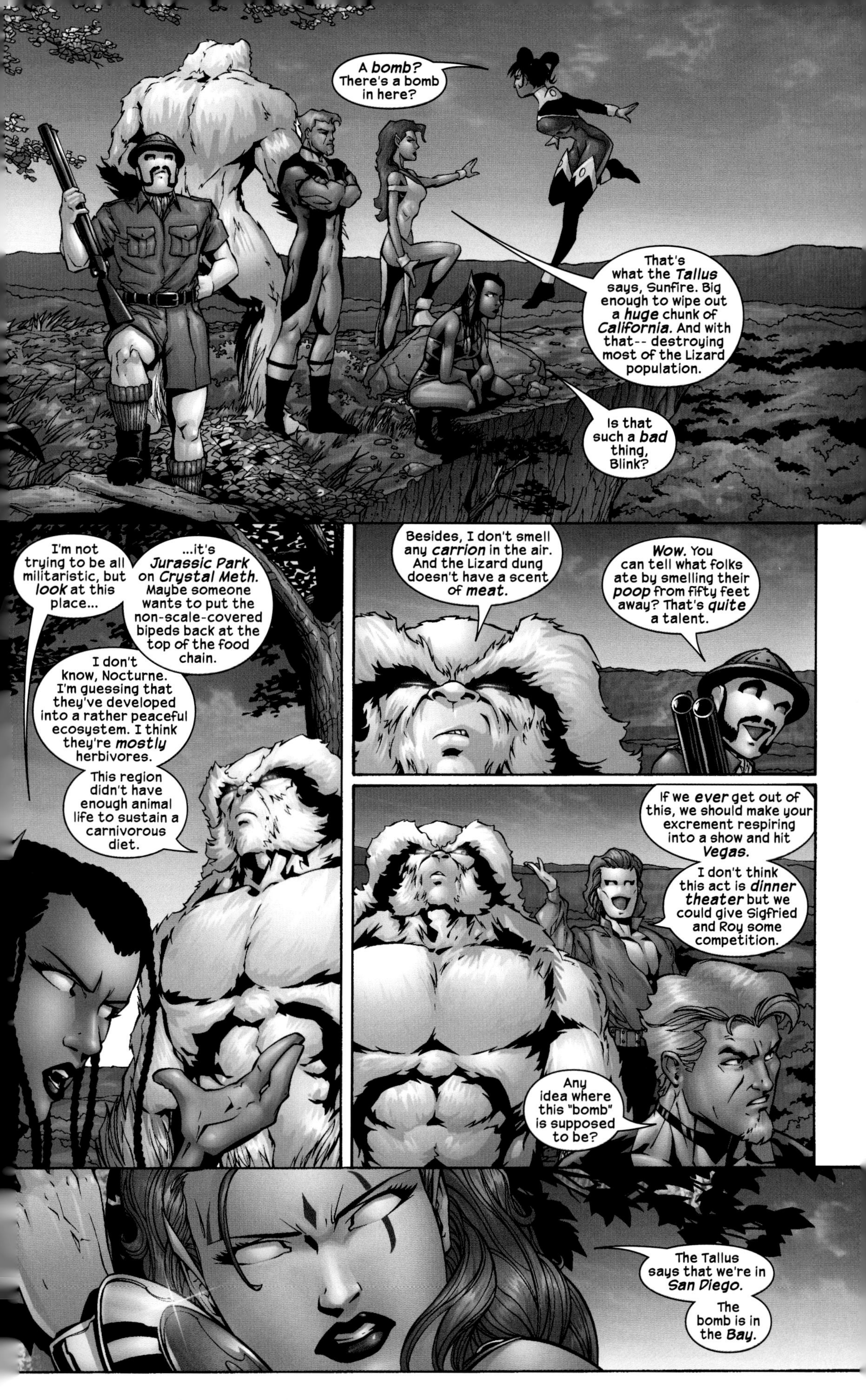
A *bomb?* There's a bomb in here?
That's what the *Tallus* says, Sunfire. Big enough to wipe out a *huge* chunk of *California.* And with that-- destroying most of the Lizard population.
Is that such a *bad* thing, Blink?
I'm not trying to be all militaristic, but *look* at this place...
...it's *Jurassic Park* on *Crystal Meth.* Maybe someone wants to put the non-scale-covered bipeds back at the top of the food chain.
I don't know, Nocturne. I'm guessing that they've developed into a rather peaceful ecosystem. I think they're *mostly* herbivores.
This region didn't have enough animal life to sustain a carnivorous diet.
Besides, I don't smell any *carrion* in the air. And the Lizard dung doesn't have a scent of *meat.*
Wow. You can tell what folks ate by smelling their *poop* from fifty feet away? That's *quite* a talent.
If we *ever* get out of this, we should make your excrement respiring into a show and hit *Vegas.*
I don't think this act is *dinner theater* but we could give Sigfried and Roy some competition.
Any idea where this "bomb" is supposed to be?
The Tallus says that we're in *San Diego.*
The bomb is in the *Bay.*

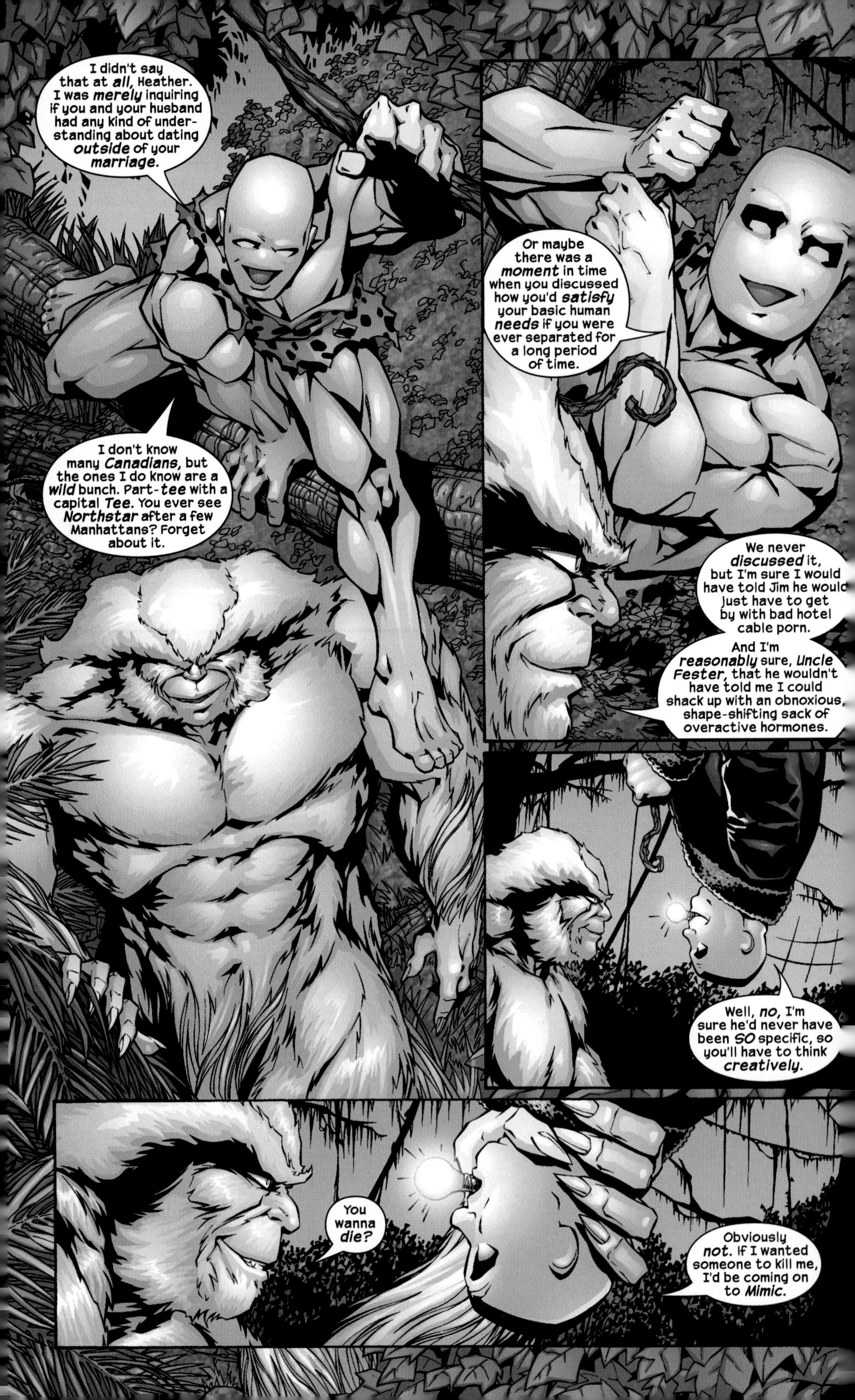
I didn't say that at *all*, Heather. I was *merely* inquiring if you and your husband had any kind of understanding about dating *outside* of your *marriage*.
I don't know many *Canadians*, but the ones I do know are a *wild* bunch. Part-*tee* with a capital *Tee*. You ever see *Northstar* after a few Manhattans? Forget about it.
Or maybe there was a *moment* in time when you discussed how you'd *satisfy* your basic human *needs* if you were ever separated for a long period of time.
We never *discussed* it, but I'm sure I would have told Jim he would just have to get by with bad hotel cable porn.
And I'm *reasonably* sure, *Uncle Fester*, that he wouldn't have told me I could shack up with an obnoxious, shape-shifting sack of overactive hormones.
Well, *no*, I'm sure he'd never have been *SO* specific, so you'll have to think *creatively*.
You wanna *die*?
Obviously *not*. If I wanted someone to kill me, I'd be coming on to *Mimic*.

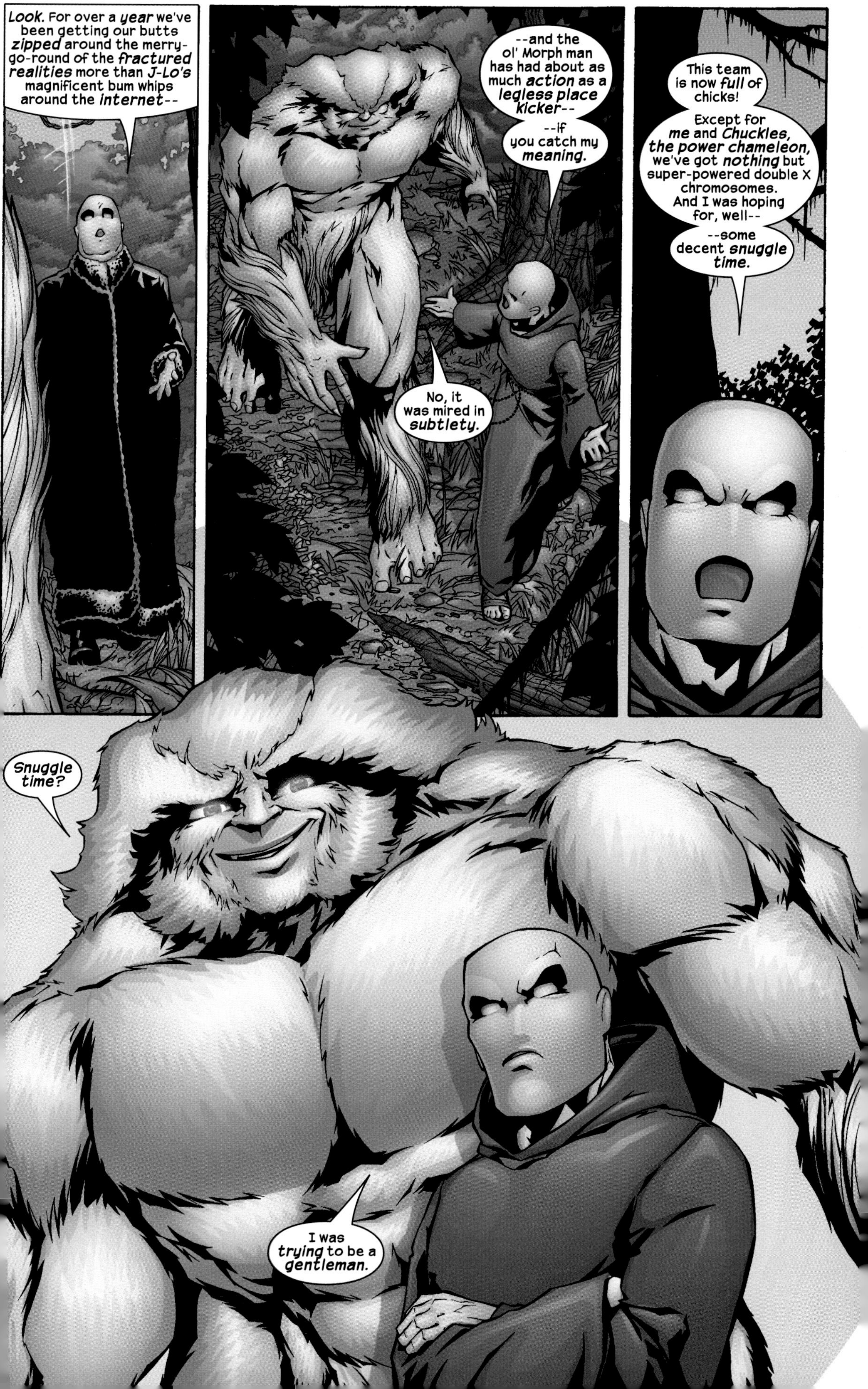
Look. For over a year we've been getting our butts zipped around the merry-go-round of the fractured realities more than J-Lo's magnificent bum whips around the internet--
--and the ol' Morph man has had about as much action as a legless place kicker--
--if you catch my meaning.
No, it was mired in subtlety.
This team is now full of chicks!
Except for me and Chuckles, the power chameleon, we've got nothing but super-powered double X chromosomes.
And I was hoping for, well--
--some decent snuggle time.
Snuggle time?
I was trying to be a gentleman.

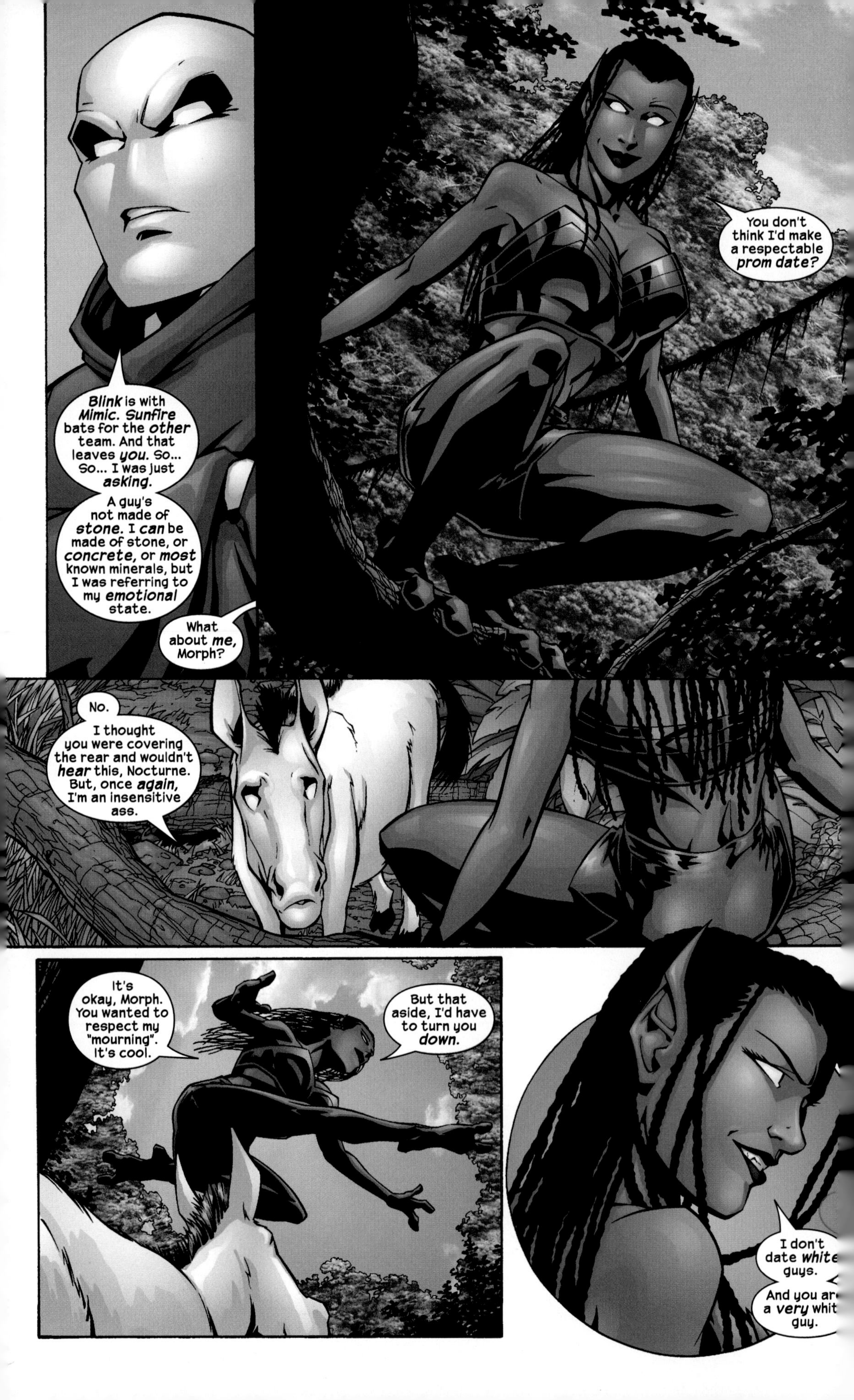
You don't think I'd make a respectable prom date?
Blink is with Mimic. Sunfire bats for the other team. And that leaves you. So... So... I was just asking.
A guy's not made of stone. I can be made of stone, or concrete, or most known minerals, but I was referring to my emotional state.
What about me, Morph?
No.
I thought you were covering the rear and wouldn't hear this, Nocturne. But, once again, I'm an insensitive ass.
It's okay, Morph. You wanted to respect my "mourning". It's cool.
But that aside, I'd have to turn you down.
I don't date white guys.
And you are a very white guy.

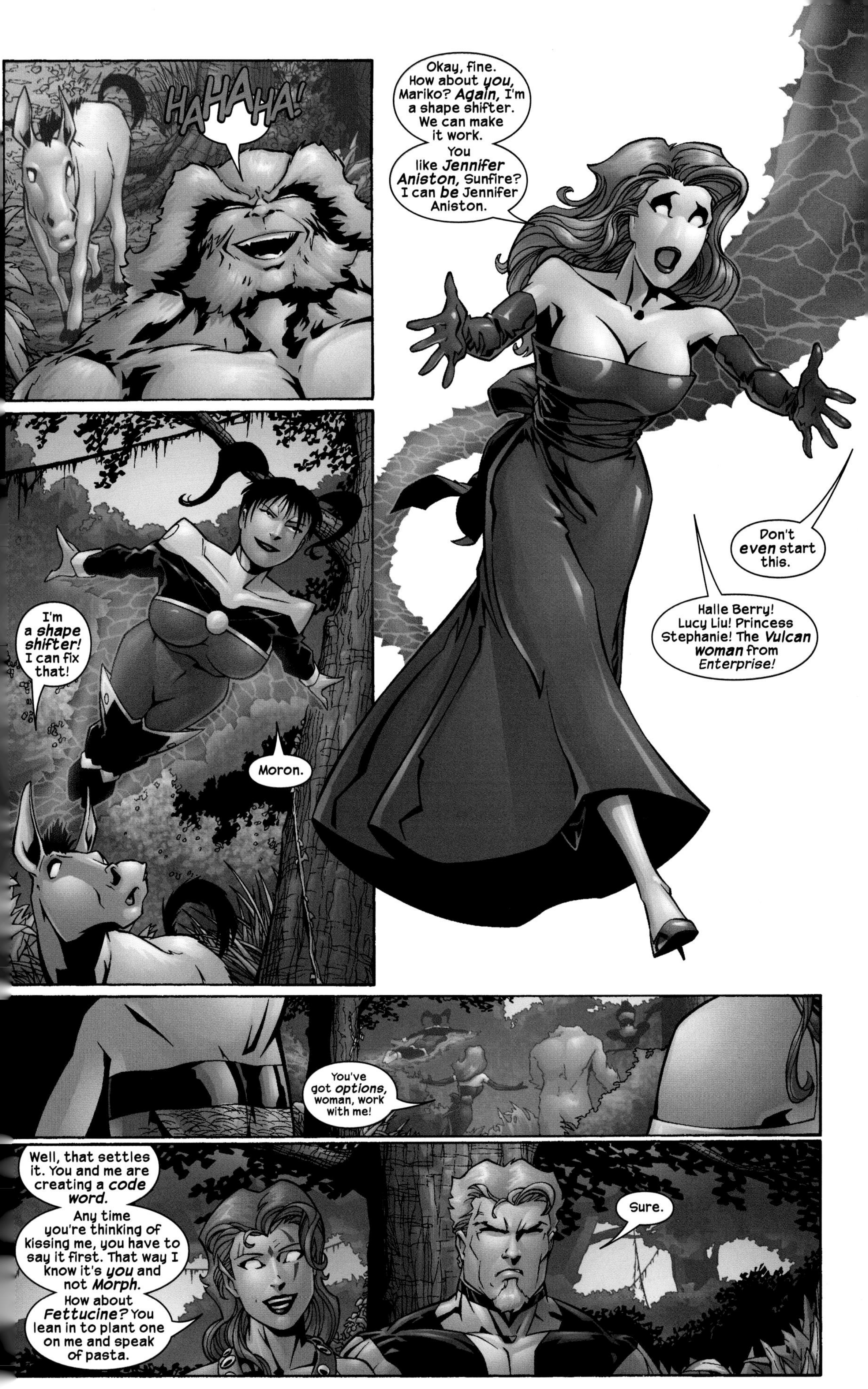
HAHAHA!
Okay, fine. How about you, Mariko? Again, I'm a shape shifter. We can make it work.
You like Jennifer Aniston, Sunfire? I can be Jennifer Aniston.
I'm a shape shifter! I can fix that!
Moron.
Halle Berry! Lucy Liu! Princess Stephanie! The Vulcan woman from Enterprise!
Don't even start this.
You've got options, woman, work with me!
Well, that settles it. You and me are creating a code word.
Any time you're thinking of kissing me, you have to say it first. That way I know it's you and not Morph.
How about Fettucine? You lean in to plant one on me and speak of pasta.
Sure.

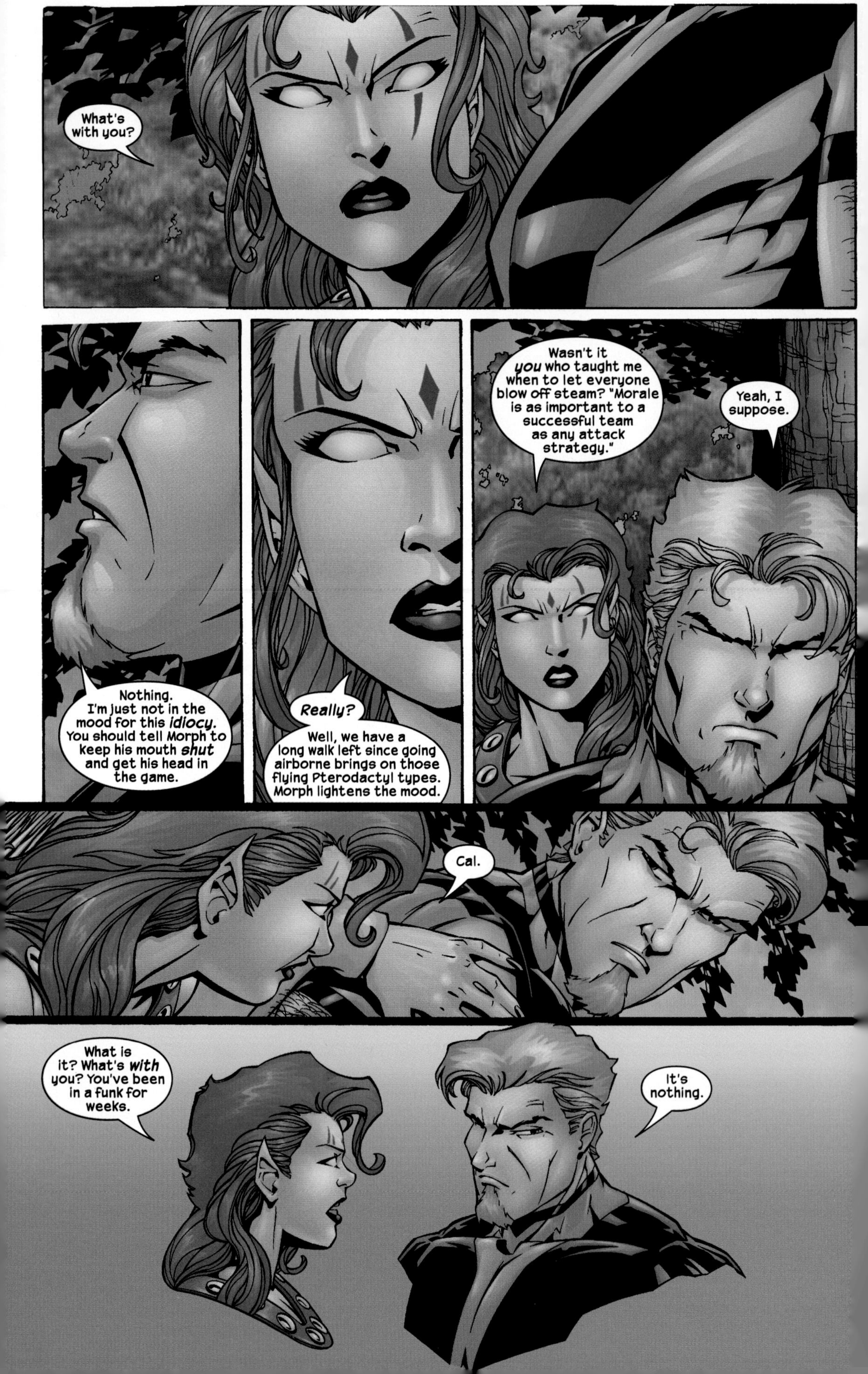
What's with you?
Nothing. I'm just not in the mood for this *idiocy*. You should tell Morph to keep his mouth *shut* and get his head in the game.
Really?
Well, we have a long walk left since going airborne brings on those flying Pterodactyl types. Morph lightens the mood.
Wasn't it *you* who taught me when to let everyone blow off steam? "Morale is as important to a successful team as any attack strategy."
Yeah, I suppose.
Cal.
What is it? What's *with* you? You've been in a funk for weeks.
It's nothing.

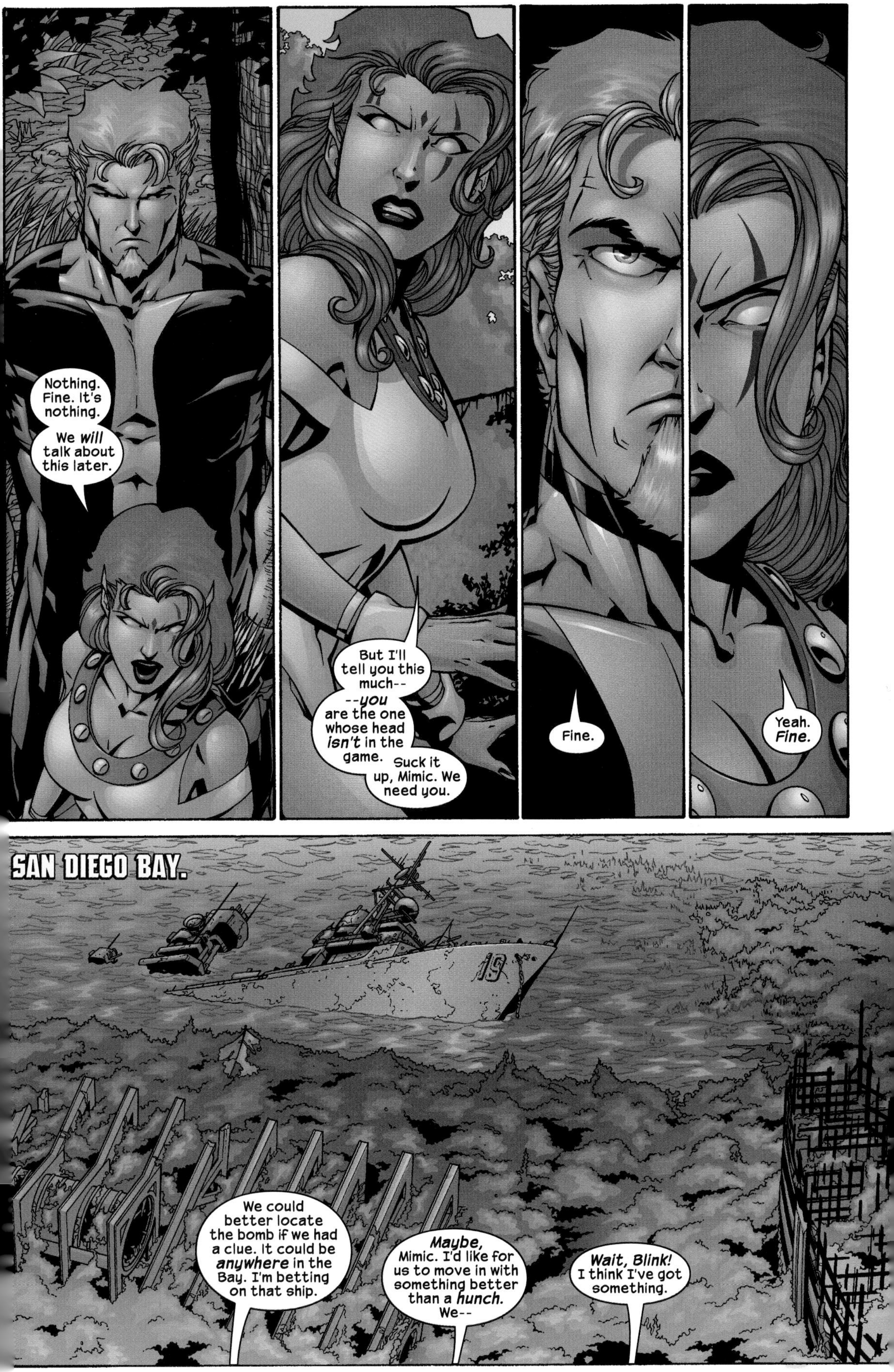
Nothing. Fine. It's nothing.
We *will* talk about this later.
But I'll tell you this much--
--*you* are the one whose head *isn't* in the game.
Suck it up, Mimic. We need you.
Fine.
Yeah. *Fine.*
SAN DIEGO BAY.
We could better locate the bomb if we had a clue. It could be *anywhere* in the Bay. I'm betting on that ship.
Maybe, Mimic. I'd like for us to move in with something better than a *hunch.* We--
Wait, Blink! I think I've got something.

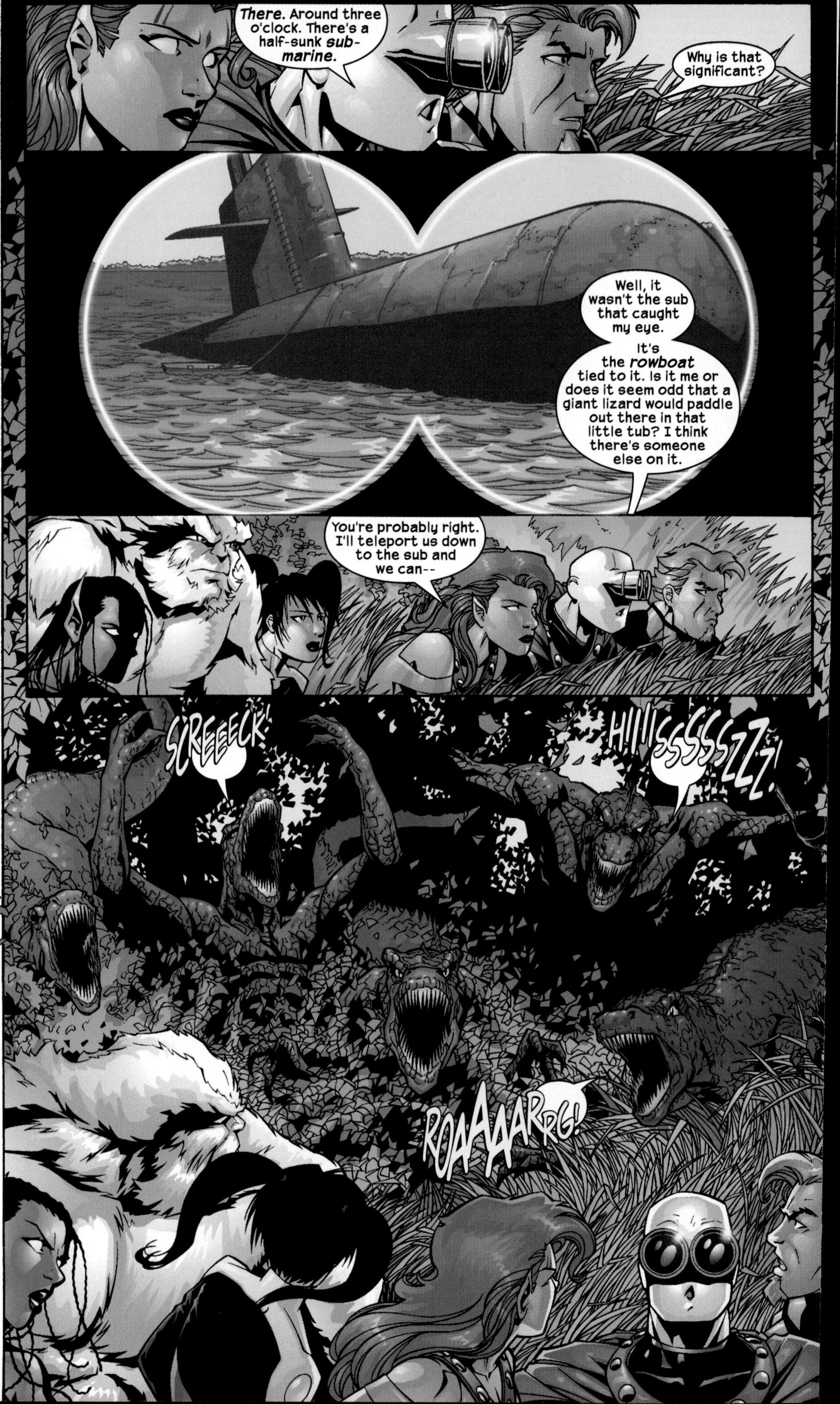
There. Around three o'clock. There's a half-sunk sub-marine.
Why is that significant?
Well, it wasn't the sub that caught my eye.
It's the rowboat tied to it. Is it me or does it seem odd that a giant lizard would paddle out there in that little tub? I think there's someone else on it.
You're probably right. I'll teleport us down to the sub and we can--
SCREEECK!
HIIISSSSSZZZ!
ROAAAARRG!

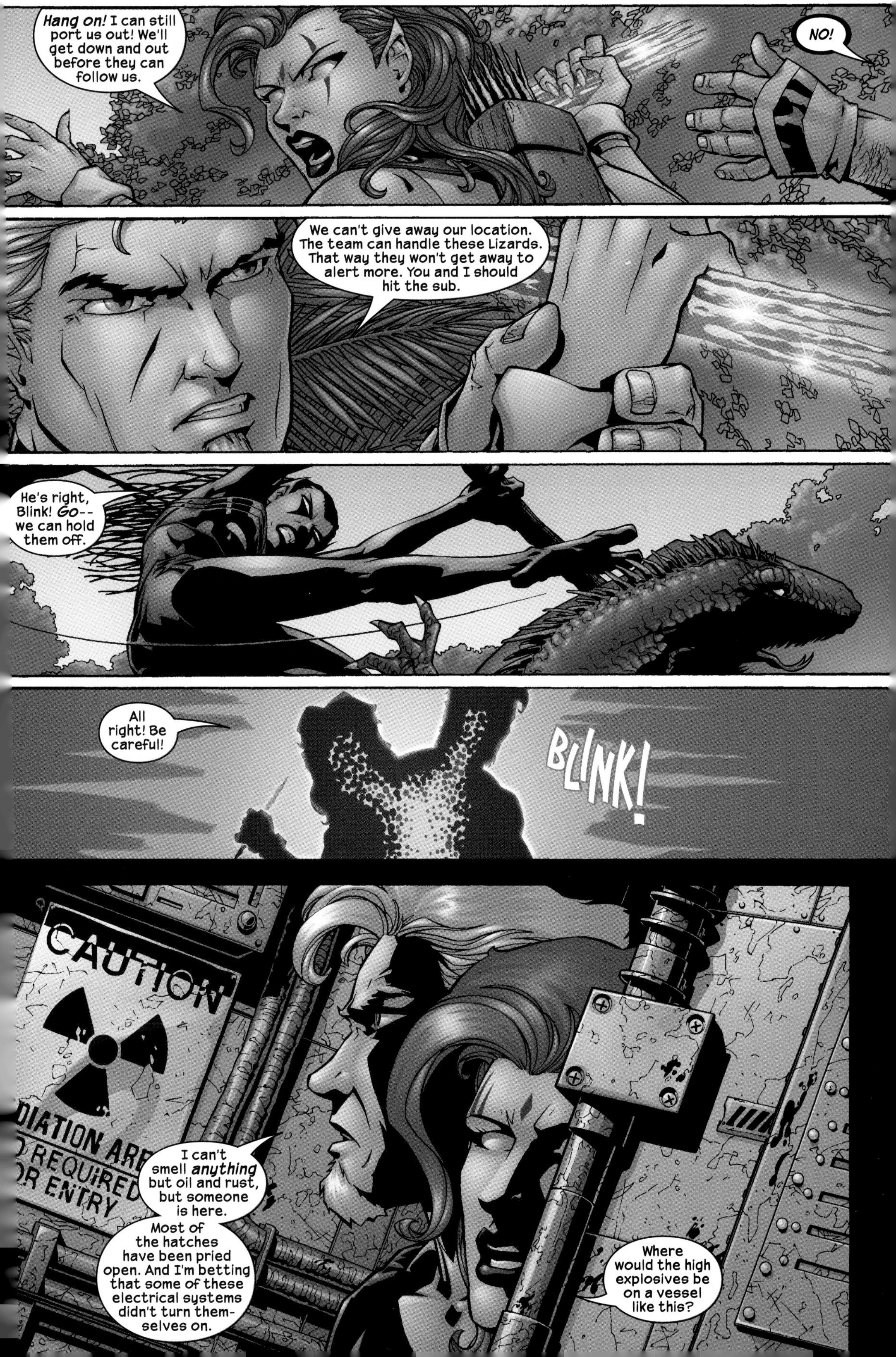

Hang on! I can still port us out! We'll get down and out before they can follow us.
NO!
We can't give away our location. The team can handle these Lizards. That way they won't get away to alert more. You and I should hit the sub.
He's right, Blink! Go-- we can hold them off.
All right! Be careful!
BLINK!
CAUTION
DIATION ARE
D REQUIRED
OR ENTRY
I can't smell anything but oil and rust, but someone is here.
Most of the hatches have been pried open. And I'm betting that some of these electrical systems didn't turn them-selves on.
Where would the high explosives be on a vessel like this?

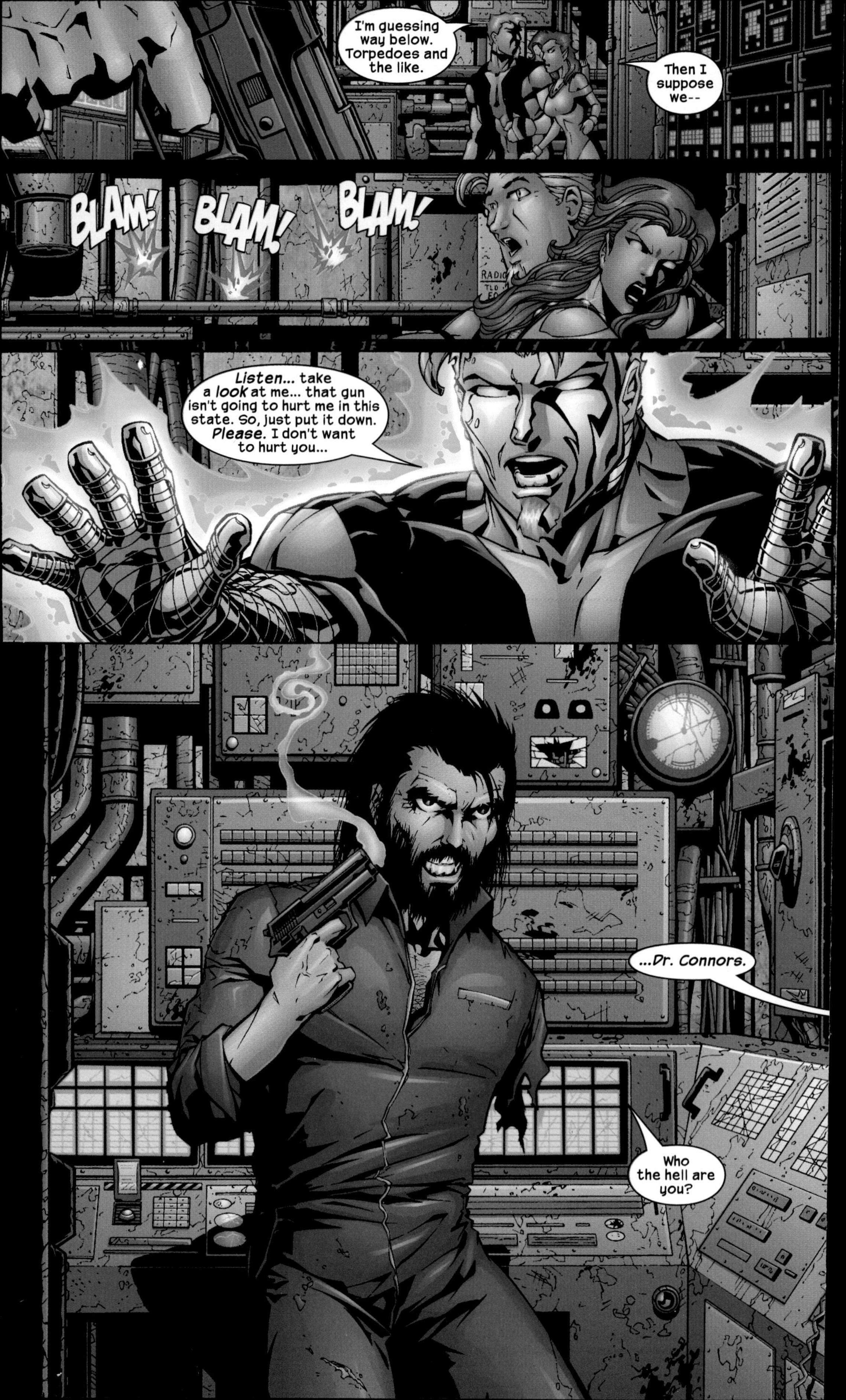
I'm guessing way below. Torpedoes and the like.
Then I suppose we--
BLAM! BLAM! BLAM!
Listen... take a look at me... that gun isn't going to hurt me in this state. So, just put it down. Please. I don't want to hurt you...
...Dr. Connors.
Who the hell are you?

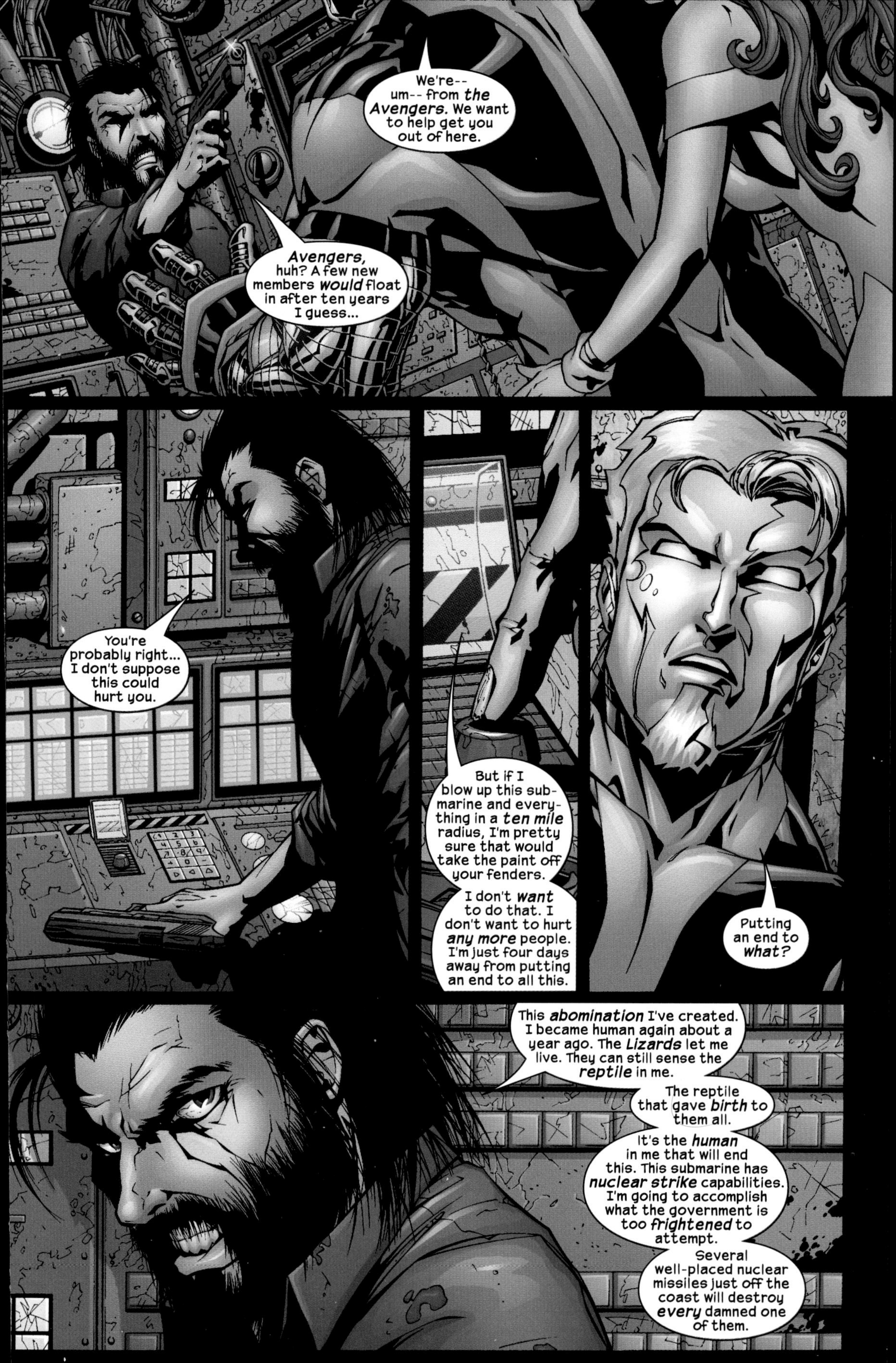
We're-- um-- from the Avengers. We want to help get you out of here.
Avengers, huh? A few new members would float in after ten years I guess...
You're probably right... I don't suppose this could hurt you.
But if I blow up this submarine and everything in a ten mile radius, I'm pretty sure that would take the paint off your fenders.
I don't want to do that. I don't want to hurt any more people. I'm just four days away from putting an end to all this.
Putting an end to what?
This abomination I've created. I became human again about a year ago. The Lizards let me live. They can still sense the reptile in me.
The reptile that gave birth to them all.
It's the human in me that will end this. This submarine has nuclear strike capabilities. I'm going to accomplish what the government is too frightened to attempt.
Several well-placed nuclear missiles just off the coast will destroy every damned one of them.

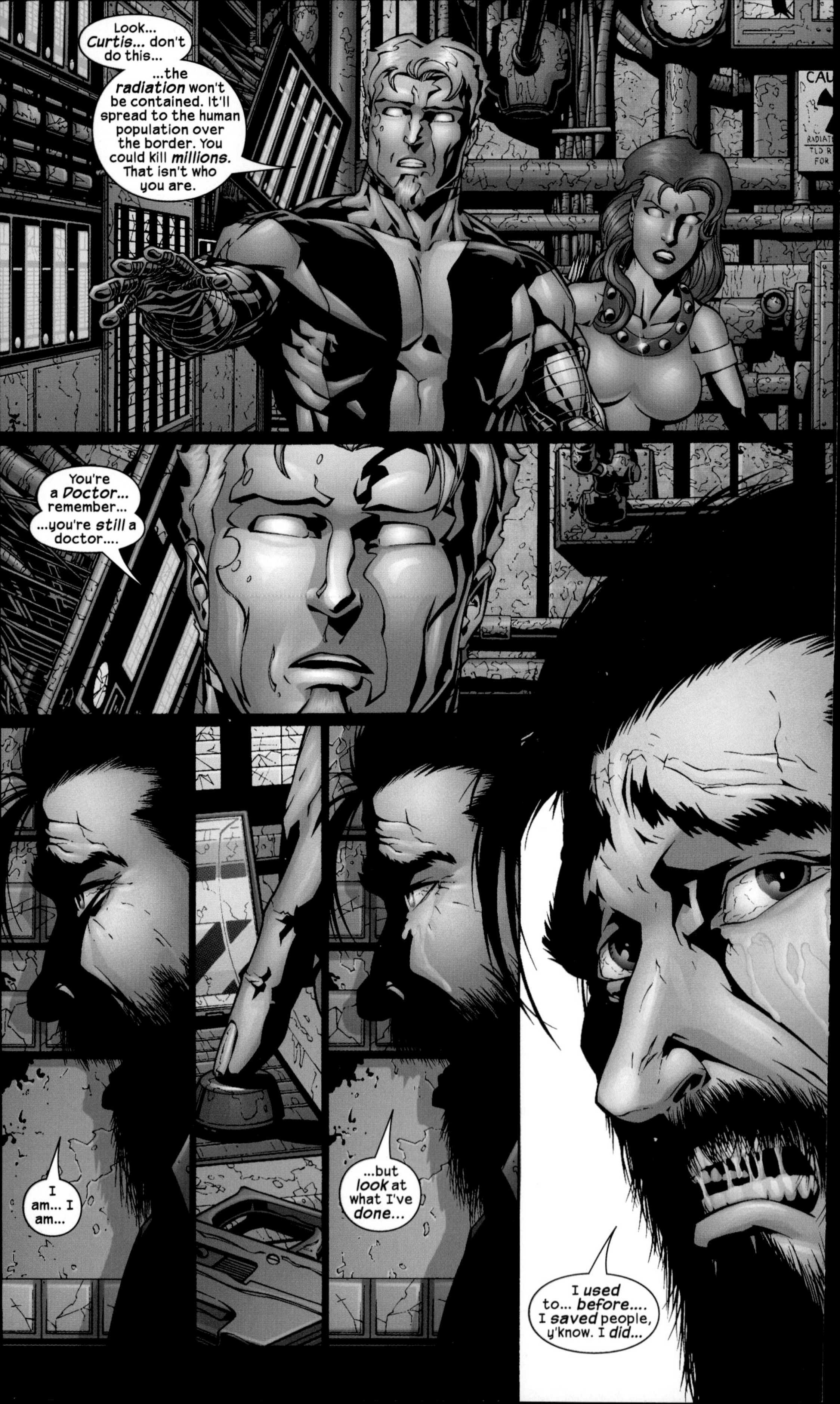
Look... Curtis... don't do this...
...the radiation won't be contained. It'll spread to the human population over the border. You could kill millions. That isn't who you are.
CAU
RADIATI
TLD R
FOR
You're a Doctor... remember...
...you're still a doctor....
I am... I am...
...but look at what I've done...
I used to... before.... I saved people, y'know. I did...

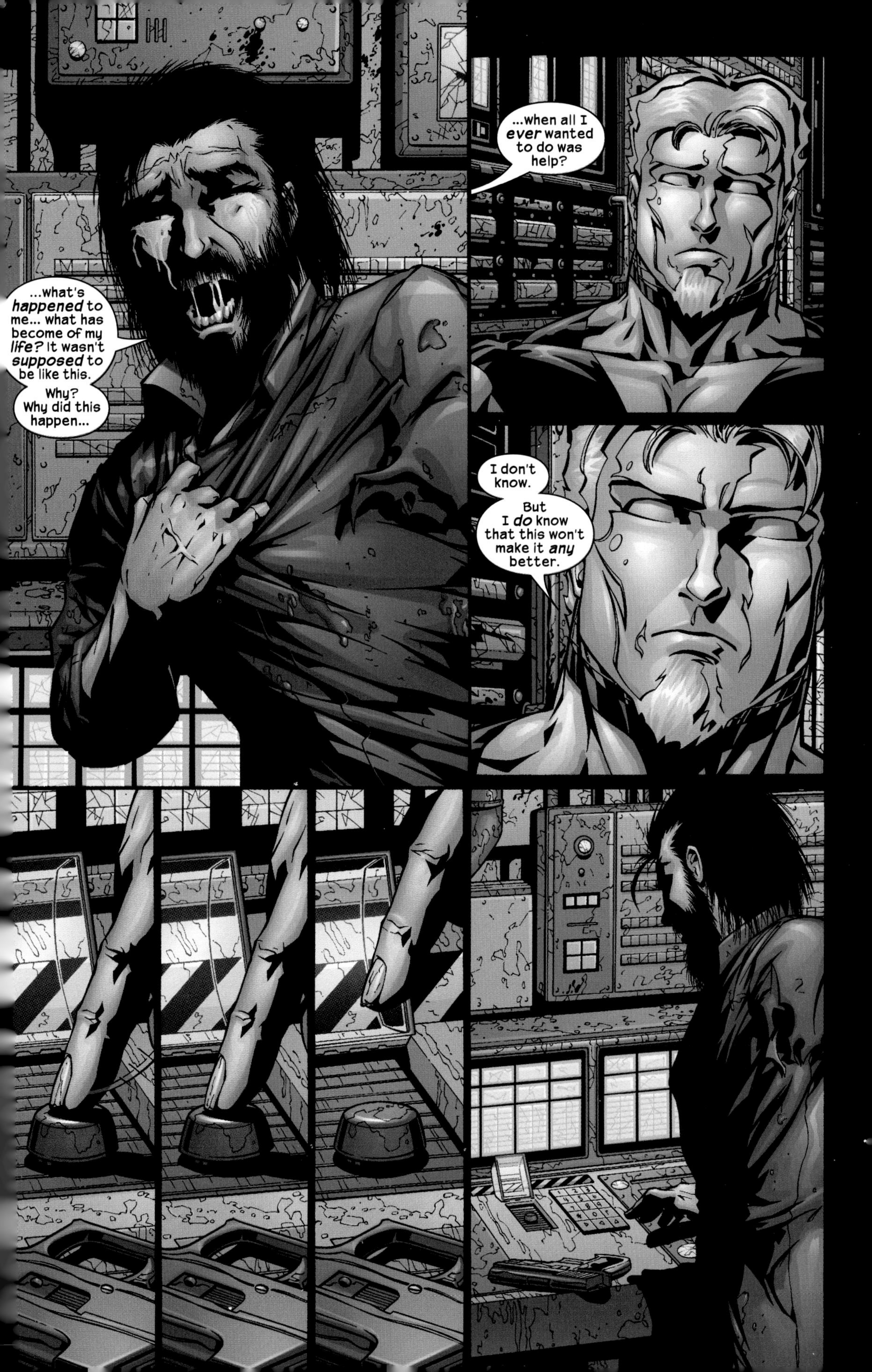
...what's *happened* to me... what has become of my *life?* It wasn't *supposed* to be like this.
Why? Why did this happen...
...when all I *ever* wanted to do was help?
I don't know.
But I *do* know that this won't make it *any* better.

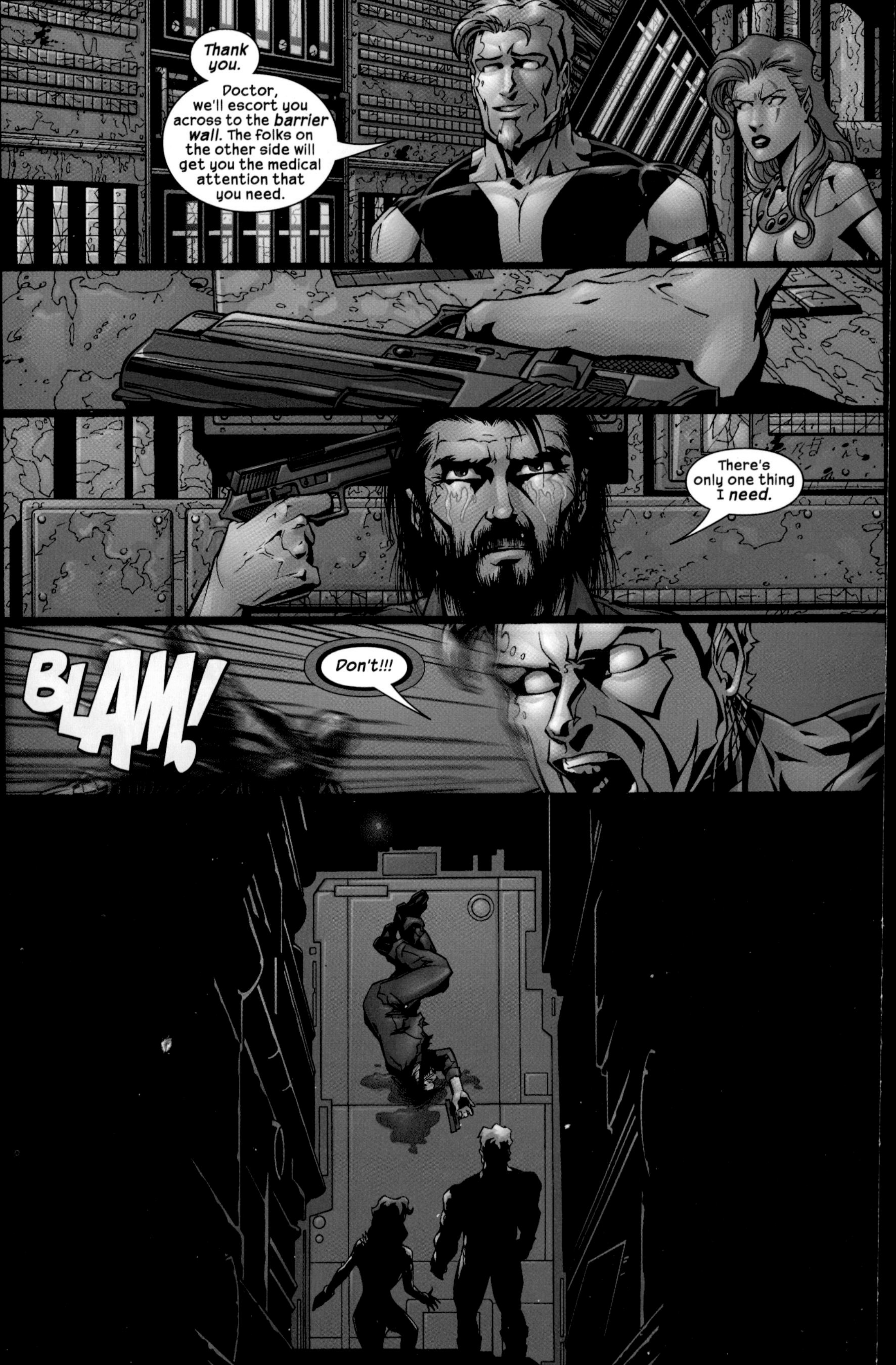

Thank you.
Doctor, we'll escort you across to the *barrier wall.* The folks on the other side will get you the medical attention that you need.
There's only one thing I *need.*
BLAM!
Don't!!!

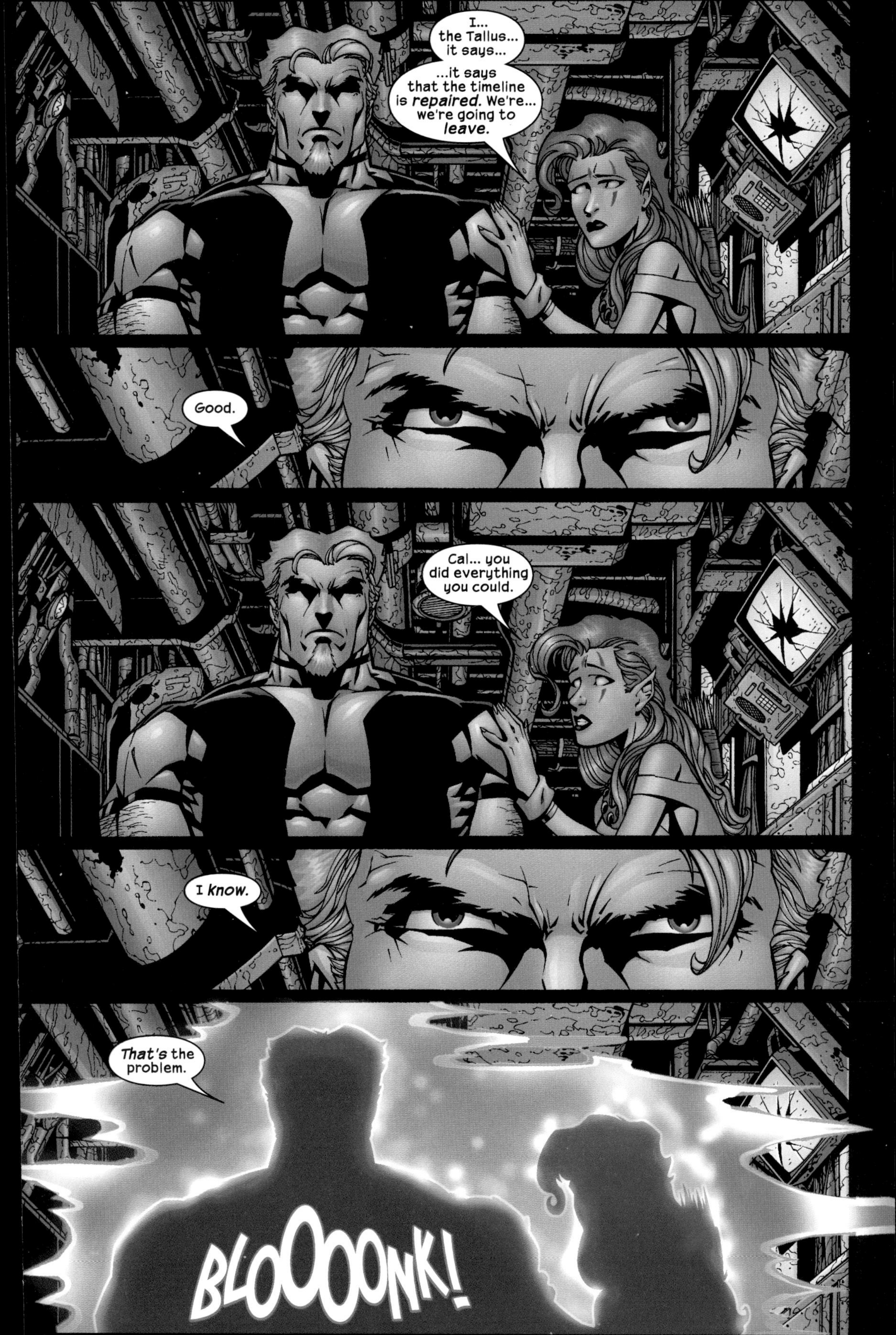
I... the Tallus... it says... ...it says that the timeline is *repaired*. We're... we're going to *leave*.
Good.
Cal... you did everything you could.
I *know*.
That's the problem.
BLOOOONK!

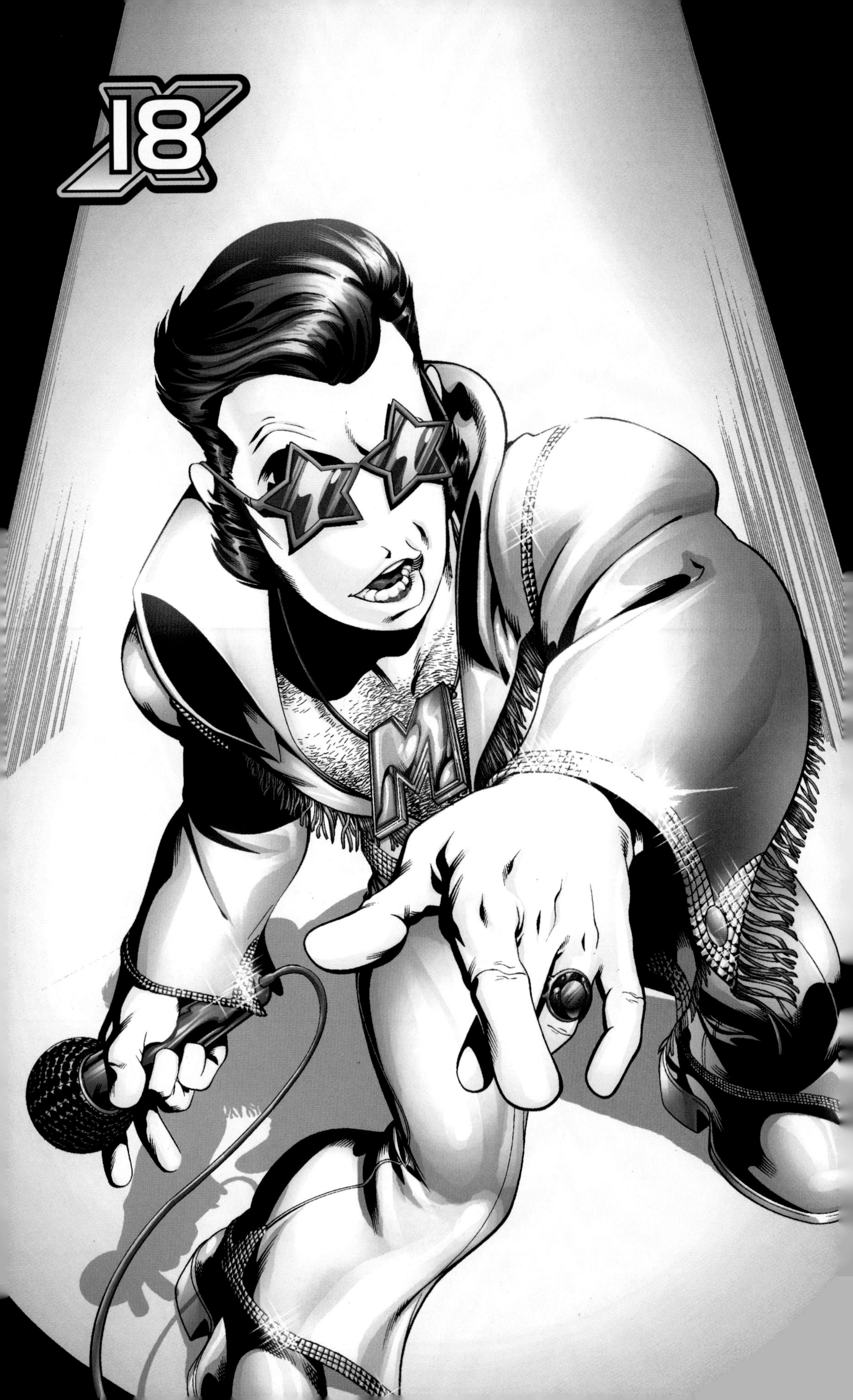
18

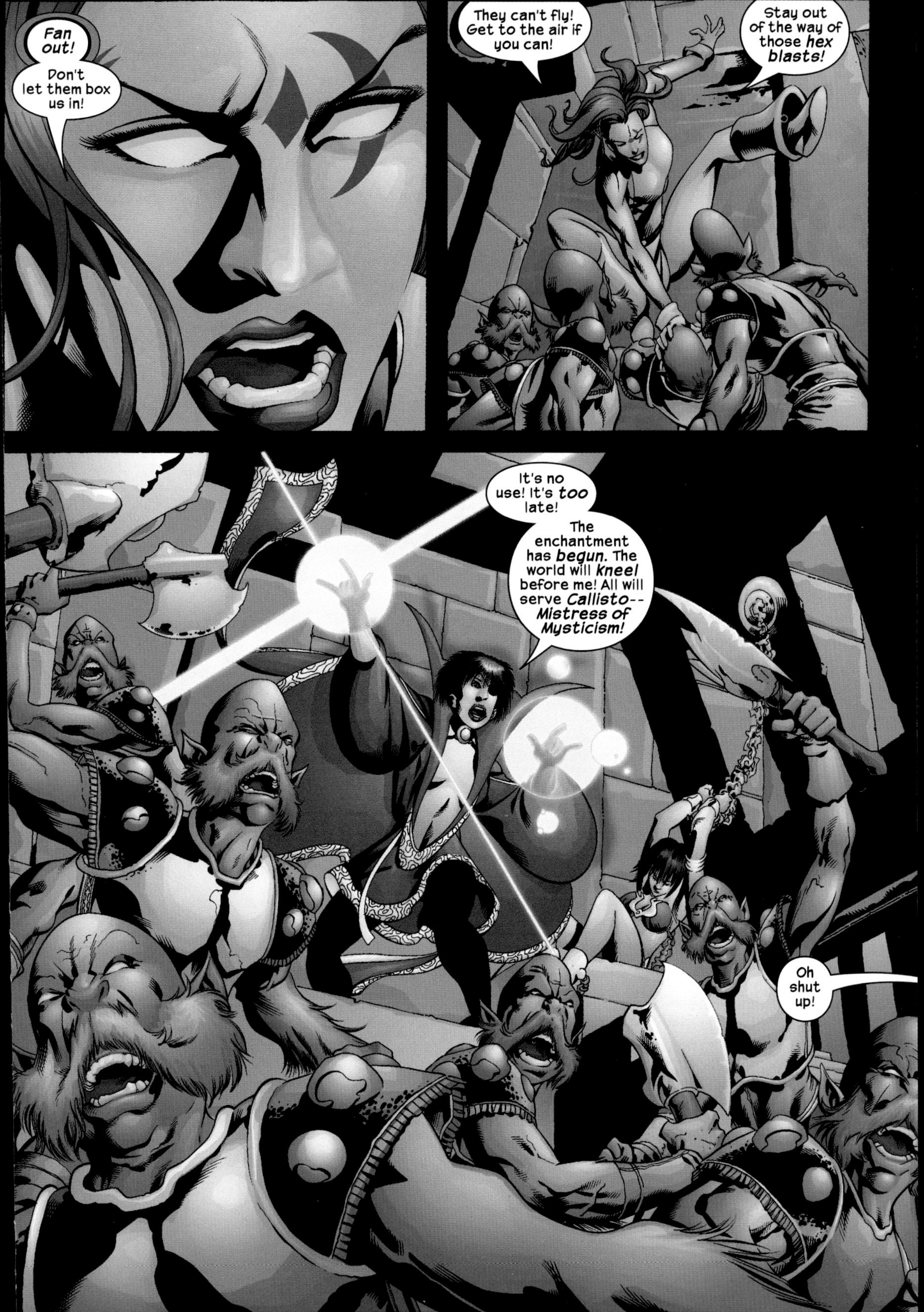
Fan out!
Don't let them box us in!
They can't fly! Get to the air if you can!
Stay out of the way of those hex blasts!
It's no use! It's too late!
The enchantment has begun. The world will kneel before me! All will serve Callisto-- Mistress of Mysticism!
Oh shut up!

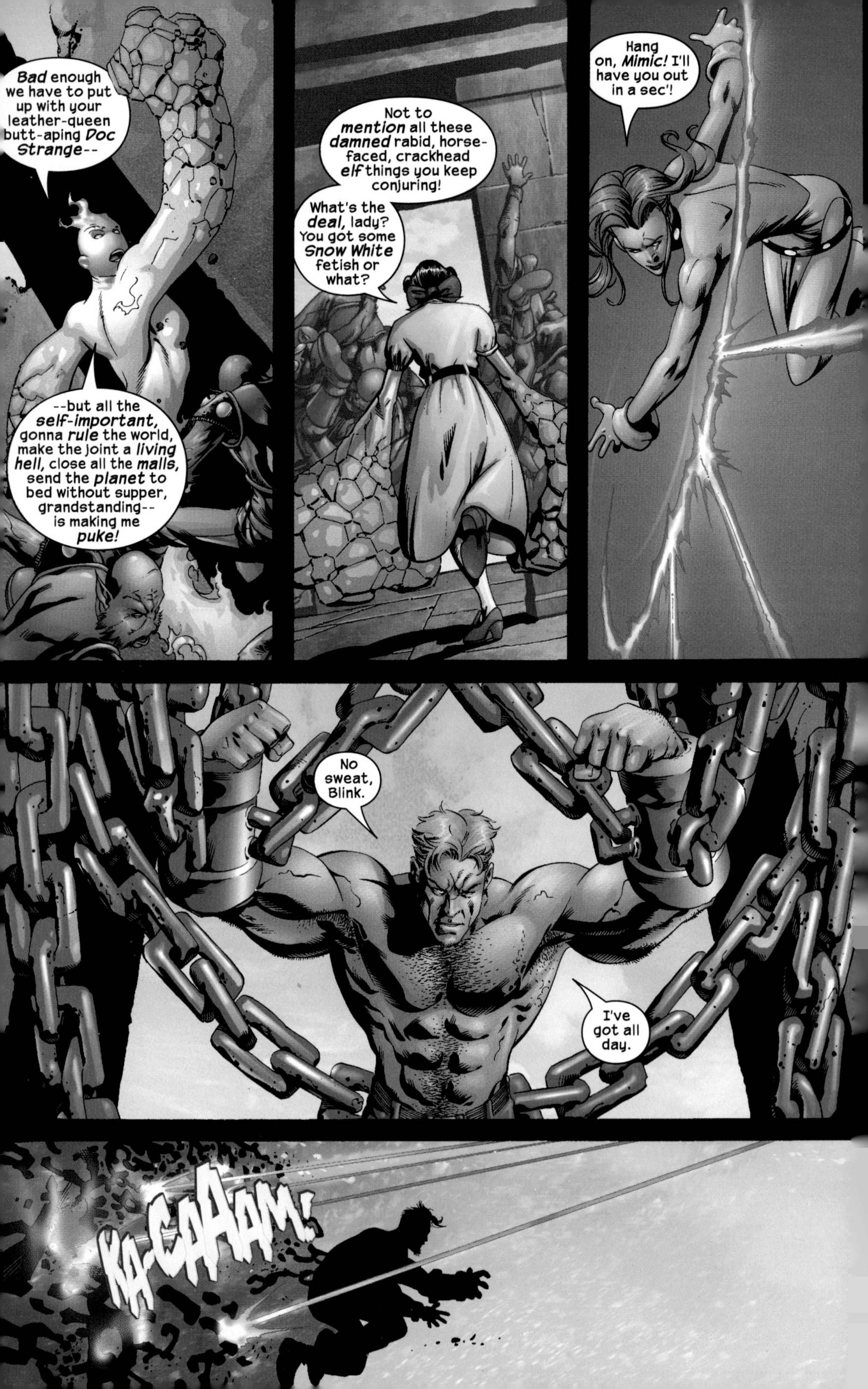

Bad enough we have to put up with your leather-queen butt-aping Doc Strange--
--but all the self-important, gonna rule the world, make the joint a living hell, close all the malls, send the planet to bed without supper, grandstanding-- is making me puke!
Not to mention all these damned rabid, horse-faced, crackhead elf things you keep conjuring!
What's the deal, lady? You got some Snow White fetish or what?
Hang on, Mimic! I'll have you out in a sec'!
No sweat, Blink.
I've got all day.
KA-CHAAM!

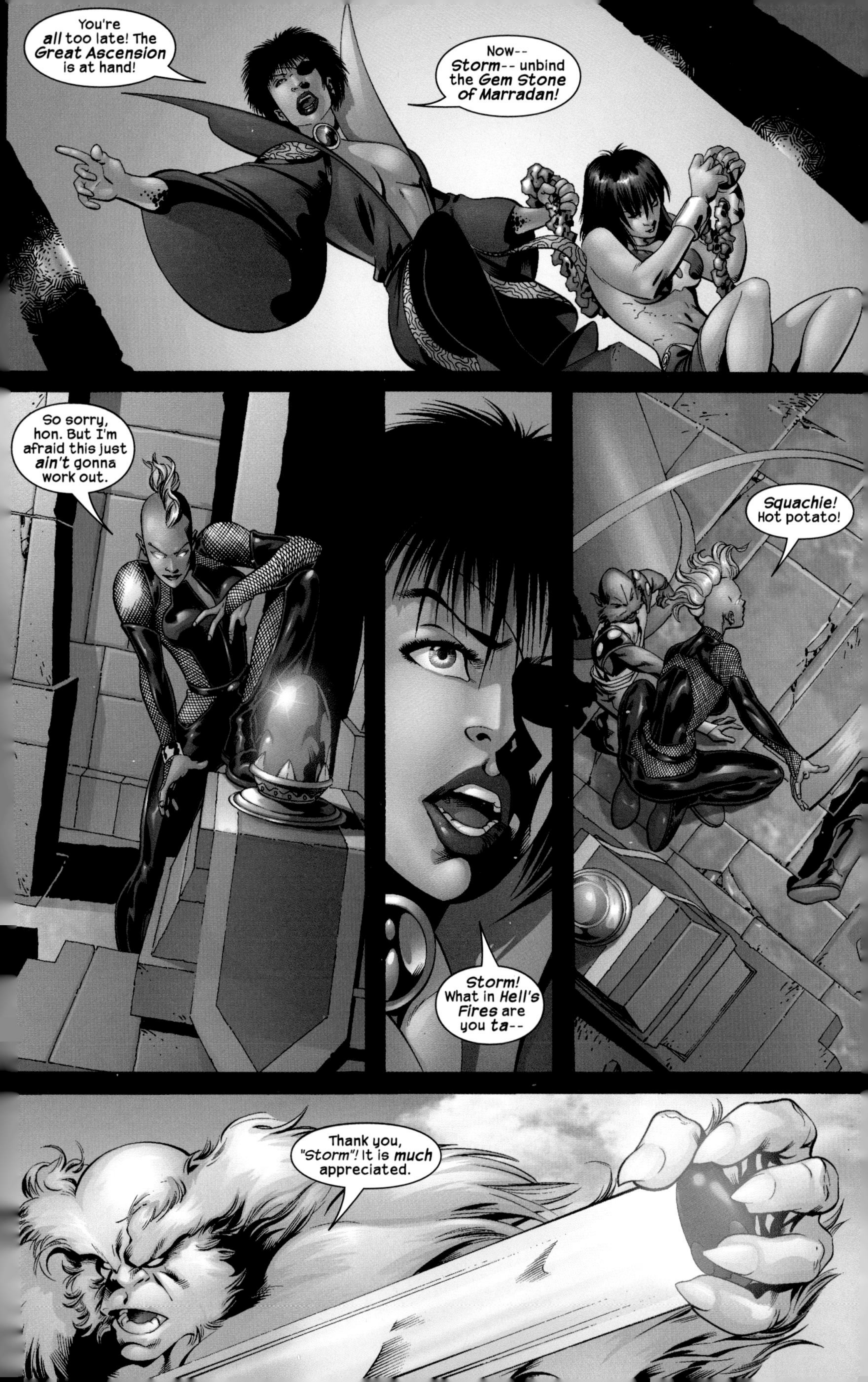
You're *all* too late! The *Great Ascension* is at hand!
Now-- *Storm*-- unbind the *Gem Stone of Marradan!*
So sorry, hon. But I'm afraid this just *ain't* gonna work out.
Storm! What in *Hell's Fires* are you *ta*--
Squachie! Hot potato!
Thank you, "*Storm*"! It is *much* appreciated.

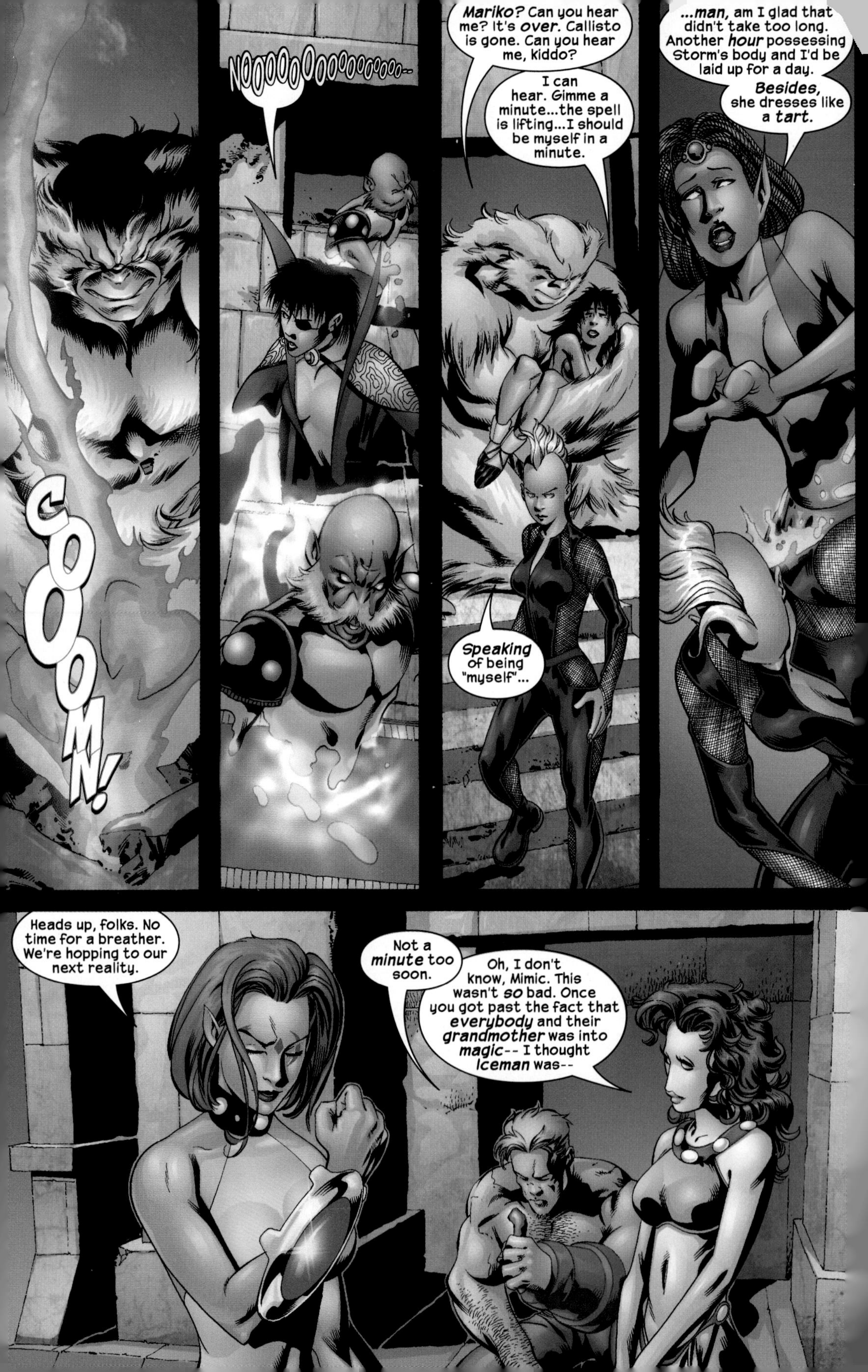

COOOOMN!
NOOOOOOOOOOOOOOOO--
Mariko? Can you hear me? It's over. Callisto is gone. Can you hear me, kiddo?
I can hear. Gimme a minute...the spell is lifting...I should be myself in a minute.
Speaking of being "myself"...
...man, am I glad that didn't take too long. Another hour possessing Storm's body and I'd be laid up for a day.
Besides, she dresses like a tart.
Heads up, folks. No time for a breather. We're hopping to our next reality.
Not a minute too soon.
Oh, I don't know, Mimic. This wasn't so bad. Once you got past the fact that everybody and their grandmother was into magic-- I thought Iceman was--

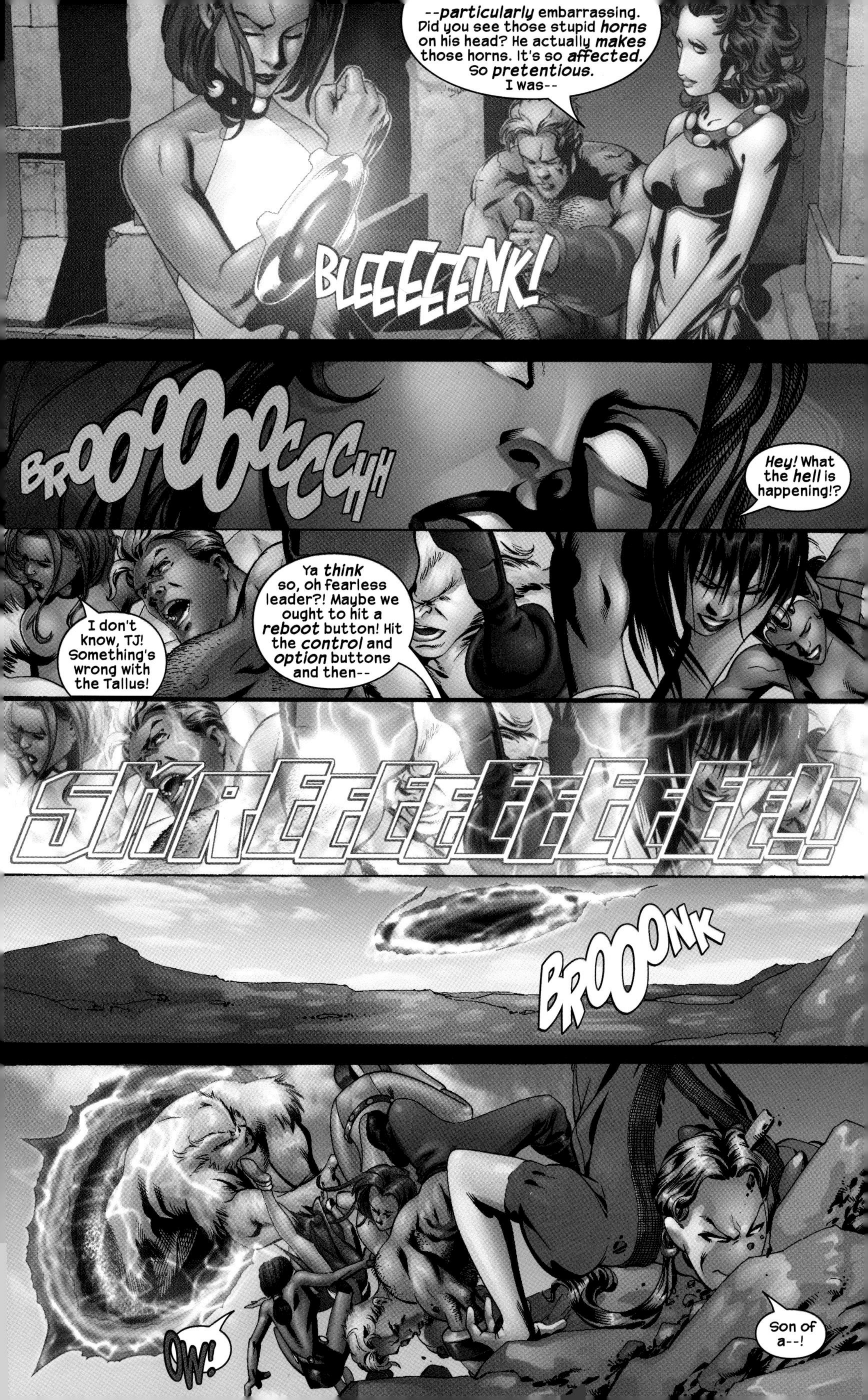
--particularly embarrassing. Did you see those stupid horns on his head? He actually makes those horns. It's so affected. So pretentious. I was--
BLEEEEEENK!
BROOOOOOCCHH
Hey! What the hell is happening!?
I don't know, TJ! Something's wrong with the Tallus!
Ya think so, oh fearless leader?! Maybe we ought to hit a reboot button! Hit the control and option buttons and then--
SHREEEEEEEEEEEEE!
BROOOONK
OW!
Son of a--!

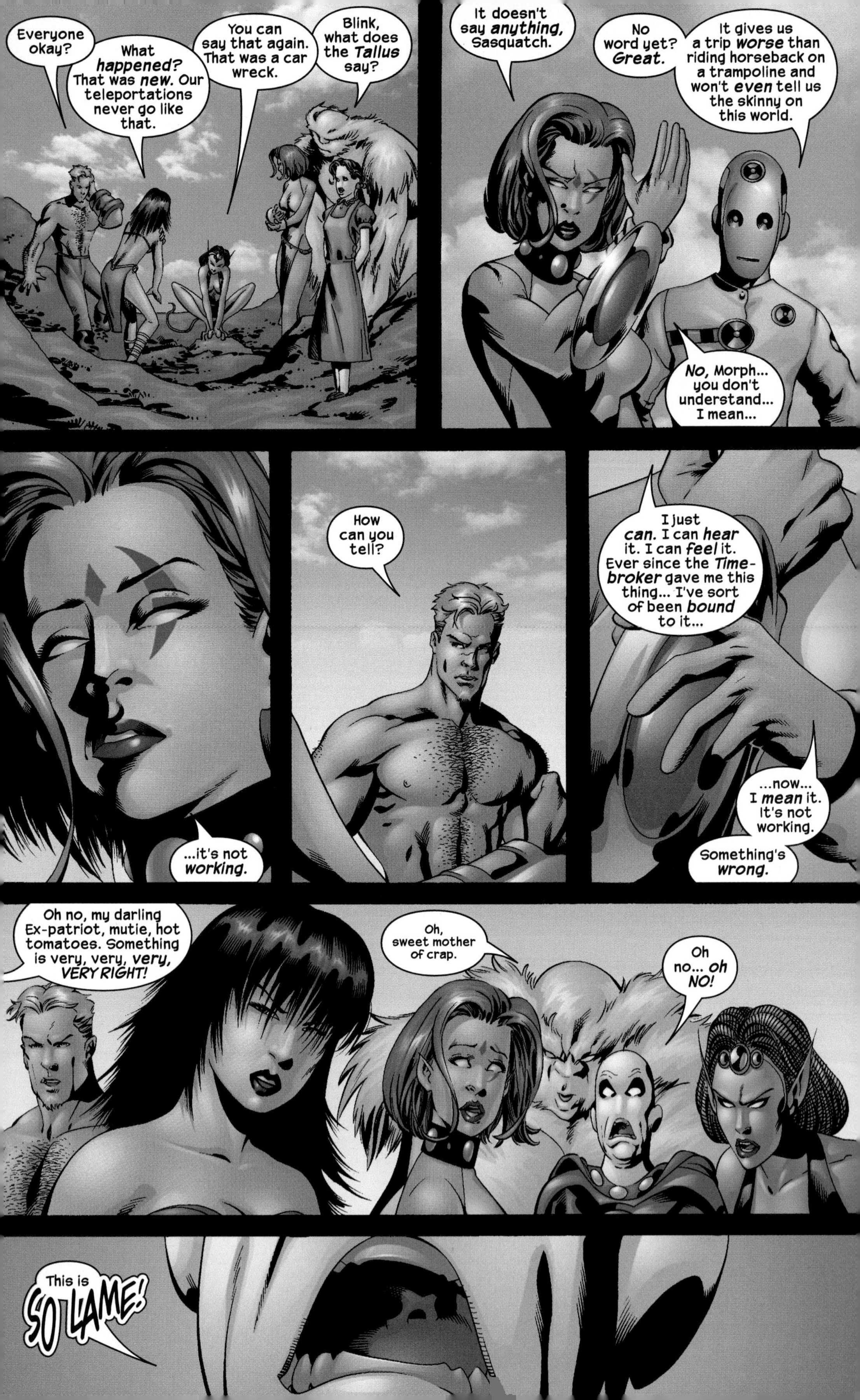
Everyone okay?
What *happened?* That was *new.* Our teleportations never go like that.
You can say that again. That was a car wreck.
Blink, what does the *Tallus* say?
It doesn't say *anything,* Sasquatch.
No word yet? *Great.*
It gives us a trip *worse* than riding horseback on a trampoline and won't *even* tell us the skinny on this world.
No, Morph... you don't understand... I mean...
...it's not *working.*
How can you tell?
I just *can.* I can *hear* it. I can *feel* it. Ever since the *Time-broker* gave me this thing... I've sort of been *bound* to it...
...now... I *mean* it. It's not working.
Something's *wrong.*
Oh no, my darling Ex-patriot, mutie, hot tomatoes. Something is very, very, *very, VERY RIGHT!*
Oh, sweet mother of crap.
Oh no... *oh NO!*
This is SO LAME!

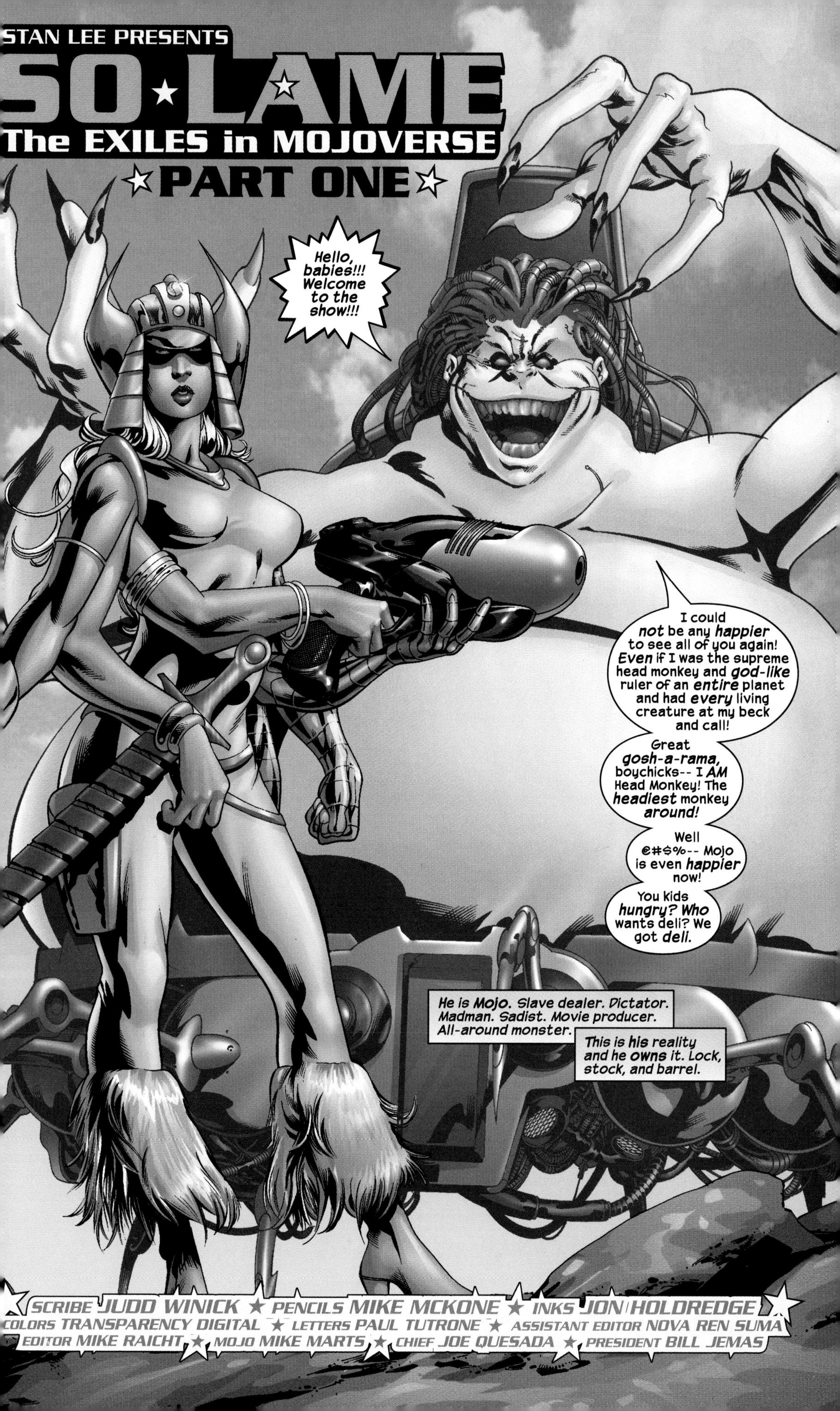
STAN LEE PRESENTS
SO★LAME
The EXILES in MOJOVERSE
★PART ONE★
Hello, babies!!! Welcome to the show!!!
I could not be any happier to see all of you again! Even if I was the supreme head monkey and god-like ruler of an entire planet and had every living creature at my beck and call!
Great gosh-a-rama, boychicks-- I AM Head Monkey! The headiest monkey around!
Well @#$%-- Mojo is even happier now!
You kids hungry? Who wants deli? We got deli.
He is Mojo. Slave dealer. Dictator. Madman. Sadist. Movie producer. All-around monster.
This is his reality and he owns it. Lock, stock, and barrel.
SCRIBE JUDD WINICK ★ PENCILS MIKE MCKONE ★ INKS JON HOLDREDGE
COLORS TRANSPARENCY DIGITAL ★ LETTERS PAUL TUTRONE ★ ASSISTANT EDITOR NOVA REN SUMA
EDITOR MIKE RAICHT ★ MOJO MIKE MARTS ★ CHIEF JOE QUESADA ★ PRESIDENT BILL JEMAS

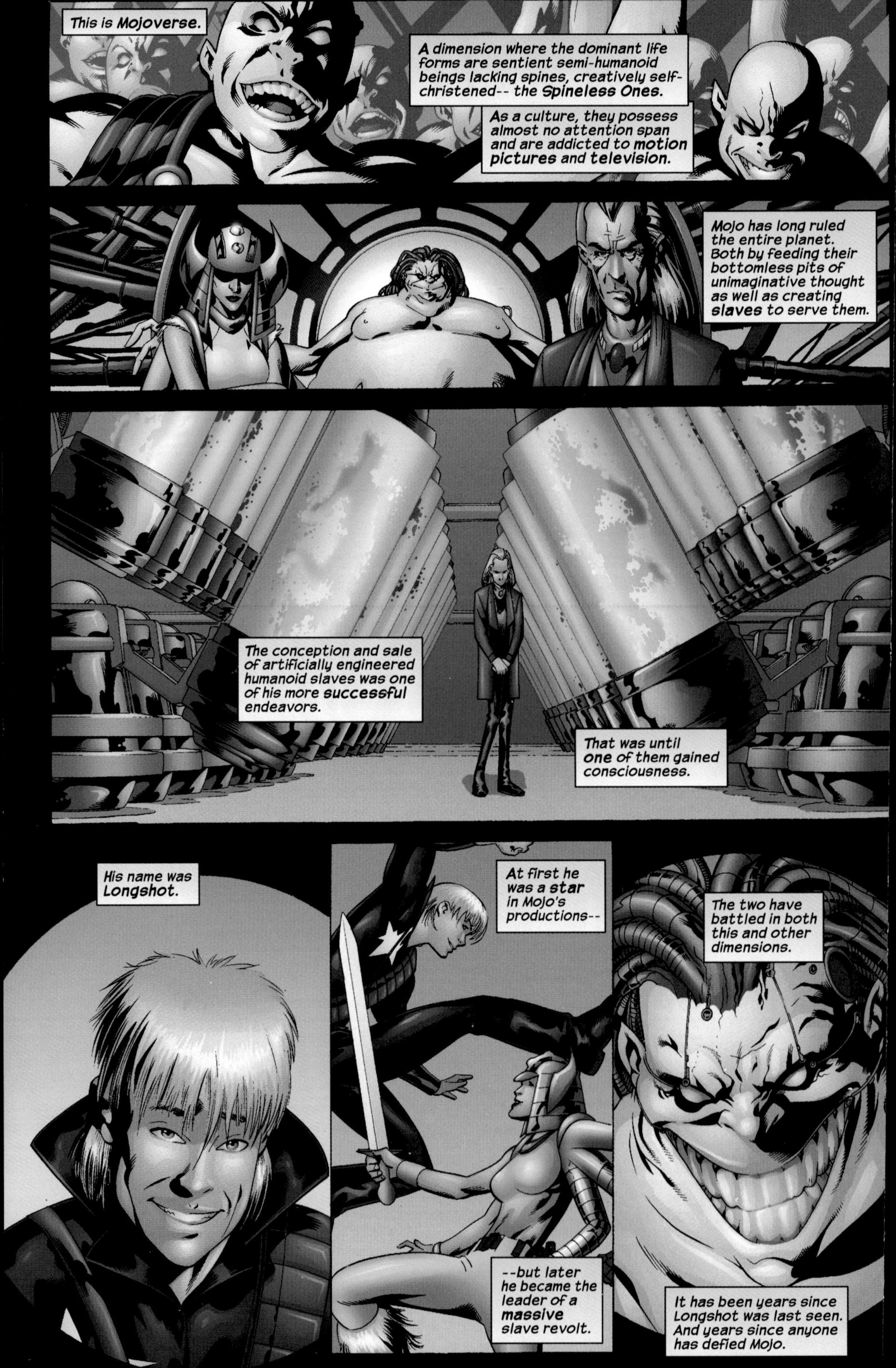

This is Mojoverse.
A dimension where the dominant life forms are sentient semi-humanoid beings lacking spines, creatively self-christened-- the Spineless Ones.
As a culture, they possess almost no attention span and are addicted to motion pictures and television.
Mojo has long ruled the entire planet. Both by feeding their bottomless pits of unimaginative thought as well as creating slaves to serve them.
The conception and sale of artificially engineered humanoid slaves was one of his more successful endeavors.
That was until one of them gained consciousness.
His name was Longshot.
At first he was a star in Mojo's productions--
--but later he became the leader of a massive slave revolt.
The two have battled in both this and other dimensions.
It has been years since Longshot was last seen. And years since anyone has defied Mojo.

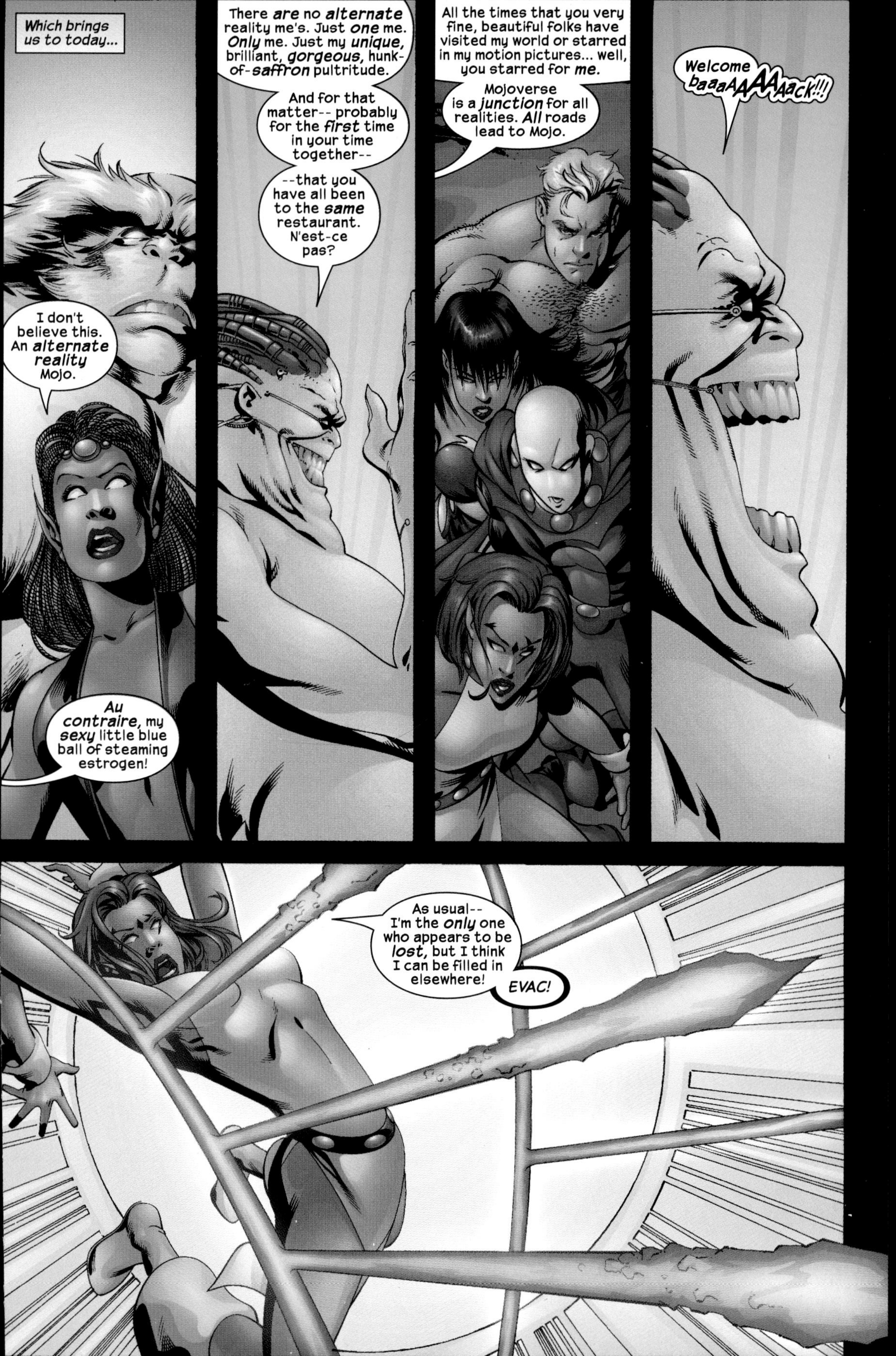

Which brings us to today...
I don't believe this. An alternate reality Mojo.
Au contraire, my sexy little blue ball of steaming estrogen!
There are no alternate reality me's. Just one me. Only me. Just my unique, brilliant, gorgeous, hunk-of-saffron pultritude.
And for that matter-- probably for the first time in your time together--
--that you have all been to the same restaurant. N'est-ce pas?
All the times that you very fine, beautiful folks have visited my world or starred in my motion pictures... well, you starred for me.
Mojoverse is a junction for all realities. All roads lead to Mojo.
Welcome baaaAAAAAack!!!
As usual-- I'm the only one who appears to be lost, but I think I can be filled in elsewhere!
EVAC!

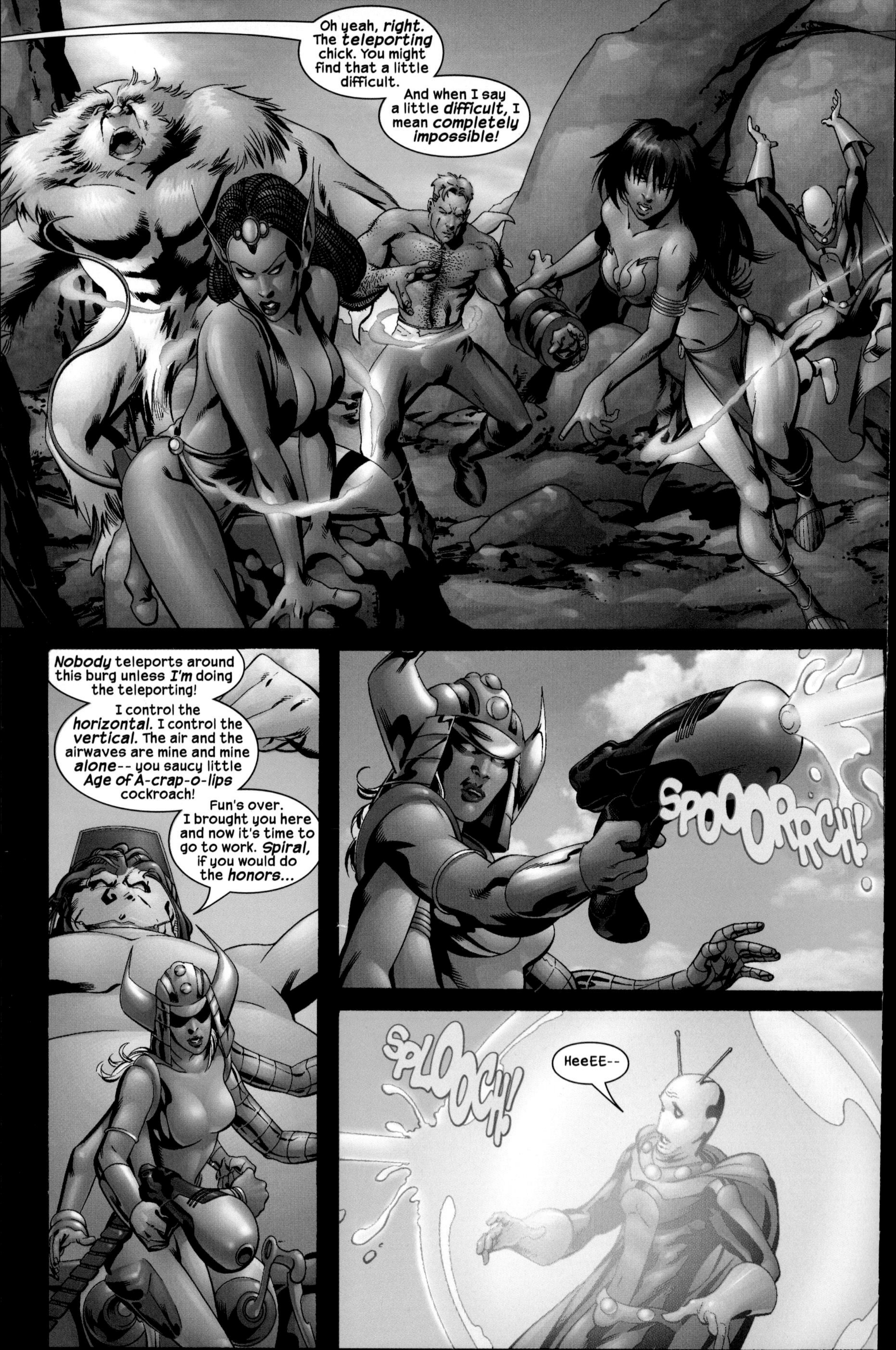

Oh yeah, *right*. The *teleporting* chick. You might find that a little difficult.
And when I say a little *difficult*, I mean *completely impossible!*
Nobody teleports around this burg unless *I'm* doing the teleporting!
I control the *horizontal*. I control the *vertical*. The air and the airwaves are mine and mine *alone*-- you saucy little *Age of A-crap-o-lips* cockroach!
Fun's over. I brought you here and now it's time to go to work. *Spiral*, if you would do the *honors*...
SPOOORRCH!
SPLOOCH!
HeeEE--

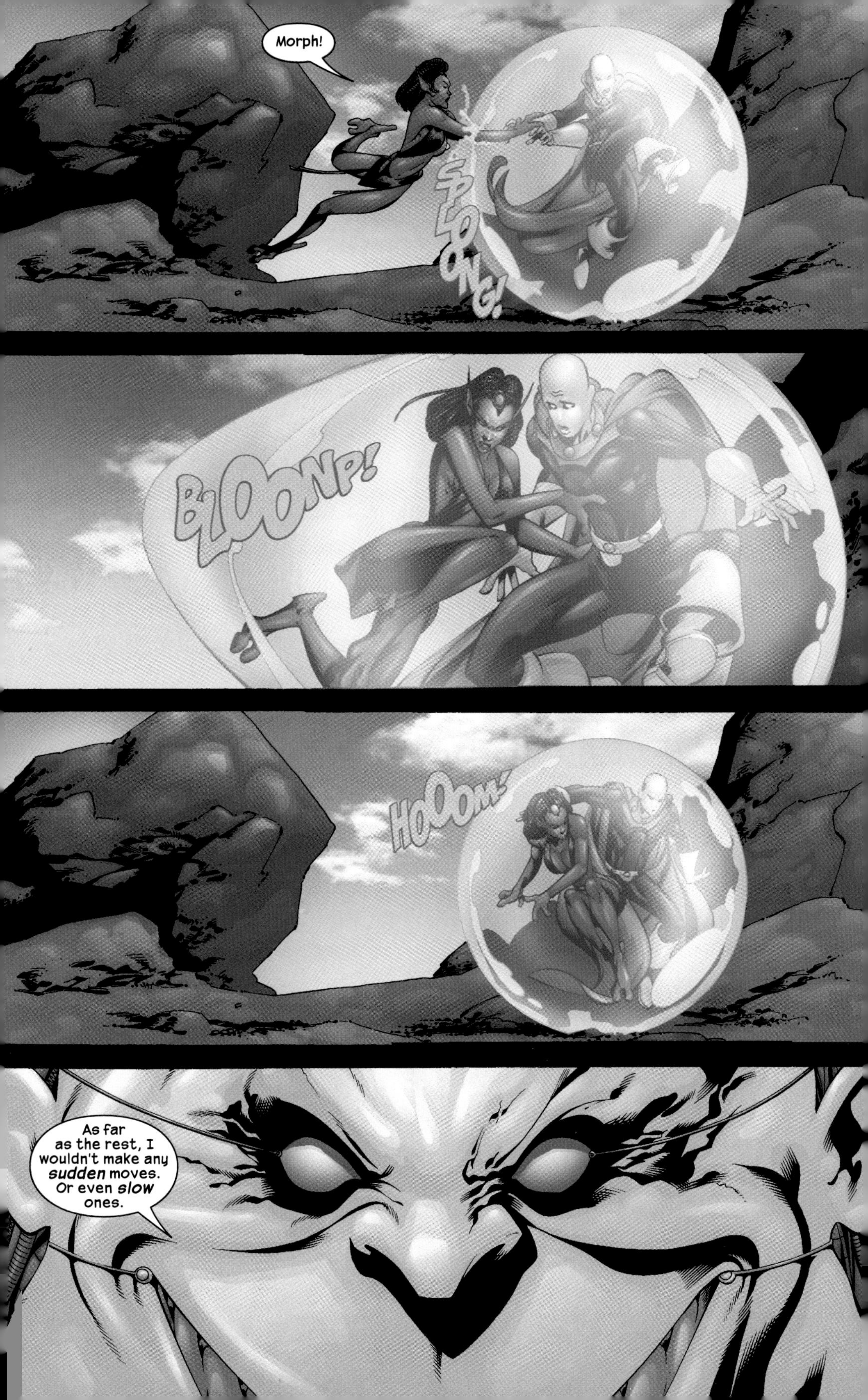
Morph!
SPLOONG!
BLOONP!
HOOOM!
As far as the rest, I wouldn't make any *sudden* moves. Or even *slow* ones.

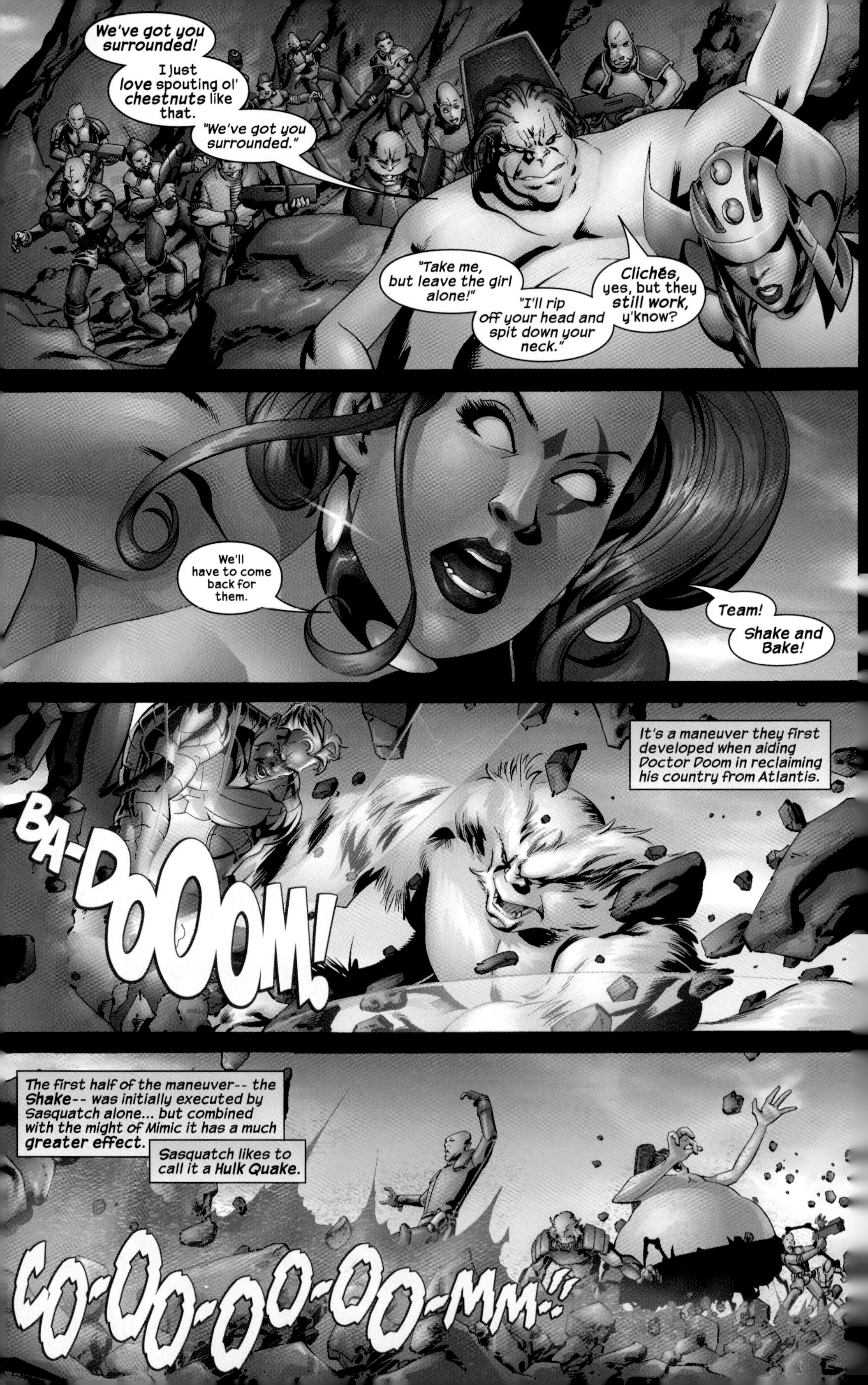
We've got you surrounded!
I just love spouting ol' chestnuts like that.
"We've got you surrounded."
"Take me, but leave the girl alone!"
"I'll rip off your head and spit down your neck."
Clichés, yes, but they still work, y'know?
We'll have to come back for them.
Team!
Shake and Bake!
It's a maneuver they first developed when aiding Doctor Doom in reclaiming his country from Atlantis.
BA-DOOOM!
The first half of the maneuver-- the Shake-- was initially executed by Sasquatch alone... but combined with the might of Mimic it has a much greater effect.
Sasquatch likes to call it a Hulk Quake.
GO-OO-OO-OO-OO-MM!!

The Bake is handled by Sunfire.

HOOOOOOAARA!

How are we going to get Sunfire out if Blink can't 'port?

Keep your head down!

I'll get her.

BWOOOAARR

Still so *weak* from the sorcery planet. I don't know if I can-- can pull this off.

Spiral! You spider-limbed cow-- *teleport* after them!

You've *jammed* all teleportation within a mile of your bloated corpulence, "Sire".

You were worried about the pink elf-girl.

We need to fall back now before we're *all* fried. You've *got* what you want!

C'mon, Mariko-- just... stay... *conscious*... a minute... longer... the army will fall back... please... *please*-- let them fall back...

FWASSHHH

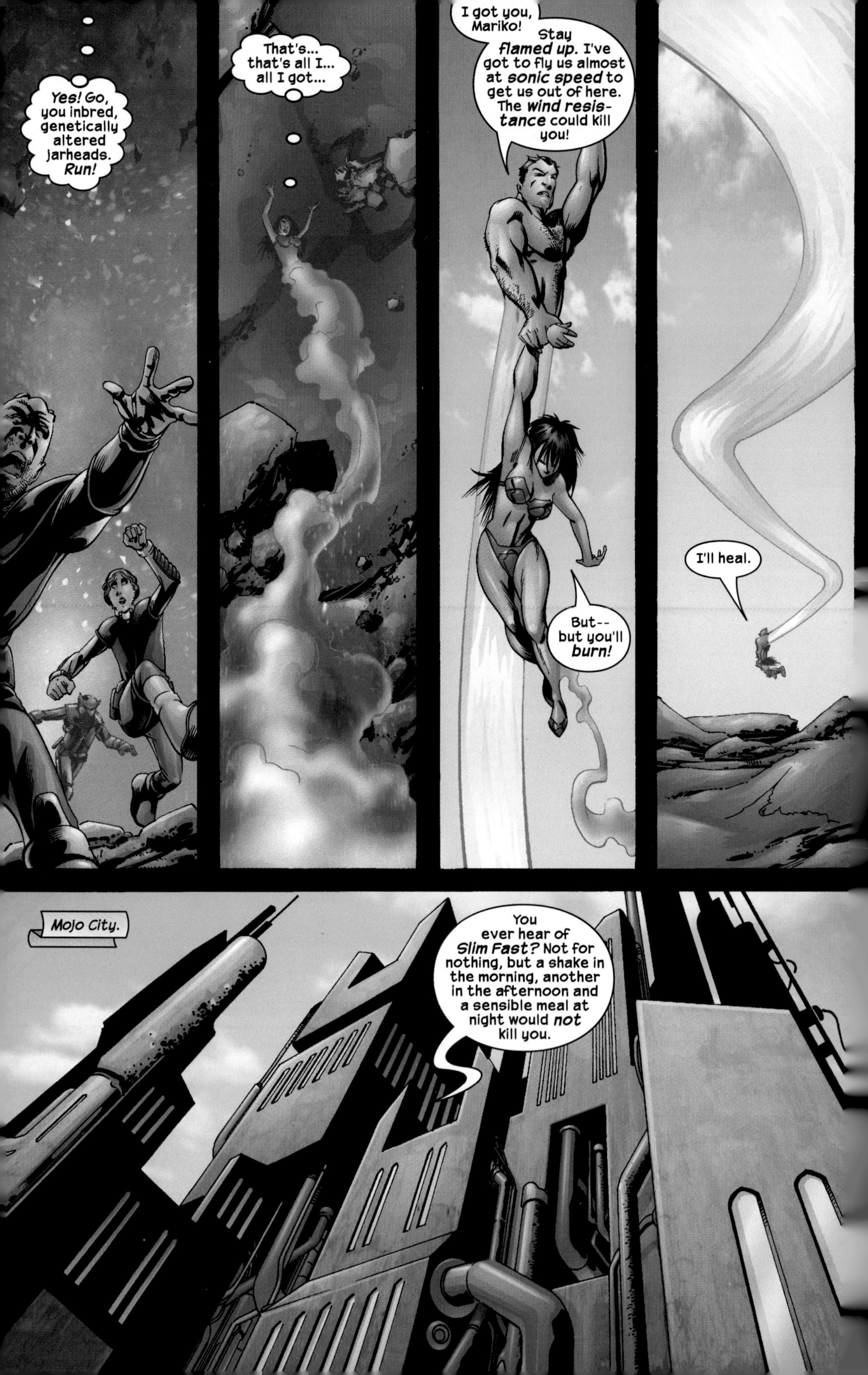
Yes! Go, you inbred, genetically altered jarheads. Run!
That's... that's all I... all I got...
I got you, Mariko!
Stay flamed up. I've got to fly us almost at sonic speed to get us out of here. The wind resistance could kill you!
But-- but you'll burn!
I'll heal.
Mojo City.
You ever hear of Slim Fast? Not for nothing, but a shake in the morning, another in the afternoon and a sensible meal at night would not kill you.

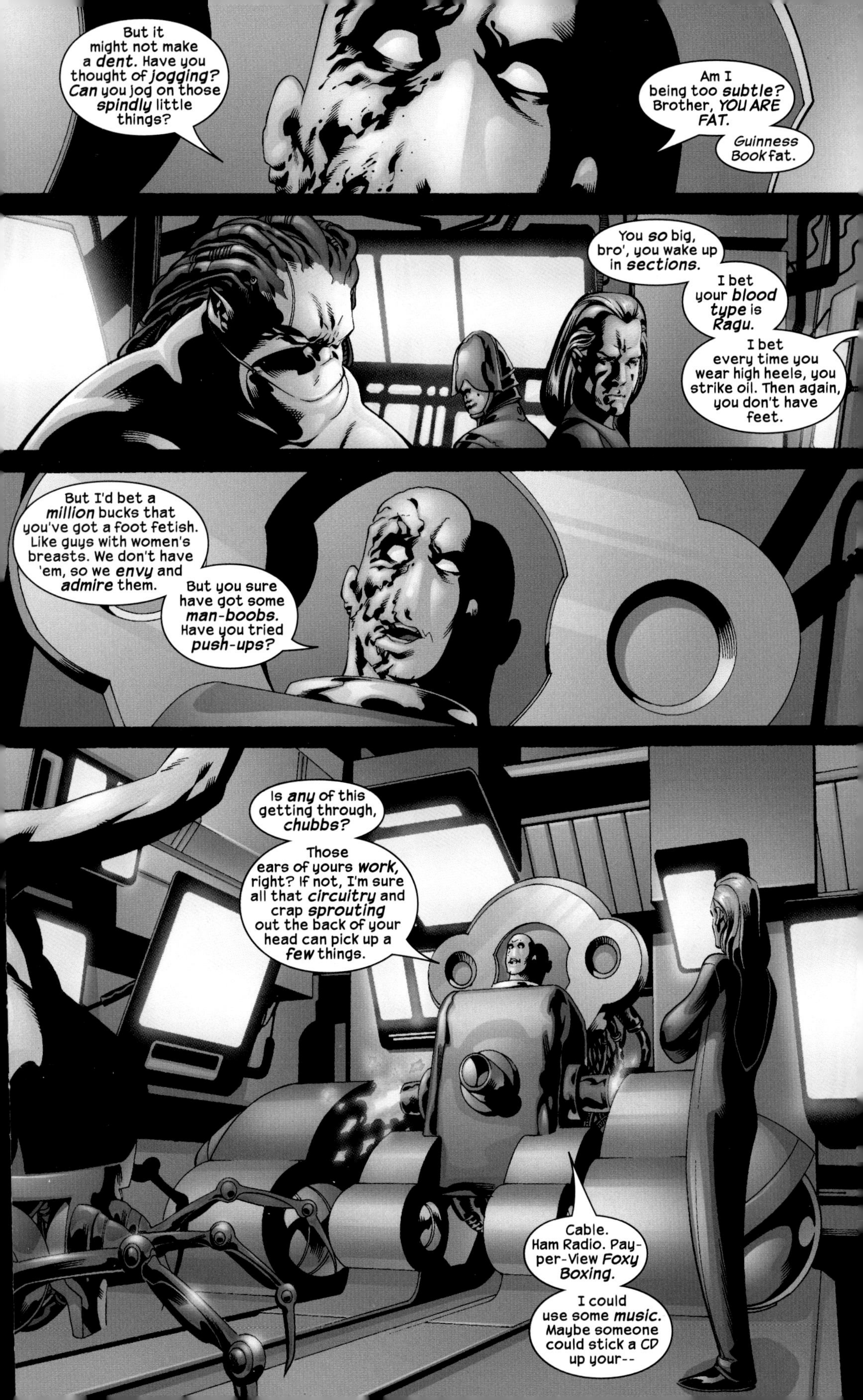
But it might not make a dent. Have you thought of jogging? Can you jog on those spindly little things?
Am I being too subtle? Brother, YOU ARE FAT.
Guinness Book fat.
You so big, bro', you wake up in sections.
I bet your blood type is Ragu.
I bet every time you wear high heels, you strike oil. Then again, you don't have feet.
But I'd bet a million bucks that you've got a foot fetish. Like guys with women's breasts. We don't have 'em, so we envy and admire them.
But you sure have got some man-boobs. Have you tried push-ups?
Is any of this getting through, chubbs?
Those ears of yours work, right? If not, I'm sure all that circuitry and crap sprouting out the back of your head can pick up a few things.
Cable. Ham Radio. Pay-per-View Foxy Boxing.
I could use some music. Maybe someone could stick a CD up your--

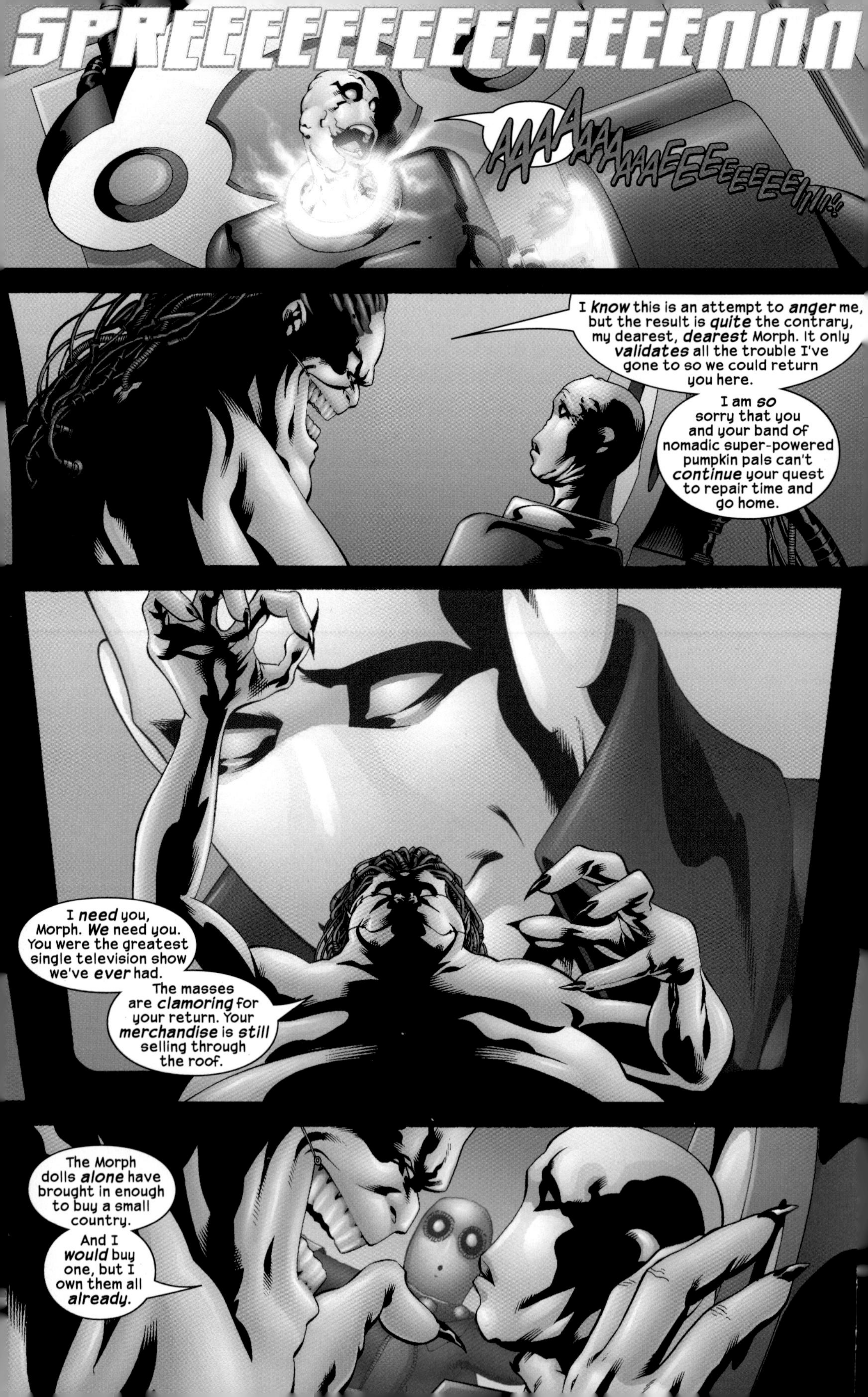
SPREEEEEEEEEEEEEENNN
AAAAAAAAAAAEEEEEEEEEEIIII!!
I *know* this is an attempt to *anger* me, but the result is *quite* the contrary, my dearest, *dearest* Morph. It only *validates* all the trouble I've gone to so we could return you here.
I am *so* sorry that you and your band of nomadic super-powered pumpkin pals can't *continue* your quest to repair time and go home.
I *need* you, Morph. *We* need you. You were the greatest single television show we've *ever* had.
The masses are *clamoring* for your return. Your *merchandise* is *still* selling through the roof.
The Morph dolls *alone* have brought in enough to buy a small country.
And I *would* buy one, but I own them all *already*.

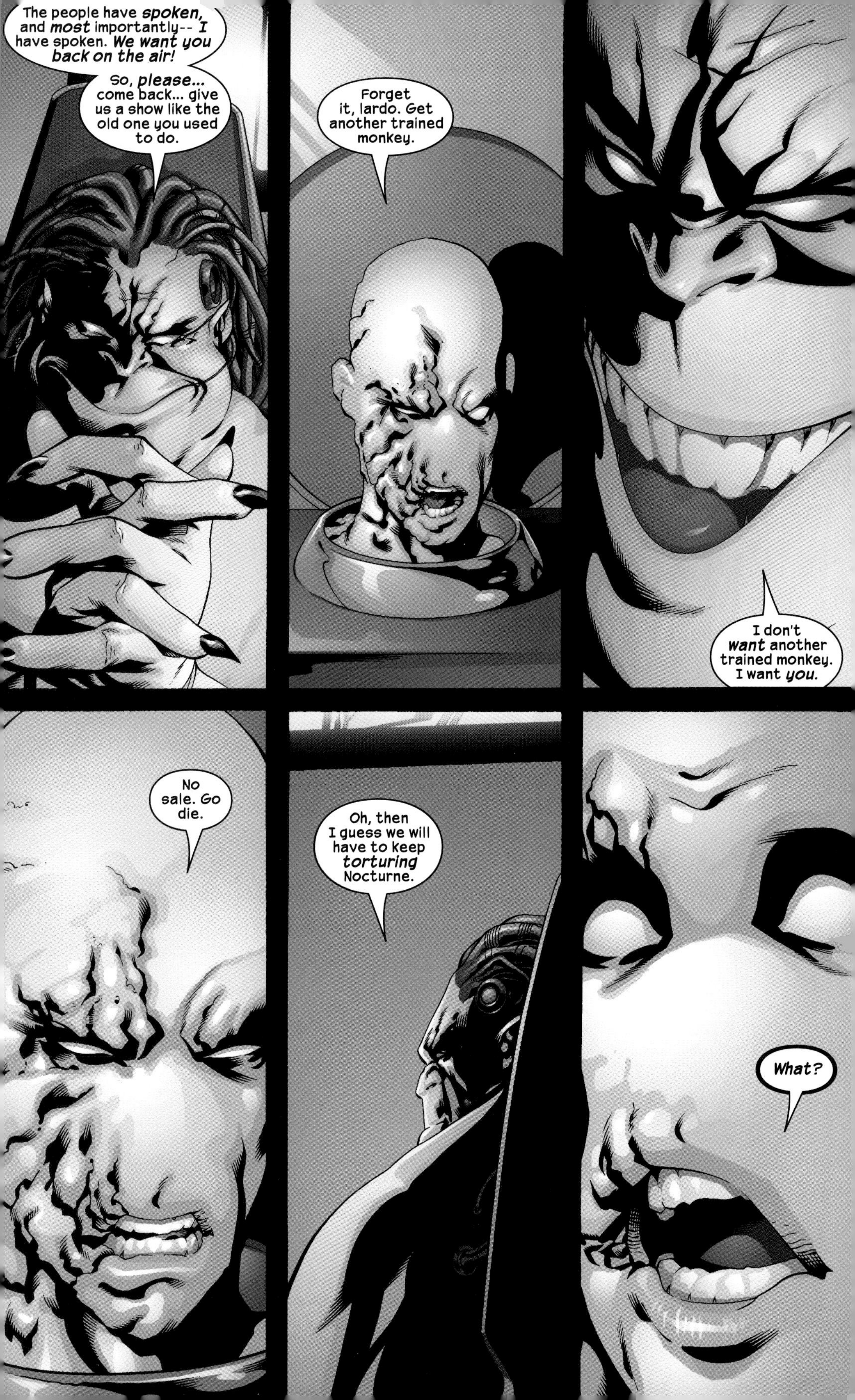

The people have *spoken*, and *most* importantly-- *I* have spoken. *We want you back on the air!*
So, *please*... come back... give us a show like the old one you used to do.
Forget it, lardo. Get another trained monkey.
I don't *want* another trained monkey. I want *you*.
No sale. Go die.
Oh, then I guess we will have to keep *torturing* Nocturne.
What?

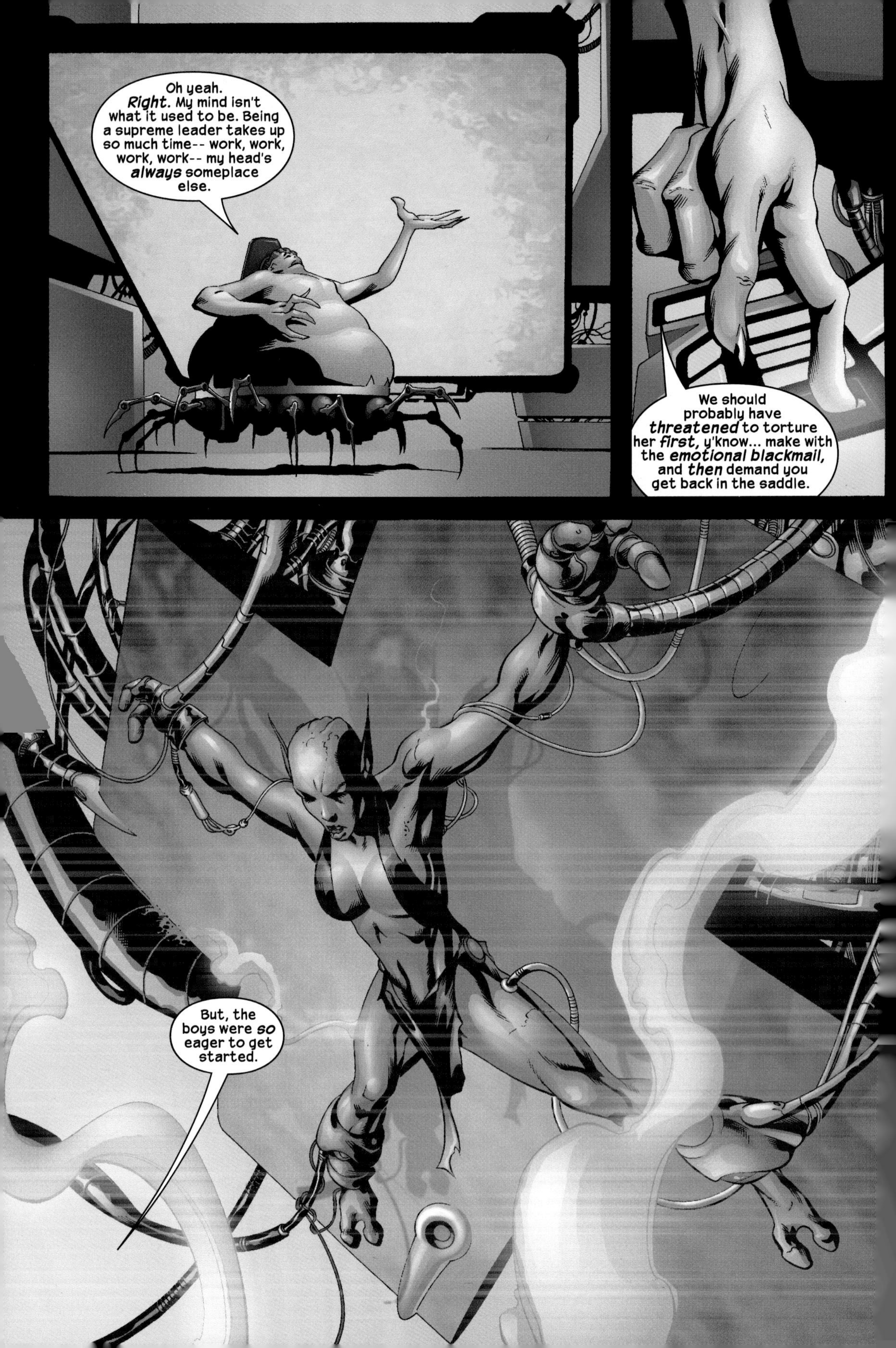
Oh yeah. Right. My mind isn't what it used to be. Being a supreme leader takes up so much time-- work, work, work, work-- my head's always someplace else.
We should probably have threatened to torture her first, y'know... make with the emotional blackmail, and then demand you get back in the saddle.
But, the boys were so eager to get started.

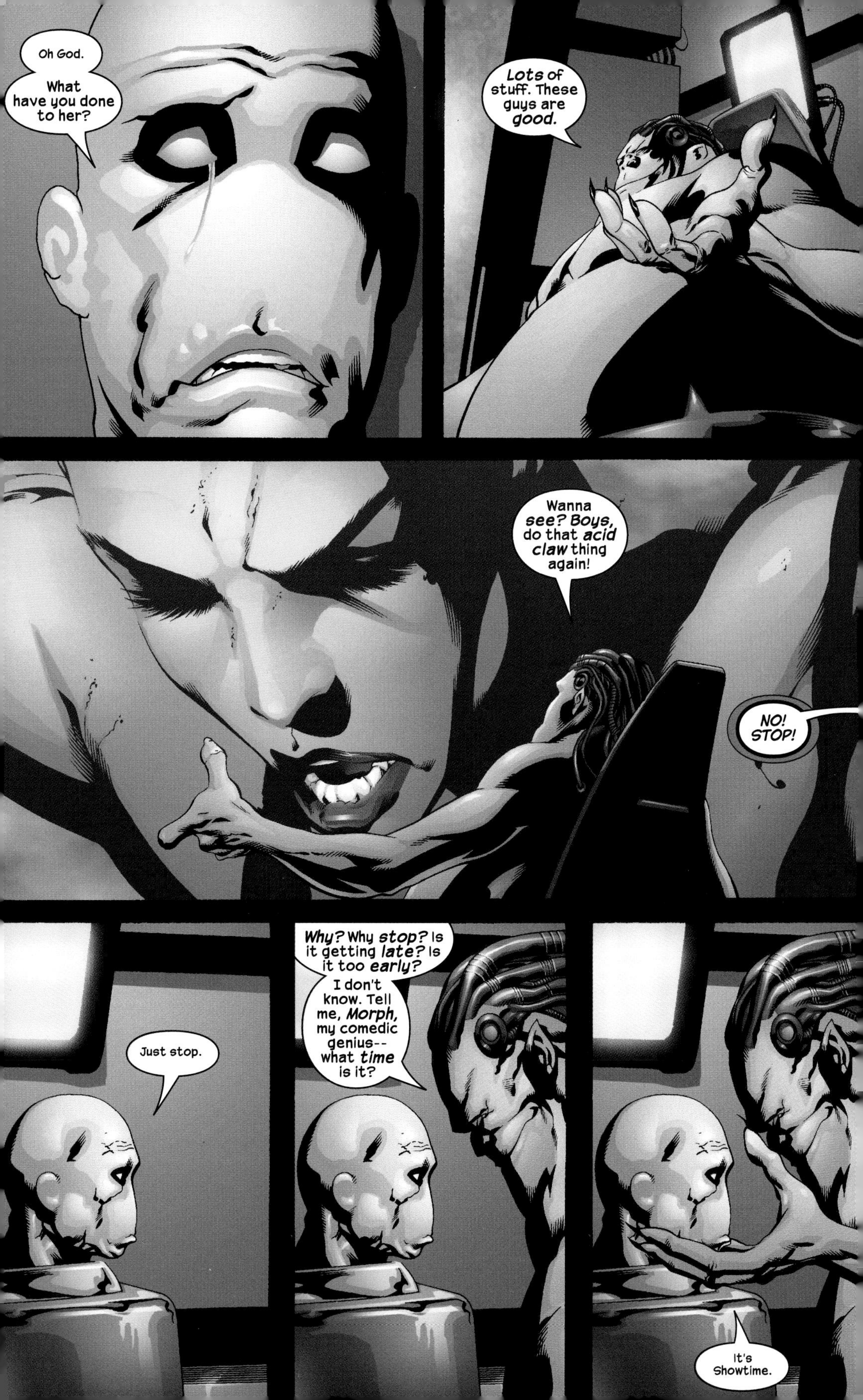
Oh God.
What have you done to her?
Lots of stuff. These guys are good.
Wanna see? Boys, do that acid claw thing again!
NO! STOP!
Just stop.
Why? Why stop? Is it getting late? Is it too early?
I don't know. Tell me, Morph, my comedic genius--what time is it?
It's Showtime.

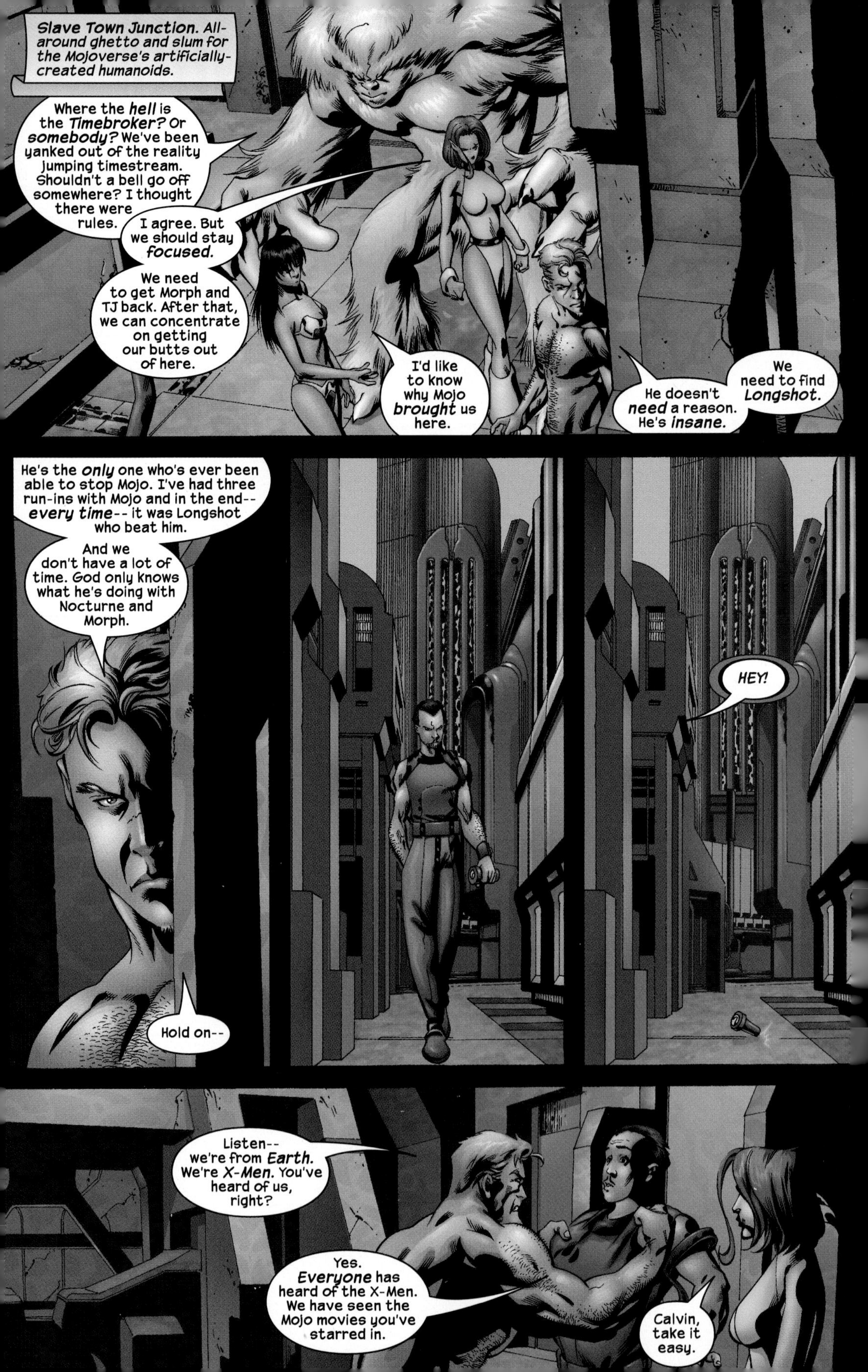
Slave Town Junction. All-around ghetto and slum for the Mojoverse's artificially-created humanoids.
Where the hell is the Timebroker? Or somebody? We've been yanked out of the reality jumping timestream. Shouldn't a bell go off somewhere? I thought there were rules.
I agree. But we should stay focused.
We need to get Morph and TJ back. After that, we can concentrate on getting our butts out of here.
I'd like to know why Mojo brought us here.
He doesn't need a reason. He's insane.
We need to find Longshot.
He's the only one who's ever been able to stop Mojo. I've had three run-ins with Mojo and in the end-- every time-- it was Longshot who beat him.
And we don't have a lot of time. God only knows what he's doing with Nocturne and Morph.
Hold on--
HEY!
Listen-- we're from Earth. We're X-Men. You've heard of us, right?
Yes. Everyone has heard of the X-Men. We have seen the Mojo movies you've starred in.
Calvin, take it easy.

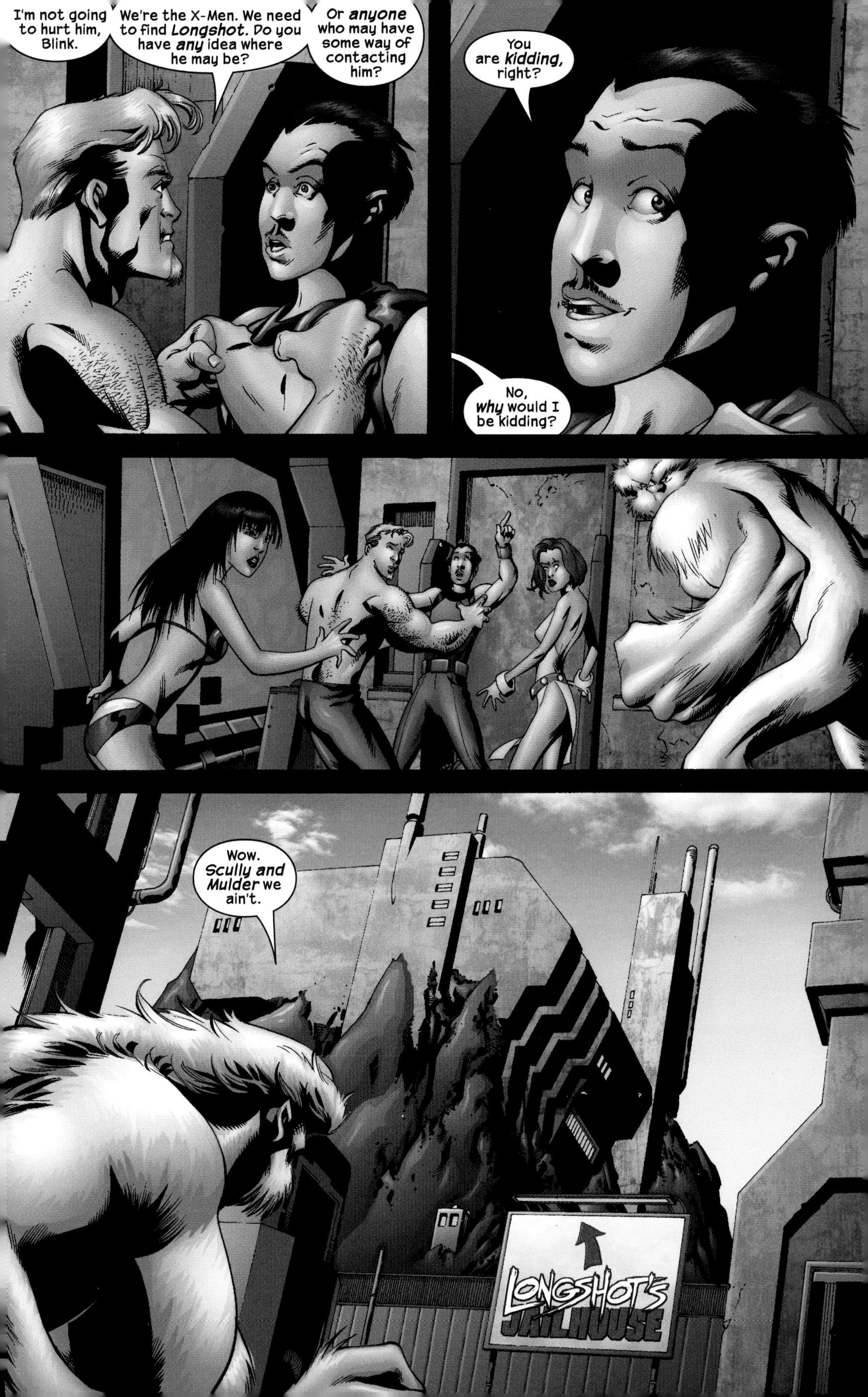
I'm not going to hurt him, Blink.
We're the X-Men. We need to find *Longshot.* Do you have *any* idea where he may be?
Or *anyone* who may have some way of contacting him?
You are *kidding,* right?
No, *why* would I be kidding?
Wow. *Scully and Mulder* we ain't.
LONGSHOT'S JAILHOUSE

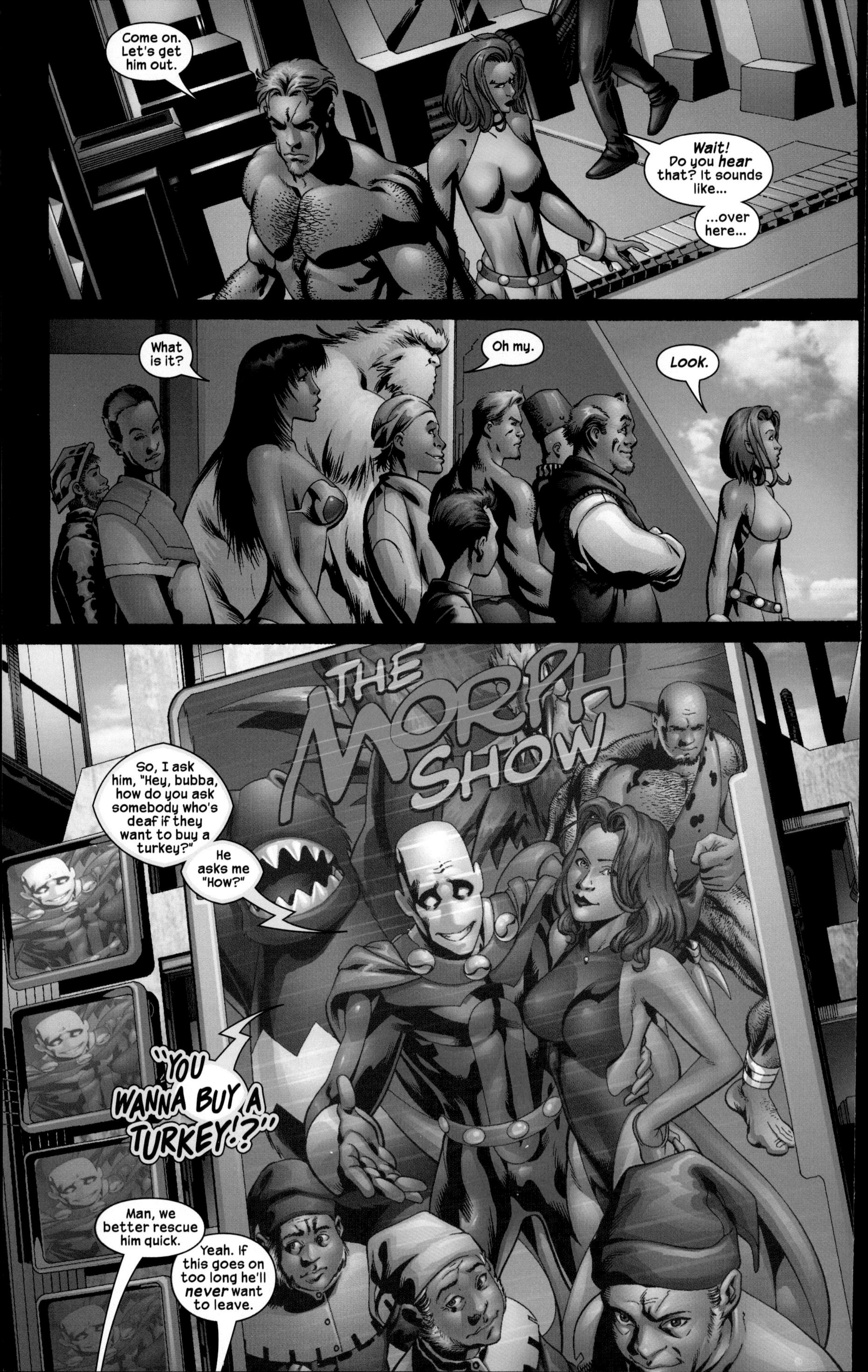
Come on. Let's get him out.
Wait! Do you hear that? It sounds like...
...over here...
What is it?
Oh my.
Look.
THE MORPH SHOW
So, I ask him, "Hey, bubba, how do you ask somebody who's deaf if they want to buy a turkey?"
He asks me "How?"
"YOU WANNA BUY A TURKEY!?"
Man, we better rescue him quick.
Yeah. If this goes on too long he'll never want to leave.

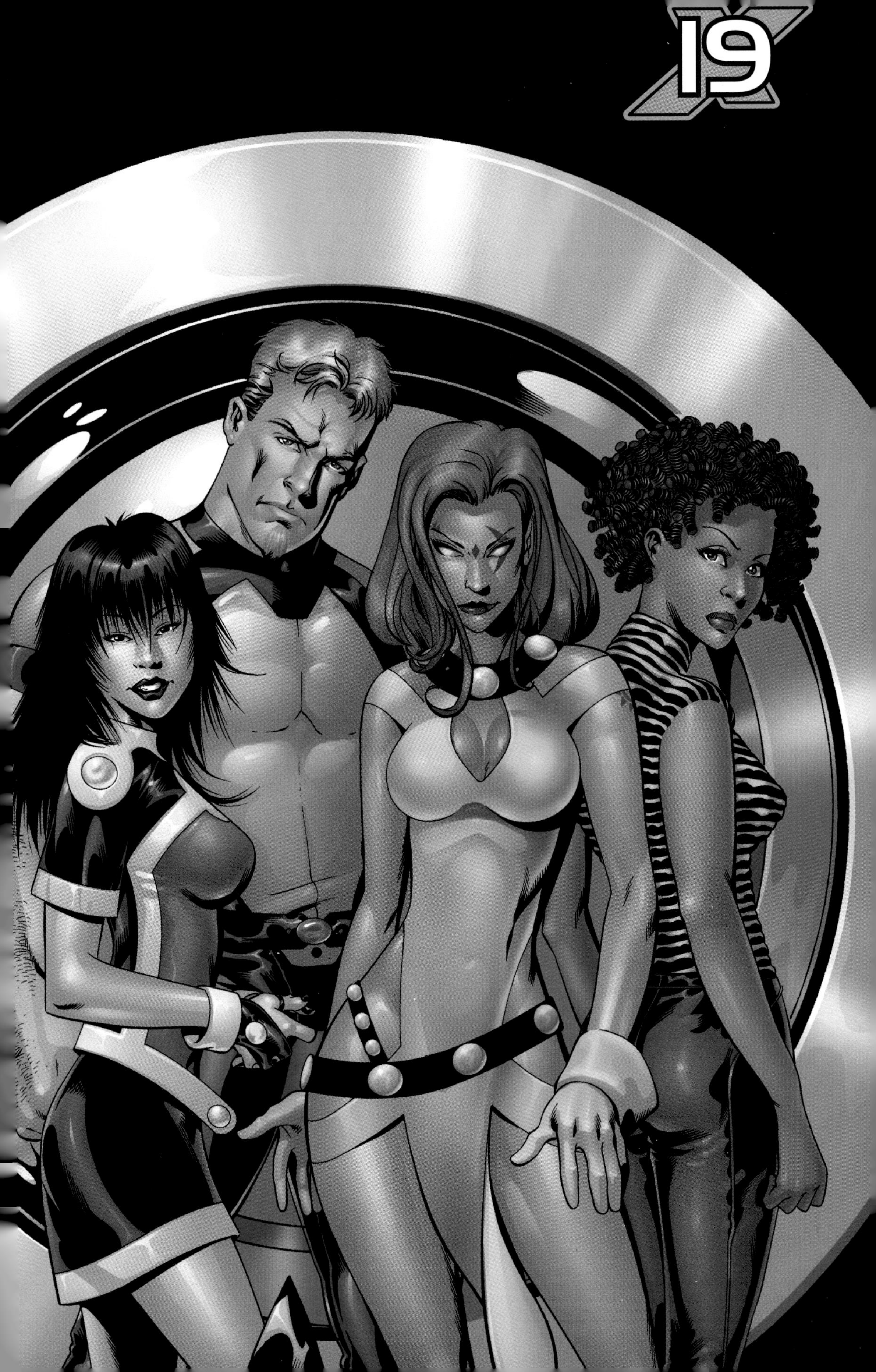
19

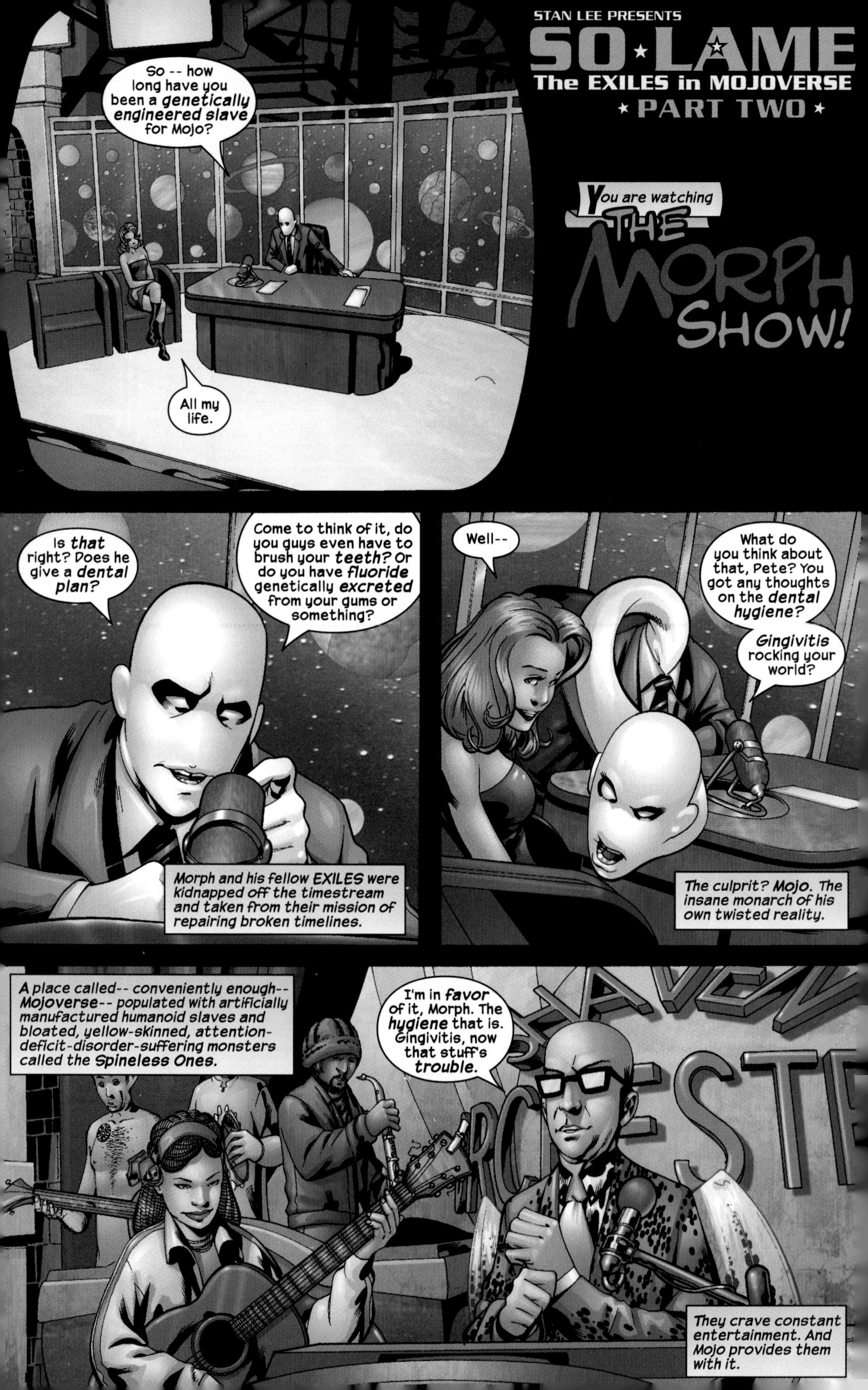
STAN LEE PRESENTS
SO★LAME
The EXILES in MOJOVERSE
★PART TWO★
So -- how long have you been a genetically engineered slave for Mojo?
All my life.
You are watching THE MORPH SHOW!
Is that right? Does he give a dental plan?
Come to think of it, do you guys even have to brush your teeth? Or do you have fluoride genetically excreted from your gums or something?
Morph and his fellow EXILES were kidnapped off the timestream and taken from their mission of repairing broken timelines.
Well--
What do you think about that, Pete? You got any thoughts on the dental hygiene?
Gingivitis rocking your world?
The culprit? Mojo. The insane monarch of his own twisted reality.
A place called-- conveniently enough-- Mojoverse-- populated with artificially manufactured humanoid slaves and bloated, yellow-skinned, attention-deficit-disorder-suffering monsters called the Spineless Ones.
I'm in favor of it, Morph. The hygiene that is. Gingivitis, now that stuff's trouble.
They crave constant entertainment. And Mojo provides them with it.

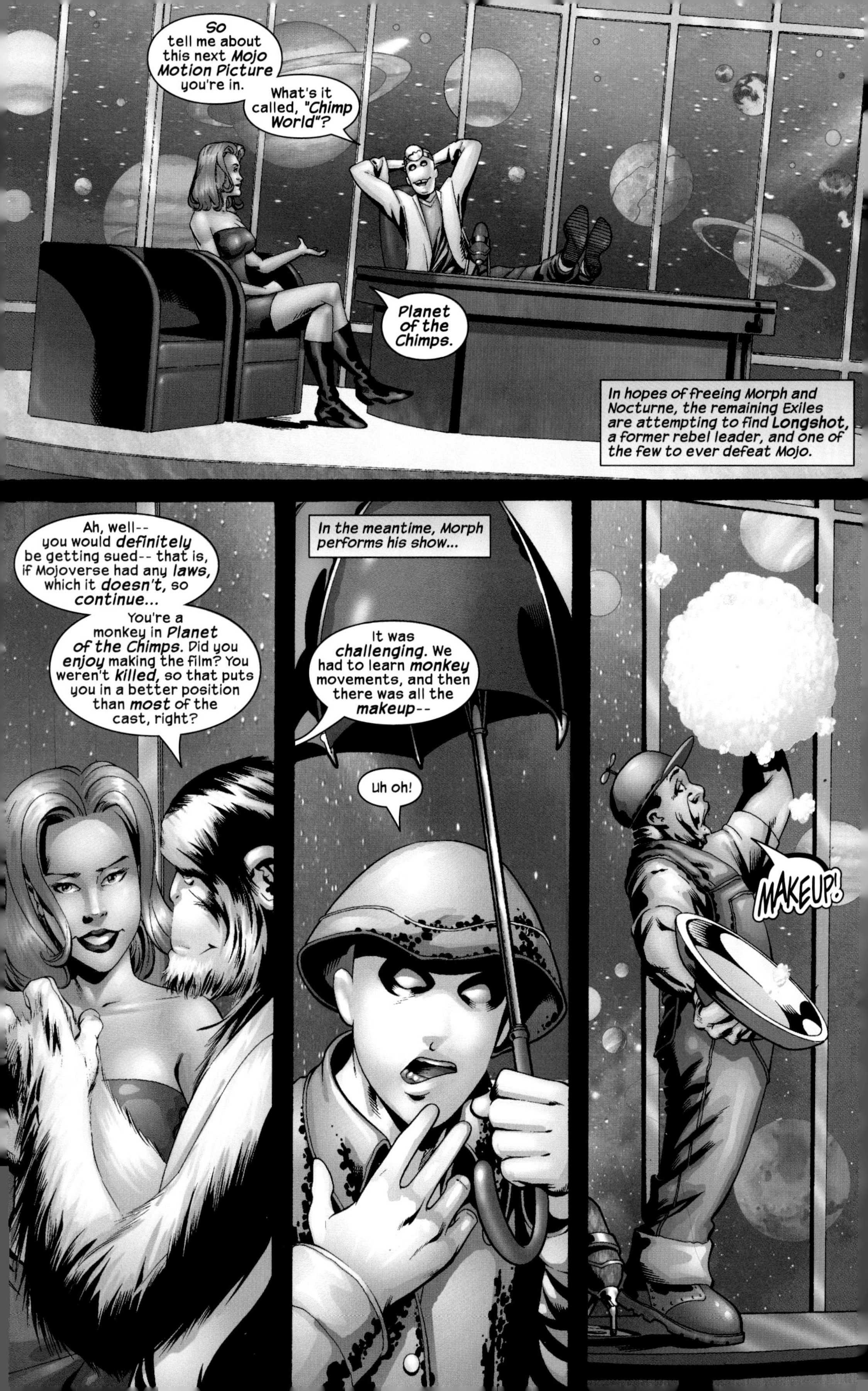
So tell me about this next *Mojo Motion Picture* you're in.
What's it called, *"Chimp World"*?
Planet of the Chimps.
In hopes of freeing Morph and Nocturne, the remaining Exiles are attempting to find ***Longshot,*** *a former rebel leader, and one of the few to ever defeat Mojo.*
Ah, well-- you would *definitely* be getting sued-- that is, if Mojoverse had any *laws,* which it *doesn't,* so *continue...*
You're a monkey in *Planet of the Chimps.* Did you *enjoy* making the film? You weren't *killed,* so that puts you in a better position than *most* of the cast, right?
In the meantime, Morph performs his show...
It was *challenging.* We had to learn *monkey* movements, and then there was all the *makeup*--
Uh oh!
MAKEUP!

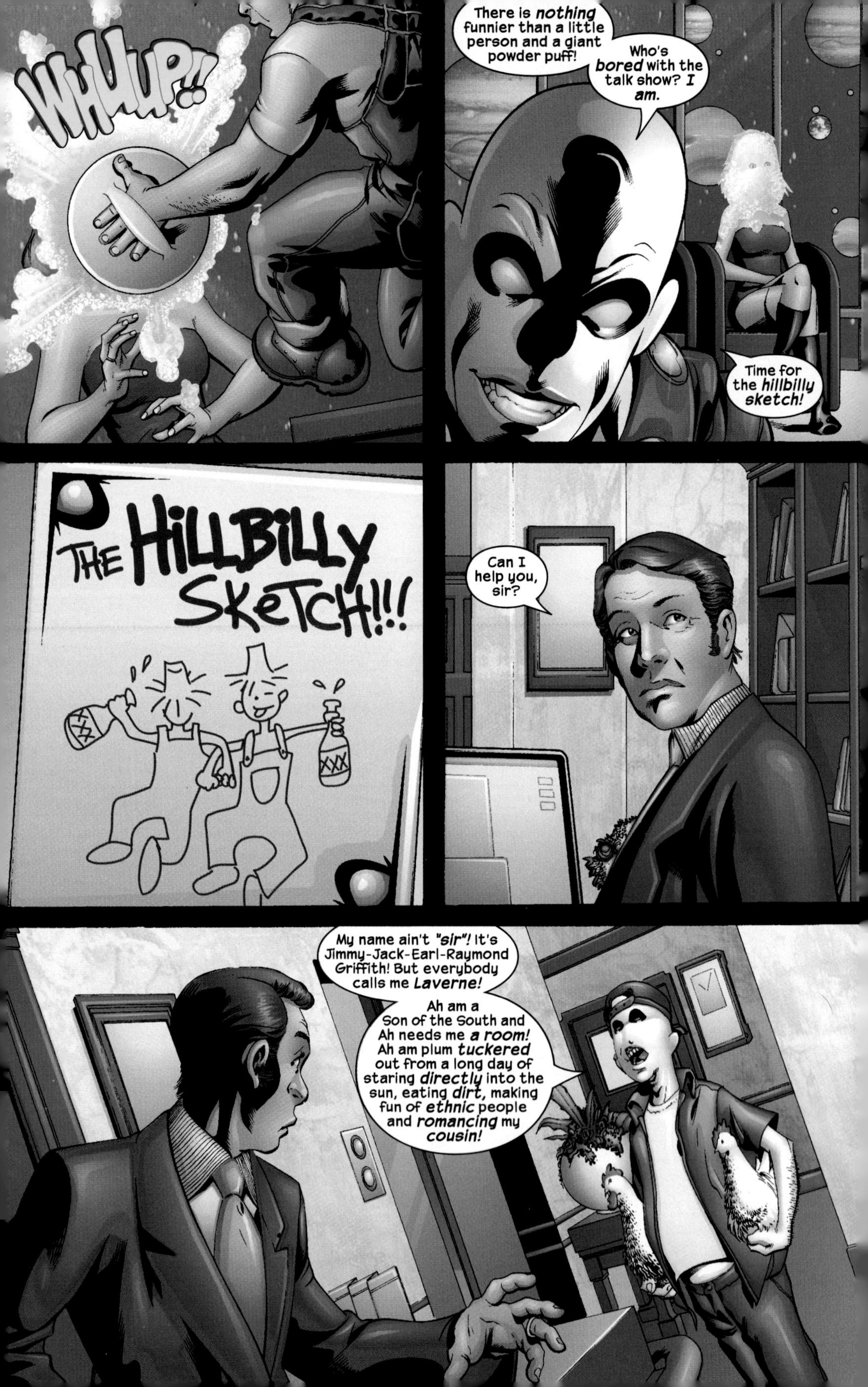
WHUUP!!
There is *nothing* funnier than a little person and a giant powder puff!
Who's *bored* with the talk show? I *am.*
Time for the *hillbilly sketch!*
THE HILLBILLY SKETCH!!!
XXX
XXX
Can I help you, sir?
My name ain't *"sir"!* It's Jimmy-Jack-Earl-Raymond Griffith! But everybody calls me *Laverne!*
Ah am a Son of the South and Ah needs me *a room!* Ah am plum *tuckered* out from a long day of staring *directly* into the sun, eating *dirt,* making fun of *ethnic* people and *romancing* my *cousin!*

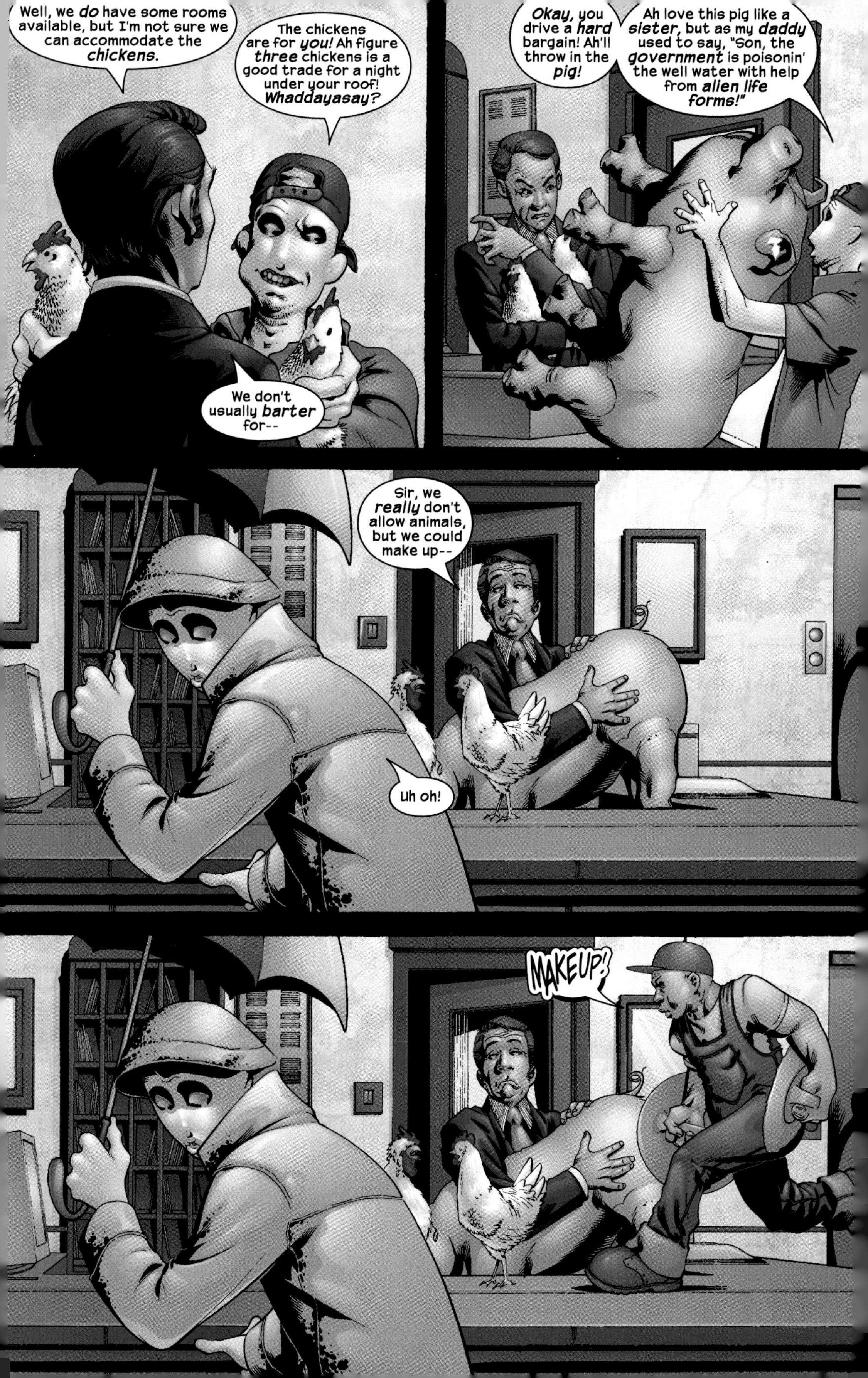
Well, we *do* have some rooms available, but I'm not sure we can accommodate the *chickens.*
The chickens are for *you!* Ah figure *three* chickens is a good trade for a night under your roof! *Whaddayasay?*
We don't usually *barter* for--
Okay, you drive a *hard* bargain! Ah'll throw in the *pig!*
Ah love this pig like a *sister,* but as my *daddy* used to say, "Son, the *government* is poisonin' the well water with help from *alien life forms!"*
Sir, we *really* don't allow animals, but we could make up--
Uh oh!
MAKEUP!

WHUP!

Kills me *every* time. We'll be back after this short break.

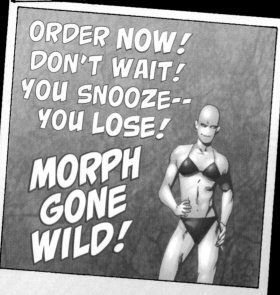

ORDER NOW! DON'T WAIT! YOU SNOOZE-- YOU LOSE!

MORPH GONE WILD!

MORPH GONE WILD! MORPH GONE WILD! COME SEE THE EXCLUSIVE PICS OF MORPH ON SPRING BREAK AS HE LOSES ALL HIS INHIBITIONS!

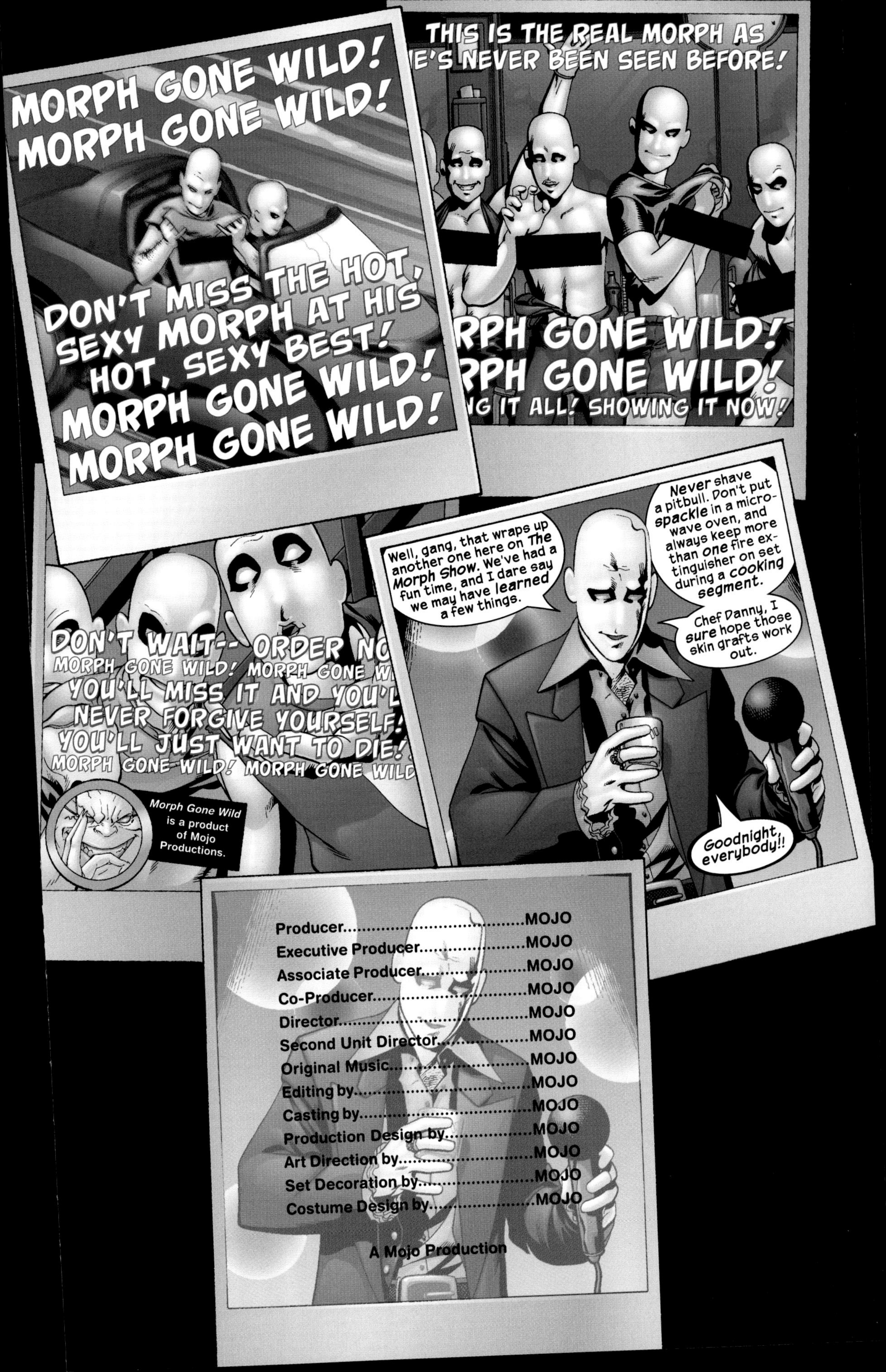
MORPH GONE WILD!
MORPH GONE WILD!
DON'T MISS THE HOT, SEXY MORPH AT HIS HOT, SEXY BEST!
MORPH GONE WILD!
MORPH GONE WILD!
THIS IS THE REAL MORPH AS
E'S NEVER BEEN SEEN BEFORE!
RPH GONE WILD!
RPH GONE WILD!
G IT ALL! SHOWING IT NOW!
DON'T WAIT-- ORDER NO
MORPH GONE WILD! MORPH GONE W
YOU'LL MISS IT AND YOU'L
NEVER FORGIVE YOURSELF!
YOU'LL JUST WANT TO DIE!
MORPH GONE WILD! MORPH GONE WILD
Morph Gone Wild is a product of Mojo Productions.
Well, gang, that wraps up another one here on The Morph Show. We've had a fun time, and I dare say we may have learned a few things.
Never shave a pitbull. Don't put spackle in a micro-wave oven, and always keep more than one fire ex-tinguisher on set during a cooking segment.
Chef Danny, I sure hope those skin grafts work out.
Goodnight, everybody!!
Producer....MOJO
Executive Producer....MOJO
Associate Producer....MOJO
Co-Producer....MOJO
Director....MOJO
Second Unit Director....MOJO
Original Music....MOJO
Editing by....MOJO
Casting by....MOJO
Production Design by....MOJO
Art Direction by....MOJO
Set Decoration by....MOJO
Costume Design by....MOJO
A Mojo Production

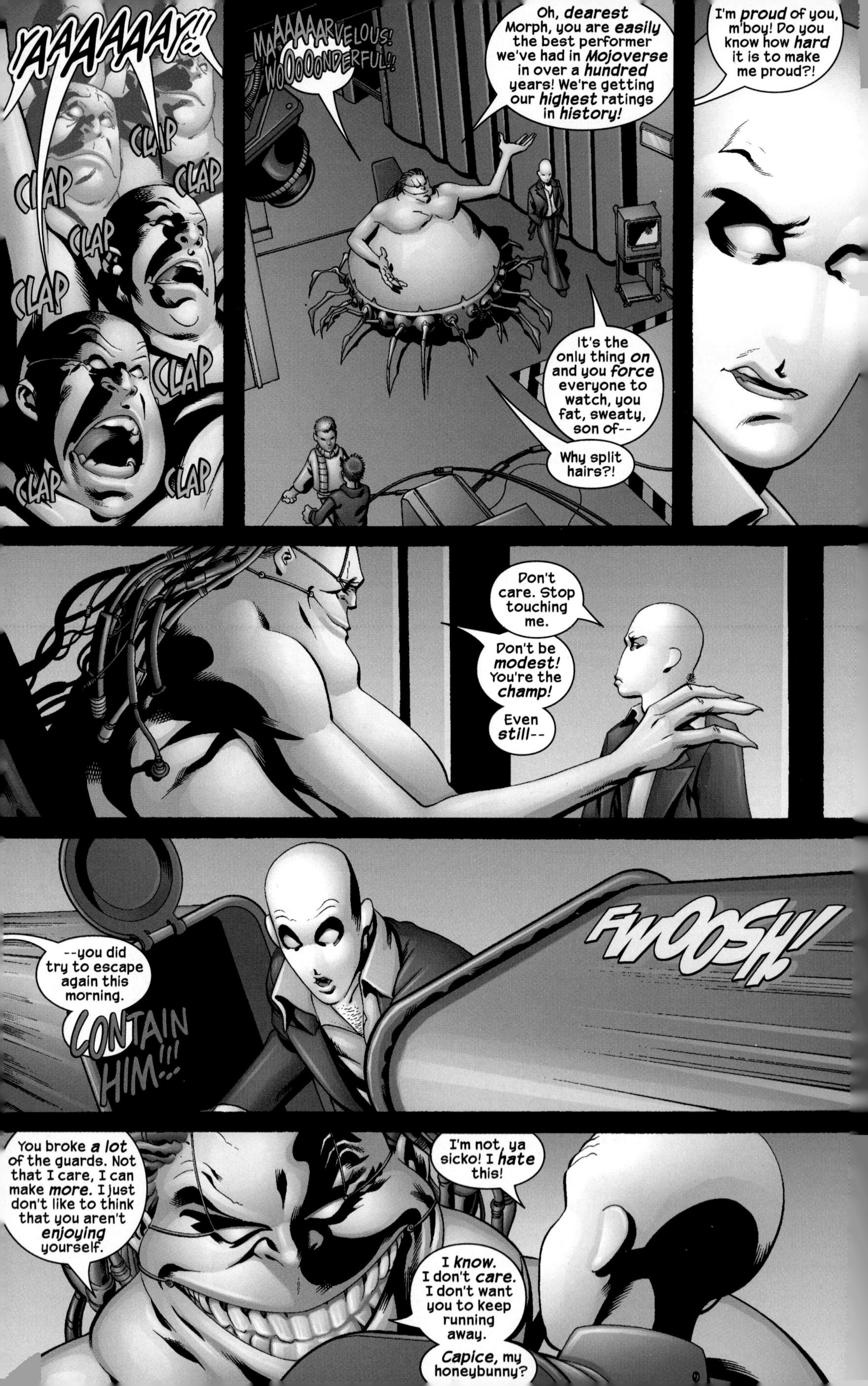
YAAAAAAY!!
CLAP CLAP CLAP CLAP CLAP CLAP CLAP CLAP
MAAAAARVELOUS! WOOOOONDERFUL!!
Oh, dearest Morph, you are easily the best performer we've had in Mojoverse in over a hundred years! We're getting our highest ratings in history!
I'm proud of you, m'boy! Do you know how hard it is to make me proud?!
It's the only thing on and you force everyone to watch, you fat, sweaty, son of--
Why split hairs?!
Don't care. Stop touching me.
Don't be modest! You're the champ!
Even still--
--you did try to escape again this morning.
CONTAIN HIM!!!
FWOOSH!
You broke a lot of the guards. Not that I care, I can make more. I just don't like to think that you aren't enjoying yourself.
I'm not, ya sicko! I hate this!
I know. I don't care. I don't want you to keep running away.
Capice, my honeybunny?

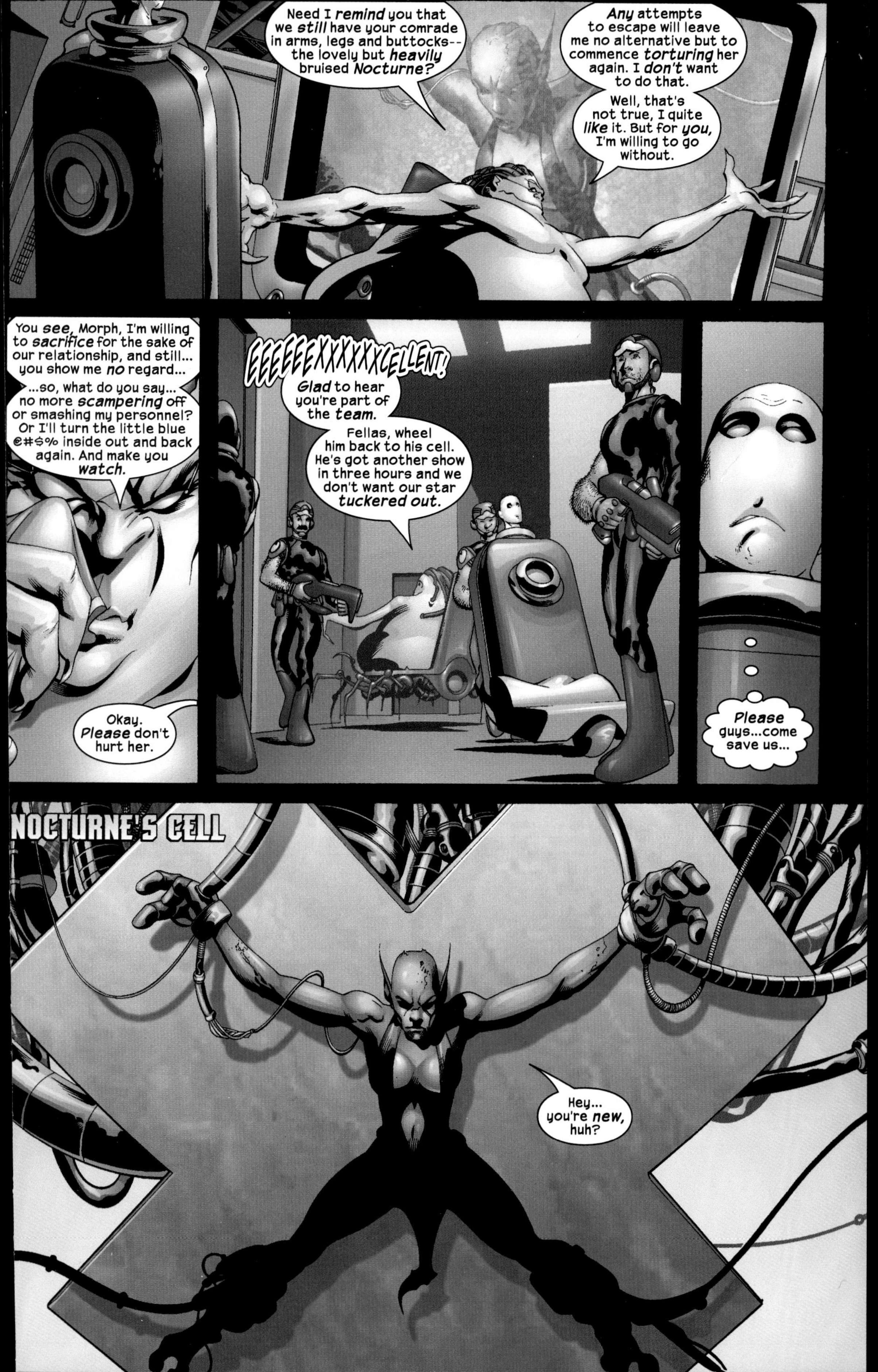
Need I remind you that we still have your comrade in arms, legs and buttocks-- the lovely but heavily bruised Nocturne?
Any attempts to escape will leave me no alternative but to commence torturing her again. I don't want to do that.
Well, that's not true, I quite like it. But for you, I'm willing to go without.
You see, Morph, I'm willing to sacrifice for the sake of our relationship, and still... you show me no regard...
...so, what do you say... no more scampering off or smashing my personnel? Or I'll turn the little blue @#$% inside out and back again. And make you watch.
Okay. Please don't hurt her.
EEEEEEXXXXXXCELLENT!
Glad to hear you're part of the team.
Fellas, wheel him back to his cell. He's got another show in three hours and we don't want our star tuckered out.
Please guys...come save us...
NOCTURNE'S CELL
Hey... you're new, huh?

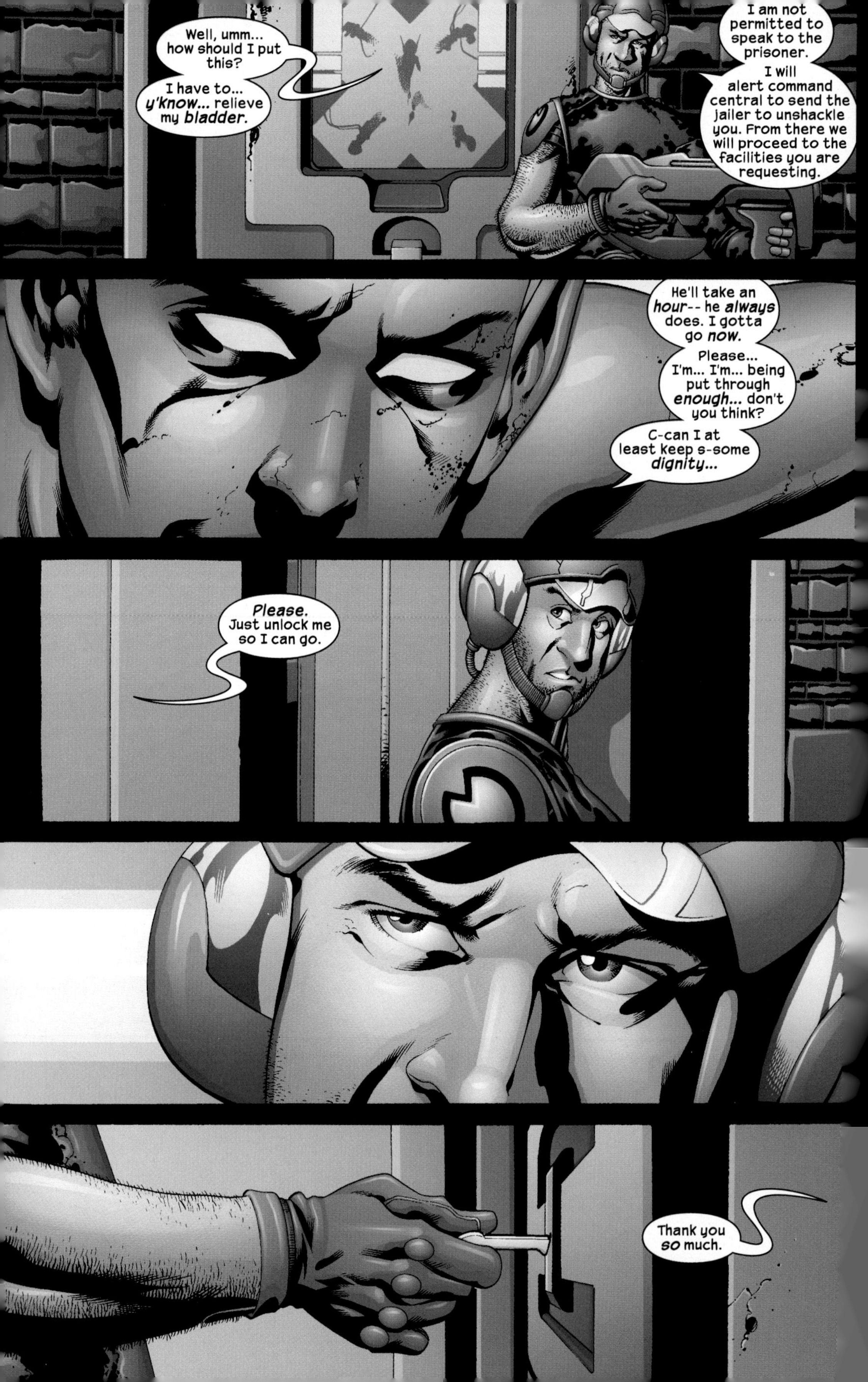
Well, umm... how should I put this?
I have to... y'know... relieve my bladder.
I am not permitted to speak to the prisoner.
I will alert command central to send the jailer to unshackle you. From there we will proceed to the facilities you are requesting.
He'll take an hour-- he always does. I gotta go now.
Please... I'm... I'm... being put through enough... don't you think?
C-can I at least keep s-some dignity...
Please. Just unlock me so I can go.
Thank you so much.

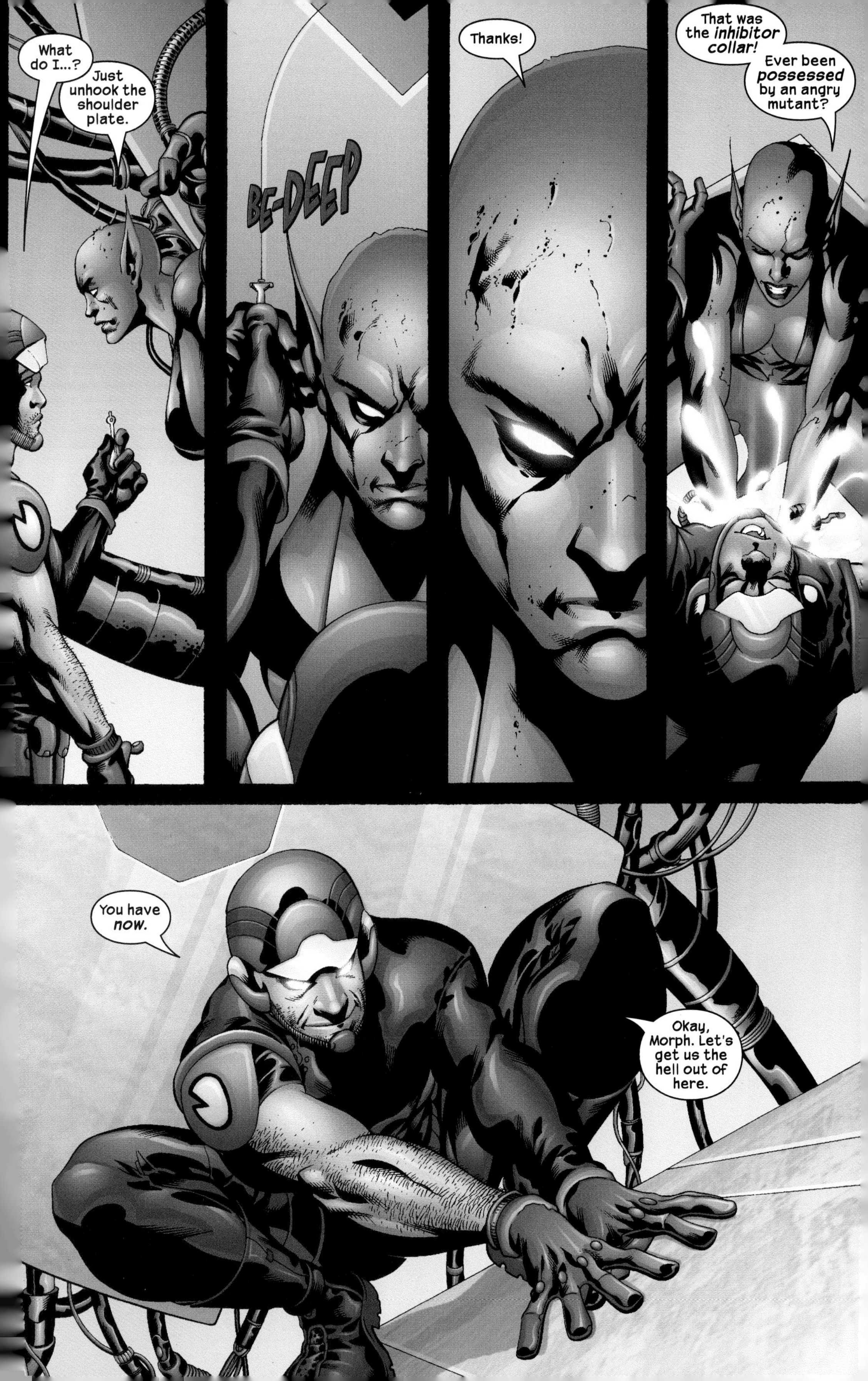
What do I...?
Just unhook the shoulder plate.
BE-DEEP
Thanks!
That was the *inhibitor collar!*
Ever been *possessed* by an angry mutant?
You have *now.*
Okay, Morph. Let's get us the hell out of here.

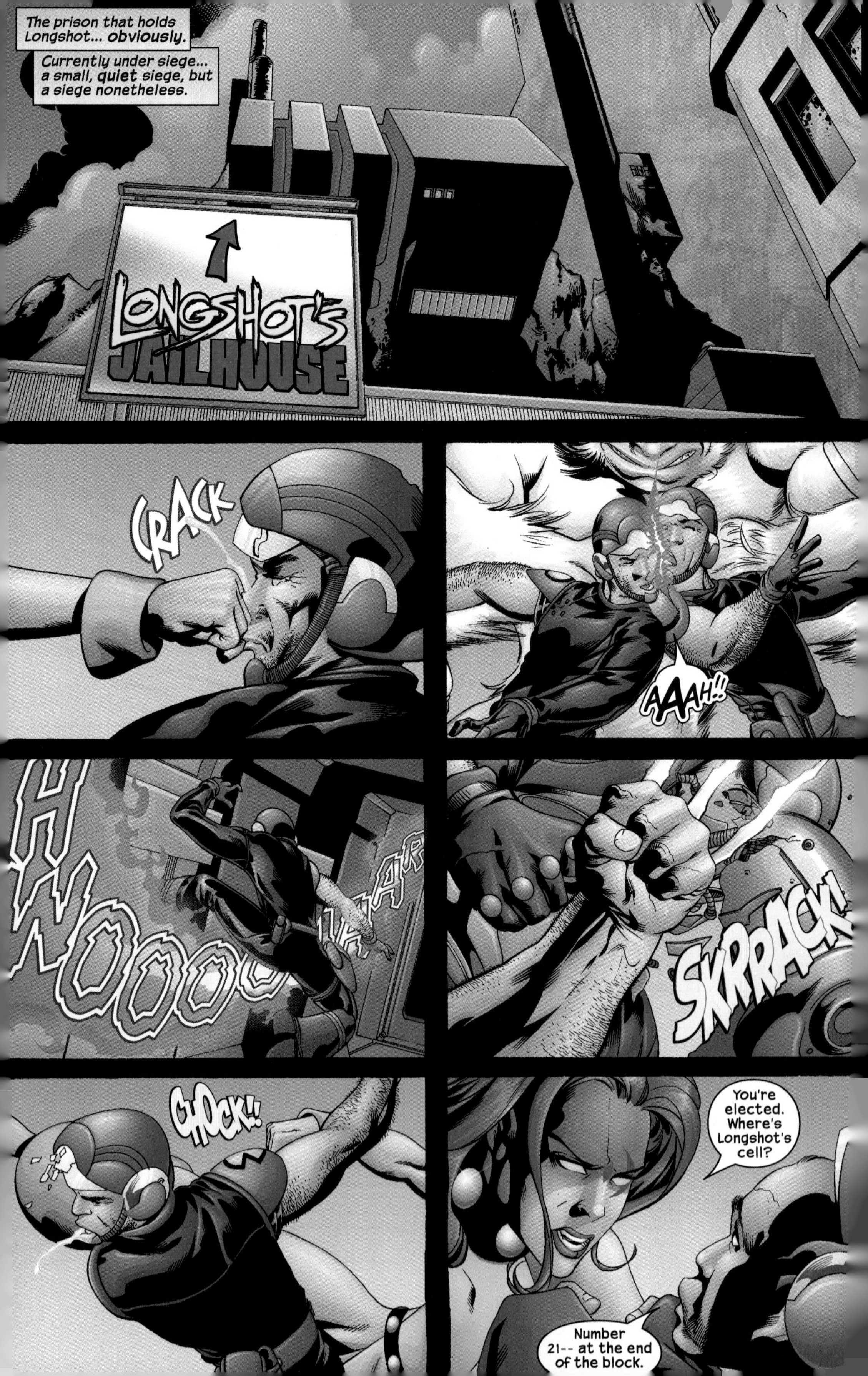
The prison that holds Longshot... obviously.
Currently under siege... a small, quiet siege, but a siege nonetheless.
LONGSHOT'S JAILHOUSE
CRACK
AAAH!!
WHOOOOOAAR
SKRRACK!
CHOCK!!
You're elected. Where's Longshot's cell?
Number 21-- at the end of the block.

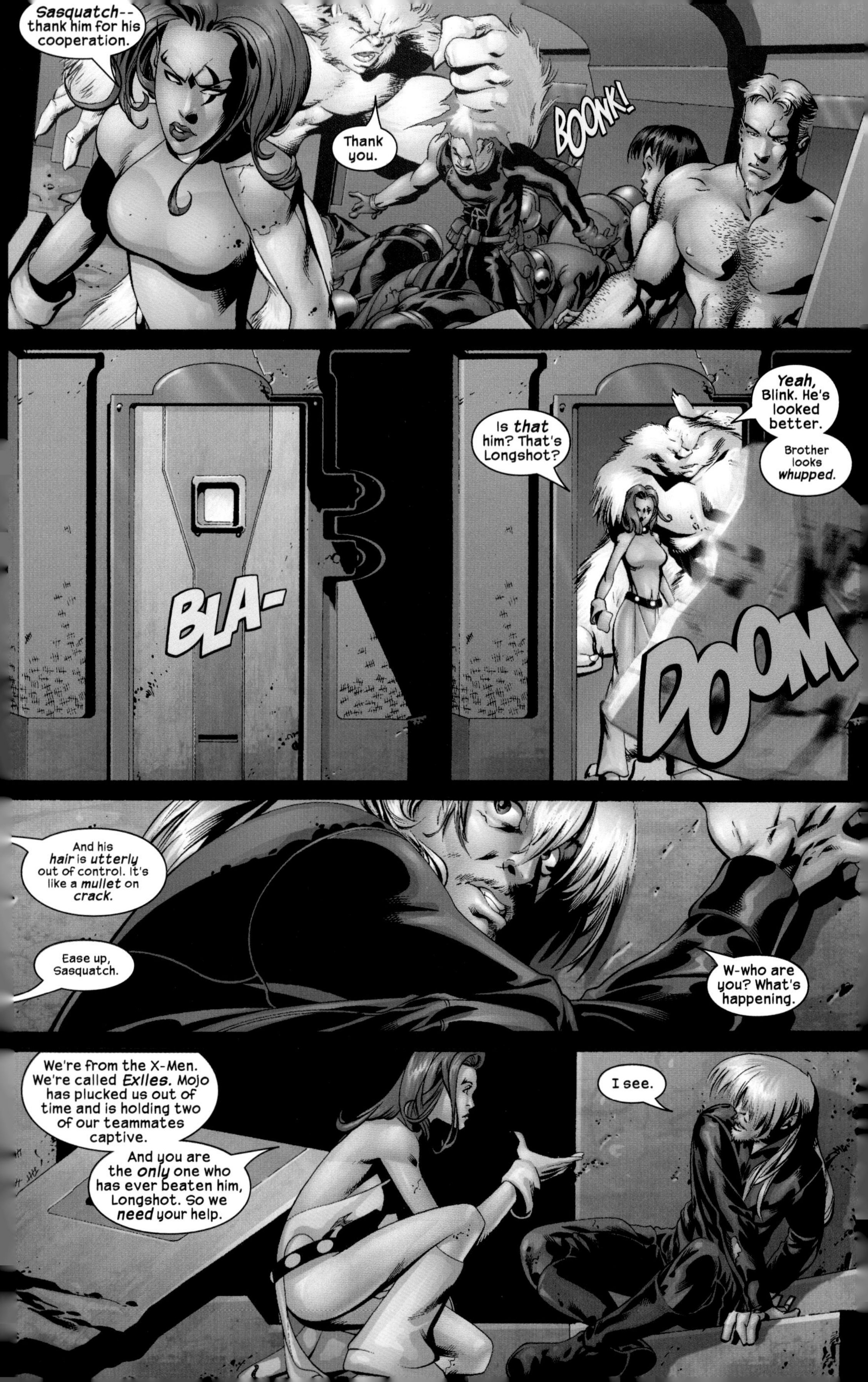
Sasquatch--thank him for his cooperation.
Thank you.
BOONK!
BLA-
Is *that* him? That's Longshot?
Yeah, Blink. He's looked better.
Brother looks *whupped.*
DOOM
And his *hair* is *utterly* out of control. It's like a *mullet* on *crack.*
Ease up, Sasquatch.
W-who are you? What's happening.
We're from the X-Men. We're called *Exiles.* Mojo has plucked us out of time and is holding two of our teammates captive.
And you are the *only* one who has ever beaten him, Longshot. So we *need* your help.
I see.

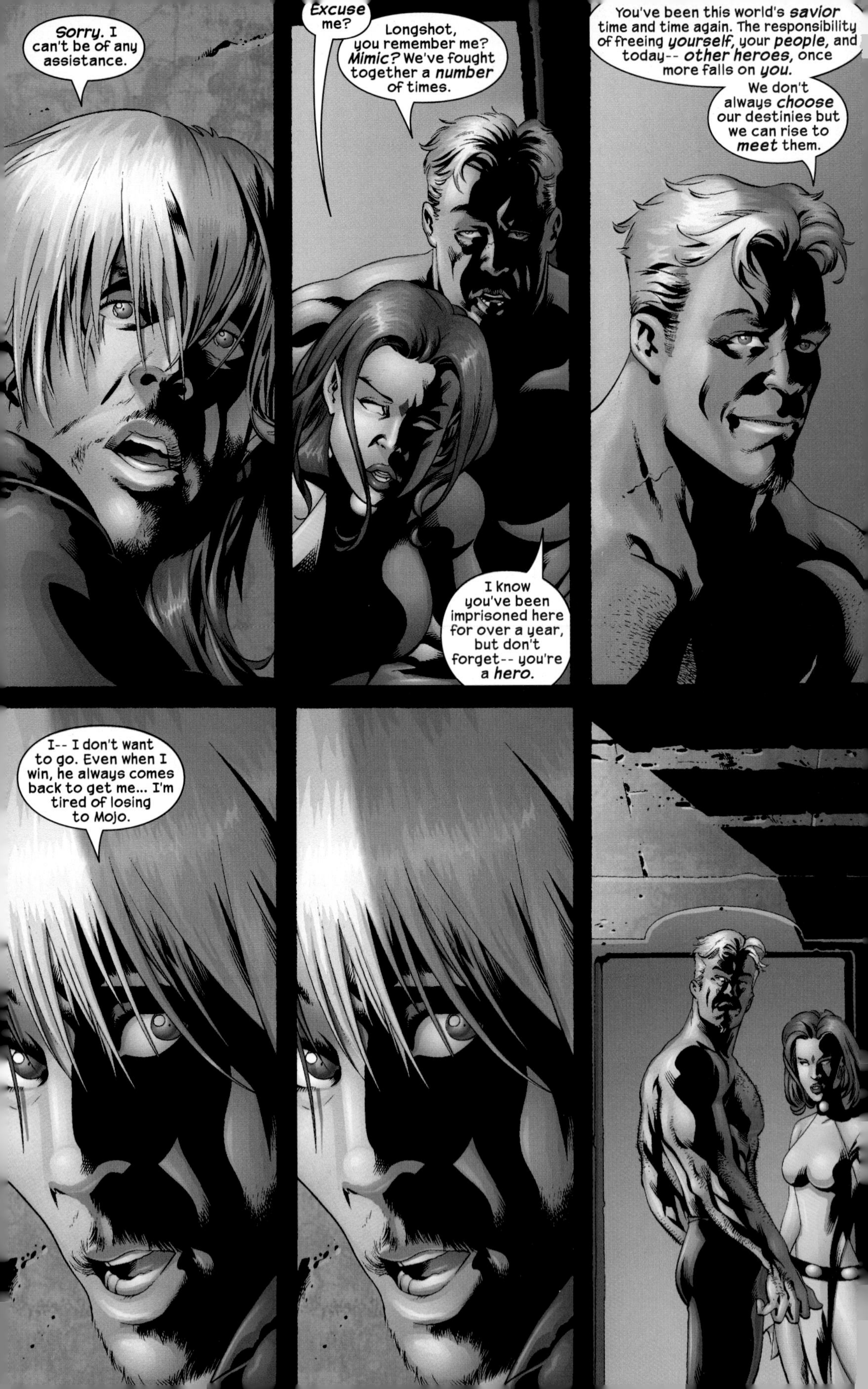
Sorry. I can't be of any assistance.
Excuse me?
Longshot, you remember me? Mimic? We've fought together a number of times.
I know you've been imprisoned here for over a year, but don't forget-- you're a hero.
You've been this world's savior time and time again. The responsibility of freeing yourself, your people, and today-- other heroes, once more falls on you.
We don't always choose our destinies but we can rise to meet them.
I-- I don't want to go. Even when I win, he always comes back to get me... I'm tired of losing to Mojo.

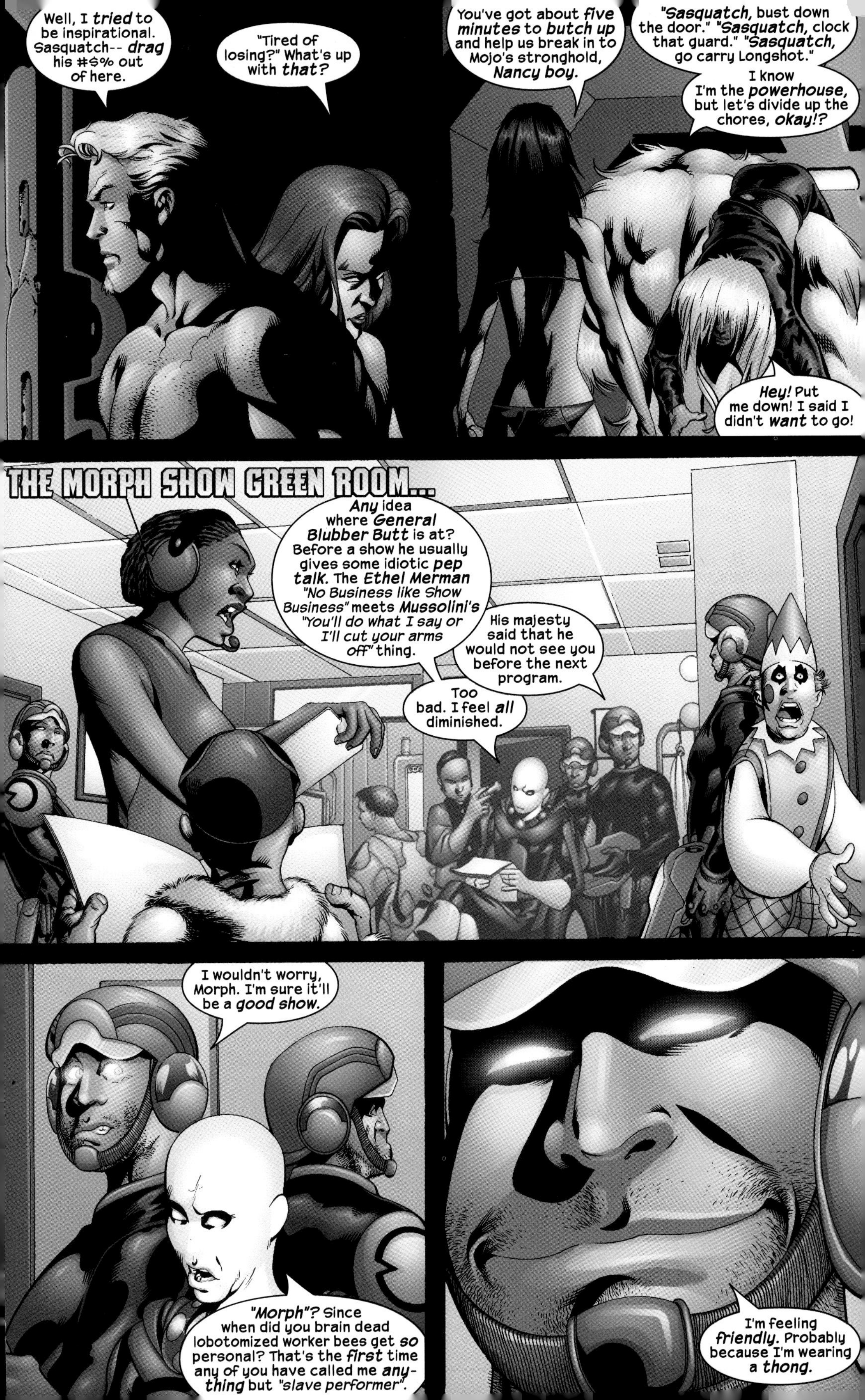
Well, I tried to be inspirational. Sasquatch-- drag his #$% out of here.
"Tired of losing?" What's up with that?
You've got about five minutes to butch up and help us break in to Mojo's stronghold, Nancy boy.
"Sasquatch, bust down the door." "Sasquatch, clock that guard." "Sasquatch, go carry Longshot."
I know I'm the powerhouse, but let's divide up the chores, okay!?
Hey! Put me down! I said I didn't want to go!
THE MORPH SHOW GREEN ROOM...
Any idea where General Blubber Butt is at? Before a show he usually gives some idiotic pep talk. The Ethel Merman "No Business like Show Business" meets Mussolini's "You'll do what I say or I'll cut your arms off" thing.
His majesty said that he would not see you before the next program.
Too bad. I feel all diminished.
I wouldn't worry, Morph. I'm sure it'll be a good show.
"Morph"? Since when did you brain dead lobotomized worker bees get so personal? That's the first time any of you have called me anything but "slave performer".
I'm feeling friendly. Probably because I'm wearing a thong.

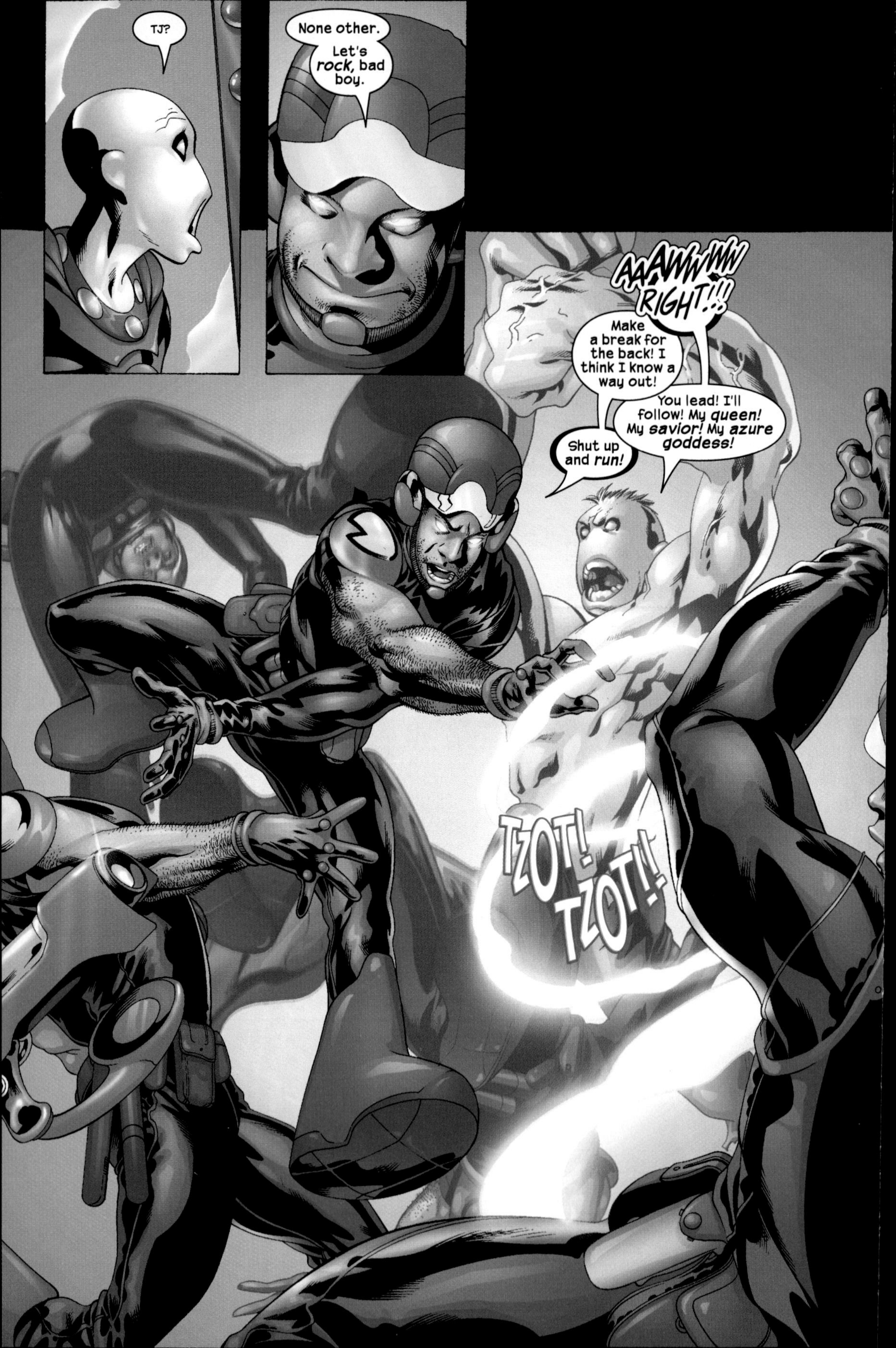
TJ?
None other. Let's rock, bad boy.
AAAWWWW RIGHT!!!
Make a break for the back! I think I know a way out!
You lead! I'll follow! My queen! My savior! My azure goddess!
Shut up and run!
TZOT! TZOT!!

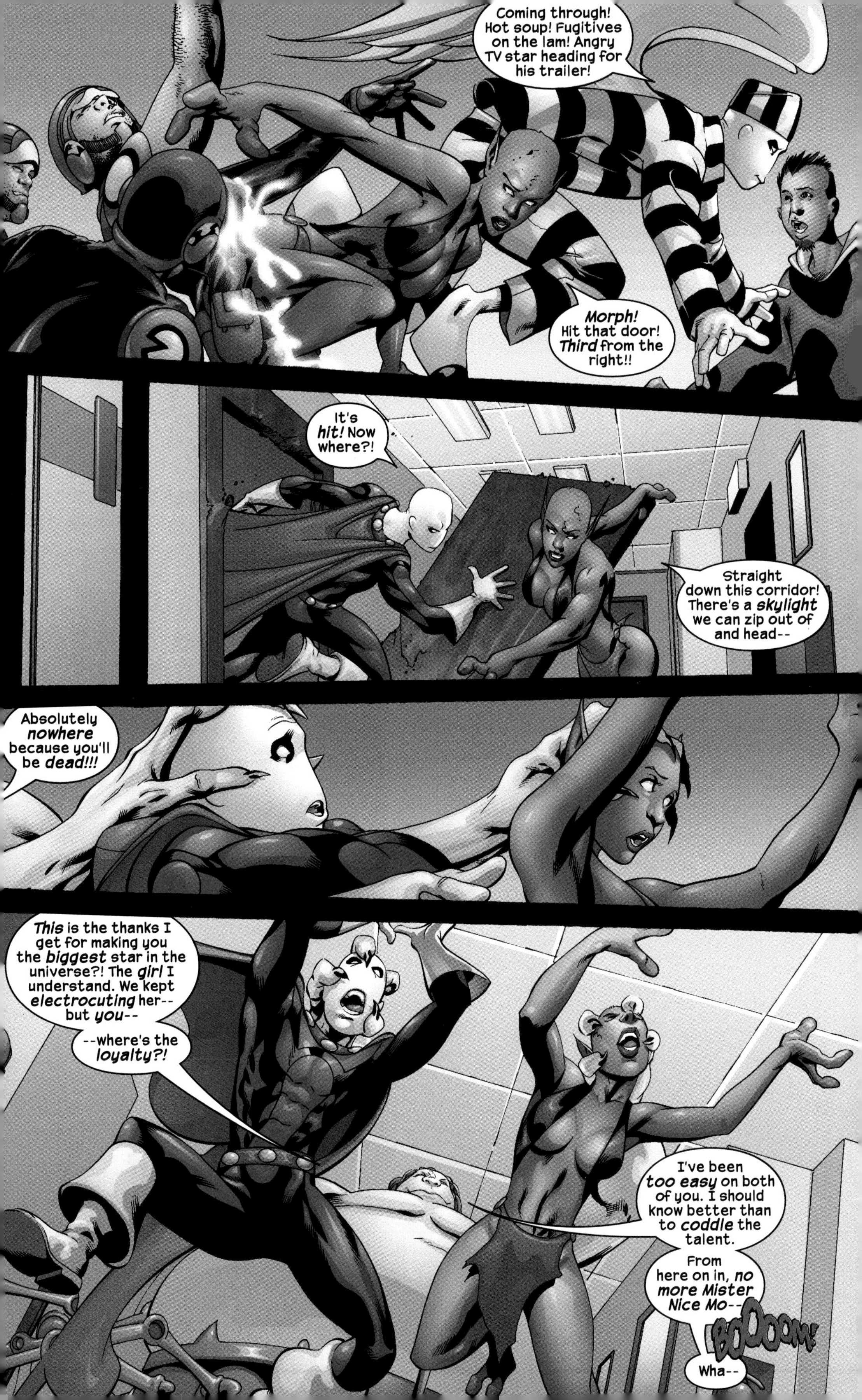
Coming through! Hot soup! Fugitives on the lam! Angry TV star heading for his trailer!
Morph! Hit that door! Third from the right!!
It's hit! Now where?!
Straight down this corridor! There's a skylight we can zip out of and head--
Absolutely nowhere because you'll be dead!!!
This is the thanks I get for making you the biggest star in the universe?! The girl I understand. We kept electrocuting her-- but you--
--where's the loyalty?!
I've been too easy on both of you. I should know better than to coddle the talent.
From here on in, no more Mister Nice Mo--
BOOOOM!
Wha--

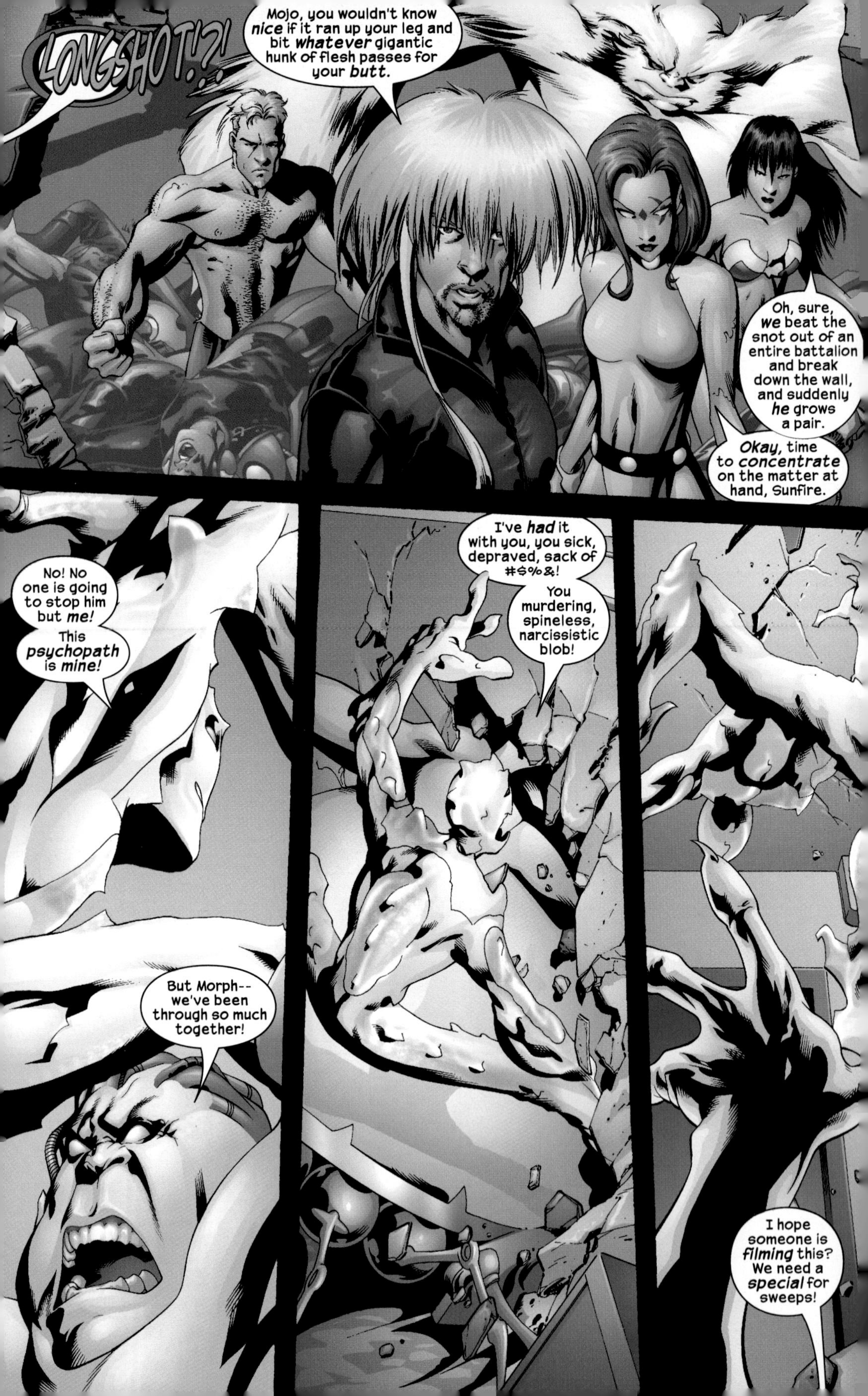
LONGSHOT!?!
Mojo, you wouldn't know nice if it ran up your leg and bit whatever gigantic hunk of flesh passes for your butt.
Oh, sure, we beat the snot out of an entire battalion and break down the wall, and suddenly he grows a pair.
Okay, time to concentrate on the matter at hand, Sunfire.
No! No one is going to stop him but me!
This psychopath is mine!
But Morph-- we've been through so much together!
I've had it with you, you sick, depraved, sack of #$%&!
You murdering, spineless, narcissistic blob!
I hope someone is filming this? We need a special for sweeps!

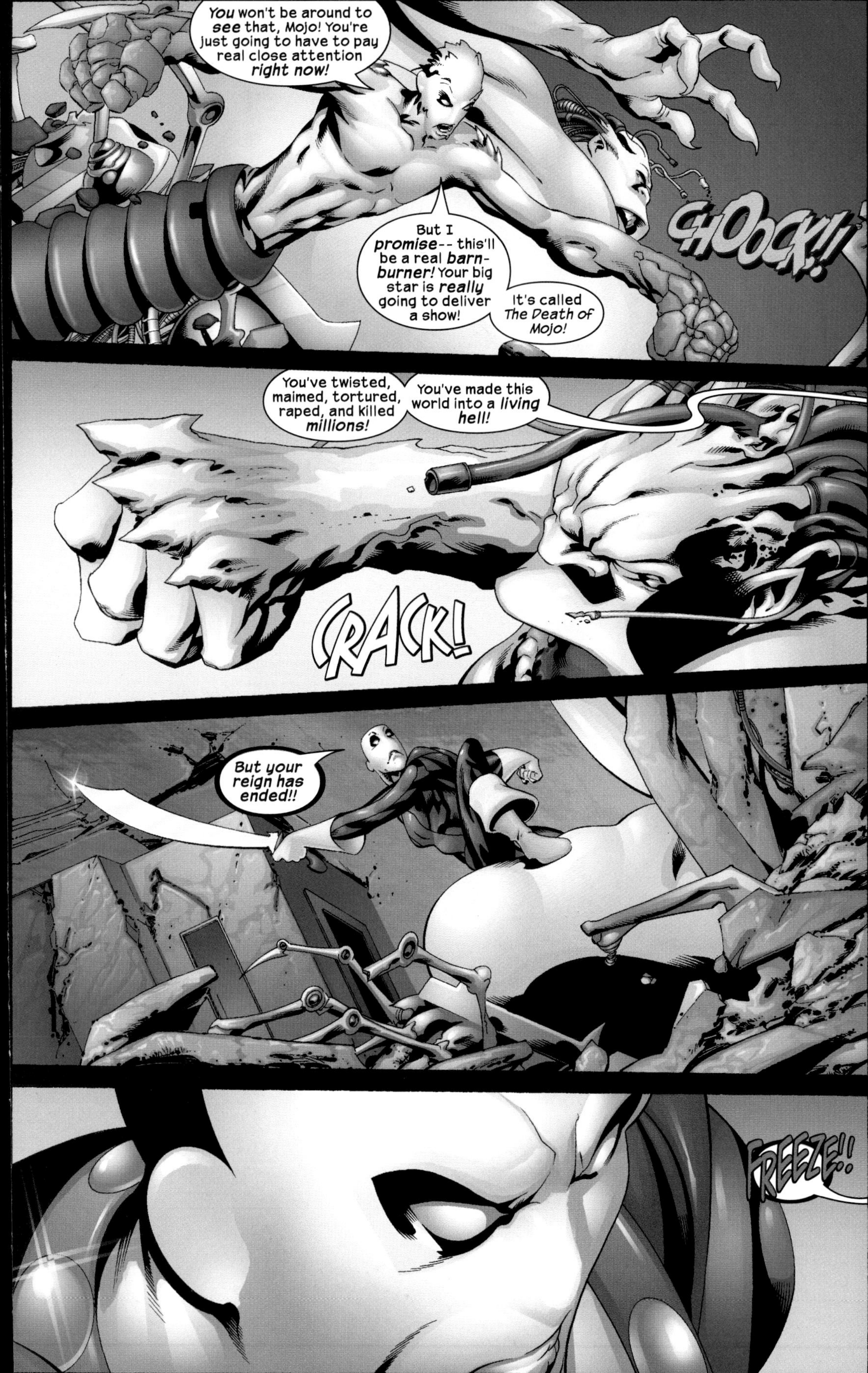
You won't be around to see that, Mojo! You're just going to have to pay real close attention right now!
But I promise-- this'll be a real barn-burner! Your big star is really going to deliver a show!
It's called The Death of Mojo!
CHOOCK!!
You've twisted, maimed, tortured, raped, and killed millions!
You've made this world into a living hell!
CRACK!
But your reign has ended!!
FREEZE!!

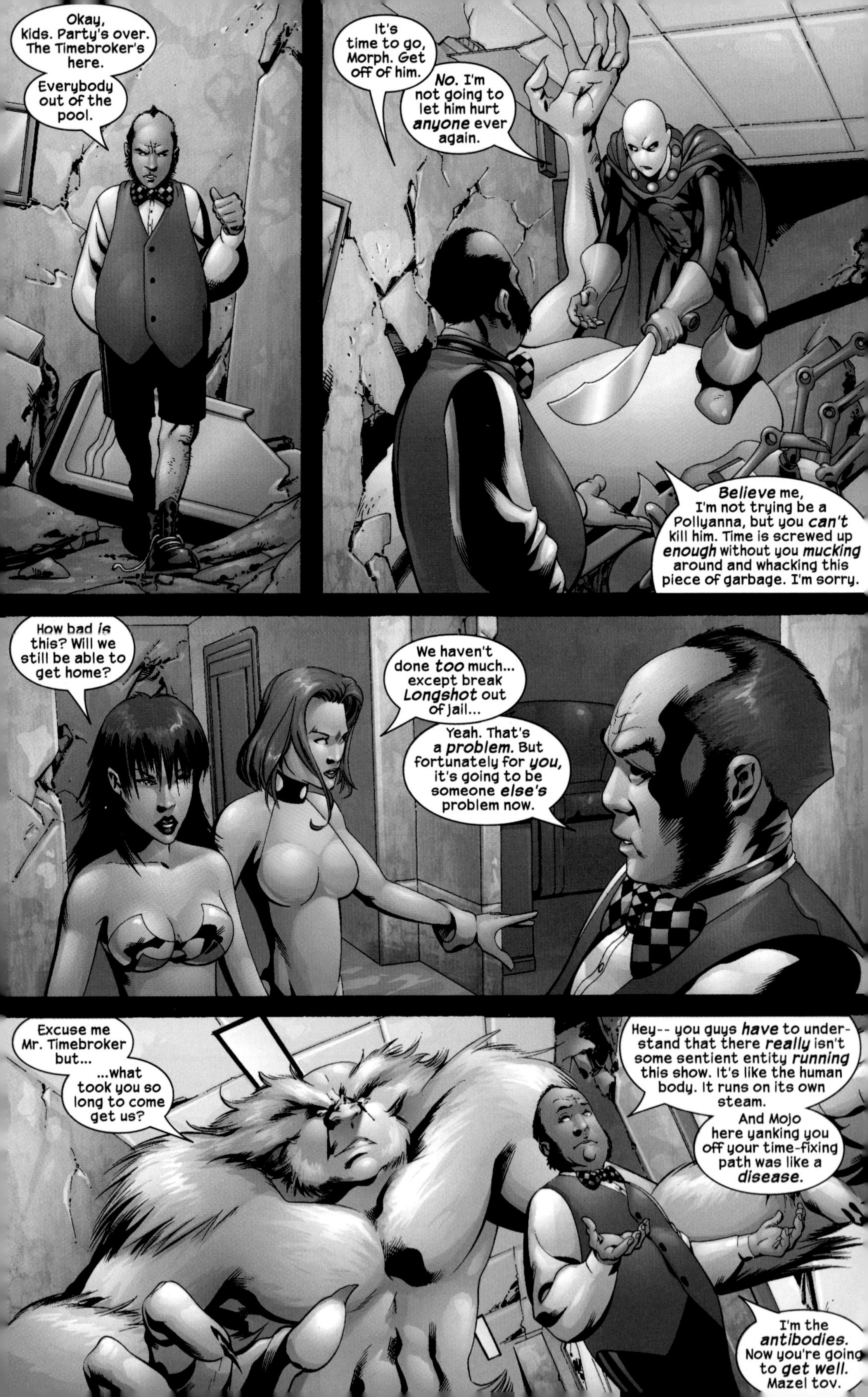
Okay, Kids. Party's over. The Timebroker's here.
Everybody out of the pool.
It's time to go, Morph. Get off of him.
No. I'm not going to let him hurt anyone ever again.
Believe me, I'm not trying be a Pollyanna, but you can't kill him. Time is screwed up enough without you mucking around and whacking this piece of garbage. I'm sorry.
How bad is this? Will we still be able to get home?
We haven't done too much... except break Longshot out of jail...
Yeah. That's a problem. But fortunately for you, it's going to be someone else's problem now.
Excuse me Mr. Timebroker but...
...what took you so long to come get us?
Hey-- you guys have to understand that there really isn't some sentient entity running this show. It's like the human body. It runs on its own steam.
And Mojo here yanking you off your time-fixing path was like a disease.
I'm the antibodies. Now you're going to get well. Mazel tov.

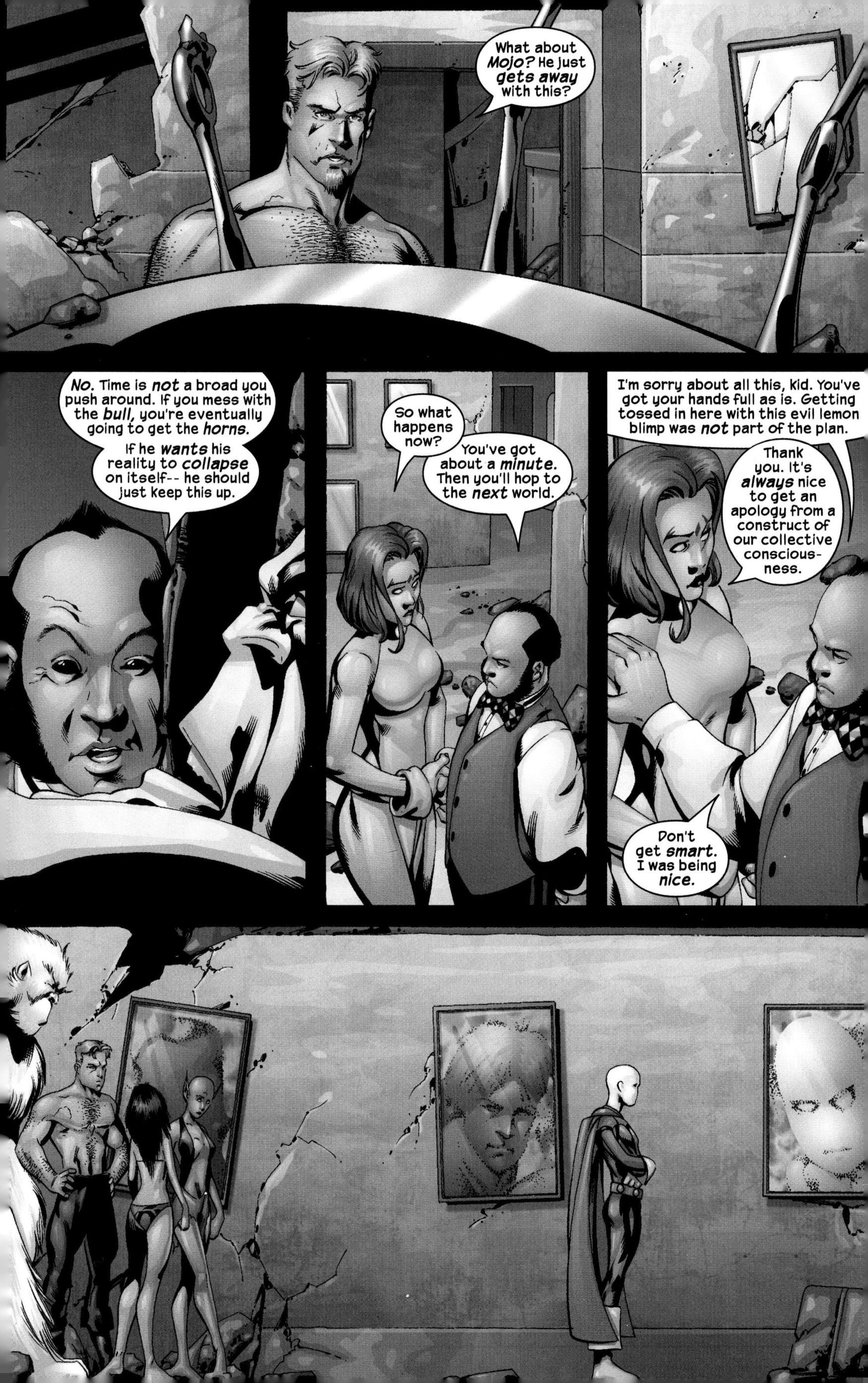
What about Mojo? He just gets away with this?
No. Time is not a broad you push around. If you mess with the bull, you're eventually going to get the horns.
If he wants his reality to collapse on itself-- he should just keep this up.
So what happens now?
You've got about a minute. Then you'll hop to the next world.
I'm sorry about all this, kid. You've got your hands full as is. Getting tossed in here with this evil lemon blimp was not part of the plan.
Thank you. It's always nice to get an apology from a construct of our collective conscious-ness.
Don't get smart. I was being nice.

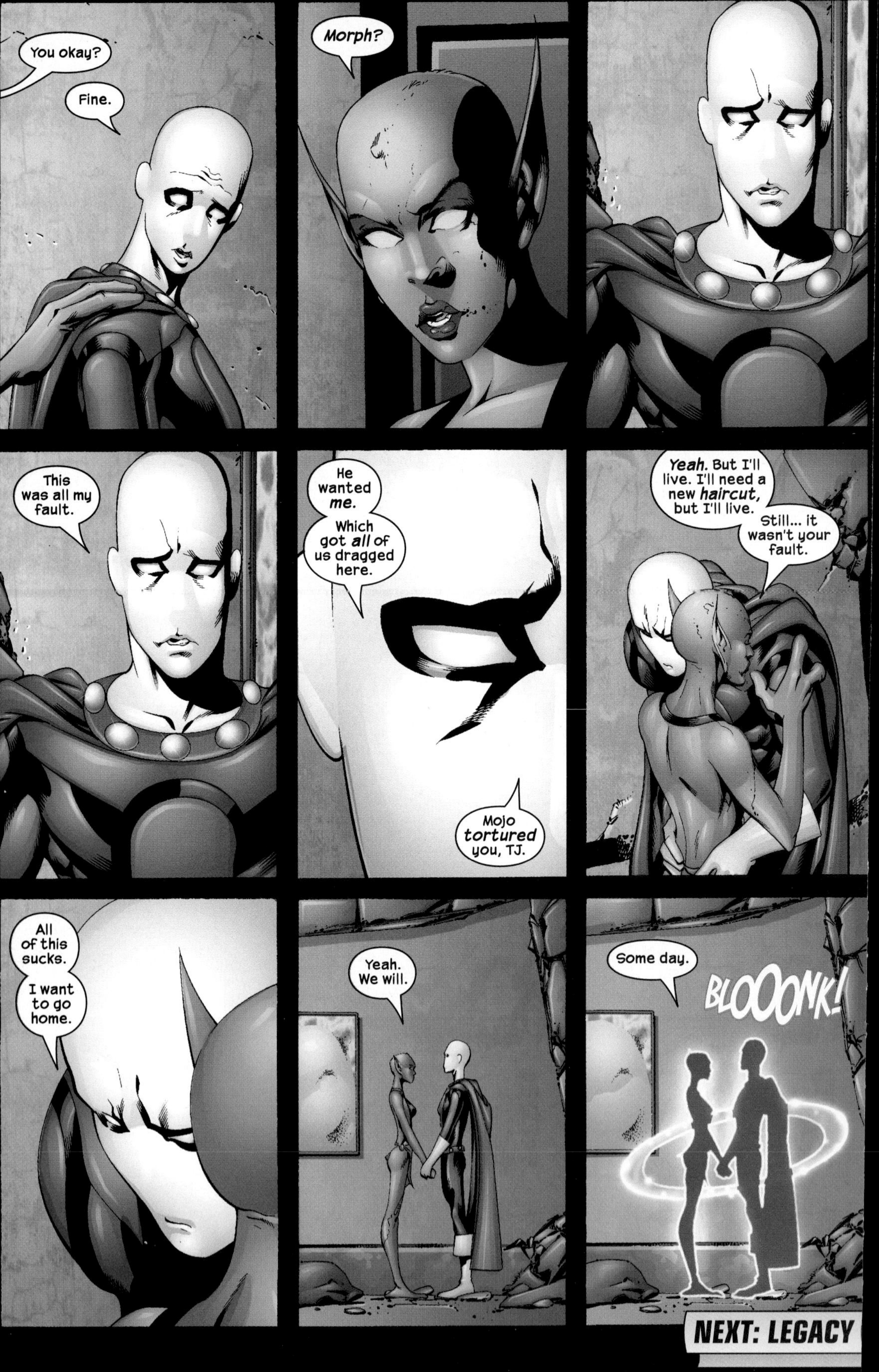
You okay?
Fine.
Morph?
This was all my fault.
He wanted *me.*
Which got *all* of us dragged here.
Mojo *tortured* you, TJ.
Yeah. But I'll live. I'll need a new *haircut,* but I'll live.
Still... it wasn't your fault.
All of this sucks.
I want to go home.
Yeah. We will.
Some day.
BLOOONK!
NEXT: LEGACY

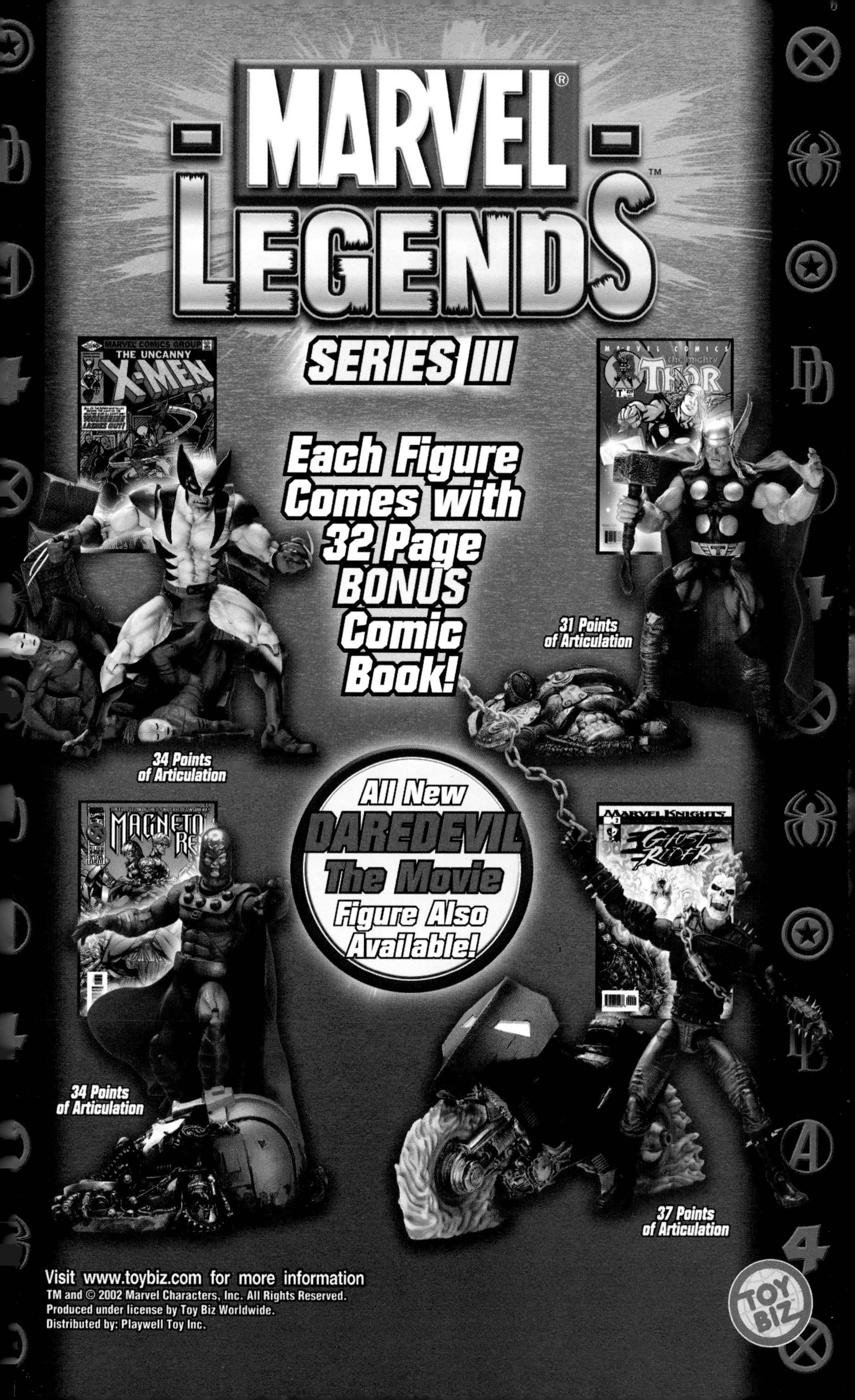
MARVEL® LEGENDS™
SERIES III
Each Figure Comes with 32 Page BONUS Comic Book!
34 Points of Articulation
31 Points of Articulation
All New DAREDEVIL The Movie Figure Also Available!
34 Points of Articulation
37 Points of Articulation
Visit www.toybiz.com for more information
TM and © 2002 Marvel Characters, Inc. All Rights Reserved.
Produced under license by Toy Biz Worldwide.
Distributed by: Playwell Toy Inc.
TOY BIZ